PEOPLE AND CONTEXTS

SOCIAL DEVELOPMENT FROM BIRTH TO OLD AGE

Henry S. Maas
University of British Columbia

PRENTICE-HALL, INC., ENGLEWOOD CLIFFS, NEW JERSEY 07632

Library of Congress Cataloging in Publication Data
Maas, Henry S.
　　　People and contexts.
　　　Includes bibliographical references and index.
　　　　1. Social psychology.　　　2. Personality.　　　3. Child
development.　　　4. Maturation (Psychology)　　　5. Life cycle,
Human.　　　I. Title.
HM251.M2665　　　　1984　　　302　　　　　　83-17622
ISBN 0-13-655845-3

For Judy
with love and appreciation
and
for our grandchildren's grandchildren
and their contemporaries of all colors and countries
with hope and concern

P-H Series in Social Work Practice, Neil Gilbert & Harry Specht, editors

Editorial/production supervision and
　　　interior design: Virginia McCarthy
Cover design: Diane Saxe
Cover photo: HUD
Manufacturing buyer: John T. Hall

Printed in the United States of America
10　9　8　7　6　5　4　3　2　1

ISBN 0-13-655845-3

Prentice-Hall International, Inc., *London*
Prentice-Hall of Australia Pty. Limited, *Sydney*
Editora Prentice-Hall do Brasil, Ltda., *Rio de Janeiro*
Prentice-Hall Canada Inc., *Toronto*
Prentice-Hall of India Private Limited, *New Delhi*
Prentice-Hall of Japan, Inc., *Tokyo*
Prentice-Hall of Southeast Asia Pte. Ltd., *Singapore*
Whitehall Books Limited, *Wellington, New Zealand*

CONTENTS

PREFACE

One purpose of this book is to present a life course view of people's social development in environments that foster or inhibit their personal growth. Social development occurs as people interact with their surroundings or contexts. I therefore decided to conceptualize the links between developmental processes and their contexts and then to describe how these interactions and other connections manifest themselves from birth to old age. When I started work on this book, no such integrated effort had been reported in a life course framework. Consequently I began this undertaking with a kind of involvement that shortly took over my academic life in the classroom and all my studies and more of my nonprofessional life than my family, friends, and I myself at times might have wished. Little that I experienced directly or read escaped the net of ideas on which I was working. This was further evidence, if I needed any, of the interplay between one's personal development and one's contexts.

Another purpose impelled me to write this book. It is intended to be useful to people who work in the human services—that is, in health and social services. The human services are preventive and remedial. Their policies, programs, and practices typically attend to people's health and continued well-being and at the same time to environmental conditions affecting people's growth and development. A book that integrates social developmental theory with concepts on contexts should have practical value. For human service workers, soundly based propositions on development, environments, and their interaction should profitably suggest directions, priorities, feasibilities, and a host of other orienting ideas in the design and provision of people-serving programs. In his introduction to Danilo Dolci's by now classic book, *Poverty in Sicily,* Aldous Huxley wrote, "Without charity, knowledge is apt to be inhuman; without knowledge, charity is predoomed, all too often, to impotence." This book aims to wed the evidence of research-observing with the provisions of people-serving in ways that will ultimately make services more potent and purposeful.

To illustrate and personalize ideas in this book I include twenty-five records and many shorter excerpts from a broad range of sources. Some are personal documents—autobiographical notes, poems, or taped interviews. Some are extracts from descriptions of human service activities intended to further people's social development and better their environmental conditions through community work, nursery schools, therapy sessions, or other means. Some are fragments of research reports—on early childhood separation, foster care, youth groups, neighborhood life, group therapy, physical and mental illness, communities in disaster, and aging—all related to phases of social development and its contexts. Because I start from assumptions about the interdependence of all people on this planet, I have selected records and brief quotations on life in Africa, Asia, European nations, and many different groups and regions in the United States and more broadly in the Americas from Canada south to Argentina. I use old as well as new sources because scholarship and specifically empirical research, especially in the several disciplines relevant to social development and its contexts, are not always thoroughly cumulative and the most recent publication is not always the most valid. My hope is that the text will involve readers in internal dialogues and group discussions. Nothing in the realm of human development should be accepted without question—that is, without a search for well founded contrary evidence.

For its contents, this book drew on more resources than the footnotes reveal. Many cohorts of students in my classes on human behavior have been active critics and modifiers of what might otherwise have appeared in print here. Early versions of this text were revised after reviews by colleagues on campuses and in other fields. Some of the book's practical implications were tested in workshops and social agencies. My thanks have previously been given to many critics. My greatest appreciation goes now to people who, except in a few cases, had nothing or little to do directly with preparing this book but rather something to do, sometimes at critical points, with preparing me to write it. In roles that tend to blur over time, all are colleagues, former students, or former teachers and long term mentors, a few of whom in recent years have died. Reduced to the shortest possible list, they are: Martha Branscombe, Tom L. Clark, Arthur Emlen, Jerome D. Frank, Henning Friis, Jay Goldsmith, Dorothy Headley-Knox, Phillip Hewett, Mary Hill, George Hougham, Mary Cover Jones, Marion Kenworthy, Joe Kuypers, Martin B. Loeb, Paul Mussen, Bernice Neugarten, Helen Harris Perlman, Norman Polansky, Daniel Prescott, Eugen Pusic, Kristine Siefert, Richard W. Small, Brewster Smith, Larry L. Smith, Richard Splane, Richard Titmuss, Peter Willmott.

The influences of some of these people were extended by others in the contexts in which we worked together: Committee on Human Development, University of Chicago, and in residence at Hull House; School of Social Welfare and Institute of Human Development, University of California, Berkeley; School of Social Work, University of British Columbia; Washington School of Psychiatry; US Children's Bureau; London School of Economics and Institute of Community Studies; and on United Nations assignments at UNESCO headquarters in Paris and in UNICEF sponsored programs in Turkey, Uganda, and the Philippines.

Finally, my thanks go to those at Prentice-Hall who transformed my manuscript into this book, especially Barbara DeVries, Virginia McCarthy, and Susan Taylor.

H.S.M.

Chapter 1
SOCIAL DEVELOPMENT AND SOCIAL CONTEXTS

Introduction: Social services aim to foster social development

Social Development
    Basic capacities: attachment, exploration, competence
    Later developments and sharing milieus

Social Contexts
    Conceptual underpinnings
    Assumptions, values, and professional purpose

Social Services, Contexts, and Development
    Residential Nurseries as Microcontexts (Record No. 1)
    Youth Groups and Youth Group Workers (Record No. 2)
    Rural Counties as Macrocontexts for Foster Care (Record No. 3)

INTRODUCTION

Social Services Aim to Foster
Social Development

A frightened woman and her two preschool children arrive at the door of a temporary residence for battered wives. The older child cradles a ragged stuffed animal, the only possession rescued from their home in their hurried departure. A social worker greets them in the large front hall.

Providing emergency support and protection for people in crises is an immediate aim of the social services. Transition houses like the one just alluded to offer short-term shelter. But the long-range purpose of such a service is to help people emerge from the critical situation with a new or renewed sense of competence. This sense of competence arises as people become aware of their choices and resources. They then experience diminished feelings of entrapment and vulnerability.

At a drop-in center for youth in an old part of the city, a cluster of streetwise teenagers talk rather freely, after a period of taunting and testing, with a social worker. They know that he knows about their involvements with drugs and prostitution. Referring to a residence for homeless youth that is still in the planning stages, he asks what, if anything, they might get out of such a place, which has been converted from an old hotel. He is looking for leads to programming for street youth, and asks them what they think is good and bad about their present lives. They talk with serious intensity, as though they welcomed the chance to describe their experiences to someone who listens and is concerned about them as human beings and not merely "problems."

Helping people in socially marginal positions participate rewardingly in their society is a major purpose of the social services. For them to do so, they need responsive environments—for example, opportunities to work collaboratively with others and enjoy the benefits of such collaboration. A responsive residence for homeless youth should include a staff of nonthreatening adults, sensitively paced resocialization programs, and sufficient openness to community members to prevent a specialized place from becoming an insulated space in its neighborhood. Institutions and institutionalization can often defeat services aimed ultimately at the social integration of residents.

In a courthouse basement, and elsewhere in family service agencies, social workers discuss with couples how to distinguish between their ruptured marital relationship and their continuing joint responsibility as parents, so that the children suffer as little as possible from their parents' separation. In a top floor conference room in the state capital, mental health workers are gathered from all around the state to consider how psychiatric patients, after a hospital stay, can continue living in rural, small-town, or metropolitan homes, remote from institutional care but with access to people who can help them at home. Different regions have or can use different kinds of supplementary services. In a local church, neighborhood residents are meeting with a city planner and a community development worker to see how traffic flow to and from a new sports stadium under construction nearby might be routed so that it is least intrusive to their neighborhood lives.

All these situations involve people's coping with changing environments or with changes in their own capacities to deal with their surroundings. In effect, the situations call for altered patterns of interaction between persons and their contexts. The social workers are concerned that these changes be negotiated in ways that foster or sustain—or at least do not appreciably reduce—people's feelings of competence and well-being.

But how interaction can change depends, in part, on people's existing capacities and developmental potentials. Changes in interaction depend also upon the options and responsiveness of people's environments. Since environments and people mutually influence each other, social workers focus appropriately on both persons and their contexts.

Underlying the nature of interaction at any given time are the ongoing processes and status of people's social development. Social development occurs in contexts more or less conducive to certain capacities or incapacities. But what is meant by social development and contexts? Clarifying these terms is the prime purpose of this introductory chapter. Amplifying the meanings of these terms, their relationships to each other, and the conceptual bases they provide for purpose and program in the social services is what this book is all about.

At the start of this section, I said that social services aim to foster social development. The significance of this proposition should become apparent in this chapter's discussions of social development and its contexts. In these times, in industrial societies as well as in many developing nations, social services have become an integral segment of people's formally organized environments. These services complement and buttress the informal support of family, friends, and neighbors. And when such contexts reflect basic caring and sharing values, people are likely to develop in socially responsible ways, ideally with ever widening views of the world and what parts of it constitute their "community."

SOCIAL DEVELOPMENT

Social development is the processes through which people become increasingly able to interact competently and responsibly—that is, with recognition of others' needs—in an increasing array of social contexts.[1] The greater the number of contexts with which people can cope, the fewer the situations in which they are overwhelmed by feelings of helplessness and stress. The more often they engage in socially responsive interaction, the more likely they are to help to generate or sustain a caring and sharing society. Such a society, including its social services, reciprocally furthers the social development of its members.

Social development occurs through the interaction of growing persons with their changing contexts. Normally, the contexts with which they may expect to cope increase in number and complexity through most of their life course. Social development occurs most effectively in contexts with which people cope success-fully—that is, in *conducive contexts.*

Understanding conducive contexts and the social development they foster seems essential for the effective provision of policies, programs, and practices in the social services, because they simultaneously address environmental conditions and the people who must cope with them. "Social workers focus on person-and-environ-ment *in interaction,*"[2] and their "central responsibility" is "to work with the inter-space between people and their social structures to help both change toward an improved quality of life."[3] Perhaps "toward a fuller social development" would serve as a less ambiguous goal. "Quality of life" provides little clarity for focused planning, intervention, or evaluation of goal attainment. Social development stipulates capacities that can be assessed; it occurs in environments that can be observed and changed.

What are the processes of social development and what are their effects? Like other strands of human development—for example, physical and cognitive develop-ment—social development is sequential. It *tends* to proceed in orderly fashion, by phases, although the sequences are certainly not followed in a lock step process. Social development is additive or cumulative in that what follows grows upon and may incorporate partially what preceded it. For example, the security that a young child experiences from attachments in a family network provides the base from which the child ventures out to explore an unknown world. Development proceeds, under favorable conditions, in the direction of increased complexity, greater differ-entiation or specialization, and better articulation or integration of social capacities.

These capacities, together with the contexts in which they develop, appear in the chart "Social Development: A Contextual-Interactional Schema." The frame-work runs the whole life course, as the row stubs in the left-hand column indicate. And like the epigenetic chart Erik Erikson prepared for *Childhood and Society,*[4] the central developmental issues for each phase are represented on a diagonal to suggest the overlapping nature of developments, and, in addition, their lifelong viability. The capacity for attachments, although most visibly based in early life, is normally used and modified across the whole life course; a major pain of old age is the loss through death of people with whom mutual attachments give life meaning. The capacity for widespread social responsibility, which seems to flourish in the middle adult years, has its germination in such earlier developments as the capacity for attachment and curiosity or exploration of the novel, reciprocity, and collabo-ration. Moreover, while Erikson's "eight stages" are based in psychoanalytic ego psychology, with their roots in intrapsychic processes, the social development schema, although obviously drawing upon some Eriksonian ideas, is focused on the interaction between personal social development and contexts. Thus, in each of the cells on the diagonal, the environment that may foster the personal social develop-ment is schematically included. How the interaction between person and context at each phase furthers and uses newly expanding capacities is dealt with on a chapter-by-chapter basis in this book. The relevance of this set of perspectives to the social services and especially social work is discussed and illustrated in each chapter. In

SOCIAL DEVELOPMENT: A CONTEXTUAL-INTERACTIONAL SCHEMA

Intrauterine life

Birth
1 Ongoing society
& living place
Neonatal responses
& influences

Somatic instabilities and rapid increments

Infancy
2 Caring social networks
Attachments

Toddlerhood
3 Curiosity & exploration
of the new
Explorable arenas

**Nursery &
primary
school age**
4 Responsive environs
Growing competence

Preadolescence
5 Reciprocity/collaboration
Caring communities
sharing culture

Somatic growth spurt and puberty

Youth
6 Productive workplaces
Intimate peer relations
New sense of self-worth

**Young
adulthood**
7 Parenting partnerships
Social supports

Middle age
8 Community options/
participant controls
Social responsibility

Somatic decrements

Old age
9 Continuities/losses
legacies
Diverse flexible social
spaces/physical places

this introduction, I shall suggest in outline some of the linkages over the life span in this contextual, developmental, interactional (CDI) approach.

Basic Capacities: Attachment, Exploration, Competence

The givens or beginnings of human social development lie in a *newborn* with potential for responding to and thus influencing her or his surroundings, and especially the contexts of a *living place and its larger society.* Both the living place, which consists of home and neighborhood, and its ongoing society, obviously antedate the arrival of a newborn. But as Chapter Two illustrates, although these contexts have affected the newcomer's intrauterine life and shaped the delivery setting into which the child emerges, the living place is itself immediately and significantly changed merely by the newborn's arrival. Ask any parents how the birth of their child has altered their home and what goes on within it. The nature of such changes is fashioned by the baby's bodily and temperamental fit with parents' and others' anticipations and capacities for accommodation. The availability and accessibility of preventive health and social services in any society may have lifelong effects upon newborns and their families. Lacking such services, a society may be incurring later debts for remedial and institutional care, as well as losses of its human resources.

During a child's first year of life, following early somatic instabilities and paralleling the course of rapid increments in growth and physical abilities, an infant normally develops *attachments* to people with whom interaction is frequent and satisfying and who reciprocally become attached to the infant. A conducive context for attachments is *a caring social network* in which the infant, normally through the family, is embedded. For attachments to develop in ways that neither thwart independent exploration nor cause the child to be neglected—that is, through neither overattachment nor underattachment—parents themselves are likely to need supportive and caring networks. In such contexts, the child's capacity for attachment is more likely to flourish, thus providing a base, although not an unchanging one, for later relationships. In fact, all through life, and ultimately for many in widowhood and old age, both capacity for attachment and the availability and changing composition of social networks should be assessed when loneliness is at issue. The social services may at times generate groups and help to link people with their members. Both psychotherapeutic and community work involves people's social networks. Networks are a source of feelings of security and social integration, sometimes in spite of and sometimes because of the obligations and other constraints they impose.

Having found a sound base in reciprocal attachments, the young child moves out to explore the surrounding world with confidence, propelled by a normal life-enriching curiosity. To be able to explore with pleasure, the child must have access to arenas which are open to exploration, offering appropriate stimuli and opportunities to examine and manipulate what is novel. Thus *curiosity* is fed in *explorable arenas* or squelched by too constraining limitations. (The dimensions of arenas that encourage the pursuit of curiosity are discussed in Chapter Four.) Curiosity and exploration may persist through a broadening life of inquiry into and engagement with ever new facets of the immediate and the universal; or curiosity and exploration may be curtailed among people who are content with the familiar and the habitual, and perhaps somewhat fearful of the novel or unknown.

In the course of pursuing questions, the young and their elders not only explore but are also likely to manipulate what interests them. In the process, they learn to cope, developing an ever-growing range of competencies. When environments, however, are unresponsive to people's coping efforts, people may cease to try. Power then seems to lie more or less completely outside themselves. They feel themselves inadequate. Given such perspectives on the interaction between the person trying to cope and the context that repeatedly fails to respond, competence is seen not merely as a personal capacity; it is basically dependent on the malleability of the environment or context. To this extent, competence is a contextual as well as personal concept. Thus, both curiosity and *competence* develop interdependently with *responsive environments.* At the other extreme, unresponsive environments may overwhelm people when coping efforts continue to be ineffectual and result in a stressful situation, generating feelings of helplessness and sometimes somatic complaints. But sometimes when stressful conditions involve many people in a neighborhood, a kind of collaborative caring may arise in what has been called an "altruistic community."[5]

Such social responsiveness reflects a shared concern in immediate social surroundings and sometimes too in macrosocieties. In fact, concern and caring are integral aspects of all the contexts discussed so far—whether they are the networks in which attachments are formed, the explorable arenas that nourish curiosity, or the social environments responsive to coping efforts. This is not to suggest that there are not also entangling constraints as well as generative facilitations, or conflict and competition as well as collaboration in these very same milieus at different times and for shorter or longer periods.

In fact, a major part of remedial social work is addressed to situations such as those of the battered mother and her children or the street youth whose lives are beset by development-thwarting conflict and constraints, as suggested in this chapter's opening descriptions. The human service workers who enter their lives may be seen as the caring part of their community responding at last. More generally, the social services are intended to provide a responsive environment in the form of essential protection and supports whenever people's normal or informal supports fail them and they cannot cope. But ideally the social services, through developmental planning and policy development, anticipate and thus minimize the occasions on which direct and remedial intervention become necessary.

Later Developments
and Sharing Milieus

Competence may develop as an individual's set of capacities for obtaining whatever that person desires, regardless of the needs of other persons. Competence assumes a different nature, however, when, first, it is manifest as effort made conjointly or collaboratively with other people, and, secondly, when the goals sought are conceived as shared or superordinate ones, transcending any single person's wants. While always, of course, some competence is exercised for the satisfaction of personal, private needs, the proportion of undertakings that are shared in their process and/or in their goals varies from society to society and from one cultural group to another within multicultural societies.

The capacity for engaging in collaborative endeavors depends, in part, on personal cognitive development which does not normally appear until children are about eight or nine years of age. Reciprocal interaction between mother and infant has been nicely studied through stop-frame analysis of films by T. Berry Brazelton and colleagues,[6] as is reported in later chapters of this book, but the continued expression of *reciprocity and collaboration* through later childhood and beyond seems to depend upon such interactions occurring in a *cultural milieu* which encourages *sharing* in a *caring community*. Research bearing on this seemingly necessary supportive field for the development and maintenance of children's cooperative and helping, or teamplay, behavior is drawn upon in Chapter Five.

Perhaps no psychological development is more intimately entwined with people's social contexts than the redefinition of their self-image beginning in early adolescence and extending through youth into young adulthood, middle, and old age. Self-images reflect people's perceptions of the appraisals they receive almost constantly from kin, peers, and other significant persons with whom they interact. Some facets and effects of *self-images* are discussed in Chapter Six, together with the search for *productive work* and *intimate relationships* in the contexts of which, during youth, the less introspectively formed and stabler self-images of later childhood are looked into, reconsidered, and modified. When capacities for collaboration and reciprocity have developed, the search for meaningful work and intimacy becomes more rewarding. Thus, self-images may reflect a greater personal sense of adequacy or power and a higher level of self-esteem.

However, as is documented in Chapter Six, the labor market favors white youth over nonwhites when jobs are available at all for large numbers of youth seeking entry to the work force. And youth's pathway toward fulfilling sexual and intimate relationships is likely to follow different routes in different societal groups. Depending on the cultural meanings attached to maleness and femaleness, heterosexual couples may have more or less of a shared partnership in contrast to a mere mating relationship. In the latter kind of sexual connection, loneliness and some of its frightening feelings and consequences may result. These issues are all part of youth's searching which is discussed in Chapter Six.

Young couples who have a child become young families—two-generation alliances of kin connected by blood or adoption. By this definition, arbitrarily set, as are most definitions, to achieve clarity about what is being discussed, a single parent and child are a family but childless couples are not. The advent of a child and the transition to parenthood for formerly childless couples mark a radical transformation in the couple's daily living. More than ever before, new parents' kin, neighborhood, and societal supports make all the difference to them in their adaptations and adjustments to the changed obligations and involvements incurred by a newborn. How such *social supports* and *young families* interact, in the beginning phases of family life—and how, without such supports, young families may be forced to break up—are the concerns of a caring society and its social services. Sharing is, at such times, a crucial social process stimulated by formal human services especially when informal resources are lacking or insufficient. Ideally, of course, human service workers anticipate the changes that occur when a first born arrives and provide many kinds of anticipatory programs for expectant couples or single mothers-to-be.

People in their forties and fifties often engage in middle-aged reappraisals of their lives and its central preoccupations to date. Parenting is likely to be at or nearing an end as a daily at-home set of activities and concerns, so that even if reappraisals are not a conscious process, many middle-aged adults are faced with the need to reapportion their time and to consider new foci. Young adult preoccupations are likely to have been, in modern times, their intimate relationships both within and outside their kinship circles as well as their means of livelihood—whether merely jobs as a source of income and attendant money worries or engagement in work one enjoys. On occasion and increasingly during affluent times when options are accessible, self-assessments in middle age result in sometimes quite radical life style changes or second chances. Job or other work-related activities may be altered, especially for formerly homebound women. In addition, new sexual alliances, marital ruptures, and second marriages, or empty nest second honeymoons with one's spouse of many years may provide new satisfactions in midlife's search for intimacy.

But a key aspect of the lives of middle-aged people, especially in Western democracies, is the degree of their feelings of *social responsibility* to their extended kinship or cultural groups, to their community (however broadly defined), and to the upcoming generations for whom the middle-aged may want to help secure a "better" world. As their own children mature and leave home, socially responsible middle-aged people may broaden their concerns and make sizable investments of their time, peaked skills, and other resources in neighborhood problems, social causes, and political concerns that extend beyond their immediate families. At some level of consciousness, they may be aware of a legacy they want to leave behind as their own lives pass beyond the midpoint and grow ever shorter.

On the other hand, for some middle-aged people, the foreshadowing of an imminent old age, occupational retirement and economic stringencies, anticipated diminutions of bodily capacities and of good health, and a host of other vaguely conceived but undesirable expectations related to aging may accelerate self-seeking midlife flings. And, for still others in the middle years, remaining as far as possible on the tracks laid down in young adulthood serves to deny the passage of time. As Chapter Eight indicates, the contexts, as well as the life styles, of people in their middle adult years are likely to be more diversified than in any previous period of life—only to be exceeded by people in their old age.

When people reach their sixties and seventies, their ways of living—as diverse as they may be—tend to reflect many aspects of their lives in young adulthood. Chapter Nine draws upon a California longitudinal study which followed the same

142 adults from, on an average, age thirty to age seventy[7]; some of the data and formulations in that study are reviewed in Chapter Nine. And while the contexts for daily living in old age make an apparent difference in how old people live, the sequence of past contexts through which people have traveled in their earlier lives continues to make a manifest and patternable difference too. Life styles in old age cannot be understood without reference to the entire framework of social developmental and contextual concepts upon which the propositions in this book rest: attachments and networks, curiosities or explorations in the novel and explorable arenas, competencies seen against the responsiveness of environments, reciprocity and collaboration in caring and sharing groups and communities, self-images reflecting appraisal of one's investments in intimate relationships and productive work, participation in family life and social supports attendant upon such family life, and during midlife transitions, the assumption of social responsibilities to human collectivities beyond one's immediate kin. Especially in old age, when personal competence may decline, the *variety and modifiability of contexts* and supports others offer become crucial. The provisions of the social services for old people reflect a society's core values about human life. But all across the life span, social contexts are integral to developmental processes, and ideas about contexts, as the term is used in this book, warrant some detailed consideration.

SOCIAL CONTEXTS

I have alluded to many kinds and dimensions of contexts throughout the prior discussion of social development. I have mentioned living places and ongoing societies into which newborns arrive, social networks, explorable arenas, and responsive environments in relation to what I call the basic social capacities. I have referred also to caring communities and cultures that value sharing, productive work places and peer groups that sanction and provide intimate relations, social supports that help new families, and communities that offer opportunities for residents to participate in socially responsible ways. In addition, there are the diverse and flexible social spaces and physical places that accommodate the continuities, losses, and legacies of old people. Each of the chapters that follow builds upon and illustrates these bare bone terms with different specific contexts or dimensions of environment. But to start with, what do they have in common?

Every environment is "a surrounding," says *Webster's New World Dictionary of the American Language.* Then, in more enlightening detail it adds that environment is "all the conditions, circumstances, and influences surrounding and affecting the development of an organism or group of organisms; often contrasted with heredity."[8]

Interchangeably with environment and surroundings, I have used the word *context.* I prefer this term because the dictionary gives it a double definition, both of which are significant in the interaction between people and their surroundings. One definition is "the whole situation, background, or environment relevant to some happening or personality." The other definition is "the parts of a sentence, paragraph, discourse, etc. that occur just before and after a specified word or passage, and determine its exact meaning." Though this second definition is literary and may seem far afield, the idea that "exact meaning" is determined by what occurs "just before and after" suggests an interdependence of the temporal parts of a total situation. If there is to be accurate understanding, one needs to consider— almost in developmental terms—what comes "just before and after." Context is thus organismic, sequential, and, perhaps most important, subject to interpretation of meaning.

People perceive and interpret their surroundings. What is involved in person-environment interaction is not merely an objectively observed setting but one that is given some personal meanings too. The term *context* thus gives a nod to the idea that the environments with (and within) which people interact are not totally objective physical and social realities, but have at least a subjective cast. On the other hand, a long-term criterion of mental health is the capacity for accurate perception or minimal distortion of one's world and one's self. There must be sufficient perceptual consensus about an environment's dimensions for people to interact with shared meanings within it.

Questions of this kind—What is environmental reality?—lead to a consideration of the theoretical and research underpinnings as well as the value assumptions that undergird the interactional approach to contexts and social development in this book.

Conceptual Underpinnings

In the sizable literature of what is now called "social ecology" and "ecological psychology," I shall refer here primarily to the work of Roger Barker and Urie Bronfenbrenner because both of them have had long-term research interests in human development (or at least child development) as well as the contexts in which development occurs. This is not to deny the importance of a long line of anthropologists, psychologists and psychiatrists, and sociologists whose studies and ideas have illuminated the complexities of person-environment interaction. Most of the early work detailed how environments influenced personality, and only in more recent decades has there been recognition of reciprocal influences between persons and their contexts. Awareness of this distinction is crucial for social workers.

In studying what he labeled "behavior settings," Barker and his colleagues focused primarily on the immediate or *microcontexts* that directly affect and are affected by people in them. "Behavior settings are independent behavior areas of a community where characteristic patterns of behavior are observed to occur; they are parts of the town that are generally recognized by the citizens."[9] In contrasting social interaction in the behavior settings of a Kansas town called Midwest and a town of similar size in Great Britain named Yoredale, Barker found evidence of differences not only between the two towns but also between the two *macrocontexts* in which they are located, the Midwestern United States of America and northern England. These differences and how they were discovered are highly relevant to this book's theses.

The behavior settings in these towns that Barker and his associates observed included stores, school classes, the post office, the railroad station, public eating places, outdoor sports, and other entertainments. Between about 500 and 600 different settings in each town were systematically observed. One of the major conclusions was that "Midwest settings are less selective, and people of all ages, sexes, and social classes associate more often on a functionally equivalent level in Midwest than in Yoredale." More specifically, the effects of these microcontext differences in the two towns are the following:

> The greater joint responsible participation of children, adolescents, and adults in the settings of Midwest reduces the differences in the functional values of these classes of people, and contributes, without doubt, to the greater self-esteem and social status of Midwest children. This often leads to a familiar, often first-naming kind of relationship between the children and adults which is in sharp contrast to the greater separation and distance in Yoredale.[10]

As an example, Barker compares summer band concerts in the two places, Midwest's town band players ranging in age from ten to forty-five while Yoredale's were professional and semiprofessional players in nearby military training camp bands. Thus, intergenerational interaction and its developmental antecedents ("before") and consequences ("after") differ in these behavior settings or microcontexts, with influences from and implications for the macrocontexts in which they are all nested.

Moreover, Barker conceives of contexts and persons being reciprocally influential. Differences in other aspects of behavior settings in Midwest and Yoredale are noted, and a generalization is made about how people form the settings they want and then, in turn, are governed by them; "A series of circular processes is initiated: of individuals creating congenial settings, and then being coerced by their own creations to behave appropriately."[11] If "coerced" suggests little play or choice for participants, the formulation seems equally static in the implication that once "created" settings do not change or are not modifiable. But the two-way or "circular" processes are recognized.

In fact, these circular processes can be planned for. Following a UNESCO-sponsored series of studies of youth growing up in cities in Argentina, Australia, Mexico, and Poland, the authors conclude:

> The children . . . should have a role to play in community maintenance and community celebration—particular functions to perform, particular places for which they are at least in part responsible. . . . The locality itself should have features that make it amenable to changes that children can accomplish. The improvements made to the small, resident-owned houses of Bystra [in Poland] and Las Rosas [in Argentina] exemplify how environments can have a form that facilitates user control. Centrally managed streets, playgrounds, and apartment yards can easily become dispiriting. The children of Melbourne and Poland might be right in their opposition to the new flat buildings. Waste

grounds offer another potential for this kind of local action—the Las Rosas pool is one example [built by neighbors]. . . .

"It is a wonderful area [Las Rosas], good, united neighbors. For Christmas we organize the Living Crèche, I played the part of the dancing shepherd, we danced the 'carnavalito' [a local dance]. The plaza is good fun. The Local Neighbors' Organization is making a swimming pool."

So reports an Argentinian adolescent, reflecting many peers' similar responses, but in marked contrast to adolescents in a western suburb of Melbourne whose environment is "distinctly limited" and who "speak constantly of their boredom."[12]

Living places become responsive to residents' wants when people are free and able to share responsibilities and involvements in local planning. Identification with one's community is nourished by such circular processes, and people's social development is fostered.

Sometimes psychologists concerned with physical and social ecology focus primarily on "the mechanisms by which the environment acts on man [sic]."[13] Rudolph Moos gives a five-part schema along "a 'positive–negative' dimension," beginning with environments that overwhelm and are "actively stressful," environments that are constraining, environments that select or favor certain people (like the behavior settings in Barker's study in Yoredale, previously reviewed), environments that elicit certain behaviors, and environments that facilitate "personal and social growth" by, for example, the "novelty and variety" they offer. These phenomena are, as Moos sees them, fitting subjects for research, but somehow the personal side of the interactional equation, "the amount of control individuals have over their environment" and the issue of "freedom of choice in selecting environments" so central to social work's concerns—are placed outside the realm of social ecological study.[14]

Urie Bronfenbrenner does not make any such distinction. Rather, he weds people and environment or human development and settings in a reciprocal relationship, from his earliest definitions on in *The Ecology of Human Development.*

Human development is the process through which the growing person acquires a more extended, differentiated, and valid conception of the ecological environment, and becomes motivated and able to engage in activities that reveal the properties of, sustain, or restructure that environment at levels of similar or greater complexity in form and content.[15]

Note that this definition of human development hinges on the person's increasingly "valid conception" of the environment and both the desire and ability to understand, maintain, or change that environment. Bronfenbrenner says that "development never takes place in a vacuum; it is always embedded and expressed through behavior in a particular environmental context."[16] Most of Bronfenbrenner's book is concerned with hypotheses, more or less well supported by research, regarding how environments affect especially child development, or "movement through ecological space—one that is both a product and a producer of developmental change."[17] Such movement, in Bronfenbrenner's conception, occurs without any reference to normative stages or an explicitly formulated sequence of developmental capacities. He is most explicit, however, about a series of "nested environments," from micro to macro, with others ("meso" and "exo") along the way. Regarding macroenvironments, in terms reminiscent of Barker's, he remarks on how "within a given society—say France—one crèche, school classroom, park playground, café, or post office looks and functions much like another, but they all differ from their counterparts in the United States."[18] Among his hypotheses, again in terms that recall Barker's behavior settings, Bronfenbrenner proposes, "The direction and degree of psychological growth are governed by the extent to which opportunities to enter settings conducive to development in various domains are open or closed to the developing person."[19]

A successful search for specificity about the "various domains" and the dimensions of conducive settings should be of prime concern to social work. Social work does address the issue of people's access to resources, for reasons that Bronfenbrenner's hypothesis on "open and closed" domains proposes. But we have still to learn what contexts foster what kinds of development. Such formulations are needed to sharpen social work's focus on environmental targets that matter—that is, have predictable effects. Also the broad assumptions underlying ideas about social development and its contexts need to be considered in the light of current statements of social work's purposes.

Assumptions, Values, and Professional Purpose

The schema of social development and its contextual requirements sketched in an earlier section of this chapter is based upon many assumptions about both a "good society" and what are considered desirable goals for people in their personal growth. The whole idea of development postulates directional change, not merely modifications or even accretions. The concept of developmental phases, one growing to some extent upon another, implies that there are progressions from, for example, simple to more complex capacities. And while biologists confirm that living organisms inherit information that orients their sequential development, such development is still influenced by environments. How or whether new capacities appear and how they are expressed in a given setting are responsive to the relevant contexts with which a person interacts. Moreover, different facets of environment presumably affect different aspects of organisms' programmed potentials for personal growth and change. And since developing organisms alter their environments, certain dimensions of environment are probably developed and supported by cohorts of people who have developed or are developing in certain ways.

The concept of macro-social development is used to refer to planned social change, in communities or nations, which affects residents' "quality of life." Macro-social development includes the formation and growth of social services and other components of a society which improve community life. The term *social develop-*

ment, in a societal context, is used to describe processes and effects that contrast with economic development or improvement in the production, distribution, and consumption of goods and services. I conceive of personal social development and macro-social development as interrelated processes, the details of which cannot be specified extensively and confidently at present because of lacks in relevant knowledge.

There are a few assumptions about contexts in relation to social development which can, however, be proposed with some confidence. Thinking of context first as community or larger society, I assume that a generally "good society" for human social development offers a variety of *options* to accommodate the individual differences among its many and diverse developing members. A "good society" provides people with *access* to these options, not reserved just for the few. A "good society" also grants maximum opportunity for public *participation* in the shaping and reshaping of important public contexts. In this way, people's competencies can be put to use and further developed. People feel socially integrated in their society, and the societal need for social control can be reconciled with people's experience of cooperation and their sense of freedom.

Reciprocally, such a society calls for the development of people with a capacity for social responsibility. They must be able to collaborate with others for the common welfare. Biologist René Dubos states categorically, "All living things, without exception, depend on other living things for their survival and development."[20] Mathematician and philosopher Alfred North Whitehead adds,

> Successful organisms modify their environments. Those organisms are successful which modify their environments so as to assist each other. This law is exemplified in nature on a vast scale.[21]

People's social interdependence is an incontrovertible assumption of life in the present day world. This requires that people be able to share goods and services, the more privileged having to moderate their personal wants and find satisfaction in sharing. The assumption also calls for the development of capacities for reciprocal caring and abilities to help alleviate, at personal cost, the stress of other people. In interdependent societal contexts, the sequence of social development I have sketched, from capacities for attachment, through reciprocity and collaboration, to socially responsible involvements in community life, is likely to be both needed and fostered. The sequence stipulates goals toward which the social services might help people move.

In fact, recent reformulations of social work purposes propose that social workers have a "dual responsibility . . . to aid in the mobilization of both the individual's inner capabilities and society's external resources"[22] or "to promote or restore a mutually beneficial interaction between individuals and society in order to improve the quality of life for everyone."[23] The latter quotation from a "Working Statement on the Purpose of Social Work" published in the National Association of Social Workers' journal, *Social Work,* continues with a set of "beliefs" regarding "environment," "individuals," and the "transactions" among them as follows:

The environment (social, physical, organizational) should provide the opportunity and resources for the maximum realization of the potential and aspirations of all individuals, and should provide for their common human needs and the alleviation of distress and suffering.

Individuals should contribute as effectively as they can to their own well-being and to the social welfare of others in their immediate environment as well as to the collective society.

Transactions between individuals and others in their environment should enhance the dignity, individuality, and self-determination of everyone. People should be treated humanely and with justice.[24]

The consonance of these values with this book's framework on social development and its contexts is apparent. These values or "should's" orient social workers, first of all, to environmental conditions. A good society should provide (a) developmentally conducive contexts (for people's "maximum realization"), (b) fundamental supports (for people's "common human needs"), and (c) informal and formal crisis and remedial services (for "alleviation of distress and suffering"). Secondly, people should be able ("competent") to further (a) their own "well-being," (b) the "welfare" of kin, friends, and neighbors in their community, and (c) the "social welfare" of the larger society beyond their local region. Such "should's" suggest the importance of people's social participation, social integration, and basic feelings of social responsibility. Note, finally, the value placed on respect, freedom ("self-determination"), and equality ("justice"). These general values are brought into clearer focus for social work's policy making, program planning, and direct intervention in the following statement of "Objectives":

Social workers focus on person-and-environment *in interaction.* To carry out their purpose, they work with people to achieve the following objectives:

Help people enlarge their competence and increase their problem-solving and coping abilities.
Help people obtain resources.
Make organizations responsive to people.
Facilitate interaction between individuals and others in their environment.
Influence interactions between organizations and institutions.
Influence social and environmental policy.

To achieve these objectives, social workers work with other people. At different times, the target of change varies—it may be the client, others in the environment, or both.[25]

Note that, as in the social developmental framework, emphases are given to social work's (a) fostering people's "competence" and "coping abilities," (b) improving access to environmental "resources," and (c) helping to make organizations and presumably other contexts "responsive to people." To do so, the "targets of change" may be "the client" and/or the client's context.

There is a clearly stated central thrust in such a statement of social work's purpose and objectives, but social workers with different educational and experiential qualifications engage in a wide range of activities. Some do intensive clinical work with emotionally troubled and developmentally blocked persons. Others engage in the planning of income maintenance programs. For the group or community worker, the social planner, and the clinician to remain in communication as members of a single profession, statements of purpose like the one just cited seem essential. People's competence, well-being, and responsive contexts—and the other elements specified—are shared basic concerns of all workers in the social services, from the professionally educated to the many volunteers in the field.

But in addition to shared purpose, objectives, and values, there should be a common knowledge base. Focused on the field as defined by professional purpose and objectives, some set of concepts and formulations with the best available research underpinnings should help to keep co-professionals in communication and, at the very least, from working at cross-purposes. And most important, the use of tested ideas leads ultimately to the most effective services. For such, of course, there must also be a developing body of practice principles which guide intervention, but these too are based, in social work, on certain assumptions about people and their contexts, how they normally change or develop, and how they may be changed by professional planning and provisions. For all these reasons, social workers need an adequately grounded and integrated set of perspectives on the subjects of their professional concerns.

The contextual, developmental and interactional (CDI) approach which this book expands upon provides one set of concepts and propositions of use to social work. An approach like this is useful to social work for a few reasons. The CDI approach addresses conceptually issues in the orbit of social work's purpose and objectives. This approach thus provides conceptual links between professional activity and formulations which derive from empirical study and have relative validity. To some extent, CDI formulations offer predictions, without which anticipatory or preventive planning is likely to be ineffective. The concepts clarify focus and offer handles for professional study and intervention. In the case of the CDI approach, the orientation is initially to normal developmental and environmental interaction, and therefore to the provision of supportive and developmental social services. These services aim to prevent or reduce crises and development-retarding stressful situations. Presumably, the ever-expanding need for remedial services can be lessened as, most important, human suffering is reduced.

Finally, and perhaps needless to say, a useful conceptual approach is one which raises questions and itself develops as new evidence accumulates. Commitment to its basic tenets gives a field of practice continuity and stability upon which policy and program can be built and then systematically or, as changed conditions and understandings warrant, radically altered. Without the support and orientation given by a valid and growing conceptual approach, workers in a field of action may find themselves buffeted about, or in turn attracted and then disenchanted by always new and unrelated perspectives. A useful conceptual approach is well-rooted in cumulative studies that have a history and literature as evidence of many years of systematic study. This underlying and ongoing process and background seem essential before significant interventions are made into people's lives. Nevertheless, little understood crises may have to be addressed in an effort to relieve people's pain, even though there is an inadequate research base. Health care in the human services has long had to operate in this fashion. But the most useful conceptual approaches for social work have a knowledge base that is steadily being advanced by study.

SOCIAL SERVICES, CONTEXTS, AND DEVELOPMENT

To illustrate links between research and the social services, and simultaneously how such services as microcontexts affect people's development, while the services are themselves affected by the macrocontexts in which they are nested, I draw upon three studies in this final section. In each of the chapters of this book I include research, practice-based, or personal records to amplify and personalize a chapter's ideas. In this introductory chapter, I use studies in which I have been directly involved, so I am able here to offer observations that go beyond the limits of the published reports.

But first, some general comments about the ideas illustrated by the records. Some social services, such as residential treatment centers and youth groups, become significant microcontexts for developing children and youth. Adult development may be furthered by services for single mothers, old people, or others who are involved in neighborhood center programs. Such services organize groups or other microcontexts which directly affect clients. But social services are themselves shaped by their macroenvironments. For example, the legislative provisions and funding of the federal government, a fundamentally influential macroenvironment, augment or curtail the size and options of public programs. Regional demographic, economic, and value differences at state and county levels, sometimes of longstanding historical origins, may transform the ways in which services are provided. Yet all services, ultimately, aim to make a difference in their clients' coping abilities, and these differences would seem to depend on the forms, as microcontexts, and services that children's nurseries, youth groups, or foster care assume. This is what each of the three following records is about.

RESIDENTIAL NURSERIES AS MICROCONTEXTS (RECORD NO. 1)

This first record comes from a study of preschool children in wartime Great Britain who were evacuated from their homes in London, threatened by air attack. There were various evacuation programs, but the one I studied through a twenty-year-after follow-up involved parents of intact families who had voluntarily sent their children out of London and into group care in the countryside. My curiosity about the possible long-term effects of early childhood separation seemed best answered by studying, in 1960–61, young adults who had experienced a year or more in one of three quite different residential situations away from their own families. While my overall findings were that most of the twenty Londoners studied "give no evidence of any extreme aberrant reactions," there was clearly a subgroup of young adults from one of the three nurseries who scored the highest on the developmental measures used to assess them. These measures included the nature of their relationships with other people as young adults and their involvements and competence in social roles.

Admittedly, twenty years after their early childhood placements, cause and effect are impossible to establish. And yet some of the hypotheses proposed by Bronfenbrenner and commented on later in this section seem to be supported by the associations or findings of this study. Clearly, if there had been very serious and enduring damage to any of these twenty adults, it would have been apparent in the projective test protocols and other kinds of assessment obtained.

From the study report, I quote first the brief descriptions of the three nurseries and then my speculations about why the one nursery may have been, if not the best, then the least damaging for these preschool children. Perhaps readers can guess, as the nurseries are described, which might have provided the most developmentally conducive context, under these special wartime circumstances, and why.

. . . three quite different wartime residential nurseries provided alumni for the group of twenty adults in this study. The three nurseries will be called Nursery N, Nursery E, and Nursery S. To characterize and compare them, three dimensions will be used. (It must be remembered, however, that nurseries, like the children in them, change over time, and only a capsule presentation can be made here. . . .) The three dimensions are: (1) numbers of children and staff; (2) children's relationships with their parents; and (3) staff orientation to the children.

In brief, Nursery N is the middle-sized one in terms of numbers of children, with the most generous supply of staff members to children. Each staff person had at least one child assigned to her. A common pattern among the three- to five-year-olds was the assignment of living groups of about five children to one staff helper. Parents could visit at any time and there were "strong contacts with parents." In a time of gasoline shortage, the fact that Nursery N was physically closer to London than either of the other two nurseries is important. With the older children in Nursery N, "We talked about parents, wrote to them. We had pictures of parents. Sunday nights were always exciting. There was a bus every Sunday. Some were very sad when Mummy had gone. Perhaps we can write a letter. We didn't put any child to bed who was upset. We took them in our rooms and talked to them. They could talk about it." This was a key to the Nursery N approach to children—the expression of feelings was encouraged, guided by a depth of psychological understanding of young children that was not present in either of the other two nurseries.

The second nursery, E, was the smallest, able to accommodate only about twenty children. Its staff consisted of a professionally untrained woman, Mrs. E, and her physiotherapist daughter, Miss E, with occasional part-time domestic help from the nearby Welsh village. Thus, the ratio of staff to children was about ten to one. Deep in the Welsh countryside, Nursery E was the most inaccessible to the London parents whose children were routed to Mrs. E and her daughter through an East End settlement house. Interviews and the log book of Nursery E indicate that parents' visits were most infrequent. The alien nature of the East End culture to Mrs. E's stern Welsh world and her approach to the children are best suggested by her own words: "Those were very interesting days and I personally loved every one of them! Bedwetter, sleep walkers, live heads, and sores. We got the better of the lot, and P was our only failure, and a doctor at the London hospital said he was incurable [as a bedwetter], poor lad. They were all fairly undisciplined—but very soon 'fell in' and we really were a very happy family—no friction anywhere." Nursery E was in marked contrast to the psychologically oriented Nursery N.

The third of the nurseries, S, was eventually the largest and had the highest ratio of children to staff. Nursery S had been a model day nursery school for the children of working mothers. Those who had been attending the school were evacuated as a unit like other school classes—starting out with forty-seven children who knew one another, their head teacher, and her three helpers. There was "no domestic help at first." Parents visited Nursery S at Christmas or Easter time, in a bus they arranged for themselves, and a festive spread was miraculously provided by Lady X, in whose home Nursery S was billeted. Many anecdotes suggest the teachers' possessiveness regarding the children in their charge during their country's time of crisis. The teachers were trained nursery school educators, not psychologists, as the head teacher remarked, "with their psychological jargon, their observations, and their graphs." These teachers told their children that they had left London because the King had wanted them to. Children's song and games, spiritual values, God and country, and the wonders of nature were central themes. The time that the busload of parents was getting ready to leave and the geese were let loose to distract the children was described with delight. In Nursery S, I was told, weeping at parting occurred among the parents, but not among the children. (The statement, not the fact, is important.)

In brief contrast, then, substitute parenting at Nursery N was open and expressive; at Nursery E somewhat firm, if not stern, and suppressive; and at Nursery S, with its faith in God, King, and denial, rather inspirational and repressive, and quite possessive.[26]

Details on the procedures used for psychological assessment are given in the published report and cannot be reviewed here, except to say that the data were reduced to ratings. The ratings were then summated for each of the three residential nursery groups separately. The research report continues as follows:

Examination of these ratings by nursery group reveal that the graduates of the somewhat firm, if not stern and suppressive small Welsh Nursery E appear as young adults to be essentially no better or worse adjusted than the graduates of the psychologically sophisticated and much larger Nursery N. The group that is clearly the best off is the one from the day nursery evacuated as a unit—Nursery S, with its faith in God, King, and denial and its rather inspirational, repressive, and possessive approach to the children.[27]

Why *might* the Nursery S group have fared the best of the three groups? In a field study like this, all that can be offered are speculative explanations, which are untested. Following is one possible after-the-fact formulation about what was empirically discovered. It makes sense in view of what is known from other sources about the importance for young children of continuity in their home environments. As long ago as the 1930s it was found that "behavior problems" of children in foster care in Kansas were "associated with the agency's policy of breaking as completely as possible all continuity with a former foster home when for any reason a child was moved into a new foster home;" testing this idea in cases involving over 500 shifts in home, Cowan and Stout found significant support for the idea that children undergoing complete breaks from former homes were less well off than those who had had some continuing connection with their past home environments.[28] In the London Study, the environmental continuity issue differentiated Nursery S from the other two.

The procedure of group residential placement following a period of day care, when children come to know the other children involved and the adults in charge, is unusual. At a day care nursery school, teachers and working mothers meet to discuss child-rearing and child-care problems, and some awareness of each others' values is communicated. Continuity in way of life and in personal relationships for the children between their day care and their residential group is provided for. "For the infant and young child," as Yarrow says, "changes result in a loss of environmental predictability. The degree of stress involved is likely to vary with the degree of unpredictability." The Nursery S placement plan seems to reduce the unpredictability of residential care. Whether this arrangement alone induces results such as the superior adjustment of Nursery S children would seem to warrant further study.[29]

My last comment on residential Nursery S as a microcontext affecting children's development brings us back to Bronfenbrenner's hypotheses on the ecology of human development. A series of his hypotheses with relevant research cited proposes that development proceeds with the least hindrance when people move to new settings if these new settings are supportively linked to their previous settings. In his terms, there may be "transcontextual dyads" (twosomes who move together) or similarity in role demands. A new situation resembles a former one when the same people are involved in both and there is good communication between the two settings.[30] How aptly these ideas find support in the evidence from Nursery S. And I cite Bronfenbrenner's late 1970s generalizations after having referred to the compatible details of a late 1930s study by Cowan and Stout as a reminder of the long and cumulative pathways systematic study follows. Such formulations may be used with considerable confidence in organizing contexts in the social services.

Continuities and similarities between former contexts and new ones can be effected in a variety of ways, and should be if such conditions foster social development.

YOUTH GROUPS
AND YOUTH GROUP WORKERS
(RECORD NO. 2)

In this exploratory study of youth groups and student group workers, their professional development is found to occur more readily in certain kinds of group situations than in others, depending on the workers' personal styles. The small group is seen as a microcontext, which affects how workers see the group members as well as how the workers perform in the group, all in patternable ways which the study's findings reveal.

In this action-oriented study, a concurrent educational program aimed to help young adult students in youth group placements become less judgmental and more cause-seeking in how they perceived the behavior of the members of their community-based youth groups. Analyses of their field work logs over an eight-month period indicated that only half of the twenty-two workers in the project became less judgmental and more cause-seeking, as desired.

Co-observers of the youth groups in the field found that the group programs differed markedly, as did the nature of member-worker interaction. Ten of the groups had activity programs, very informal meeting procedures, and membership open to anyone who wanted to join. These were categorized as "open groups." The group workers tended to be very active participants in these open groups. The twelve other groups had religious, ethical, or social purposes, regulated themselves by parliamentary and other formal procedures, usually called for the voting in of youth applying for membership and used initiation rituals for their inception, and were classified, for study purposes, as "closed groups." In these latter groups, the group workers had a rather peripheral role as advisors. The co-observers' field records showed that workers in open groups initiated twice as much of the group interaction as did workers in closed groups. Moreover, group members addressed three or more times as much of their interaction to open group workers as they did to closed group workers. Clearly, open groups required more active involvement of their workers than did closed groups. But type of group was not apparently associated with which of the student workers changed his perception of members in desired ways. Of the eleven workers who became less judgmental and more cause-seeking about youth group members' behavior, six worked in open groups and five in closed groups.

Were some student workers more psychologically oriented to judging and blaming other people? The young adult students' autobiographical reports about their own adolescence, together with their responses to a personality inventory, differentiated what were called x-type and y-type workers. The x-type students tended to report themselves as feeling self-confident and, at the same time, markedly critical of others; x-type students expected other people to change their ways.

The y-type workers tended to report a lower sense of their own capacities, showed a relatively uncritical acceptance of others, and were likely to adapt or otherwise modify their own behavior to meet external pressures rather than expecting or trying to effect environmental change. Admittedly, this kind of dichotomous classification into x-type and y-type is an unrefined reduction of human complexity into an oversimplified mold, and yet for a first, exploratory study the procedure seemed justifiable and yielded plausible findings.

The personal distinctions between x-type and y-type, considered by themselves, shed no light on the differences in the student workers' changes in perception. Five of the x-type workers changed in desired ways as did six of the y-type workers. But when the changes were examined against the type of group placement and *x* or *y* typing *combined,* a pattern emerged. The x-type workers in activity-centered or open groups showed the hoped for professional development, but the x-type workers in closed groups did not. By contrast, the y-type workers in the formal or closed groups changed desirably, but the y-type workers in open groups did not. Given these discovered differences in the "fit" between contexts and developmental status, what explanations might be offered? It was speculated that x-type workers experience less frustration in open than in closed groups and thus find the former kinds of context more conducive to their own professional development. Conversely, y-type workers feel more competent in clearly structured or closed groups than in unstructured or open groups. In the latter context, members' demands upon them may seem excessive and threatening. They may become anxious, and development is less likely to occur under such conditions.[31]

The question of compatible placements for students or beginning social workers has not been studied in any systematic way. In the language of this book, such placements may be seen as more or less conducive contexts for professional development, as these contexts interact with personal capacities and predilections which have still to be specified. Social agencies provide microcontexts which foster the social development not only of their clients but also of their staff members. A complexity which must be remembered, however, is that every microcontext has a reciprocally interactive and influential relationship with the macrocontext in which it is located. Two such relationships, between foster care services and their macrocontexts, are described in the third and last record in this chapter.

RURAL COUNTIES
AS MACROCONTEXTS
FOR FOSTER CARE
(RECORD NO. 3)

Living places like the three residential nurseries in Record No. 1 and work settings like the open and closed groups of Record No. 2 are not the only kinds of context affecting people's social development. Another kind is macrosocietal. Social policy is planned at state and federal as well as at local levels. Direct service practitioners sometimes consider and try to deal with the effects of macrosocial forces on their practice and its outcomes. Thus, useful studies bearing on social development illuminate relationships between large societal modifiabilities and people's development, as well as between microcontexts and the kinds of interaction and development they induce.

As an example of what I mean, I conclude this chapter with a record of macrosocial processes in two rural counties of two different North Central states as part of a nationwide field study of foster care. The study aimed to discover how the different macrocontexts, ranging from farm counties to metropolises across the United States, differentially affect children's experiences in foster care. The study took two research teams from New England to the Pacific Northwest, and from the South Atlantic states through Texas to the Southwest, with stopoffs in Central and Mountain states, for a total of nine locations. In each of the nine counties, both the children in foster care and their macrosocial contexts were the double focus of study. The assumption that the outcome of a child welfare "case" depends only on the child's parents and foster parents, on the child him- or herself, and the caseworker is, of course, as any experienced child welfare worker knows, a myth. The social structure, culture, and related policies and provisions of the macrosociety in which the child welfare agency operates also make a difference as to what can happen in foster care.

In the illustrative excerpts from the study report, one rural county is called Norden, with Abbotsford as its county seat. The other rural county is Granger, with its county seat in Daleville. Norden was in the richer of the two North Central states—a state which in the late 1950s emphasized institutional care for dependent children, in keeping with the dominant values of its quite homogeneous population. Thus, two thirds of Norden's children in foster care were found in privately sponsored institutional placements. By contrast, two thirds of Granger's children in foster care—all of them known to Mrs. Camilla Jones, the committed county public welfare director—lived fairly well-integrated lives in the community in foster families. The quoted excerpts start with a "typical" child in foster care in each of the two counties.

Karl Bayer, thirteen years old, lived with about fifty other boys and girls in the Abbotsford Home for Children. Abbotsford is the county seat of Norden County, with a population of about 5,000. Like most other thirteen-year-old boys and girls in Abbotsford, Karl attended the eighth grade class at the public school and every Sunday morning went to St. John's Lutheran Church. But the other children and their parents and just about everyone in town knew that Karl was "different," for he was from the Home.

About two years ago, Karl arrived at the Home from a county across the state after he had succeeded in "exploding" two prior foster placements. His first had been in a large private institution for dependent children outside Walloon, where he lived for a year and a half following his eighth birthday. Karl's second placement was with a foster family in Walloon for almost twelve painful months. Increasingly during these years Karl's vacillating demands for attention were followed by violently distrustful responses to any and all adults . . .

Gary Olsen was twelve and a half years old and lived with the Meads, just outside Daleville. Like Karl, in Norden County, Gary was white, Lutheran, of average intelligence, and free from physical disability or disease. Like Karl, Gary was one of four children of parents who no longer lived together. Again, Gary's father was in his late forties and earned his living by unskilled work, in this case farm labor; Gary's mother, in her late thirties, was thought to be remarried. These were the similarities. But community reactions differentiated the situations of the two boys.

Mrs. Jones placed Gary and his three brothers in two different foster families when Judge Swanson removed them from their father for "neglect." This was almost three years ago. Actually, Mrs. Jones had known about, and kept a watchful eye on, the Olsen family ever since, a year before, Gary's mother had deserted the family and Mr. Olsen's drinking had become worse. Farm neighbors—mostly the families for whom Mr. Olsen had worked—were able to help on an informal basis just so long. Judge Swanson removed the children until, he said, Mr. Olsen could give evidence that he had mended his ways. . . .

Computed from the histories of all the children in care in these two rural counties—children like Karl Bayer and Gary Olsen—the percentages in Table 1-1 indicate important differences in foster care in the two macrocontexts. In Norden, not only were most of the children in institutional care but also they averaged twice as long in care as did the Granger children. This occurred even though the Norden children tended not to be placed until after they had entered school.

By contrast, Granger children, most of whom when placed went into foster families, were discovered to need substitute care earlier in their lives, while still pre-

TABLE 1-1 Placement, Length of Care, and Separation Ages of Children in Norden and Granger Counties

	NORDEN COUNTY (ABBOTSFORD)	GRANGER COUNTY (DALEVILLE)
Type of placement, by percentage of children in care on April 1		
In foster family care	25	67
In institutional care	67	17
In adoptive homes	8	17
Average (median) number of years since first separation from parents, for all children under study	5	2½
Age at which children first entered care, by percentage of all children under study		
As preschoolers (0–5 years)	19	40
As school-aged children (6–10 years)	44	16

schoolers. Were Granger County people more aware of and concerned about how their local families cared for their children? Or in Granger were people less reluctant than in Norden to act upon evidence of family neglect or abuse of their children? Portraits of the local judges who made decisions about involuntary placements appear as Record No. 23 at the end of Chapter Eight; the marked difference in their values about family autonomy and community responsibility may well reflect the macrosocial values in which they worked.

Do differences in some of the social processes and structures of Norden and Granger help to explain differences in the ways their children's services were provided? I present field observations and other facts on population composition, the economy, and values in these two rural counties as of the time the study was made. I start with Norden County where institutional care and later and longer placements characterized its child welfare programs.

Norden is located in a state which calls itself the "richest agricultural area in the world." But this rich agricultural area was rapidly changing, and the change could be seen in the redefinition which it sought for its economy. For the same brochures which declared this to be "the richest agricultural area" went on to invite "industry, science, and commerce" to communities where people who "know how to work" would be awaiting them.

Here, in a region central to avenues that carry core-cultural values across the farm lands, the problem of securing industry which could absorb the growing town populations being surplused off the farms was being faced directly. Still, the concern was with adjusting the economy in the interests of those who, having grown up in the small communities of the state, had a pride in their local areas and wished to continue to live, work, and raise their families there. Thus Norden was not in the market for new people; rather, it sought industry to better the life of those who already were in and of the county.

What had economic changes meant to Norden and its people? The predominant German Lutheran stock, whose ancestors predated the Civil War, still were anchored to the milk herds and creameries that make Norden the dairy spot of the state. And even the appearance of agriculturally oriented industries, like the large farm machinery plant, had not changed its ethnic make-up. The visitor immediately felt the homogeneity of these people, of whom one resident said, "Here one is either Lutheran or German or both, or an outsider." Even new occupations had tended to spring from grass-roots beginnings so that the industry one saw in Norden was not so much outside industry but, as it were, "inside industry." Still, and this is in contrast to Granger, the total Norden County population had increased, particularly in the decade and a half since the Second World War. But the evidence indicated that the newcomers too, coming mostly from neighboring rural counties, tended also to be "either Lutheran or German or both." Coupled with this is another contrast to Granger County; in Norden only about one in thirty-five of the local inhabitants was listed as foreign born (almost all of these, by the way, were either German or Danish).

These facts indicate something about Norden as a community which contrasts it with Granger. Norden had felt itself to be progressing steadily for a hundred years. It had been relatively closed to any but people much like those who had grown up there in the past several generations. Yet it had continued to grow and to thrive, with the pattern of its growth being largely conditioned by social dynamisms which not only affected internal conditions but deflected and modified the influences toward change which came from without. New residential areas had grown up on the periphery of Abbotsford, and commercial and industrial concerns had added office buildings and factory additions. And the evidence indicated, as we have noted before, that Norden, unlike Granger, was tending to hold its young people. . . .

The daily happenings in and around Granger County are in some ways not very different from happenings in other parts of rural America today. Still remote from the main lines of commerce and communication, Granger's rural ways changed slowly. The Big Missouri, scene of an expanding network of Federal engineering projects, is more than a hundred miles west of Daleville. And the new interstate highway, linking the state capital to the east with the state's largest retail and whole-sale center to the west, would by-pass Daleville and barely permit the traveler a glimpse of the city's tree-lined streets and stone churches.

The people who settled Granger County were like many of those one finds sprinkled westward across the Northern United States. They raised livestock, and grain from the rich soil of the river valleys, and congregated for their worship and their social and commercial activities in the towns which dot the right of ways of the Northern Pacific—one of the proud empire-building railroads of an earlier era. They were largely Scandinavian and other Northern European folk—Norwegians and Swedes, with a sizable proportion of Germans and Danes interspersed among them. But in Granger County, we found enough Southern and Eastern European stock— Russian, Austrian, Hungarian, Czech, and Polish—and enough Catholicism alongside the predominant Lutheranism for this to be an area in which differences among people were visible and accepted. Significant too for this feeling of openness to difference in such a relatively small community was the fact that one out of four-teen of Granger's inhabitants was still counted by the U.S. census-takers as foreign born. For the child in need of substitute parents, also in his own way different, Granger's air of acceptance of difference was relevant.

The children of Granger have grown up in this social setting amidst an agri-cultural economy. But there is a breadth to the horizons of the Granger countryside which makes it difficult for local youths to keep the locus of their life ambitions within the county's boundaries. There is a challenge in a landscape of level fields that invites exploration of what lies beyond them. And just as the whistle of the Northern Pacific once lured away young men during the drought and depression days of the thirties, so the flow of traffic along the east-west artery now takes with it an increasing number of Granger County youth, as often as not in cars which prosperous postwar years have enabled them to purchase for themselves. It was a tribute to the agricultural wealth of Granger County that it had prospered so well in the postwar years and had held many of its human resources close to the soil. Still, with the consolidation of farms and with the advent of more machines that replaced farm hands, agricultural employment was shrinking. And with this dwindling of opportunity in agriculture came a declining population in Granger County. . . . It was here that we observed children like Gary Olsen, children who had been deprived of homes of their own and for whom the community assumed the responsibility of foster parenthood.

In short, in the county which was ethnically more heterogeneous and economically less well off, foster family care was available to more of the children needing care. People in Granger seemed sympathetically responsive to economic hardship. The report concludes:

. . . Norden seemed to stress independence of the individual, while Granger had had more growth experience that stressed the importance of interdependence. Wounds of the great depression were recalled as much more painful in Granger than in Norden. And Granger seemed more receptive to visible ethnic differences within the community, having had a wider range of social experience in its history.

Finally, in terms of orientation to the dependent child and his family, Granger seemed to accept the children of our study more into the larger "we," while Norden relegated them more to a "they." If the depression of the thirties brought crises to a larger number of people in Granger than in Norden, dependency conditions were thus more normal to Granger than to Norden. But most of all, the dependent child in Granger was initially one of the community's own, while most dependent children in institutional treatment in Norden came there from outside the community, often after many other foster care experiences. Thus the dependent child in Norden, being seen as different, was in a situation that tended to consign him to a "they" position in this homogeneous, independence-oriented, and highly personalized community. Consequently, his social and psychological problems of personal identity—knowing his worth, place, and direction—seemed greatly enhanced.[32]

Child welfare resources, timetables, and developmental experiences for children in care differ in these two counties. Foster families may be easier to find and more frequently used in less affluent and less urbanized places, especially where the value of getting ahead personally has not displaced a sense of interdependence among diverse neighbors. In an interdependent community, other people's children remain visible. Children whose own parents cannot care for them receive community support. Children needing placement remain in care a shorter time when there are concern and help for the social conditions and capacities of parents in trouble. Children may thus return to their own family more promptly, or move into an adoptive home or some other permanent placement. Such formulations suggest the complex interplay of macrocontexts, microcontexts, and social development, with social services an integral part of the setting.

Differences in the residential nurseries and in the youth groups, as reported in the first two records, covary with differences in how people involved in them change over time. Propositions like these should, of course, be discussed and questioned in the light of other evidence. Many studies of interaction between social development and contexts are reported in this book, especially those having relevance for the human services.

Generally, differences among people's developmental potentials and capacities both generate and require a great diversity of contexts and options within them. In multicultural countries, regional variations of kinds merely suggested by the excerpted fragments on Norden and Granger appear and seem to persist. The great range of individual differences among human beings from birth on, as discussed in the next chapter, makes the study of macrosocietal dimensions important for an understanding of social development.

NOTES

[1] Definitions serve as boundary setters and specifiers of a field for study in books of this kind. For different views of social development, see Robert B. Cairns, *Social Development: The Origins and Plasticity of Interchanges* (San Francisco: W. H. Freeman, 1979); Robert A. Hinde, "Social Development: a Biological Approach," in Jerome S. Bruner and Alison Garton, eds., *Human Growth and Development: Wolfson College Lectures, 1976* (Oxford: Clarendon Press, 1978), pp. 1–32; and Zick Rubin and Willard Hartup, eds., *Children's Relationships: Their Role in Social and Emotional Development* (forthcoming), papers from a 1981 conference sponsored by the Committee on Social and Emotional Development, the Social Science Research Council.

[2] Chauncey A. Alexander, "Social Work in the 80's: Issues and Strategies," *The Social Worker/Le Travailleur Social*, 50 (1982), p. 65.

[3] "Working Statement on the Purpose of Social Work," developed by participants at the second meeting on conceptual frameworks, in *Social Work*, 26 (1981), p. 6. Reprinted with permission.

[4] Erik H. Erikson, *Childhood and Society*, 2nd ed. (New York: W. W. Norton, 1963), p. 273.

[5] Allen H. Barton, *Communities in Disaster: A Sociological Analysis of Collective Stress Situations* (Garden City, New York: Anchor Books, 1970).

[6] T. Berry Brazelton and others, "The Infant as a Focus for Family Reciprocity," in Michael Lewis and Leonard A. Rosenblum, eds., *The Child and its Family* (New York: Plenum Press, 1979), pp. 29–43.

[7] Henry S. Maas and Joseph A. Kuypers, *From Thirty to Seventy: A Forty-Year Longitudinal Study of Adult Life Styles and Personality* (San Francisco: Jossey–Bass Publishers, 1974).

[8] *Webster's New World Dictionary of the American Language*, College Edition (Cleveland: World Publishing Company, 1964).

[9] Roger G. Barker and Associates, *Habitats, Environments, and Human Behavior* (San Francisco: Jossey–Bass, 1978), p. 94.

[10] Roger Barker and Louise Barker, "Behavior Units for the Comparative Study of Cultures," in Bert Kaplan, ed., *Studying Personality Cross-Culturally* (Evanston, Illinois: Row, Peterson and Co., 1961), p. 474.

[11] Barker, "Behavior Units," p. 475.

[12] Kevin Lynch, ed., *Growing Up in Cities* (Cambridge, Mass.: M.I.T. Press (with UNESCO, Paris), 1977), pp. 24, 57, 118, and 123. On urban environments for the young, see also William Michelson, Saul V. Levine, and Ellen Michelson, eds., *The Child in the City: Today and Tomorrow*, volume I, and William Michelson and others, eds., *The Child in the City: Changes and Challenges*, volume II (Toronto: University of Toronto Press, 1979). In addition

to Roger Barker's previously cited studies of small town contexts in the Midwest and in Yorkshire, England, see the report of a two-year inquiry into the uses and meanings of space and pathways in and around a small New England town called "Inavale," as its children see it, in Roger Hart, *Children's Experience of Place: a Developmental Study* (New York: Halsted Press, 1977).

[13] Rudolf H. Moos, *The Human Context: Environmental Determinants of Behavior* (New York: Wiley, 1976), pp. 29–31.

[14] Moos, *Human Context,* pp. 29–31.

[15] Urie Bronfenbrenner, *The Ecology of Human Development: Experiments by Nature and Design* (Cambridge, Mass.: Harvard University Press, 1979), p. 27.

[16] Bronfenbrenner, *Ecology,* p. 27.

[17] Bronfenbrenner, *Ecology,* p. 26.

[18] Bronfenbrenner, *Ecology,* p. 26.

[19] Bronfenbrenner, *Ecology,* p. 288.

[20] Rene Dubos, "The Mysteries of Life," *Propaedia: Outline of Knowledge* (Chicago: Encyclopaedia Britannica, 15th ed., 1977), pp. 128–29.

[21] Alfred North Whitehead, *Science and the Modern World* (Middlesex, England: Penguin Books, 1938), p. 238.

[22] Alexander, "Social Work," p. 65.

[23] "Working Statement," p. 6. Reprinted with permission.

[24] "Working Statement," p. 6.

[25] "Working Statement," p. 6.

[26] Henry S. Maas, "The Young Adult Adjustment of Twenty Wartime Residential Nursery Children," *Child Welfare,* 42 (1963), pp. 60–61. Quoted with the permission of the Child Welfare League of America.

[27] Maas, "The Young Adult," p. 69.

[28] Edwina A. Cowan and Eva Stout, "A Comparative Study of the Adjustment Made by Foster Children after Complete and Partial Breaks in Continuity of Home Environment," *American Journal of Orthopsychiatry,* 9 (1939), pp. 330–38.

[29] Maas, "The Young Adult," pp. 69–70. The Yarrow quotation is from Leon Yarrow, "Maternal Deprivation: Toward an Empirical and Conceptual Reevaluation," *Psychological Bulletin,* 58 (1961), p. 481. For a more recent review of this issue, see Michael Rutter, "Maternal Deprivation, 1972–1978: New Findings, New Concepts, New Approaches," in Stella Chess and Alexander Thomas, eds., *Annual Progress in Child Psychiatry and Child Development 1980* (New York: Brunner/Mazel, 1980).

[30] Bronfenbrenner, *Ecology,* pp. 211–217, hypotheses 27–42.

[31] Henry S. Maas, "Personal and Group Factors in Leaders' Social Perception," *Journal of Abnormal and Social Psychology,* 45 (1950), pp. 54–63.

[32] Henry S. Maas and Richard E. Engler, Jr., *Children in Need of Parents* (New York: Columbia University Press, 1959), pp. 10–12, 15–22.

Chapter 2
NEWBORNS, SOCIETIES, AND LIVING PLACES

Introduction: Newborns enter ongoing societies

Newborns
>   Newborns in social interaction
>   Societal provisions and neonatal life

Human Societies
>   Options and human variability
>   Access and human groups
>   Controls and human needs

Living Places and Space
>   Shared space and social interaction
>   Place as identification
>   Residents' own controls
>>   Redevelopment Planning in the East End—Local People Lose (Record No. 4)
>>   Living Place versus Larger Society: The Strathcona Story (Record No. 5)

INTRODUCTION

Newborns Enter Ongoing Societies

Each child is born into an ongoing society. Each society regulates, at least in informal ways, the activities of the persons attending a child's delivery. "Society is everywhere a control organization. Its function is to organize, integrate and direct. . . ." wrote Chicago sociologist Robert Ezra Park as a baseline for his studies in human ecology.[1]

At the delivery of babies, in parts of the world you know well, who is likely to be present with the mothers-to-be? A midwife, relatives, and neighbors? Or nurses, physicians, and other professional specialists, but no relatives or other persons who intimately know the parturient woman? Societal norms or official codes specify who is admissible to settings in which babies are born. Are the attendants only women, or women and men? Is the child's father present? If so, is he only an observer or is he a participant in the delivery? Do most births in a given society include the same kinds of participants, or can there be variations among those present at different births?

Is the parturient women propped up on high cleared ground, or is she on a metal-framed bed with stirrups and sterile tools lined up on a high table close by? The setting, including the instruments, used for a child's birth reflects the technology and services of the society into which the child is born. In regard to such settings, does a society offer alternatives or options, or is the setting essentially the same for all persons? Is there easier access to the "better" settings for women of higher social position in a society? Or are alternatives selected only after considering the expected ease or difficulty of the delivery, regardless of the woman's social status? Has she been prepared to participate actively in her child's birth, or is she heavily sedated and unaware of what is being done to and for her? Societies differ in the range of *options* they offer, in the ease or difficulty of *access* to the options for all persons, and in the degrees of *control* participants can enjoy. In this chapter I introduce the three fundamentals in an interactional view of social development: first the neonate and then the macrosociety and the living place into which the child is born.

NEWBORNS

Differences among societies in their options, access, and controls—issues I shall discuss in some detail in this chapter's later section called "Human Societies"—are more than matched by differences among people, even from the moment of their birth. Most newborns can, of course, both see and hear at birth, despite myths to the contrary. But there is a wide range among newborns in their perceptual capacities, cycles of attention and inattention, responses to changes in light and sound, and their bodies' abilities to control, for example, the position of their heads. Thus, from the outset, the appropriate environmental supports and other surrounding conditions which best "fit" or accommodate different babies will vary. Similarly, studies of how neonates and their mothers interact during the first forty-eight hours or so of extrauterine life reveal differential beginnings in the human processes and development of attachments, curiosity and competence, and reciprocity—terms which are elaborated throughout this book as central and lifelong aspects of human social development.

Newborns in Social Interaction

Extrauterine life often begins with clearly proactive newborns—that is, with newborns who are initiators of social interaction. The newborn's proactivity is an important assumption, opposing the widely held belief that newborns are only reactive—that is, that they merely respond to what is being done to or for them. People who believe that newborns are primarily reactive emphasize the importance of environments and minimize biopsychological impulses and needs. People who are committed to proactive perspectives may stress development and learning to the neglect of or inadequate attention to the person's contexts. But an appropriate framework for human service workers requires a relatively balanced approach to persons *and* their environments, starting with an understanding of the social interaction of neonates in whatever living places and ongoing societies they are born into. My opening observations on their delivery settings, which may be more or less technologically advanced and variously staffed or peopled, illustrate how societies and regional values and custom provide very different starting places for different newborns. But human variabilities and individual differences are apparent among newborns themselves.

In observations of over one hundred infants "at delivery, beginning from the moment that the head was delivered," Packer and Rosenblatt report, "There was great variation in the interval after birth before the baby first opened his eyes, and in the total length of time for which the eyes were open during the first twenty minutes." Apparently, from the start, neonates differentially initiate their connections with whatever surrounds them. By the end of the observation period, "the majority showed evidence of response to sound, and of the ability to follow briefly a bright object or human face. . . . It is striking that more babies tracked the examiner's face at delivery better than they did a string of beads, and were more likely to turn if the examiner talked at the same time."[2] Thus quickly in their extrauterine lives newborns may become social beings, originating and engaged in two-way social interaction with other human beings. And still, each newborn communicates in a unique style.

During the first thirty-six to forty-eight hours, infants and their mothers begin to pattern the ways in which they interact with one another. The upsurge of emotional bonding and gratifications in being physically close to each other normally mark the start of what, before or by about three months, is apparent in the infant's attachment behavior—looking toward or for the mother, smiling at her, or crying when she leaves. Extending beyond the neonatal period but as early as ten months of age, infants in day-care centers—who thus have an early awareness of and access to agemates—may show preference for playing with certain children rather than others, and may show separation reactions when parted from familiar peers.[3] In such behavior, one sees the earliest orientations to later friendships and loving relationships, and to being part of a social network in which affection and mutual services are exchanged. Within the interactions and ambience of such networks, a sense of self as worthy or lovable begins to take seed. But such remarks take us beyond neonatal life. They appear in this text as a reminder that development has both antecedents and sequels over a life's course.

The influence of newborns on their mothers' earliest interactions with them may differ according to the cultural milieu into which the infants are born. For example, at California's Stanford University Medical Center, in the 1970s, forty white newborns and their mostly college educated, American-born mothers were systematically observed within two days of the babies' birth. Generally, these mothers were found to be more talkative, smiling, and otherwise stimulating with their female firstborns than with their male children.[4] By contrast, in an Atlanta, Georgia, hospital, low-income black mothers were observed to engage in more talking, touching, kissing, and rocking with their heavier and larger males than with their female newborns. "This fact . . . suggests that in this population large male infants are most valued."[5] Thus, obliquely, cultural values may affect how the characteristics of newborns influence their mothers' behavior with them. In such circumstances, a cycle of interaction may start with longlasting repercussions, both in parent-child relationship and on each of the developing persons in that relationship.

Within any cultural context, there is, of course, always individual variation. And the important theme, for present purposes, is not such formulations as the sex preferences by mothers with different values. Rather, early interactions between mother and newborn—interactions initiated by either the proactive neonate or the mother—typically lead to accommodations by either person. Present-day students of neonatal behavior stress both "the adaptability of the newborn" and the fact that "the baby exerts a powerful influence" on the mother.[6] Biological states are also crucial. In the Atlanta study of black mothers and babies, it was also observed that "Infants whose mothers received more drugs were generally more passive" and "The mothers responded to these more passive babies by stimulating them more and by spending more time holding them and feeding them."[7] Were the larger newborns the ones whose delivery required more medication for the mothers?—medication which "does alter the nature of mother–infant interactions." Might this fact account for the apparent preference for the larger and heavier male children? The correlates of differing patterns of mother–neonate interaction are just beginning to be decoded.

Generally, there is a tendency for mothers, at least initially, to engage in more interaction with young children who are not themselves self-starters. For example, in a comparison of mother–child communication involving mentally handicapped (Down's syndrome) babies and normal babies, "The Down's children did not take the initiative in interaction as much as the normal children and the mothers of the Down's children tended to be more directive in interactive situations." This occurred despite the finding that "the Down's children were by no means inactive and unresponsive in interaction with their mothers," and there was "an enormous range of ability in the Down's children. . . ." Continuing to use an interactional perspective, this report recommends that mothers of Down's babies be encouraged "to reduce the 'pressure' and sit back a little" so that the children have "more opportunity to follow their own play activity" and "practice taking the lead in interaction," thus learning about their effects on their environments.[8]

Pacing of the mother's interaction with her newborn is a central issue in the development of synchrony or appropriately timed give-and-take in the early communications between infant and caretaker. Brazelton and his colleagues have been studying such reciprocal interaction for years. I discuss some of this work at some length in the next chapter.[9] Note here merely that such early interaction feeds into two-way parent–child attachments and ultimately into a later level of social development, discussed as reciprocity or the ability to take the role of the other and, in the process, respond sympathetically and lovingly, with concern for the welfare of others.

Though mothers may attempt, for a while, to compensate for their newborns' passivity, as in the cited study of Down's syndrome children, more typically, if babies' responses are slow or inadequate, mothers are likely to interpret this, after a period of trying to evoke activity, as a turn-off signal and the relationship may suffer. Thus, more typically, as Osofsky and Danzer's large-scale study indicates, mothers who are more attentive and sensitive have newborns who are more responsive. Or, they ask, does the more responsive baby awaken greater responsiveness from mothers? These researchers conclude this is a "chicken–egg relationship," probably as good a formulation as we are likely to have on the earliest mother–infant interaction.[10] Coupled with ample evidence of marked temperamental differences among newborns which call for differences in maternal response, it is clear that developing mutually accommodative communication processes calls for much work on the part of both parent and child; typically both parties in this dyadic relationship will have to make adaptations so that these early and initially unstable rhythms can become synchronized. Human service workers may be able to help in early efforts, assisting mothers with the observations of a third party and the kinds of practical suggestions that more experienced mothers have to offer. It is likely that early failures at synchronous interaction which persist will become later sources of disturbance and referral for remedial care.

In Chapter Seven, in the section on starting family life, an examination of transitions to parenthood will bring us back to newborns and their family contexts. The family contexts that newborns enter are almost universally responsive to macrosocietal forces. Social policy and provisions must address whatever significantly affects beginning life.

Societal Provisions and Neonatal Life

To see the newborn's "world" only as the familial context is to be very shortsighted. At least, what goes on between newborns and their immediate caretakers is itself highly vulnerable and inevitably responsive to impingements from the larger society and its cultural milieus. When social structural and cultural value changes occur as rapidly as they have in the postwar world, almost universally, then the experiences of newborns are bound to reflect the ambiguities or uncertainties and tensions that rapid social change occasions. We have yet to discover just what effects, in fact, such radically changing conditions have upon neonates. Still the issues—if not their solutions—warrant brief review.

Generally, when societies and cultures undergo sizable changes over relatively short periods of time, there is a weakening of the informal resources that formerly made daily life familiar, predictable, and comfortable under stable circumstances. For example, intergenerational communication suffers, the assumptions and values of parents fail to retain their meanings for their children, and grandparenting is more often at odds with the adult children's parenting. Shared neighborhood goals may cease to be common ones as special interest groups arise. Thus former family and neighborhood supports to young parents when their firstborn arrives may suffer. As a result of the loss of informal supports, formal provisions through the human services are more extensively required.

Probably the most dramatic of postwar social and cultural changes relevant to newborns is the ongoing reorganization in the status and roles of women. This issue will come up repeatedly in this book and especially in the chapter on young family life. Briefly, here, note that pressures toward increased equality for women with men in the labor market probably influence early mothering and neonatal life in countless ways, some advantageously and others not so. Cultural expectations and societal reinforcements once made a woman's firstborn the realization of a major life goal and an unconflicted attainment of her socialization as a female. If for most women the first birth is still a fundamentally happy occurrence, for increasing numbers of women the newborn's entry into her life is experienced as a mixed blessing, especially if she lacks appropriate supports of many kinds. For one thing, the baby cuts into her wage earning and complicates the work or career to which she may be more or less committed. Thus, governments are being urged to develop family social policies that help the newborn's family economically and require work places to allow parents some time off, with at least partial pay, to precede delivery and/or to care for newborns. Systematic studies of the effects on newborns and their parents of such provisions have yet to be made, but existing theory suggests that parental and neonatal life would profit from such opportunities.

Another major societal change is at least the awareness and concern in postindustrial nations regarding worldwide disparities between the have and have not regions and countries, recently called the North–South issue. Newborns delivered in parts of the world where food supplies are grossly inadequate have a very different start from their more fortunate agemates who happen to be born in food-abundant areas. Moreover, even within the latter areas, the maldistribution of wealth and other resources among families impinges on public consciousness far more extensively now than in pretelevision days and in times when other mass media were less involved and involving. It is widespread public knowledge that nutrition affecting newborns must begin prenatally. It is perhaps less well known that improved prenatal and neonatal food intake may effect changes in more than such biological measures as body weight and general physical health. World Health Organization efforts to have mothers breast-feed their babies, instead of misusing powdered milk and other baby foods, have been backed by relevant health statistics. But beyond the purely somatic gains, for example, in one program in which food was supplemented, mothers were found to arise earlier from their post-partum recoveries and both parents were discovered to increase their playful interaction with their newborns.[11] Improved nutrition may have unanticipated efforts upon social development as well as upon physical growth and health.

In addition to adequate food, appropriate housing is a central issue. With population expansion and much migration worldwide from rural regions to towns and cities, housing deficits have increased. Squatter settlements of overcrowded shanty towns fringe many of the growing cities in developing nations, and inner city slums in many wealthy nations provide newborns with rat-infested, over-populated homes as their first living places. Neighborly supports sometimes found in such quarters may ease somewhat but hardly fully compensate for the multiple disadvantages neonates suffer under such conditions.

Rapid social change has also brought with it marked increases in the disruption of family life. Increasing proportions of newborns arrive to single mothers, some still in their early teens. Single mothers of any age need emotional, social, and often economic buttresses to be able to engage in a relatively stable starting relationship with their babies. Rising marital separation and divorce rates mark the need for human services of both preventive and compensatory kinds, especially for new parents and their neonates who lack helpful extended kin or other informal network involvements.

Societies and their governments that value children and family life may develop family policies providing such economic supplements for young families as family loans or starting allowances, insurance benefits for working women who are pregnant and who after delivery spend a few months at home with their newborns, and/or children's allowances which begin with the birth of a child. National population size goals are likely to be an important determinant of the provision of such programs, although merely the availability of such supplements has not been found to increase childbirths as expected. Other provisions are at issue, too. The availability of health care, with its educational programs, for prenatal examinations, preparation for delivery, hospital or midwife services, and post-partum maternal and infant care is obviously also essential.

In societies lacking such public provisions, human service workers at regional and neighborhood levels may participate in the development of local programs—for example, self-help groups for parent education and shared infant care. Fathers' participation in childbirth and child care and women's increased sharing of early newborn responsibilities with other women—for example, in housing cooperatives of single mothers or in neighborhood groups of women living in nearby separate units—generate new milieus for newborns. Newborns may thus have repeated early interaction with adults other than and in addition to their mothers. The long-term effects of such early experiences are just beginning to be patterned in studies of, for example, alternate family styles.

These observations on variations in macrocontexts that neonates enter at birth serve as an introduction to the following section on human societies. Human social development is differentially influenced, in ways documented repeatedly in this book, by differences in societal and cultural contexts. This fact, coupled with the innate proactivity of human organisms (see my opening comments on newborns' proactivity in social interaction, early in this chapter), suggests that certain properties of societies may be especially important for people's optimal development. These societal properties—of central concern to human services workers—may be grossly categorized as the options, access, and controls a society provides. Their significance is explained in the next section.

HUMAN SOCIETIES

Options? Access? Control? Why single out these three facets of the complex collectivities which are human societies? To respond, I must discuss some assumptions about human beings who compose and both change and are changed by their societies. These assumptions about human behavior and social conditions suggest goals for human service workers and other participants in community life.

Options and Human Variation

I begin with an example of what I mean by societal options. Housing for old people should protect them from the disturbing, noisy activities of children and young families. Such housing should include special physical facilities, such as low kitchen cupboards for the less agile aged, and generally foster a harmonious life for homogeneous-by-age elderly residents, or so argue some social planners. Old people should be housed in heterogeneous or age-integrated communities, where the young and old can interact, each enriching the others' lives, not confining old people to association with only other old people, or so argue planners with completely different prejudices. After considering studies of elderly people's ways of life and housing preferences, however, one becomes convinced that no single design can accommodate the widely diverse interests, capacities, and life styles of the elderly. "The needs of [old] people for differing locations, physical settings, on-site services, age integration, neighborhood contexts, and social contacts vary widely, and undoubtedly enter into housing choice," concludes one review of relevant research.[12] Both age-integrated and age-segregated dwelling areas are needed, as well as many other variants in housing design, so that choices may approximate what is wanted and needed by the elderly.

The ideal of societal options for the meeting of human needs is a response to the extensive variability, personal uniqueness, and lifelong changes of human beings, based in part on human choices. Developmental psychologist Jerome Kagan writes,

"We must distinguish among variation within one person in different times and places, variation among persons in the same time and place, and variation among persons from different societies."[13] From a microbiologist's vantage point, René Dubos comments on human variation as follows:

> All human beings have fundamentally the same anatomical structure, operate through the same physiological processes, and are driven by the same biological urges. Yet no two human beings are alike, and what is perhaps more important, the individuality of a person living now is different from that of anyone who has ever lived in the past or will live in the future. Each person is unique, unprecedented, and unrepeatable. . . .[14]

Human uniqueness and variability are in part genetic, *homo sapiens* having become so geographically mobile and thus engaged in mate selection far from places of birth and peoples of origin. Human uniqueness and variability are also, of course, in part environmental, *homo sapiens* being so adaptable, creating tools and other artifacts to cope with a wide spectrum of terrestrial and extraterrestrial climates and physical conditions. Thus, as biologist Julian Huxley observes, *homo sapiens* has become "more variable than other species," manifesting "a degree of variation that would be staggering if it were not so familiar" with differences among individuals "as profound as those which distinguish the major groups of the animal kingdom."[15]

Change, moreover, is a constant process all through the life of each individual—bodily change, psychological change, and social change usually varying in pace and nature with a person's developmental stage, genetic inheritance and health, and social conditions. "Since sequences in development usually lead to increasing differentiation of the person and his behavior, the older we get the more complex we should become and thus the more distinctive from other persons. In short, diversity among people should increase with age."[16] More succinctly put, on the issue of lifelong change, gerontologist David Schonfield gives "gerontology's principal generalization" as follows: "Individual differences increase with age."[17]

Individual differences seem to proliferate with the range and access of opportunities or options a society offers its members for choice. "The latent potentialities of human beings," writes Dubos, "have a better chance to emerge in a living form when the social environment is sufficiently diversified to provide a variety of stimulating experience, especially for the young. . . . For this reason, we must shun uniformity of surroundings as much as absolute uniformity in behavior," and, in practical terms, Dubos then concludes:

> Creating diversified environments may result in some loss of efficiency but in my opinion diversity is vastly more important than efficiency because it is essential for the germination of the seeds dormant in man's nature. Since the physical and social environments play such a crucial role in the shaping of individuality, environmental design should aim at enlarging the range of choices as much as possible. The word *design* as I use it applies to social planning, urban or rural development, and all the practices that affect the conduct of life.[18]

In brief, societal options encourage the expression and growth of the multiple potentials in people, complicating and thus enriching their societies and ultimately the world community.

Access and Human Groups

Although societal options are available, their accessibility to some segments or groups of people in a society may be very limited. In choosing new workers, an employer may select men over women. In choosing new tenants, a rental agent may pick women over men. And both rental agent and employer in the United States today are likely to prefer "mature" adults over equally qualified applicants in their early twenties, "stable" married couples over "unattached" singles, whites over blacks, English-speaking over Spanish-speaking applicants, Christians over Jews and Moslems, persons of middle-class over working-class origins, childless women over single mothers, straights over gays, native born over foreign born, the beautiful and handsome over the plain and homely, and the manifestly unhandicapped over the obviously handicapped—although none of these attributes may in any way affect the applicants' abilities to do the job or pay the rent and care for the housing unit.

The distribution of social power—that is, the capacity to gain access to what one needs or wants—is more uneven in some societies than in others, although in most if not all societies the world round the more affluent have greater social power and easier access to more options than the poor have. And the effects of having easier access or greater social power are likely to be incremental, intrafamilial, and intergenerational, because the more power one has, the more one tends to accrue for oneself, one's children, and other kin. In an effort to equalize social power, human service workers aim to increase accessibility for the less powerful.

I enumerated above illustrations of a dozen attributes that influence accessibility to jobs and housing in the United States, despite Equal Rights legislation and moral codes forbidding such discrimination. Elsewhere in the world too, in Western Europe, the Near East, East Africa, and Southeast Asia, I have seen evidence of preferential treatment and restrictions influenced (but not always in the same ways) by these same attributes: age or generation, gender, marital status, race, ethnicity, religion, social class, parental status, sexual orientation, place of birth, bodily attractiveness, and somatic functioning. These attributes are foci around which people structure their societies, forming coalitions and such special interest groups as "youth" or "senior citizens," women's rights groups, or Parents without Partners. Through associations, members ease their accessibility to goods or services denied them as individuals. Human service workers participate in the organization of people who are discriminated against and relatively powerless. Community workers provide information and other services for a great variety of self-help groups.

Organizations of people who have had accessibility problems sometimes cross societal boundaries and link up with similar groups in other parts of the world. Although North American accessibility patterns are, of course, not all worldwide, women's rights have become a universal issue and there are many international formal and informal alliances. Job discrimination against women in so-called Western societies need not be documented here—women's lower salaries and the preference for men especially in better paying jobs are well known. In Eastern European communist societies, the position of women seems no better. To the question, "Does socialism liberate women?" Hilda Scott's well documented study replies, "In all the socialist countries women still do most of the low-skill, poorly paid work, and the majority of women do work of this kind."[19] There is no evidence that social power for women is any greater in socialist than in capitalist nations, and typically, in developing countries in the Third World, women lack the options men enjoy.[20]

In addition to the moral reprehensibility of limited access for certain groups in any society, it is a both personally and societally damaging condition. It cheapens a group's sense of its own value. It lowers group members' self-regard and thus may reduce their confidence in their ability to cope. Societies consequently lose the suppressed contributions of the people they put down. One way of beginning to reverse feelings of powerlessness among excluded people is to help them improve the accessibility of options. This is a process in which human service workers repeatedly engage, when, for example, they work with employers to hire handicapped persons or participate in the development of cooperative housing and various child care programs for single parents. I shall discuss improving access for groups of people who are discriminated against in chapter four, on coping and responsive environments, as well as in subsequent chapters.

Controls and Human Needs

Central to any society and its integrative processes are social controls. If "options" and "access" highlight the individuality and subgroup differences of human beings, social controls remind us that people who are members of a society from which they derive specifiable rights owe, in return, specifiable responsibilities. If belonging to a society provides protection and responses to other needs, membership also entails obligations which reduce people's freedom of action and choice. For controls involve the apportioning of a society's always limited resources for meeting both basic and expanding human needs and wants. Societies vary, of course, in how equitably among their peoples apportionment is made, how and for whom access is limited, and how and by whom acceptable options are decided upon.

The idea of social controls should not, however, evoke thoughts of only formal constraints such as the law, the police, and other legal or quasilegal and custodial agents. Schools and churches teach conformity too. And controls include informal socialization processes also—for example, customs, traditional rituals, or gossip which may very effectively keep people in line. But societal controls as integrating forces in a society are not limited to barriers or deterrents to undesired behavior. Controls encompass also supportive or helpful processes and provisions, benefits or rewards for membership in a given society. Granted the central purpose of social controls, to keep a society connected and well functioning, what better ways to ensure members' attachment and involvement—their being unalienated—than to provide as many options and as much access to what is needed and wanted as resources allow.

Under any circumstances, there are some basic human needs and wants regarding which every society provides both supportive and deterrent controls. To amplify Park's statement, with which this chapter began—"Society is everywhere a control organization"—the survival needs of the people for food and drink (subsistence) and for protection from adverse natural conditions and enemy attack give primary shape to social organization, always in the light of available and accessible environmental resources. Here are some examples of what I mean.

To use a faraway but clearly differentiated pair of situations, inner Java's specialized wet rice high-yield terraces accommodate surrounding dense populations; outer Java's diversified slash-and-burn farming areas maintain only dispersed, thinner populations in what anthropologist Clifford Geertz calls "two types of eco-systems" and quite differently organized and controlled societies. More pointedly, citing Julian Steward, Geertz observes:

> If the main game animal exists in large herds, say, bison or caribou, it is adaptive to engage in cooperative hunting on a fairly sizable scale. Considerable numbers of people are likely to remain together throughout the year, following the herds as they move, driving them in mass surrounds, and so on. If, however, the game is of the sort which occurs in small scattered groups and does not migrate, it is better hunted piecemeal by small groups of men who know their immediate territory extremely well—large population concentrations being impossible at any rate. In the first situation, Steward argues, the elementary community will tend to be a relatively large, multifamily group, while in the second it will tend to be a small, localized patrilineal band.[21]

Similarly, in more complex, modern societies—more immediately familiar to most readers—social organization and its controls vary in response to the available resources for ultimately meeting subsistence needs. In various kinds of farming regions, logging or mining communities, factory towns, and in metropolitan trade centers, community controls are likely to differ in many ways that human service workers must attend to if their messages are not to go awry. Forms of family life, a prime force in the processes of social control, vary in response to the ways in which family members provide the food.

Of course, societies control the satisfactions of more than merely subsistence and security needs and wants. They address also affiliative or associational and sexual needs, related to what Abraham Maslow called needs for belonging and love,[22] or William Schutz called needs for inclusion and affection.[23] Social controls address sexual behavior and group life of every kind: "the most basic requirement of social organization" is "a code regulating the relations of the sexes," writes British economist Joan Robinson.[24] Beyond basic needs of this kind, however, efforts to compile all-inclusive lists of needs and wants inevitably fail because they differ among people in different societies and change within lifetimes lived in rapidly paced eras such as the present. Thus, relevant controls must change too.

Changes in controls probably occur as the survival of a society becomes more assured or more threatened. In "better" times, societal controls may become less essential, since nonconformity seems less dangerous in a comfortable, thriving social order. Conversely, controls tighten when societies suffer economic or political strains. Thus, tolerances and perhaps options too increase or diminish as the apparent security is perceived as changing.

Because control measures have varying degress of effectiveness in satisfying human needs and wants, and at the same time integrating a society, an expanding body of policy research examines whether, in fact, specific control programs have expected consequences. In some such programs, human service workers convey the supports, monitor the constraints, and participate as observers of effects. As agents of social control, most human service workers spend most of their time at the microsocietal level, that is, people in their living places. There one can tell to which human needs a society is effectively responsive and of which it is neglectful, which wants are changing and what provisions should, as a result, be changed. It is thus important for the socially concerned to understand community life. Much of this book is addressed to this level of society, and I now present some introductory ideas about it.

LIVING PLACES AND SPACE

Habitats, human settlements, or what I prefer to call living places are the dwelling areas in which people sleep, eat, and store their clothing and other possessions. There they may share their daily lives with their cohabitants—members of their families, friends, neighbors, acquaintances, and people who provide special services.

To start with, note that living places are simultaneously (1) space shared with others, sometimes sparsely populated but increasingly, the world over, crowded by many occupants, (2) places to which people may become attached and with which they are identified, and (3) regions that, providing more or less access to options, strongly influence the lives and development of residents. In turn, residents, for their own individual and collective betterment, should be able to exercise controls over their living places, especially to prevent untoward local influences on their lives.

Shared Space

Objectively, a living place is a space, a territory, a turf. Its spatial opportunities for residents' activities is dependent on the numbers of other people who share the same space and the space's physical facilities. I shall shortly and briefly review some influences on residents of densely or sparsely populated living spaces, but I must remind you first of the great variety of living places, both as compounds and as single household units. Such matters are important to human service workers because what people can do on their home ground is spatially determined. For example, the opportunities a crawler or toddler has to explore the immediate environs with or without the surveillance of older persons, the settings lovers seek or others want for privacy, the size of a neighborhood's public gatherings, and the risks on local streets of ambush and violence are all at least in part a matter of spatial arrangements.

Shared space differs in a cluster of thatch-roofed dwellings and the open market place that are a rural village in East Africa, or corrugated metal lean-tos, squeezed into a shanty town fringing a developing Southeast Asian nation's capital. (Governments sometimes remove such untidy squatters' shacks from the environs of their most visited urban centers lest the poor be too visible.) Living places include a checkerboard of crowded, noisy streets and densely tenanted, tall buildings in a North American metropolitan neighborhood; a large, centuries-old town square faced by a church and encircled by squat stone houses and narrow lanes in Western Europe; a small remotely spaced temporary settlement of nomadic people in a desert, or of Eskimo igloos in the far North. The basic living space accommodates a household unit: a large wooden building shared by single parents in San Francisco, or a crowded dark box of an apartment housing three generations of assorted kin and boarders in southside Chicago or Manhattan's Harlem; or an isolated, multigenerational family farmhouse on the prairie, near a road that extends flatly past a few similar farmhouses and a one-room schoolhouse to one or more stores, a place of worship, and a government agency of some kind.

The basic living shelter or enclosure is usually grouped more or less closely among others of its kind, becoming the basis of a neighborhood. Homes may be tiny or massive, appearing in seemingly infinite designs, but although the options are multiple, housing for the poor, in addition to other inadequacies, is likely universally to lack sufficient enclosed space for all its occupants. The effects of crowding are known to be destructive. Thinking generally of human population density, René Dubos speculates:

> The design of human settlements and homes may compensate to some extent for insufficient space, but there are limits to such compensation. Beyond these limits, overcrowding is likely to produce irreversible damage. It may even, eventually, change the prospect of nuclear warfare from a threat to a temptation—the salvage from an evil life. In the absence of a world holocaust, crowding will probably lead to the evolutionary selective survival of persons best adapted to regimented life. The two alternatives to population control are thus nuclear destruction and social regimentation of the ant-hill.[25]

If a household unit is small and overcrowded, it lacks a private area or "backstage." As a result, sleeping, meal preparation, television watching, and the coming and going of household members or visitors all occur simultaneously within a limited and quite public space. In a well-designed study of the effects of overcrowding in the home, researchers report residents suffering from "physical withdrawal, psychological withdrawal, a lack of effective planning behavior, and a general feeling of being 'washed out'," all associated with "poor physical health. . . . generally getting insufficient sleep, catching infectious diseases. . . . and not being cared for by others when one is sick," and the writers conclude, "The effects of crowding as measured by P/R [persons per room] tend to be largely explained or interpreted by the experience of excessive demands and lack of privacy."[26]

Concerned with the effects of household space on family life, Canadian sociologist Dorothy E. Smith observes that in some housing projects, such as one designed by Frank Lloyd Wright, "Indoor and outdoor play areas are included in [an] individual household unit," thus screening a family from its neighborhood. "But," she continues:

> . . . in many neighborhoods play areas for children are communal. This is particularly likely when space in the home is markedly limited. In the *vecinidadad* (Lewis 1959, 1961), the children played in the interstices between dwellings. Kerr (1958), in her study of an English slum, describes how children were kept outside the house as much as possible during the day. If they were not on the street, they were sent to the cinema (see also Spinley, 1953). If the boundaries of the household largely circumscribe the local lives of the adult members, while the children occupy the territory between, then there is a lack of coincidence between adults' and children's worlds and the latter may develop a pronounced autonomy.[27]

That is, children's autonomy from adults. Children's interdependence with playmates is likely to be strengthened in such spatial arrangements.

In contrast to overcrowded space, space shared by too few presents its own problems. The children of socially isolated farm families living in the rugged and relatively inaccessible mountains of Norway were contrasted with seven- to fourteen-year-old agemates who lived in towns in families of similar socioeconomic conditions. Using a battery of projective tests and other measures, psychologists Anna von der Lippe and Ernest Haggard describe the isolated children, who only had other family members in their daily lives, compared with the "control" children in town as follows. The isolated mountain children showed more conflicting and ambivalent feelings toward their parents, on whom they were so dependent for daily interaction. The isolated children tended not to express their feelings openly in daily behavior and also displayed "less involvement in their play with [their favorite] animal." When the animal had to be sold, in the test situation, "they brushed the matter off more easily than the urban children." In summary, the isolated mountain children were "less differentiated and more inflexible and intolerant of indirect impulse expression than the urban children," who, by contrast, showed "a more extensive, richer fantasy life, more psychological insight and better emotional contact with others. . . ."[28]

The monotony and understimulation of sparsely shared living places may take their toll. In the broad range between too thinly peopled or isolated areas and densely populated regions, there lies a variegated social milieu to accommodate optimal human development. Within that range, there may be sufficient variation appropriate to the different needs and tolerances for social stimulation of widely differing people.

Place as Identification

Living places are, of course, much more than merely shared space. Residents of some duration, whether by choice or entrapment, develop strong feelings about where they live. Home territory evokes also protective responses from most residents, almost as though boundary between body and nest were indistinguishable. No matter what the deficits of living places as seen by outsiders, residents with an insider's views may develop not only lasting attachments to place but also an identification with it. The latter is strengthened by others' tendencies to identify people, in part, by their living place—whether it is the east or west side of town, or a certain region of a country.

Evidence of residents' attachment to and identification with their living places is widespread. Concerned with urban land use many decades ago, Walter Firey noted the "symbolic quality" and feelings of attachment inhabitants invested in a neighborhood such as Beacon Hill or the largely Italian North End of Boston: "the area has a certain retentive power over those residents who most fully share the values which prevail there."[29] In Bethnal Green in London's working-class East End, a Mr. Lamb says, "I suppose people who come here from outside think it's an awful place, but us established ones like it. Here you can just open the door and say hello to everybody."[30] And Jane Jacobs writes of the denizens of American big cities, "Even the most urbane citizen does care about the atmosphere of the street and district where he lives, no matter how much choice he has of pursuits outside it; and the common run of city people do depend greatly on their neighborhoods for the kind of everyday lives they live."[31]

Describing a working-class community called Dagenham outside London, British sociologist Peter Willmott says of its residents,

> Many of them are not oppressed by the architectural monotony and dreariness which fill the visitor with gloomy amazement that people could live in such a place, let alone enjoy it. The inhabitants express affection for it. Mr. Brooks, a toolmaker is an engineering factory, went to Dagenham when he was 16, and is now 38.
>
> > 'I know Dagenham seems monotonous to people from outside,' he said, 'but when you've been living here a while, the roads develop their own personalities—there are landmarks which you get to recognize in different turnings. Anyway, it's not the outside of the houses that matter, it's what's inside them. I've got a number of good friends here. Lots of the people round here know me. I get on extremely well with the shopkeepers in the district. My roots are here now and I'm very happy indeed.'
>
> Time and again, people said similar things. 'I like the district and I like the neighbours,' 'I like Dagenham, I like it very well.' 'In my opinion it's a nice

place to live.' 'I like it here. It's ideal if you're a working man.' To report this contentment is not, of course, to excuse bad architecture or town planning, nor to imply that Dagenham's faults do not matter, rather to draw attention to human resilience and the vitality of traditional social patterns.[32]

The issue of local attachment and identification becomes particularly important when social planners and other human service workers bring their own perspectives to bear on a neighborhood. Outsiders may see and appraise a living place by very different criteria than are used by its daily occupants. And what seems like desirable or undesirable change may vary with whose interests are at stake. Thus, the power residents have to control their own living environs is crucial.

Residents' Own Controls

Since living places as shared space may so influence residents' lives and become sources of attachment and identification, people should be able to participate in decisions about local improvements or the prevention of unwanted changes. Living places may symbolize a world of completely uncontrollable and alienating forces, or, on the other hand, local participation may strengthen people's sense of competence and engagement.

City planner Jane Jacobs, concerned primarily with American metropolitan living, puts it as follows:

> We shall have something solid to chew on if we think of city neighborhoods as mundane organs of self-government. Our failures with city neighborhoods are, ultimately, failures in localized self-government. And our successes are successes at localized self-government. I am using self-government in its broadest sense, meaning both the formal and informal self-management of society.[33]

In their living places local people may want, through neighborhood associations, to minimize outsiders' intrusions. As examples of such communal issues, community development specialist Michael Hirst cites the flow of local versus nonlocal traffic, outsiders' commercial or industrial interests in parking space rather than the neighborhood's residential quality, absentee landlords' concerns versus local homeowners', and the efforts of government agents, such as school teachers, social workers, and police who, working but not living in the community, may "exacerbate feelings amongst local residents of helplessness, frustration in the lack of control over their lives and environment."[34]

Plans to provide local participation may, of course, founder. Living places are minisocieties with limited powers to control larger societal forces, and before I turn to "The Strathcona Story," which concludes this chapter, British sociologist Peter Marris's report on a failed exercise in local participatory democracy is worth reviewing. The scene is East End London and what were then five boroughs. Marris neglects to tell us that the population involved is many hundred thousands, but it is a part of a working-class world where stability and neighborliness are integral.

REDELOPMENT PLANNING
IN THE EAST END—
LOCAL PEOPLE LOSE
(RECORD NO. 4)

Downstream from Tower Bridge, a mile from the financial heart of the city, the Thames winds between wharfs and docks, warehouses, and large moorings, once the centre of the port of London. These Victorian docks are falling idle as cargo handling moves down the estuary to Tilbury, where the techniques are modern. Five thousand acres of obsolete docks, warehouses, and a huge gasworks made redundant by piped natural gas, interspersed with enclaves of shabby terraced cottages and public housing, lie open for redevelopment in the heart of the capital. Four-fifths of it is in public hands. "All the essential ingredients are present for something 'big' to happen here," observed Peter Walker, the Conservative Government's Secretary for the Environment, as he announced a planning study.

From the outset, the choice of a plan was to be responsive to democratic consultation. But the first exercise in participatory planning was absurdly clumsy. A team of consultants was appointed to draw up examples of how the banks of the commercial river might look by 1990, mixing private and public housing, offices, industries, and open spaces in every conceivable proportion with more adventurous proposals—a monorail, yacht harbour, fun fair, or safari park—enhancing somewhat randomly one conception or another. Five of these national plans, each representing a different future, were then presented to the residents of London's East End through an extensive sequence of pamphlets, reports, exhibitions, and social surveys designed to elicit a choice among them. Understandably, most people were bemused by the brightly colored mosaics which mapped these possible distant futures, and scarcely a thousand responded. Embarrassed planners tried to interest East Enders in a vision of lions roaming across the Isle of Dogs or lectured on advanced transport technology near closed subway stations and people sleeping in the street. But the whole exercise was eventually put aside, and the process of planning started afresh.

A new structure evolved, with a planning team responsible to the five boroughs in which the dockland lies, and an advisory council on which local groups were represented. By this time residents alerted to the issues had set up their own action groups and had recruited professional help; these were recognized and incorporated in the advisory council. However, the new consultative structure worked scarcely any better than the old. The action groups soon lost faith in the advisory council, whose power to influence decisions was vague and its discussions unminuted. The planning team resisted any independent initiative from local residents, protesting against "a participation exercise which would militate against observing the tight timetable . . . agreed for the preparation of the main strategy." In general, although the public would be informed and sometimes consulted about each stage in the development of the plan, the officials maintained that active participation by the affected residents was only practicable in detailed local design, when the 'commanding factors' determining the project had already become 'fixed points in public discussion.' This policy made mutual frustration inevitable, for if crucial decisions were taken over the residents' heads, when the implications became evident in the rebuilding of the immediate surroundings the residents were bound to raise all the issues which the planners would wish to take as settled.

So the hope of a genuinely participatory process faded and with it the ideal of communities revitalized by shared responsibility for their future. . . . The first major decision . . . [then] taken about the development of dockland ignored the advice of the planners as much as the wishes of the local residents, preempting the logical sequence of an integrated plan. A Texas company was interested in acquiring much of the largest disused complex of docks for a trade mart—a permanent wholesale market where manufacturers would rent space to display their goods and negotiate sales. The project was unattractive to the people of the area. The few jobs that would be open to them were mostly custodial or cleaning; the company had, besides, a reputation for hostility to trade unions. The supplying of the market would generate heavy traffic in the surrounding residential streets and houses would have to be pulled down for road widening. Socially, economically, and physically, the scheme was an alien intrusion. The planners were not against a trade mart, but they considered it should be sited elsewhere, on the other side of the river, where it would not overwhelm an already overburdened street pattern, fit better with the existing pattern of use, and involve less public cost in improving the traffic flow. They argued that no decision should be taken in advance of their study of the overall principles of the plan, but the company wanted the Surrey site, the borough council wanted the tax revenue, and the national government, in the face of economic recession, was anxious for any investment. The company demanded a decision within a year without a public hearing, or they would withdraw. It also invited several parties of local councillors and community leaders to its Texas headquarters for a round of sightseeing and lavish barbecues.

The politicians understandably succumbed to this pressure. If the borough council concerned wanted the trade mart, the other four councils were ready to go along with it in return for equal sympathy for their own favourite schemes when the time came. The national government refused appeals to review their decision. Thus, the political authorities, which had conceived the idea of a comprehensive, democratically responsive redevelopment plan, were the first to abandon it in the face of economic realities.[35]

Perhaps if these residents or their local political borough council had had an ongoing planning unit, they could have actively worked on improvements with time on their side, long before outsiders became aware of available space. Then they would not have been merely and belatedly reactive. The Strathcona Story, which follows, has a very different sequence, set of participants, and ending.

LIVING PLACE VERSUS
LARGER SOCIETY:
THE STRATHCONA STORY
(RECORD NO. 5)*

Every living place is interconnected with other and larger sections of its society, much as living tissue interacts with all other parts of the organism. Ultimately, each living place has weaker or stronger interchanges with the entire world community— effects exacerbated in times of crisis such as wars or major economic avalanches which may reach catastrophic proportions even in the remotest of villages. Obviously, residents' own controls can cope with some problems, but not all. The constellation of factors auguring well for community efforts will vary with the nature of the problem under attack. Under any circumstances, the number and integration of the local people involved as well as their information and other problem-targeting resources create basic differences in the likelihood of their success. The Strathcona Story provides a nice contrast with the London dockland fiasco presented above.

In the Strathcona Story,[36] which follows, a quite racially homogeneous and strongly intranetworked inner city neighborhood, occupying a small land area, succeeds not only in stopping a locally unwanted urban renewal program but also in starting an ongoing neighborhood association which continues, after its first major success, to attend to community development issues. The original crisis began with higher levels of government and metropolitan commercial interests offering residents neither options nor effective access to decision-making power. The neighborhood, with its traditionally strong Chinese family base, had also many other internal organizational ties, but it had no alliance geared to the threat of demolition of their homes and their own bodily removal and relocation. Whatever the deficits of their shared space in Strathcona, most residents were clearly attached to it and identified with it. Residents' opposition to government at municipal, provincial (the Canadian equivalent of the American state), and federal levels, and a part of their success story are here reported, from an insider's view, by a resident member of the community. As an observer of the later stages of this community effort, I experienced vicariously some of the excitement of the hard work and successful outcome of this project.

Early History

Strathcona is one of Vancouver's oldest residential neighbourhoods. Most of the houses in the area were built about the turn of the century, but some date back to the origins of the City itself. The Strathcona School was originally built in 1890 as the East End School.

---

*This section is dedicated to the residents of Strathcona who fought to preserve their homes and the community, and to all those others who helped Strathcona to survive as a residential neighborhood in the urban core.

The early residents of Strathcona were Anglo-Saxon. However, the area soon became inhabited by large numbers of Italians and Jews, as well as Scandinavians, Ukranians, Russians and Yugoslavs. The old Hastings Auditorium (828 East Hastings) used to be called the "Italian Hall" and was the center of Vancouver's pre-World War II Italian community. Benny's Italian Market (Union and Princess) dates back to 1915. The Gibbs Boys Club building (Heatley and Pender) was originally built in 1921 as the Schara Tzedeck Synagogue. The Ukrainian Canadian Center (Hawks and Pender) dates back to 1928. The church at Princess and Pender was built as the Swedish Lutheran Church and served as the Ukrainian Catholic Church before it became the Chinese Catholic Church. The Russian People's Home on Campbell Avenue, adjacent to the Russian Orthodox Church, was built by the Yugoslav community. The Yugoslavs had their own center on Keefer Street.

Compared to the Europeans, the Chinese were latecomers to Strathcona. There were some Chinese and Japanese living in the area in the 1930's, however it was not until after the repeal of the Chinese Exclusion Act in 1947 that Strathcona became increasingly Chinese. The area served as a gateway for post-war Chinese immigrants. Housing prices were low and the area was adjacent to Chinatown.

In 1947, Strathcona was only about 28 percent Chinese. By 1957, this figure had reached about 50 percent. Strathcona today is about 75 percent Chinese. It contains less than ten percent of Greater Vancouver's sixty thousand plus Chinese. There are large numbers of Chinese living in neighbourhoods well outside of the Chinatown-Strathcona area.

Urban Renewal

In 1957, the City of Vancouver embarked upon a twenty year urban renewal plan. A major focus of this program was "comprehensive redevelopment" for Strathcona, the clearance of all existing homes and replacement with public housing, high rises, and row housing. Union Street was to be the Southern border of the new Strathcona as the blocks of homes below it were to be demolished for a major City freeway system.

The rationale for the urban renewal was that Strathcona, in addition to having old and run-down housing, was in a strategic location being adjacent to the Downtown, Waterfront and False Creek areas. The City wanted high density development for Strathcona.

Commencing in 1958, the City placed a freeze upon the entire area. Property values were frozen. No major redevelopment and home improvement permits were allowed. No regular public works maintenance was carried out. The neighbourhood was left to await the bulldozer.

The first phase of urban renewal began in 1959 with the construction of 159 units of public housing at MacLean Park. An entire block of homes was then demolished as a new replacement park. Ten acres of land and homes were then cleared in preparation for the 376 unit Raymur Place Housing Project at Campbell Avenue.

Acquisition and clearance for Scheme II Urban Renewal began in 1965 with the expropriation and clearance of homes in five blocks for an extension to Mac-Lean Park, senior citizens housing and an extension to Strathcona School.

The urban renewal schemes met strong opposition from Strathcona residents and Chinatown leaders. It was pointed out that the urban renewal would destroy the community and threaten the livelihood of Chinatown. The expropriation of homes for $6,000–$8,000 was argued unfair and discriminatory.

The protests were of no avail as the City continued with its urban renewal. In August 1968, the City prepared Scheme III, the final and complete bulldozing of the entire neighbourhood. Fortunately, this scheme was never implemented as the Federal government reassessed its urban renewal involvement across Canada.

Rehabilitation and Neighbourhood Improvement

The third and final urban renewal proposal had also sparked a last ditch effort among Strathcona residents to stop the bulldozing of their neighbourhood. In December, 1968, six hundred persons attended the founding meeting of the Strathcona Property Owners and Tenants Association, SPOTA. The purpose of the new organization was to "ensure that the people who live in the area would be fully informed and their interests and community will be protected." In briefs to City Hall, SPOTA argued for a revised renewal scheme which favoured rehabilitation and preservation.

In the Fall of 1969, SPOTA was asked by the senior governments to join in a four level committee to investigate rehabilitation for Strathcona. It was the first time in Canada that a committee had been charged with that responsibility. It was also the first time that a citizens group had been invited to participate in such a capacity.

In July 1971, after almost two years of meetings, studies and negotiations, the Committee agreed upon a series of recommendations. They called for a $4.9 million Rehabilitation scheme, with two million dollars each in new public works and grant-loan housing rehabilitation assistance. The Strathcona Rehabilitation Project officially began in February 1972 and operated out of a site office on Hawks Avenue. During the three years of implementation, the three levels of government, site office staff and the community worked closely and informally together.

In the summer of 1973, the Federal government introduced national programs for neighbourhood improvement and rehabilitation based largely on the Strathcona experience. The new programs, NIP and RRAP, which the City of Vancouver has already chosen for certain areas include additional and expanded features of the Strathcona Project. The new programs are also meant to recognize a meaningful role for citizen involvement in the neighbourhood improvement process.

With the completion of the Rehabilitation Project in 1975, Strathcona displays a new look and spirit. Two hundred and thirty three houses were improved under the Project, with the majority of homeowners expending sums above and beyond the grant-loan assistance. Of the original $2 million allotted for housing rehabilitation assistance, less than $700,000 was spent. This resulted because the grant-loan scheme excluded more homeowners and failed to attract more landlords than had originally been estimated. The new sidewalks, sewers and streets were installed but overran their $2 million budget by $500,000.

With strong community initiative, a new linear park was funded by the Rehabilitation Project. Vacant lots were used in the park development to connect the existing parks in the neighbourhood. The Linear Park also involved blocking off streets and thus curtailing heavy truck and non-residential traffic through the community.

Another worthwhile development during the Rehabilitation Project was the Home Improvement Centre (717 East Pender). Initiated by Strathcona students, this Centre offered free design services and home improvements, and operated repair workshops for the elderly and lower incomed. It operated under OFY and LIP funding.

For members of SPOTA, rehabilitation of their neighbourhood did not end with the Rehabilitation Project. Mid-way through the Project in 1973, SPOTA initiated plans for non-profit housing on infill lots throughout the neighbourhood. These lots which had been acquired by the City under urban renewal were sold to the Provincial government at SPOTA's request. The Province was to lease the land for non-profit housing.

SPOTA began its housing program with a seven unit cooperative on five vacant lots of 730 Union Street. After several months of delay by City zoning officials, the Project began construction in the Fall of 1974. Five months later the seven families moved in. Financing of the cooperative came under the Federal government's non-profit housing program.

In the Fall of 1975, SPOTA began Phase Two of the Infill Housing. This involved three units of housing on double lots at 8 different Strathcona locations. The first families started moving into the new units in the Spring 1976. Financing for this phase came under the Provincial government's non-profit housing program.

The third and final phase of the Infill Housing involves the construction of single units on 16 remaining small lots. Construction is to begin in the Summer of 1976.

Future SPOTA housing plans include non-profit housing on the vacant land opposite the Strathcona School. This site was acquired by the City under urban renewal and then sold to a developer for $210,000, about one-third of the cost of the land assembly. In 1971 the City sought to buy it back for three times the amount to locate a large firehall there. After strong Strathcona-Chinatown protests which culminated in a large rally in December 1972, civic officials re-declared the land for housing. In February 1974, SPOTA and another organization were chosen by the City to develop non-profit and senior citizens housing on the site. Although the two organizations submitted detailed housing plans to the City in the Fall of 1974, no City action has been taken because of a legal suit filed by the private developer demanding market value for the land. At the present time, the "Firehall site" is a parking lot operated for and by the Vancouver Police Department.

During its years of existence, SPOTA has not only been involved in rehabilitation and new housing, but has also been concerned with many other community matters. The organization has worked closely with other Strathcona groups in social services and recreational and educational concerns. The organization has participated in many festivals and conferences. It has assisted students and researchers interested in neighbourhood improvement and rehabilitation.

For SPOTA neighbourhood improvement will not end with the Rehabilitation Project and the new housing. It is a continuous process. Other problems will be encountered.

Whatever the future, there has been one central principle throughout the Strathcona experience; and that is that citizens MUST participate in those decisions which affect their community. This principle has been fought for by SPOTA, as it has by many other neighbourhood organizations across Canada.

Hayne Wai
1 June 1976

As this chapter is being written, more than a decade after the 1968 founding of SPOTA, that organization continues to be a vigilant observer of living place changes and needed changes as well as planning coordinator for local residents. New options and needs for collaborative decisions are constantly arising. There are always plans being worked on by the professional and volunteer staff. Housed in an old former residence in Strathcona, SPOTA serves as a visible reminder of past collaborative effort and a present link in the chain of access between local people and outside powers—for example, social planning and other offices in City Hall. Residents' own controls are coordinated and at times mobilized by SPOTA.

Strathcona, as a living place, combines sections of ethnic homogeneity—at present primarily Chinese and Italian—within a shared space that has a multiethnic mosaic history. A map of this seventy-block area designates many "Landmarks of Old Strathcona." They are illustrative of North American urban development. The sites bear testimony to an inner-city neighborhood's past and residual immigrant populations.

LANDMARKS OF OLD STRATHCONA

1. Vancouver Chinese Public School
2. Ukrainian Canadian Centre–1928
3. The Italian Hall
4. Lord Strathcona School–1890
5. Synagogue–1914
6. Schara Tzedeck Synagogue–1921
7. Sacred Heart Rectory–1905
8. Russian People's Home
9. Russian Orthodox Church
10. St. Francis Xavier Chinese Catholic Centre

11. St. Francis Xavier Chinese Parish–1903
12. Benny's Italian Market–1915
13. The Fountain Chapel Church–1908
14. Chinese United Church

In addition, the community is more than a living place with which many residents are strongly identified; it is also a place of business. Its shops, ethnic restaurants, and other commercial ventures employ many local residents and attract a steady flow of outside city-dwellers and city-visitors as customers. Thus, the community is identified by residents as both home and workplace. In their opposition to relocation plans, residents could justifiably assert that "urban renewal would destroy the community and threaten the livelihood of Chinatown." Living places that are also working places for many residents doubly tie local people to their home territory.

As *The Strathcona Story* indicates, only a small percentage of the city's Chinese live in Strathcona. It attracts widely extended family members and otherwise associated persons from many parts of the city and its environs who come to visit kin and friends. Moreover, some of these visitors use the markets and other ethnic services—for example, the Chinese language school for children. And there are parallel facilities that involve the city's sizable Italian population. This living place thus finds support among many nonresidents who are strongly interested in what happens to this shared inner city space.

In each living place, the effectiveness of residents' own controls depends upon a unique and changing constellation of local conditions and external forces. Among the latter, outside Strathcona, as we have seen, there are both supportive and oppositional groups. But internally, despite some divisiveness which seems irrelevant to the urban renewal issue, Strathcona is united in protecting its turf. Residents' shared identification is rooted in the many available options for locals who choose to live there, its readily accessible inner city location for the visitors upon whom its economy relies, its ethnic ties and honeycomb of associations (some in conflict), topped by shared commercial interests, and its adequately sized and manageable space that serves many purposes. The exercise of residents' own controls through indigenous organizations like SPOTA, which is competently staffed by human service workers, is obviously strengthened by the internal conditions enumerated above.

Any fuller analysis of Strathcona's social structure and community coping strategies would have to include some of its myriad social networks. Some networks are primarily cultural, some economic, and some political, paralleling the divided and conflicting Chinas in Asia. But such complexities take us beyond the limits of this chapter. Enough has been said about societies and living places to suggest what different beginnings newborns might have, for example, in a Strathcona being torn down—as long-term residents await relocation—and a Strathcona whose networks are organized and committed to retain and improve its living place. Chapter Three addresses ideas about social networks and some of their implications for the development of infants and other people.

NOTES

[1] Robert Ezra Park, *Human Communities: The City and Human Ecology,* Collected Papers of R. E. Park, II, edited by E. C. Hughes and others (Glencoe, Illinois: The Free Press, 1952), p. 157. Also in Robert E. Park, *On Social Control and Collective Behavior,* Selected Papers edited by Ralph H. Turner (Chicago: University of Chicago Press, 1967), p. 83. Park is considered the founder of human ecology, the study of relationships between people and their environments.

[2] M. Packer and D. Rosenblatt, "Issues in the Study of Social Behaviour in the First Week of Life," in David Shaffer and Judy Dunn, eds., *The First Year of Life* (Chichester: Wiley, 1979), pp. 10–11.

[3] Willard Hartup, "The Origins of Friendship," in Michael Lewis and Leonard A. Rosenblum, eds., *Friendship and Peer Relations* (New York: Wiley, 1975).

[4] E. B. Thoman, P. H. Leiderman, and J. P. Olson, "Neonate–mother Interaction during Breast-feeding," *Developmental Psychology,* 6 (1972), 110–18, p. 113 and Table 7, p. 116.

[5] Josephine V. Brown and others, "Interactions of Black Inner-City Mothers and their Newborn Infants," *Child Development,* 46 (1975), p. 685.

[6] Packer and Rosenblatt, "Issues," p. 20.

[7] Brown, "Interactions," p. 684.

[8] Olwen, H. M. Jones, "A Comparative Study of Mother-Child Communication with Down's Syndrome and Normal Infants," in David Shaffer and Judy Dunn, eds., *The First Year of Life* (Chichester: Wiley, 1979), pp. 192–93.

[9] T. Berry Brazelton and others, "The Infant as Focus for Family Reciprocity," in Michael Lewis and Leonard A. Rosenblum, eds., *The Child and its Family* (New York: Plenum Press, 1979).

[10] Joy D. Osofsky and Barbara Danzer, "Relationships between Neonatal Characteristics and Mother-infant Interaction," *Developmental Psychology,* 10 (1974), 124–30.

[11] A. Chavez, C. Martinez, and T. Yaschine, "The Importance of Nutrition and Stimuli on Child Mental Development," in Joaquin Cravioto and others, eds., *Early Malnutrition and Mental Development* (Uppsala, Sweden: Almquist and Wiksell, 1974).

[12] M. Powell Lawton and Lucille Nahemow, "Ecology and the Aging Process," in Carl Eisdorfer and M. Powell Lawton, eds., *The Psychology of Adult Development and Aging* (Washington, D.C.: American Psychological Association, 1973), p. 637.

[13] Jerome Kagan, Richard B. Kearsley, and Philip R. Zelazo, *Infancy: Its Place in Human Development* (Cambridge: Harvard University Press, 1978), p. 8.

[14] René Dubos, "Biological Individuality," *Columbia Forum,* 12, (Spring 1969), p. 5.

[15] Julian Huxley, *Man Stands Alone* (New York: Harper, 1941, reprinted 1970), p. 8.

[16] Henry S. Maas and Joseph A. Kuypers, *From Thirty to Seventy: A Forty-Year Longitudinal Study of Adult Life Styles and Personality* (San Francisco: Jossey-Bass, 1974), p. 2.

[17] David Schonfield, "Retirement and the Commitment to Activity: Motivation," in Blossom T. Wigdor, ed., *Canadian Gerontological Collection I: Selected Papers* (Canadian Association on Gerontology, 1977), p. 53.

[18] Dubos, "Biological Individuality," p. 9.

[19] Hilda Scott, *Does Socialism Liberate Women? Experiences from Eastern Europe* (Boston: Beacon Press, 1974), p. 212.

[20] See, for example, "Observations on the Subordination of Russian Women" in Andrea Lee, "Russian Journal: I. Summer and Fall," *The New Yorker,* 56 (June 30, 1980), 72–87, especially pp. 75–76, and Dusko Doder, "Phoney Divorces, Feeble Feminism Mark U.S.S.R.," *The Washington Post,* reprinted in *The Vancouver Sun,* Friday, September 12, 1980, p. A6. Regarding the Third World, see, as one example, Beatrice B. Whiting on urban women's "working long and exhausting hours" in "Changing Life Styles in Kenya," *Daedalus,* 106 (Spring 1977), p. 221.

[21] Clifford Geertz, *Agricultural Involution: The Process of Ecological Change in Indonesia* (Berkeley: University of California Press, 1971), pp. 7–8.

[22] See his distinction between "B-love (love for the Being of another person, unneeding love, unselfish love) and D-love (deficiency-love, love need, selfish love)" in Abraham Maslow, *Toward a Psychology of Being* (Princeton, New Jersey: D. Van Nostrand, 1962), p. 39. Also, Abraham Maslow, *Maturation and Personality* (New York: Harper, 1954).

[23] William Schutz, *FIRO: A Three-Dimensional Theory of Interpersonal Behavior* (New York: Rinehart, 1958).

[24] Joan Robinson, *Freedom and Necessity: an Introduction to the Study of Society* (London: George Allen and Unwin, 1970), p. 121.

[25] René Dubos, "Environmental Determinants of Human Life," in David C. Glass, ed., *Environmental Influences: Third of a Series on Biology and Behavior* (New York: Rockefeller University Press and Russell Sage Foundation, 1968), p. 148.

[26] W. R. Gove, M. Hughes, and O. R. Galle, "Overcrowding in the Home: an Empirical Investigation of its Possible Pathological Consequences," *American Sociological Review,* 44 (1979), p. 78. See also the four-part exchange between authors Walter R. Gove and Michael Hughes and their critics Alan Booth and his colleagues over the differences in findings between the Gove Chicago study and the Booth Toronto study in *American Sociological Review,* 45 (1980), 864–86. See especially Gove's final remarks which include quantitative evidence (in Table 2, p. 885) "that our measures of psychiatric symptoms, the experience of crowding, self-esteem, manifest irritations and positive affect are distinct factors . . ." (p. 884) in "The Pursuit of Preconceptions: a Reply to the Claim of Booth and his Colleagues that Household Crowding is not an Important Variable (Reply to Booth, Johnson, and Edwards)," pp. 878–86. For a review of research on crowding and how "perceived similarity" of co-residents may reduce damaging effects, see James A. Russell and Lawrence M. Ward, "Environmental Psychology," *Annual Review of Psychology,* 33 (1982), 651–683, p. 675.

[27] Dorothy E. Smith, "Household Space and Family Organization," in D. I. Davies and Kathleen Herman, eds., *Social Space: Canadian Perspectives* (Toronto: New Press, 1971), pp. 64–65.

[27a] Oscar Lewis, *Five Families: Mexican Case Studies in the Culture of Poverty* (New York: Basic Books, 1959), and *Children of Sanchez: Autobiography of a Mexican Family* (New York: Random House, 1961).

[27b] Madeleine Kerr, *The People of Ship Street* (London: Routledge and Kegan Paul, 1958), pp. 64–65.

[27c] Betty L. Spinley, *The Deprived and the Privileged* (London: Routledge and Kegan Paul, 1953).

[28] Ernest A. Haggard and Anna Von der Lippe, "Isolated Families in the Mountains of Norway," in E. James Anthony and Cyrille Koupernik, eds., *The Child in His Family* (New York: Wiley–Interscience, 1970), pp. 482, 484–85.

[29] Walter Firey, "Sentiment and Symbolism as Ecological Variables," *American Sociological Review* 10 (1945), 140–48.

[30] Michael Young and Peter Willmott, *Family and Kinship in East London* (London: Routledge and Kegan Paul, 1957), p. 85.

[31] Jane Jacobs, *The Death and Life of Great American Cities* (New York: Vintage Books, 1961), p. 117.

[32] Peter Willmott, *The Evolution of a Community: a Study of Dagenham after Forty Years* (London: Routledge and Kegan Paul, 1963), p. 110. Quoted with the permission of the author, Peter Willmott.

[33] Jacobs, *Great American Cities,* p. 114.

[34] Michael A. Hirst, "The Geographical Basis of Community Work," *Community Development Journal: an International Forum* 15 (1980), 53–59.

[35] Peter Marris, "The Ideology of Human Settlements," in *People and Places: Social Work Education and Human Settlements* (New York: International Association of Schools of Social Work, 1976). Quoted with permission.

[36] Hayne Wai, *The Strathcona Story* (Vancouver, British Columbia: Strathcona Property Owners and Tenants Association (SPOTA), 1976). Quoted with permission.

Chapter 3
NETWORKS
AND
ATTACHMENTS

Introduction: Attachments develop throughout life in social networks.

INTRODUCTION

Attachments Develop Throughout
Life in Social Networks

Almost all infants become a part of their caretakers' networks. Such networks are composed of the kin, friends, neighbors, acquaintances, and/or service givers of either one of the infant's parents or of both parents jointly. During the first year of the child's life, reciprocal attachments normally develop between not only the infant and parent(s) but also between the infant and other network members who frequently interact with the baby. "Reciprocal" in this context means that the baby becomes attached to the older person, and the older person becomes attached to the baby. While adult network members may originally have been linked to one or both of the infant's parents, the members come in time to include the child in their relationships. Thus, infants become a part of networks in which their caretakers are central members.

The mother's sister drops by, the father's workmate and "buddy" visits, or the nine-year-old child next door asks to borrow some potatoes. Each of them, in the course of the visit, peers into the crib, and the baby's smile engages the visitor. Each stands over the crib for a few minutes and "plays" with the baby, who responds with vigorous arm and leg movements, almost reaching out to be picked up. Each of the visitors succumbs to the baby's apparent entreaties, holding the baby for longer or shorter times, as the baby touches a face, cuddles, or makes sounds suggesting happiness. The baby holders make approving remarks: "What a wonderful kid!" "A real little person!" "More fun than anything!" The visitors leave, but the neighbor's nine-year-old returns in an hour, and thereafter visits daily after school. The baby's aunt volunteers to "sit" regularly, so the mother can get out and shop or run other errands a few times each week. The father's friend asks whether the cigar smoke bothers the baby, wonders what kind of toy the baby would like, and asks if he can bring his girlfriend to see the baby. He drops by more often than the Friday night card game sessions, and almost always inquires upon arrival what "new tricks" the baby is up to. The baby, in turn, becomes responsive whenever the friend appears. "The kid knows me!" the friend exclaims jubilantly.

How do such experiences modify the subsequent social behavior of all the participants in such events? How is the infant affected? What is the effect on the adults, or on the neighbor's nine-year-old? Or on an infant's older sibling who may find visitors' exclusive involvements with the baby troublesome? Or on the infant's parents who enjoy seeing others enjoying their baby, as well as their baby's responsiveness?

And what if, by contrast, a baby often cries demandingly, will not be readily pacified, and usually repels visitors with negative reactions or nonresponsiveness? What social interaction, attachment, and network effects might such an infant generate?

Studies of early attachments and of social networks have proliferated in recent years, but they have remained, for the most part, separate spheres of inquiry. Network research has usually been matrixed in anthropology's or sociology's studies of community life or work. Attachment research has been conceptually rooted in psychological inquiry of infant and early childhood development, focused until quite recently on how the child (and not the "parenting person") is affected. Studies of failure in the development of attachment, and research on separation, loss, and mourning have been done in psychiatry. Thus several separate disciplines have addressed different facets of the attachment-network nexus.

One purpose of this chapter is to strengthen relationships between current views of network and attachment, and to consider some of the consequences of their conceptual partnership for the human services. Although attachments normally begin in infancy in whatever networks are available to the child, capacities for attachment develop and are modified throughout the life course. During life periods such as adolescence and old age, and following transitional events such as the birth of a first child and widowhood, changes occur in one's needs for networks, their composition, and the kinds of mutuality they involve. At the same time, personal capacities for attachment become more or less salient. The efficacy of direct services may depend on clients' capacities for attachment; furthering the development of these capacities is sometimes a primary goal of counseling. Network concepts are being put to work in both community development and family therapy. The human services could profit from a better linking of attachment as a developmental process with social network as its context.

SOCIAL NETWORKS

Before discussing the concept of social network, I shall present illustrations from two community studies, one done in Boston's West End before its primarily Italian-American residents were evicted by urban redevelopers, the other in a working class public housing development of some 27,000 units accommodating over 90,000 residents in Essex outside London. (The British call such a London County Council-planned development a "housing estate.") Both the Boston and the British records describe living-place networks, in contrast to, for example, occupational or work-place networks.

Living-place Networks

First, here are some of sociologist Herbert Gans' observations on what he labels "peer group life" among working class Italian-Americans in Boston. In this community family members tend to live close by and friends may become godparents. Thus familial, friendship, and neighborly roles overlap in what I discuss later as a multiplex network. Under such circumstances, attachments among the people involved are likely to be strong. Neighborhood centers and church groups try to provide roughly comparable contexts, especially for people who are not otherwise affiliated. What aspects of the informal relationships described in the Boston and the British living-place network (Record No. 7) might be adapted for use in human services addressed to fostering attachments through group programs?

BOSTON WEST END PEER GROUP
LIFE (RECORD NO. 6)

The basis of adult West End life is peer group sociability. By sociability I do not mean the entertaining and party-giving of the middle class. Nor do I mean the informal conversational activity that the middle class ranks well below occupational, familial, and self-improvement activities in importance. For the West Ender, sociability is a routinized gathering of a relatively unchanging peer group of family members and friends that takes place several times a week. One could almost say that the meetings of the group are at the vital center of West End life, that they are the end for which other everyday activities are a means.

Membership in the group is based primarily on kinship. As already noted, brothers, sisters, and cousins of the husband and wife—and their spouses—are at the core. The group also includes godparents and friends who may come less regularly. . . .

Included among other unrelated individuals are friends of long duration, as well as more recent friends. Though the latter may be newcomers to the group, they are likely to have been known to the group before, because, as already noted, everyone knows of everyone else. Consequently, nearly everyone is a potential friend who can join a peer group at any time. This happens most often after people have extended help to each other, met at ceremonial occasions, or have had prolonged contact, for example, as hospital patients. . . .

Much of the conversation is devoted to the exchange of reportage—and gossip—about people known to the group. As noted earlier, every peer group is tied, through kinship, friendship, or other connections, to many other groups and individuals in a giant network that extends far beyond the West End. Thus, someone may have a report about someone else, even if he does not know the individual personally. . . .

The exchange of news has a number of functions. It keeps people up-to-date on what is going on among present and potential peer group members, and defines or redefines the place of the reporter and his audience in this large group. It also provides for social control, since deviant behavior is reported and evaluated quite fully. And, at the same time, it considers new ideas that might be useful to the group. Moreover, it supplies information about services and "experts" in a culture that suspects or rejects the professional expert provided by the outside world. Thus the constant flow of news holds the network of peer groups together and makes it easier for West Enders to do without formal community organizations—either their own or those of the outside world. Finally, the reportage and gossip provide entertainment and drama about one's own group of the kind that is available about other groups in soap operas and similar mass media fiction.[1]

In this record, one sees vividly a small part of "a giant network" which may provide tangible help and emotional supports as well as the enjoyment of good times together.

The residents of Dagenham, whom British sociologist Peter Willmott quotes in his community study come primarily from, and retain ties in, the working class boroughs of London's East End, although the Dagenham housing estate is about five miles outside of London. There, "working wives regularly exchange visits with friends nearby who help with their children." Peter Willmott quotes Mrs. Roberts: "Mrs. Bacon next door pays my rent, does the bagwash and puts it out to dry," she says, "I know if the children come home she'll be there to see to them."

NEIGHBORS' NETWORKS IN
DAGENHAM (RECORD NO. 7)

Mrs. Palmer explained: "The children are on their own for about half an hour, from half past four till five, when I get home from work, but they're always in full view of the neighbours. If they want anything Mrs. Jordan over the road sees to it for them. Mrs. Jordan gets the groceries for us."

In other words, if going out to work keeps some wives apart, for others it is made possible by their being together already. And the practical help the wives receive in this situation provides one illustration of the kind of neighbourly give and take that goes on.

The people who help, in this and other ways, live close at hand. There are exceptions. Mrs. Davies said, "I've got one friend who comes in. She's not a neighbour. We speak to the neighbours, but that's all. My friend lives on the estate, about ten minutes' walk away. She comes for tea once a week and I go round to her. It's a regular thing. I met her through the children going to the same religious classes." Mrs. Barton said likewise, "I've got a friend round in York Avenue. Every week I go round to her one afternoon and she comes here another. I used to work with her back in Stepney before I was married and we kept in touch after we moved here."

For most people, however, it is not like this. In fact, the radius of friendship is extremely localized. Apart from relatives, people seldom seem to maintain contact with, or exchange visits with, others if they do not live close at hand. Most of the friends who visit them are drawn from amongst people living in the dozen or so houses nearby. The friendships that bring wives, and to a lesser extent husbands, into each other's homes are of a piece with the day-to-day meetings in the garden or street. "I see Mrs. Jones every day to speak to," said Mrs. Knight; "she doesn't come in as a rule, but we walk up to the shops together, or like today when the laundry called and I went over to pay her and stopped for a little chat." And Mrs.

Taylor explained, "Mrs. Braddock lives next door. We go shopping together near enough every day and we go to the school together to collect the children. She doesn't come in much; she usually calls me over the back there and we have a talk over the garden fence."

Of course, people choose their friends, but they usually choose them from among people they see often as neighbours. Frequently, the friends who are selected live next door or across the road.

"I know the women on either side best," said Mrs. Salmon, "because they're the ones I mostly see. Sometimes they come in here or I go in there."

Mrs. Gibson's closest friends are two of her neighbours.

"We've got some good friends, particularly Mrs. Gordon over the road and Mrs. Wheeler who lives just down the street. If I'm ever fed up I go in to Mrs. Gordon for a friendly cup of tea and a chat and then we go to Mrs. Wheeler, the three of us are just like that."

The links between the women are not only those of companionship, but are often built upon mutual aid in their day-to-day tasks. Mrs. Page has a friend living two doors away.

"If we happen to run short," she said, "we always run in to each other, and if she ever buys anything excessive she asks me to use it up. If I go out she sees to the workmen or the laundry man or the rent man, and I do the same for her. If you needed her help she'd always be there."

"I've got two very good friends," Mrs. Jarvis said. "Mrs. Barker, who lives opposite, has got a spin drier and she uses my sewing machine. I put my washing in her spin drier and she uses my sewing machine when she wants to. Then the lady next door on one side is another friend of mine. We always help each other out."

The men have less to do with each other, but often their friendships, too, develop out of shared interests around the home. Apart from an occasional trade union meeting, most men seem to see little of their workmates outside working hours. Even when people share their employer, or even their job, as well as their residence on the estate, they do not apparently have much to do with each other unless they also live very near. Contacts like this are common:

"We hadn't been here a fortnight," said Mr. Gray, "when the turf that I'd ordered came, and I had the job of putting it down. The chappie down at the bottom of the garden came and said, 'Why don't you borrow my fork?' Then when I started to do it, he said, 'Let me help you.' It turned out that that was his line of business. He's quite a pal of mine now. He helps me with the garden; I help him with photography; it's my hobby and he's just taking it up."

Mr. Dover's great hobby is woodwork; at the time he was interviewed he was busy on a pelmet he was making for a friend living next door and he had just finished a toy train for the son of another. He relies on Fred, another friend who is also a neighbour, to help when needed. "Just today I was sawing a log for the engine of this train and Fred sees that my saw is blunt and lends me a sharp one. Anything at all I want he'll lend it to me if he has it. I'm the same with him. The other day he knocked when I wasn't here and borrowed my steps—we take each other for granted that way."

How do these patterns tie in with those with relatives, described earlier? Some people live in the thick of extended families, others are isolated from kin. Some people, it is now apparent, have friends among their neighbours with whom they give and receive help. What is the connection? Have friends taken the place of relatives for the couples whose kindred are not near?

It is not like this. Some couples, of course, have friends at hand, but not relatives. Others have relatives nearby and see little of other people, and others see little of either. But many both belong to extended families and have a good deal to do with their neighbours as well. Mrs. Rank often has neighbours in; her mother also lives around the corner and is seen every day. She is not unique. Of the 209 people in the general sample who had been visited by relatives in the previous 24 hours, 37% had also been visited by friends or neighbours, against 28% of the 668 who had not been visited by relatives. The two kinds of relationship, in other words, are not mutually exclusive. On the contrary, those with relatives at hand are rather more likely to have friends in their homes as well. This is exactly what we found in Bethnal Green also.[2]

In this record of an English suburban "local network," residents' get-togethers seem smaller and are perhaps less effusive than the Boston Italian-American gatherings. Moreover, while Gans says "the meetings of the group are at the vital center of West End life" in Boston, Willmott conveys no such impression about the interchanges of the working class women or men in Dagenham. Are such differences a function of the different cultural styles of the residents in the two living places? Or do they reflect differences in the focus of observations? Note that in both places, however, concrete services are mutually rendered; emotional support is offered, especially if, as Mrs. Gibson says, one is "ever fed up"; and sociability and home visiting occur on a regular "every day" or "every week" schedule. In all of this, one is able to count on someone's help "if we happen to run short." There are also repeated exchanges: "He helps me with the garden; I help him with photography." Tangible services, together with a modicum of sympathetic feelings, must lighten the lives of all these people.

Living-place networks among friends and neighbors are not, of course, total social networks. Perhaps some general attention to what the term "social network" means—and does not mean—is appropriate, now that some limited illustrations have been presented.

Conceptions and Misconceptions of "Network"

While immediate and extended family members, friends, and neighbors, as in the two illustrations, are typically the people who matter most in life, other network members are sometimes important too—for example co-workers or people who work (serving as "functionaries") in local stores, health centers, or other frequently used facilities. In fact, just who should be included in a person's network is often uncertain. Anthropologist J. A. Barnes, in an article to which the origins of the term "network" are traced, says, "The elements of this social field are not fixed, for new ties are continually being formed and old links are broken or put into cold storage."[3] Thus, the boundaries of networks tend to be blurred, and their exact memberships may be unclear. Secondary ties, persons who are once removed, such as one's brother's friend who is also a lawyer, may be excluded today, but tomorrow in a crisis she may become an important link in the network. In addition, as Barnes and others have noted, networks, in their informality, may have only very loose, if any, organization or hierarchical structures, so there is no central coordination of members' behavior.[4] Instead, shared mores and values may provide informally some unifying orientations, but people who are many links away from one another in a network may not share any common values. Still, despite the uncertainties and imprecision of its meaning and application in everyday life, the term "network" proves useful in considering the social contexts of human behavior, at least when the term's use is not overextended.

For example, the word *network* should not be used interchangeably with such terms as *support system* or *helping community,* as though there were never conflicting, constraining, demanding, nonsupportive, and unhelpful relationships in social networks. Sophisticates in network terminology recognize "asymmetrical" ties in which the ideal of reciprocity—equal giving and taking—fails; one member may become unable to share burdens or even carry his or her own. Conformist pressures in networks may become personally stifling for mavericks or creative people. It may not always be desirable for networks to be strongly tied together, or cohesive. Networks tend to become cohesive when there is high internal "density" or "multiplexity." *Density* refers to extensive overlapping in relationships in which not only are many A's and B's close to each other but also both are close to C's. *Multiplexity* occurs when within any paired relationship many roles are involved, one's cousin being also one's babysitter and also closest confidante. Such network cohesion may inhibit freedom of movement. There is good evidence, for example, for "the superiority of loosely knit social networks as supportive milieus for persons undergoing abrupt life transitions."[5] If, for example, a married couple is in a dense network in which all friends are shared by both spouses, should a sudden separation occur, one of the spouses may become friendless. The asymmetrical helpfulness of a tight network is nowhere more sharply illustrated than in developing nations; the Filipino or Ugandan who leaves a rural home to try to "get ahead" in town may no sooner begin to enjoy some economic success than friends and kin from the countryside invade his room in town. Although helpful to the newcomers, network obligations may destroy the new emancipation and small accumulated resources of the original emigré to the town. Network must not be thought of in oversimplified, undifferentiated, or romantic terms as it is not always socially desirable and supportive for all members.

On the other hand, there are, of course, many advantages to network membership, and people who have no or few interpersonal links may suffer in many ways for their social isolation, especially in crises. The record of Dee Rodgers, with which this section on social networks ends, illustrates some effects of lack of close ties on a newcomer to a city. She suffers not only from loneliness for adult companionship but also the lack of help she needs with her very young children. Of course, network members enjoy more than simply "help." From several sources, the following desirable "functions" emerge, most of them portrayed in the earlier illustrative passages on community life in Boston and Dagenham:

> Attachment or emotional support and concern
> Exchange of services (task assistance, material aid)
> Guidance (information, referrals, etc.)
> Social integration (value sharing, expectation setting, evaluative feedback, maintenance of social identity)
> Sense of alliance (or belonging)
> Reassurance of worth
> Opportunity to provide nurturance[6]

Note that "attachment"—and its feeling component—heads the list of a social network's functions. The idea of interpersonal tie is the essence of most definitions of the term: for example, "The individual's social network consists of those persons with whom he maintains contact and has some form of social bonds."[7] As attachment is central to network, so within networks, human attachments begin.

In the Boston living-place network described earlier in this chapter, the presence of social bonds and strong attachments is implicit. The British record emphasizes exchange of services or "mutual aid," but emotional support creeps in too: "If I'm ever fed up I go in to Mrs. Gordon for a friendly cup of tea and a chat and then we go to Mrs. Wheeler, the three of us are just like that." The information-giving functions of the network are stressed in the Boston report on the exchange of news and gossip. Easily inferred from the description are the network's value-sharing and identity-maintenance functions, the sense of belonging the group generates, the opportunities provided for ingroup nurturing, and the reciprocal reassurance of worth such nurturing confers.

Lack of Network

Persons lacking network memberships or unsupported by their networks appear in disproportionately large numbers in some specialized welfare and mental health services. People who suffer from psychiatric problems, contrasted with "various normal control populations," have "networks characterized by fewer linkages overall, fewer intimate relationships, greater asymmetrical and dependent relationships, and lower scores on indices of perceived support."[8] Social competence is necessary in order to enter into, participate, and remain in a social network. In child welfare, parents whose children are thrust into foster care and protective services sometimes lack such competence or else are unrooted and socially isolated people because of social conditions; they lack the kind of informal support that network members may give in an emergency to a relative or friend.[9] Such parents have nowhere but formal agencies to turn to when they are unable to care for their own child for even a brief period. Once involved in the formal arrangements of specialized welfare services, the needs for informal network relationships may diminish.

Preventive programs that help link networkless newcomers to neighborhood groups offer the promise of keeping families intact. Such groups provide not only services and guidance; in time they offer the newcomer emotional support, a sense of belonging, and an opportunity, in return, to help others—the rewards of network members. The burgeoning of self-help groups and neighborhood networks, sometimes with the consultation or assistance of human service workers, is amply reported in the professional literature.[10]

How a newcomer to a community may merely be launched by a formal agency's help with first linkages to a new network is illustrated in the record of Dee Rodgers. Note how the social worker's information-giving and linking services allow a newcomer to resume parenting with the support not only of a formal child care program but also of "some girl friends."

DEE RODGERS: A BRIEF
NETWORK-LINKING SERVICE
(RECORD NO. 8)

Mrs. Dee Rodgers (Mrs. R.) was visited five times in response to an initial complaint by a neighbor that she was leaving her two preschool children, Annie, 18 months, and Joe, 2½ years, alone, locked in the apartment for half a day or more at a time. On my first visit she talked to me only through the half-opened door, the two children clinging to her skirt. She said her husband was away, the children were all right, and she wanted nothing to do with social workers. I said it was late in the day, she was probably busy making supper, and I should stop by tomorrow morning. The neighbor told me Mrs. R. had lived in the house only three or four months and seemed to have no friends.

Since Mrs. Lake, in my single-parents Thursday-night group, lives right across the street, I told her that Mrs. R. was a newcomer who seemed to know no one in the neighborhood. Mrs. Lake phoned me early the next day, saying she had visited Mrs. R. and that Mrs. R. wanted to see me tomorrow.

I found that Mrs. R. was indeed without friends in the city, having just moved here, she said, from Marysville. She felt unable to go out on the street with the two children and sometimes just had to get away without them. Her husband had gone "up north" to log and periodically sent her money on which she managed adequately. Her only pastimes were sewing and watching TV. She knew nothing of the community, including the Canby Street Day Care Center. Moreover, her attitude about looking into such places was one of anticipated rejection.

Having arranged for us to visit the day care center when Mrs. R. expressed an interest in seeing it, I was nevertheless not too surprised when she failed to appear. When I visited her at home later that day, she said she had not been feeling well. On that visit she told me spontaneously about the small Indian village in which she'd grown up until age 10, then of the series of foster homes and finally group home for teenagers in which she'd lived until she married at age 16. I noticed that her approach to her children seemed somewhat screened by her preoccupations with herself; her expectations for their behavior seemed beyond their capacities at times, and at other times she seemed to treat them like dolls. We talked about young children and their needs and also about the difficulties of being a single parent with personal needs that young children could not fulfill.

After a visit to the Canby Street Day Care Center, Mrs. R. put Joe's name on the waiting list for one morning a week. For Joe's required health checkup, I introduced Mrs. R. to the Bluevale Pediatric Clinic, which she used for Annie, too. On my last visit, Joe was starting at Canby Street on a one-morning-a-week schedule, and Mrs. R. had joined a group of mothers who used the Center's sewing machine. They also bought some material collectively and exchanged clothing patterns. Mrs. R. remarked, "I have some girlfriends now." I left my agency telephone number in case she wanted to speak with me again.[11]

Note that when Dee Rodgers has made relationships with "some girlfriends," she seems more comfortably able to assume parental responsibilities. It is as though interaction with peers provides a salutary balance to the many hours daily a single parent must attend to very young children. The theoretical relationships between attachment behavior as parent, and significant experiences with agemates, are explored more fully in the last section of this chapter, in a report on a study of the mothers of young schizophrenic women. Clearly, however, even from a short record like Dee Rodgers', one is reminded of the important interplay of network membership with other facets of people's daily living.

ATTACHMENTS IN INFANCY
AND LATER LIFE

Attachment is an emotional bond between two people, recognized by participants through their desire to be close to each other. Attachment is observable to other persons by what psychologists call "proximity-seeking behavior." Attachment is likely to be shared, or reciprocal—the adult attaching to the child as well as child to adult—in its earliest form, in the ties between an infant, his or her caretaker(s), and other persons. Signs of an infant's growing attachment normally first become apparent between about the third and seventh month of a child's life. A child's crying when mother leaves, smiling and lifting arms at her approach, visually, or later bodily, following her when she moves away are all proximity-seeking behaviors indicative of attachment.

Children who have failed to make such attachments may indiscriminately respond to almost anyone who approaches and never show any fear or other concern about strangers or unfamiliar persons. I have visited large and understaffed "orphanages" in Turkey and elsewhere in which, on entry to the grounds, playing children run up to any newcomer, pulling at a visitor's hands or clothing to be picked up and held, and then just as suddenly seem to want to get down and run off. They communicate no sense of either pleasurable or unpleasurable feelings about the encounter. They seem to want contact but do not know what to do with it when it occurs. Such children are "deprived" and suffer the effects of a lack of any early, enduring, and intensive attachments. Such attachments, some conditions for their development, and their going awry as "overattachments" as well as "under-attachments" are considered in the following sections.

Early Multiple Attachments

Recent studies have revealed the active part infants play in initiating attachments, inducing relationships by attracting and responding in various ways to persons in their parents' network or otherwise in the infants' orbit. Note that it is not only to their primary caretakers that infant attachments occur. Observational studies in Uganda, Scotland, and elsewhere make the development of multiple attachments a more understandable process, although whether the single relationship with the "parent" must come first is not clear from all the evidence.

Of the twenty-eight children in psychologist Mary Ainsworth's intensive study done outside Kampala, Uganda, "only five babies were looked after exclusively by their mothers. In all other instances the mother shared her duties to some extent with other figures—other adults or older children in the household or neighbors."[12] In her "summary of the development of attachments" during each of the four quarters (or three-month periods) of the children's first year, Ainsworth reports for the third quarter when the children were from twenty-seven to thirty-nine weeks old:

> Of the fourteen who were attached to their mothers, ten were described as having clear-cut attachments to other familiar members of the household—father, grandparent, aunt, uncle, sibling, or nursemaid, and an eleventh child—Perero—at least "liked" his father, who was home on weekends only. . . . On the whole, however, it appears that Ganda babies who have the opportunity to develop an attachment to another adult in the household will do so in the third quarter, if not earlier, and very soon after a clear-cut attachment to the mother has been formed. Attachments to young siblings seem to develop more slowly, but both William and Aida appeared to be somewhat attached to siblings in this quarter.[13]

Attachments to noncaretakers are more fully reported in a Scottish observational study by H. R. Schaffer and Peggy Emerson. Repeated observations of 60 Glasgow children in their working-class homes, from their earliest months until they were a year and a half old, reveal the following:

> . . . we also observed attachments to be formed to individuals who have never participated in routine care activities. . . . Satisfaction of physical needs does

not appear to be a necessary precondition to the development of attachments, the latter taking place independently and without any obvious regard to the experiences that the child encounters in physical care situations.[14]

Regarding their evidence of infants' multiple attachment to noncaretakers, Schaffer and Emerson further generalize:

> Investigators have ... generally isolated the child's relationship with the mother from his total social behavior and studied it without reference to any other social relationship also formed by him. A wider focus is needed, however, in order to appreciate that the usual view is too simple .... a person's constant presence in the infant's immediate environment is no guarantee that interaction will occur and the necessary stimulation be offered. The most available person has, of course, the best opportunity of providing such stimulation and for this reason the mother is, more often than not, the infant's principal object. Yet not every mother will avail herself of this opportunity; personality factors and practical considerations may prevent her from doing so and thus allow other people, more responsive if less available, to become the child's principal attachment objects. ... Whom an infant chooses as his attachment object and how many objects he selects depend, we believe, primarily on the nature of the social setting in which he is reared and not on some intrinsic characteristics of the attachment function itself.[15]

After reviewing these same two studies, by Ainsworth and by Schaffer and Emerson, in a chapter called "Focusing on a Figure" in the first of his three volumes on *Attachment and Loss,* British psychoanalyst John Bowlby adheres to his early formulations about mother-infant attachment, concluding, "Because the bias of a child to attach himself especially to one figure seems to be well established and also to have far-reaching implications for psychopathology, I believe it merits a special term. In the earlier paper I referred to it as 'monotropy'."[16]

On whether children are innately "monotropic" and whether "the bond with the mother (or mother-surrogate) is different in kind from the bonds developed with others," psychiatrist Michael Rutter's book-length review of maternal deprivation research concludes:

> The evidence on that point is unsatisfactory but what there is seems not to support that view. Two issues are involved. The first is whether or not the main bond differs from all others. It is suggested here that it does not. The chief bond is especially important because of its greater strength, but most children develop bonds with several people and it appears likely that these bonds are basically similar. The second concerns the assumption that the 'mother' or 'mother-surrogate' is the person to whom the child is necessarily most attached. Of course in most families the mother has most to do with the young child and as a consequence she is usually the person with whom the strongest bond is formed. But it should be appreciated that the chief bond need not be with a biological parent, it need not be with the chief caretaker and it need not be with a female.[17]

Bowlby's commitment to the idea of monotropism in the face of questioning, if not contrary evidence, illustrates how, on issues so close to the self—issues of a kind this book addresses—objectivity even by serious scholars may not always be possible.

By contrast, Schaffer and Emerson offer some practical observations about their findings on multiple attachments in infancy:

> The data of the present report suggest strongly that such individuals as fathers, grandmothers, and even siblings need not play quite the minor subsidiary role generally allotted to them, but that from the beginning they may assume important positions in the infant's world. Once the view has been accepted that the child–mother relationship does not necessarily exhaust the infant's attachment behavior, a linkage becomes possible between the family setting and one aspect of personality growth. . . . The purpose of these remarks is not to challenge the importance of the mother vis-a-vis her children, but to stress the fact that other people in the infant's environment may also play important roles.[18]

In a period of steadily increasing numbers of working mothers and of other women whose interests and capacities extend beyond fulltime mothering, of fathers who share the responsibilities of parenting in ways that were once considered "unmasculine," and of families whose compositions change within boundaries far more permeable than the tightly closed, middle-class nuclear family of former days, such evidence of multiple attachments in the lives of infants is, at the very least, timely.

Synchrony in Early Attachments

Not enough is known as yet to be able to specify the conditions most conducive to the development of early attachments in ways that provide a sound basis for later personal relationships. Recent studies have revealed the active part an infant plays in initiating attachments, inducing interaction by attracting, or responding engagingly to, certain persons. The continuance of an initiated connection depends on many factors, but one that has special relevance in the interactional framework of this book is the fit in the rhythms of interchange or "synchrony" (sympathetic timing) of the young child and the other person. Affectional ties and proximity-seeking behavior grow out of a complex interactional process, providing in that process early elements of what later in life may become central developmental capacities. I call your attention to the process of synchrony not only because it seems to foster attachment but also because it contributes to the development of capacities for mutuality or reciprocity, as illustrated later in this section.

Inborn temperamental characteristics differentiate in readily observable ways the behavior of tiny neonates cribbed behind glass in hospital nurseries. Activity-passivity levels, intensity of reactions, low or high thresholds of response to external stimulation, the degree of stabilized timing of sleeping and waking phases, and the periodicities of hunger mark some of the uniquenesses of each baby. Some of the infant's timed or rhythmic behavior calls for response from other persons. There are various ways in which other persons can time their responses to fit—or help the infant gradually to adapt—into a mutually compatible sequence of interactions. The alternations of active sucking and passivity of the infant at the breast may be matched by a composed and receptive woman during the infant's active sucking phase and more playful or otherwise communicative behavior during the infant's nonsucking pauses. Adaptation to the rhythms of the infant's cyclical behavior may be more or less complete; totally out-of-sync adult interaction guarantees infant displeasure.

As the infant grows, of course, adaptation and learning regarding synchrony occur in both persons, so that mutual accommodations may be achieved. Clearly this early rhythmic patterning of interplay between two people models later, and all through life, mutual or reciprocal exchanges—in conversations, in nonverbal game play, in sexual relations, in bartering and bargaining, and in peace negotiations. Such reciprocity is fundamental to all human interaction and its residua in personal relationships.

Many observations of synchrony or timed reciprocity are reported in the research literature. The report of a Harvard study using films of what goes on between a mother and her infant during the first months of the child's life notes,

> Short cycles of attention and nonattention seemed to underlie all periods of prolonged interaction. Although we thought we were observing continuous attention to her (mother's) stimuli, on the part of the infant, stop-frame analysis uncovered the cyclical nature of the infant's looking-not-looking in our laboratory setting. Looking away behavior reflects the need of each infant to maintain some control over the amount of stimulation he can take in via the visual mode in such an intense period of interaction.[19]

About this cyclical behavior, the authors remark, "The most important rule for maintaining an interaction seemed to be that a mother develop a sensitivity to her infant's capacity for attention and his need for withdrawal—partial or complete—after a period of attention to her."[20] Under the heading, "Allowing for Reciprocity," a foreshadowing of later phases of social development appears:

> When the mother can allow for the cyclic turning away from her, which seems to be necessary for the infant, she can be assured of longer periods of attention when he turns back to her. One of our mothers was particularly striking in her capacity to subside as he decreased his attention to her. She relaxed back in her chair smiling softly, reducing other activity such as vocalizing and moving, waiting for him to return. When he did look back, she began slowly to add behavior on behavior, as if she were feeling out how much he could master. She also sensed his need to reciprocate. She vocalized then waited for his response. When she smiled, she waited until he smiled before she began to build up her own smiling again. Her moving in close to him was paced sensitively to coincide with his body cycling, and if he became excited or jerky in his movement she subsided back into her chair.

We felt she was outstanding in her sensitivity to the importance of reciprocity in this interaction. Whether she felt the danger of overloading him and cutting short their communication, or whether she sensed that pacing her behaviors decreased habituation effects and increased the value to him of each behavior as a signal, she brought out clear evidence of a more intense communication system between them. She provided an atmosphere that led to longer periods of interaction. She seemed to teach him an expectancy of more than just stimuli from her in the guise of her sensitivity to his needs and his cues. As she allowed for these, she seemed to be teaching him now to expand his own ability to attend to stimulation, for "long-term intention" as well as "long-term interaction." Thus her role took on deeper significance as she established not only the climate for communication but gave him the experience in pacing himself in order to attend to the environment. [21]

The report concludes, "This interdependency of rhythms seemed to be at the root of their 'attachment' . . ." [22]

In a developmental analysis of peer interaction among toddlers, other researchers note this same kind of "act/watch rhythm of interaction" when children are manipulating toys in a small group. These researchers interpret the pauses which punctuate the action as a time for the child "to process the feedback deriving from the actions." [23] Whatever the explanation for this cyclical kind of behavior, begun in the first weeks of life, it is apparently an important element in the development of feelings of attachment. It may play a part in the connective or dysjunctive interaction of toddler playmates or other later interpersonal relations. Manifest as synchrony in the early growth of attachment between an infant and another person, it is a process to which I shall return in later chapter discussions of reciprocity and social responsibility.

Under- and Overattachments

Normally, feelings of mutual attachment develop between infants and one or more persons in the networks of their immediate living places without cause for public or private concern. But obviously, there are great differences within that normal range in the qualities of the attachments formed. Any given attachment between an infant and another person may undergo changes, even momentarily, for example, by intensifying when an infant feels threatened. Attachments may also fail to develop adequately from the outset because of longlasting social network lacks or larger societal deprivations, repeated or enduring physical separations, and personal incapacities for synchronous interaction—for example, the seriously troubled parent's or an autistic child's.

Problems in attachment are often thought of grossly and only as nonattachments, or ruptured attachments and losses. Evidence of the extreme effects of nonattachment used to be called "marasmus," a condition in which infants physically waste away, unable to take in or hold down food, seeming to atrophy and many eventually dying. This dreadful condition occurred in large, colorless institutions with grossly inadequate numbers of caretaking staff for the large numbers of crib-confined, inadequately tended, unstimulated and essentially uncared for, apathetic babies. Some of the complexities of inadequate attachment were causatively labeled in the 1950s and 1960s "maternal deprivation." At that time it became clear again that attachments were problematic not only in their absence; they might develop damagingly as warps of varying kinds when a caretaker was present. The nature of relationships rather than merely the absence of an "attachment figure" called for inquiry, concern, and appropriate change.

A few distinctions by way of definitional clarifications should be made concerning under- and overattachments. Attachments are subjectively experienced as feelings of attraction, and, typically, of concern for the other. Attachments are objectively seen as behavior that brings people physically close to each other or otherwise into supportive communication. *Underattachment* is a condition in which interpersonal links are so weak and nonsupportive as to provide no help even in a crisis. The newcomer to a neighborhood, like the single mother, Mrs. Rodgers, in the record in the first part of this chapter, is suffering from underattachment. By contrast, *overattachment* is a condition in which relationship constraints are so binding that people become unable to develop or exercise personal competence independently without feelings of conflict or betrayal. As underattachment results in the neglect of children—or neighbors—so overattachment stunts personal development.

Overattachment tends to perpetuate itself, as in the relationships of the mothers and their schizophrenic daughters in Record Number 9, below. Overattachment resembles, but is not the same as, what occurs in a time-limited situation, under catastrophic threat, when people may pair intensively or a small group becomes exceedingly cohesive in an effort to survive. An example of the latter is a wartime bomber crew under enemy attack, when teamwork geared to the crew's survival deindividualizes persons so completely that they become one with their roles.[24] Rather, by overattachment I mean the kind of enduring relationship found in a family that psychiatrist Lyman Wynne described as "pseudomutual."[25] In such a family, expectations of a double-bind variety are overwhelming, and a child may have no escape except through an immobilizing schizophrenic break. No normal privacy, no autonomy, no separateness or secrets are possible—only entry into another world of hallucinations where network members cannot follow.

Human service workers who think of attachments as multiple linkages in social networks may address problematic conditions such as under- or overattachments through network-work. In the description of the social worker's interventions in the situation of Mrs. Rodgers (the record ending the "social networks" section earlier in this chapter), a problem in child neglect apparently related to underattachment was alleviated by referral and network linking for this single, newcomer parent. In situations of overattachment, the warping condition sometimes develops in a twosome relationship in association with a lack of satisfying and less constraining linkages elsewhere in the network. All eggs are heaped in one consequently misshapen basket. Human services which can provide mutually but not overly engaging network relationships for persons in overattached situations may help the persons release one another in the growth-stunting vice of overattachment. An illustration of such a service follows.

In this demonstration project, reported as *Maternal Dependency and Schizophrenia,* seven mothers and their seven inpatient daughters were seen over an extended period in a therapy group in a psychiatric hospital in Washington, D.C.[26] One effect of the group meetings was that the mothers developed peer relations with one another, the first attachments of this kind some of them had had in many years, if ever; some mothers engaged in social activities in the city together or visited one another. Simultaneously, and perhaps as a result (how could one know?), as the mothers became friends, they seemed able to release their schizophrenic daughters from the overattachment that probably played a part in the younger women's psychoses. (The relationships children develop with agemates, about ages eight-and-one-half to ten or eleven, similarly help the children to attenuate any overinvolvements they may have with their own parents.) New network linking may, in short, relieve the undesirable social conditions and psychological effects of either under- or overattachment.

In the following paragraphs, which end this chapter, are some of the relevant conclusions of the demonstration study of mothers and daughters in one small therapeutic group.

MOTHERS' AND SCHIZOPHRENIC DAUGHTERS' GROUP: SOME EFFECTS OF LONG-TERM THERAPY IN A PSYCHIATRIC HOSPITAL (RECORD NO. 9)

The mothers reported changes in their relationship to their daughters. All of them seemed to be less beset with the feeling that they were not doing enough for their daughters. Some—Mrs. Knowland, Mrs. Angell, and Mrs. Roper—could show some negative reactions toward daughter without as profound guilt reactions. Daughter, on the other hand, showed (most clearly in Karen Knowland) a definite tendency to let go of mother, and greater warmth toward father. She was able to defy mother pertinently and on current issues when on visits home. Mrs. Knowland reported Karen's "putting her foot down" in relation to mother's overclose supervision of all her activities.

In discussing their relationship with daughter there was still a pronounced tendency to describe it in terms of daughters' fulfillment or failure to fulfill mothers' wishes, or the daughters' affection for the mother. For example, Mrs. Link helplessly complained of her daughter's calling the telephone operator and saying, "Call the police, I'm being neglected," and of daughter's preference for father. Two mothers reported an improved relationship because daughter was "sweeter" and "more open."

Three of the mothers, Mrs. Tenant, Mrs. Roper, and Mrs. Link, had a close physical tie to the patient before the onset of the illness, fondling and cuddling the daughter, often sleeping with her. They talked to the observer, both in the interview and in postsession conversations of how much they missed this physical contact. One of them reported that when the daughter was sicker, she, the mother, could not have sex relations with her husband. These three mothers now were jealous of daughter's newly developed interest in father.

These mothers stated their increased awareness of treating their daughters like babies. Mrs. Tenant expressed her "loving Tina too much" as a sin, for which she was being punished. Mrs. Angell resolved that "instead of smoothing things over, to go about a rehashing of upsetting things with Astrid, which is necessary to let them out." Mrs. Roper stated, "Everything doesn't now revolve around Rae." Mothers reported they felt free to skip a visit to the hospital, when it was inconvenient, or they were particularly resentful.

The group seemed to have in part replaced daughter as the focus toward which mother's thoughts and feelings turned in distressing moments during the day. This occurred most often when it or the mother missed a session. Five of the mothers indicated that they got emotional support from the group. They gathered at each others' houses at intervals. Four of them held long conversations over the phone during the week, and derived comfort from this and from being able to talk in the group. This apparently relieved the husbands of some of their wives' emotional demands.

The mothers reported differences in how they felt toward each other in and outside the group situation. They would ally with or resent other group members bitterly during the session. They all reported that after the session each felt a bond of fellowship: "We would do anything for each other."[27]

The theoretical linkage between social network membership and inadequacy in primary attachments, illustrated in this group study report, has practical implications for human service programs in social network development. The professional literature in this field has expanded in recent years.[28]

Drawing upon some of these ideas, reviewed earlier in this chapter, I wonder how human service workers who had previously seen any of the mothers in this group had acted. Were they aware of the mother's overattached or symbiotic relationship with her daughter? Had the worker inquired about the mother's living-place network, such as the ones described at the beginning of this chapter in Boston's West End or among neighbors in Dagenham? A sensitive worker would have picked up on the mother's solitary life or sense of loneliness, perhaps her sadness at having no nearby friends (with her daughter in the psychiatric hospital), and then considered with the mother what she might do to relate in a satisfying way to, for example, her neighbors. The focus would be, perhaps, on the mother's low self-esteem, her feeling unworthy of peer relations, her sense of inadequate social skills, or whatever seemed to be an impediment to the formation of peer relationships. But a worker might not engage a client in this area of concern unless guided by a formulation such as the one proposed: That lacking adequate peer relations, parents may overattach to their child, thus impeding normal development. Conversely, when parents' own peer relations prove satisfying, their attachments with their own children are more likely to be mutually supportive in a balanced way, conducive to continuing personal development.

By contrast with the mother–daughter overattachment seen in the therapy record, human service workers are more often involved in problems of what on the surface seem like underattachments—for example, child neglect or a married couple's splitting. Considering only under- and overattachments, however, one may remain focused on warps or developmental malformations, and I do not want to close this chapter without balancing the pathology perspective with a preventive one.

A preventive approach would start with the recognition of family needs for social network supports with the birth of a first child. During pregnancy, medical checkups, and throughout the course of maternal and child health involvements, families' social-psychological as well as biological situations can be assessed. Are parents engaged in extranuclear family networks which provide attachments and emotional supports, exchanges of services such as infant care, guidance and referral to other needed resources, sharing of mutual concerns and a sense of belonging, some reassurance of personal worth during a major life transition, and perhaps some nurturance of the young parents themselves? Young parents often could profitably use a bit of parenting.

In these times, when childless couples' former freedoms are curtailed by a baby's birth, when women have their work lives interrupted and men feel the new economic pressures a child's birth may bring, young parents—for all their joy with a new baby—inevitably also have new strains. Young parents are likely to need what good social networks can provide, especially in groups of other new parents who are peers or equals. Relationships in such contexts may become multiplex (see this chapter's earlier section on "conceptions and misconceptions of networks"). New parents' groups may provide a base for an infant's or young child's multiple attachments, with the parent of an agemate or, in a year or two, the agemate him- or herself. The development of skills in synchronous interaction may be accelerated for the young by the presence of others with varying natural paces and rhythms of communication. Opportunities for life enrichment increase with the greater variety and choice of relationships possible in expanded networks. But the fundamental principle that the human services should address preventively is that when family life begins, supportive social networks should be available from the outset. The formation of local new parents' groups becomes a prime vehicle for such purposes, especially for parents who are not well embedded in a natural network of their own.

The human services should as normally develop such groups as they offer other kinds of prenatal and postnatal family health care. This is preventive network linking, which may for some parents require more service than merely the announcement of such a group's formation. But early efforts of this kind can have long-term payoffs in terms of human development. It is conceivable, for example, that having been engaged in a program of sharing with other parents some of the joys and pains of caring for a newborn, and maintaining some of these group relationships, a few of the mothers who appeared in the therapy group with their schizophrenic daughters, about twenty years later, might never have had to participate in such a group.

NOTES

[1] Herbert J. Gans, *The Urban Villagers: Group and Class in the Life of Italian-Americans* (New York: The Free Press, a division of Macmillan Publishing Co., Inc., 1962), pp. 74–79. Reprinted with permission.

[2] Peter Willmott, *The Evolution of a Community: A Study of Dagenham after Forty Years* (London: Routledge and Kegan Paul, 1963), pp. 60–64. Quoted with the permission of the author, Peter Willmott.

[3] J. A. Barnes, "Class and Committees in a Norwegian Island Parish," *Human Relations,* 7 (1954), p. 43.

[4] Edward J. Jay, "The Concept of 'Field' and 'Network' in Anthropological Research," *Man,* 64 (1964), pp. 137–38.

[5] Benjamin Gottlieb, "Social Networks and Social Support in the Design of Preventive Interventions," *Helping Networks and the Welfare State: A Symposium* (Toronto: Faculty of Social Work, University of Toronto, May 1980), p. 120.

[6] Roger E. Mitchell and Edison J. Trickett, "Task Force Report: Social Networks as Mediators of Social Support—An Analysis of the Effects and Determinants of Social Networks," *Community Mental Health Journal,* 16 (Spring 1980), pp. 30 and 32.

[7] Bert N. Adams, "Interaction Theory and the Social Network," *Sociometry,* 30 (1967), p. 64.

[8] Mitchell and Trickett, "Social Networks as Mediators," p. 36.

[9] Henry S. Maas, "Children's Environments and Child Welfare," *Child Welfare,* 50 (1971), 132–42; Norman A. Polansky, M. Chalmers, E. Chalmers, E. Buttenweiser, and D. P. Williams, "Isolation of the Neglectful Family," *American Journal of Orthopsychiatry,* 49 (1979), pp. 149–52.

[10] A. Gartner and F. Reissman, *Self-help in Human Services* (San Francisco: Jossey-Bass, 1977); L. H. Levy, Self-help Groups viewed by Mental Health Professionals: A Survey and Comments," *American Journal of Community Psychology,* 6 (1978), pp. 305–13; R. W. Tyler, "Self-help Groups: Thoughts on Public Policy," *Journal of Applied Behavioral Science,* 12 (1976), pp. 444–48.

[11] Henry S. Maas, "Social Work with Individuals and Families," in Walter A. Friedlander, ed., *Concepts and Methods of Social Work* (Englewood Cliffs, New Jersey: Prentice–Hall, 1976, 2nd edition), pp. 16–17.

[12] Mary D. S. Ainsworth, *Infancy in Uganda: Infant Care and the Growth of Love* (Baltimore: Johns Hopkins Press, 1967), p. 96.

[13] Ibid., p. 376. In a publication a decade later, discussing "other attachment figures," Ainsworth cautions, "A baby may both enjoy and derive security from all of his or her attachment figures, but under certain circumstances (e.g., illness, fatigue, stress), is likely to show a clear preference among them." Mary D. S. Ainsworth, "Infant-Mother Attachment," *American Psychologist,* 34 (1979) 932–37, p. 936.

[14] H. R. Schaffer and Peggy E. Emerson, "The Development of Social Attachments in Infancy," *Monograph of the Society for Research in Child Development,* 29, no. 3 (Serial no. 94) 1964, pp. 66–67. Quoted with the permission of the Society for Research in Child Development.

[15] Ibid., pp. 70–71.

[16] John Bowlby, *Attachment and Loss, Volume 1, Attachment* (New York: Basic Books, 1969), p. 309.

[17]Michael Rutter, *Maternal Deprivation Reassessed* (Middlesex, England: Penguin, 1972), p. 125.

[18] Schaffer and Emerson, "Development of Social Attachments," p. 72.

[19] T. Berry Brazelton, Barbara Koslowski, and Mary Main, "The Origins of Reciprocity: the Early Mother-infant Interaction," in Michael Lewis and Leonard A. Rosenblum, eds., *The Effect of the Infant on its Caretaker: The Origins of Behavior* (New York: Wiley, 1974), pp. 59–60. Reprinted with the permission of the publisher.

[20] Ibid., p. 59.

[21] Ibid., pp. 66–67.

[22] Ibid., p. 74.

[23] Edward Mueller and Thomas Lucas, "A Developmental Analysis of Peer Interaction Among Toddlers," in Michael Lewis and Leonard A. Rosenblum, eds., *Friendship and Peer Relations: The Origins of Behavior*, Volume 4 (New York: Wiley, 1975), p. 233.

[24] Donald W. Hastings, David G. Wright, and Bernard C. Glueck, *Psychiatric Experiences of the Eighth Air Force: First Year of Combat (July 2, 1942–July 4, 1943)* (New York: Josiah Macy, Jr. Foundation, 1944).

[25] Lyman C. Wynne and others, "Pseudo-Mutuality in the Family Relations of Schizophrenics," *Psychiatry*, 21 (1958), pp. 205–20.

[26] Joseph Abrahams and Edith Varon, *Maternal Dependency and Schizophrenia: Mothers and Daughters in a Therapeutic Group, A Group-Analytic Study* (New York: International Universities Press, 1953). Reprinted with the permission of the authors and International Universities Press.

[27] Ibid., pp. 186–88.

[28] See, for example, Alice H. Collins and Diane L. Pancoast, *Natural Helping Networks* (Washington, D.C.: National Association of Social Workers, 1976); Charles Froland and Diane L. Pancoast, eds., *Networks for Helping: Illustrations from Research and Practice* (Proceedings of the Conference on Networks) (Portland, Oregon: Portland State University, November 1 and 2, 1978); *Helping Networks and the Welfare State: A Symposium* (Toronto: Faculty of Social Work, University of Toronto, May 13–15, 1980); Morton A. Lieberman, Leonard D. Borman, and associates, *Self-help Groups for Coping with Crisis* (San Francisco: Jossey–Bass, 1979).

Chapter 4
CURIOSITY, COPING, AND RESPONSIVE ENVIRONMENTS

Introduction: Young children explore accessible arenas and learn to cope in environments they can manage.

INTRODUCTION

Young Children Explore Accessible
Arenas and Learn to Cope
in Environments They Can Manage

From a base of attachments with one or more persons, a healthy ten-month-old may crawl, and some months after a first birthday, toddle off to explore the immediate world. Long before this, during the first fifteen or so weeks of life, curiosity orients children to touch, under their own close scrutiny, their own hands and other parts of their body, and they try to grasp and examine a colorful rubber ring hanging within reach. They turn in the direction of a puppy's crying or voices from a television set. When children become ambulatory, such distant sounds attract them, and they approach close enough to reach for the puppy's wagging tail or the television's tempting display of knobs. Then, more or less quickly, one exploration—its workings temporarily discovered—is abandoned for another inquiry. Why?

Why all this activity? Why these efforts to see how things feel, move, work? Some psychologists like Jean Piaget, who is quoted later in this chapter, offer developmental explanations as to what lies behind and prompts exploratory behavior in infants and young children. Other psychologists stress characteristics of external stimuli that initiate exploration. From a purposive or teleological point of view, in which the future as well as the past is considered, it is apparent that human organisms would not be able to cope with their environments if they did not first explore them and try to understand how they can be manipulated to satisfy both need and desire. Consequently, young children whose milieus drastically cut off curiosity's pursuits may, in simple survival terms, become the least able to cope.

For this reason, the arenas that children first explore should ideally be inviting to them and yet not so overwhelming in the multiplicity or complexity of their attractions or so frightening as to deter profitable inquiry. What seems novel and appealing to an infant may, under other circumstances, seem strange, threatening, and something to be avoided. A flight of stairs, accessible to a child of about eleven months, can be a source of discovery and accomplishment as the child turns backwards on them or slides down. But if the stairs are tackled prematurely, resulting in a fall, they may temporarily become a deterrent to further adventure. When successfully managed, such an exploit breeds a feeling of competence which encourages further conquest.

Confined to a household where shouts and physical violence repeatedly assault a child, whether from a perpetually glowing television screen or from the child's cohabitants in a living place, young ones are not encouraged to go forth and discover more. Rather, they may withdraw and hide. By contrast, children's functional competence and feelings of competence develop in settings that encourage and enable them to bring about desired effects. That is why, basically, competence is not merely personal capacity. Competence is embedded in an equation or transaction of person and environment. It is equally contextual and personal. In an overwhelming world, no one is competent.

Through the development of appropriate social policies and programs, human service workers aim to increase people's abilities to control their environments. Much of this is done through providing options and access which make social contexts more readily manageable. For example, as ombudsmen or advocates, human service workers may ease access to hearings before a rent board for tenants who had not known how or felt able to report their complaints. Brought together by a school social worker, a group of physically handicapped school-aged children and young teens may, through their own collaborative efforts, bring about changes in a school which then better accommodates their special needs. Of course, much of social casework is intended to improve, through a wide variety of approaches, the capacities of clients to modify the conditions in their lives which have, in the past, defeated them.

CURIOSITY AND EXPLORABLE ARENAS

Curiosity is a fundamental orienting force in human development. It attracts the young child and other people to what seems new and unusual or incompletely understood in their daily experience. It transports them beyond the habitual and the familiar, potentially extending their understandings and sensory appreciations. It thus expands their lives and involvements, increasing their personal complexity. It augments their interest as sources of curiosity to themselves and to other people.

Curiosity leads the infant and young child into accessible arenas. It fosters the development of autonomous behavior, which is physically independent of people to whom the children are attached. Still, the sense of security in their attachment provides the base for their explorations of the unfamiliar.

Curiosity ought not be thought of as creating only activity or physical adventure in previously unknown spheres. To value curiosity is not simply to reflect the bias of Western society's commitments to action, or its growth into scientific inquiry for the purpose of controlling and exploiting the environment. Curiosity may also prompt the contemplation of a lotus blossom or quiet musing on the meanings of life. Curiosity as an English word derives indirectly from the Latin word *cura* or caring. It is the antithesis of lack of interest, boredom, and apathy. These are unpleasant—or certainly not optimal—states for homo sapiens in any culture.

Finally, by way of introduction to what I elaborate later, curiosity has its environmental requisites at both immediate and remote levels. For the young child, if curiosity is to be fully expressed, there must be accessible, explorable arenas. At a macrosocietal political level, curiosity is related to the public's freedom of inquiry and the scientist's freedom for research. The full pursuit of curiosity at any age requires no less than a free society.

From Attachment to Exploration

In a study of relationships between attachment and exploratory behavior among one-year-olds, Mary Ainsworth and Sylvia Bell make their observations in a room whose floor is "marked off into sixteen squares to facilitate recording of location and locomotion" between a heap of toys at one end and mother sitting at the other end, with a female stranger sometimes seated somewhere on an opposite wall in between.[1] The presence and behavior of the adults is varied by experimental design during eight "episodes" or sets of conditions. Placed in the middle of the triangle, at whose three angles are mother, toys, or stranger, in which direction and how far will the baby move when the mother is present? When the child is alone? When the stranger is present? Ainsworth's and Bell's conclusions regarding the fifty-six white, middle-class, family-reared, one-year-olds are:

> One of the conditions which facilitates approach and exploration of the novel is the presence, in reasonable but not necessarily close proximity, of the mother—the object of attachment. The infants of the present sample showed little alarm in the preseparation episodes of the strange situation. Their attachment behavior was not activated; they tended not to cling to the mother or even to approach her. They used her as a secure base from which to explore the strange situation. . . . The presence of the mother can tip the balance in favor of exploring the novel rather than avoiding it or withdrawing from it.
>
> Absence of the mother tends to tip the balance in the opposite direction with a substantial heightening of attachment behavior and concomitant lessening of exploration. . . . Provided that there is no threat of separation, the infant is likely to be able to use his mother as a secure base from which to explore, manifesting no alarm in even a strange situation as long as she is present. Under these circumstances the relative absence of attachment behavior—of proximity-promoting behavior—can not be considered an index of a weak attachment.
>
> Attachment behavior is heightened in situations perceived as threatening, whether it is an external danger or an actual or impending separation from the attachment object that constitutes the threat.
>
> When strongly activated, attachment behavior is incompatible with exploratory behavior. On the other hand, the state of being attached, together with the presence of the attachment object, may support and facilitate exploratory behaviors.[2]

Such conclusions reconfirm and amplify a series of previous studies. In the early 1940s, Arsenian showed that eleven-to-thirty-month-old institutionalized children's fearful behavior in a new situation, such as a strange room, could be reduced by mother's presence, indicating her "security value."[3] Harriet Rheingold's findings

> demonstrate that an unfamiliar environment had distressing and inhibiting effects upon the behavior of infants nine to ten months of age. . . . The results show, too, that the presence of a familiar social object reduces the strangeness

of a strange environment. Although it cannot be said that the environment is now familiar, it may be surmised that the strangeness is transmuted into novelty and as such supports the normal volubility and curiosity of children.[4]

Together, these and other studies support the theoretical connections between young children's attachments, a resultant sense of security, and the children's ability to cope with a new or strange situation. Attachment thus seems to provide a tap root for the healthy growth of curiosity and exploratory behavior.

Curiosity and exploratory behavior develop through infancy and early childhood in far more complicated ways than can or should, for the purposes of this book, be reviewed here. However, the early intertwining of curiosity and efforts to cope with an explored environment are of immediate interest, because a major purpose of many human service programs is the increase of people's abilities to manage their environments and their resultant feelings of competence. Drawing briefly on Jean Piaget's work, I can clarify the early curiosity–coping connection. Observing the infant behavior of his own children, Laurent and Jacqueline, Piaget remarks

> Just as, at 4 to 6 months, the child strikes, shakes, rubs, etc., the unfamiliar object which is offered to him, so also, at 8 to 10 months, he displaces it, swings it, shakes it, etc. . . . Nevertheless they [*the behaviors at the two periods*] do not seem to us to be identical because, however delicate the evaluation of such characteristics may be, their orientation is different. At the beginning of the third stage, in effect, the new object does not interest the child at all as a novelty. Its novelty only arrests his curiosity fleetingly and the object immediately serves as aliment to habitual schemata [*that is, "food" for the child's existing cognitive patterns or understandings*]. Interest is consequently not centered on the object as such but on its *utilization*.[5] (italics mine)

In short, the explorations that curiosity generates begin to be aimed not merely at making sense of but also at making *use* of objects. Prompted by the attractions of curiosity, as simultaneously the demands of attachments for staying close to familiar others diminish, young children move out into their world to see how they can make new things work as extensions of themselves in an attempt to get what they want out of their environs. Curiosity behavior has become inseparable from learning to cope, and there is obviously much new coping to learn as young children begin to explore strange situations in a world that, being almost totally unknown, invites discovery.

Young children's curiosity and attachment behavior continue to develop in interdependent ways through the third year of life. Between the ages of two and three years, children spend less time physically close to their parent or caretaker, increase and elaborate their social interaction with strange adults—as well as with agemates if opportunity allows—and extend the amount of time they spend exploring playthings and, specifically, focusing on and manipulating a single toy.[6] These findings appear in a short-term longitudinal and crosssocietal investigation of children in Stanford, California, and four Israeli kibbutzim by psychologists Eleanor Maccoby and S. Shirley Feldman. The study's experimental design was "patterned as closely as possible upon the 'strange situation' developed by Ainsworth with one-year-olds"[7] (which I reviewed earlier in this chapter), thus ensuring cumulative findings on the linkage and development of attachment and exploratory behavior.

When they begin nursery school, young children may be attracted to the new arena by their curiosity or held back by their uncertain attachments to a parent and a familiar living place. In a study that follows sixteen children, aged about three to four years, during their initial adjustment to nursery school, repeated measures indicate that the children who have a "positive" reaction to school entry give evidence of decreased or the same level of attachment and/or increased or the same level of exploration. By contrast, the children who show distress at nursery school entry increase their attachment scores and/or decrease their exploration scores.[8] The two sets of behavior counterbalance each other, one going up as the other goes down.

Some of the three-year-old California children in the previously cited Stanford–Israeli study were followed beyond the experimental situation into a nursery school. There, those children who had previously been most attached to mother and "able to accept the stranger easily" became the ones "who were most likely to interact with adults, and remain near them, in the nursery school."[9] Thus, a pattern of coping in a test situation shows continuity from the laboratory into a real life setting, linking children's antecedent, familial attachments, and their subsequent relationships with extrafamilial adults. Interaction with other children in the nursery school and manipulative play have, however, in the Stanford study, no predictable connection with the earlier observations of curiosity in the experimental setting. Nor, surprisingly, are any major differences found in the observed behavior of the California and the Israeli children, despite the differences in their socialization and geographical milieus. Are social and physical contexts irrelevant to the interdependent development of attachments and explorations by the young and other people? Is curiosity unaffected by the arenas available for its pursuit? Or are some contexts more conducive than others to exploration?

Explorable Arenas

I have been able to tease ten environmental conditions that are likely to affect children's curiosity behavior out of what is known or surmised about this aspect of children's development. The task has not been easy because there is still no systematic theory or widely used conceptual framework for understanding the psychosocial environments of children and other people. Of all the problems in research on child care, moreover, "the lack of awareness of the context of child development stands out as the most glaring," says Kenneth Keniston, and contextual studies are "notoriously difficult, time-consuming, and expensive."[10] Much of the existing contextual research focuses on the effects of depriving environments—bad institutional care, absent parents, economically disadvantaged homes, and so forth—but the policy and program implications, for what *should* optimally be done, do not always emerge clearly from analyses of what *is* being done that is bad for children. To learn that X seems to cause damage to young children is not to discover what Y's or Z's would foster their development. What follows, therefore, is grounded only in limited and often gross evidence. Hopefully in the years ahead there will be more refined answers.

Imagine, while reading what follows, a child's living place, or a group care setting, or a street scene where children are playing. A child is poised in the center of such an arena. What in that milieu arouses the child's curiosity and/or encourages explorations? By contrast, what might distress children or make them become indifferent and withdraw from an arena? To begin with, there are human or social climate conditions in any such milieu. Each is also a geographic place, occupying physical space with certain material features. In addition, any boundaried place exists in its own larger social environment or society. Immediate social climate, material conditions, and macrosocietal forces are all likely to influence children's explorations in any arena. The ten conducive conditions—all working interdependently in life spaces but separated out and treated distinctively here for descriptive and analytic purposes—may be labeled and listed, prior to the discussion of each, as follows:

SOCIAL CLIMATE	MATERIAL FEATURES	MACROSOCIETAL CONDITIONS
Openness	Complexity/multiplicity	Innovative variety: options
Concern	Spaciousness	Structural flexibility: access
Demonstration	Object responsiveness	Political freedom: controls
Personal advantage		

"Social climate" encompasses the interaction patterns and underlying values of children's caretakers, as well as the children's own response potentials in any arena, whether the caretakers are always physically present or not. The caretakers may, directly or indirectly, be more or less nonrestrictive or "open" regarding the children's behavior (openness). They may provide emotional support and attention (concern). They may themselves model curiosity arousal and exploring (demonstration) for the children's imitation or learning. The children themselves may be high or low in response potential, depending on whether they are biologically, psychologically, and/or socially disadvantaged or advantaged (personal advantage).

Physically, an arena may be a barren setting, or it may include complex, novel, and varied stimuli of a less than overwhelming nature for the children involved (complexity). Its space, often shared, may be physically confining or unlimiting (spaciousness), and what attracts children in the arena may or may not respond to their exploratory manipulations (object responsiveness).

Regarding broad social conditions, the arena's ambient society may, economically, produce only limited and standardized artifacts or innovative variety. The society may rigidly allow little mobility and access for members, or it may be characterized by structural flexibility. Finally, opportunities for public inquiry may be drastically curtailed, or a large measure of political freedom may exist. Evidence on the relationship of these conditions to the expression of children's curiosity follows.

Parents' openness, or nonrestrictiveness, their concern for their children expressed as emotional support and interest, and their demonstration, or modeling, of exploratory behavior characterize the parental behavior of the more curious first-grade boys in a study by Saxe and Stollak.[11] Mothers' support and interest are linked with children's curiosity in two other investigations, one by Collard[12] and one by Gershaw.[13] To explain the effects of sex differences on curiosity, an early 1960s study draws on research on parents' greater restrictiveness with girls, on the assumption that girls' "more highly structured environment" might limit their information-seeking or exploratory behavior.[14] In still another study, among forty pairs of preschool children and their mothers, the more curious children are oriented to exploration by mothers who respond positively to the children's curiosity, answering their questions while themselves engaged in exploring; by contrast, the more authoritarian mothers are less likely to interact with or orient their children toward exploring the novel materials.[15] Parental openness, concern, and demonstration are thus repeatedly found to be conditions conducive to children's curiosity behavior.

Moreover, obverse kinds of parenting, typified as authoritarianism, seem to reduce children's curiosity in interesting ways that invoke the dynamics of what Adorno, Sanford, Frenkel-Brunswick, and Levinson called "the authoritarian personality."[16] People who tend toward authoritarianism find ambiguous situations troublesome; they want immediate and final, if not simplistic, answers because they do not enjoy the suspense and irresolutions of an inquiry period, when they must endure uncertainties and the unknown. Thus, Endsley and colleagues find their more authoritarian mothers less likely to interact with and orient their preschool children toward the exploration of novel materials. Such mothers have, in the terms of the Berkeley (Adorno et al.) study of authoritarians, an "intolerance of ambiguity." And interestingly enough, greater "tolerance of ambiguity," as well as other positive traits, are found in the more curious fifth graders in studies by Maw.[17] Democratic orientations clearly seem to foster, and be otherwise associated with, children's and adults' arousal and pursuit of curiosity.

In group settings and classrooms, more curious children appear in "open schools," which aim "to develop critical techniques of inquiry" and in which "exploration is encouraged," rather than in "traditional schools," which stress "competence, obedience, and hard work."[18] Note that such "openness," coupled with support, is not the indifference of a laissez-faire approach; it is not at all an "anything goes" milieu, because it values, for example, children's learning "the knowledge and techniques necessary to participate in the society thoughtfully, creatively, and with intellectual curiosity."[19] In such milieus, there is also openness to adverse criticism and change which authoritarians, in settings which accommodate their preferences for stasis and certitude, will not brook. Note also that findings that link "open schools" and children's curiosity and creativity (production of novelty) do not establish that open classroom environments "cause" the children's behavior. Quite probably parents who themselves share the schools' "open" values selectively place their children in such schools. In the present context, however, this probability does not alter the proposition that an "open" social climate, whether at home and/or outside it, fosters exploratory behavior in children.

A fourth condition in a holistic view of milieus conducive to exploration is the children's having sufficient biological health and psychosocial advantage for their curiosity to be arousable. Patricia Minuchin's study of four-year-old disadvantaged children in a Head Start program reveals a low level of exploratory behavior, associated with their poor concept formation and their low expectation of coherence or support in their environment.[20] Roberta Collard finds institutionalized infants exploring less than home-reared infants, and both institutionalized and lower-class infants engaging in less social play and showing fewer schemas than more advantaged middle-class infants, although results depend less on such gross macroenvironmental conditions than on the infants' prior experience and specifically on "whether someone played with them."[21] In Marian Seligman's study of preterm and fullterm eight-month-olds, matched for conceptual age, the biologically disadvantaged infants explored *familiar* objects longer than did their fullterm peers.[22] Thus, relevant conditions of the children themselves, in the total person–environment equation, influence their exploratory behavior—and specifically relevant are any biopsychosocial conditions that inhibit the arousal of their curiosity.

How the disadvantaged limit their own explorations is vividly described by Kurt Goldstein with his organismic, or holistic, perspectives. He writes of the hospitalized brain-damaged patients with whom he worked for decades in Germany:

> They do not stroll about, for strolling about contains in it many dangers of abrupt stimulation. Thus, the patient avoids it, and may even resist going to a known goal by an unfamiliar route, even if accompanied by a friend. He tries at all costs to avoid the unknown.[23]

These intellectually impaired patients limit their environmental options to the routinely familiar and manageable. New and unexpected experience may throw them into a highly anxious and personally disorganized or "catastrophic" state. By contrast with the delight in novel and puzzling situations which engage healthier persons' attention, Goldstein's brain-damaged patients must keep their surroundings in familiar and routinized order, thus making their environments manageable, as, for example, in the following passage:

> ... the patients under my observation were supposed to look after their personal belongings. Nothing was more illuminating to me than the wardrobes and the closets of these people and the extreme care with which innumerable odds and ends, the accumulation of ten years' residence, were always arranged. Everything had its appointed place; and not only that—it had to occupy that place in a definite way. Looking more closely, one discovered a utilitarian motive behind this formal geometry—namely, that of bringing each article within the patient's reach with a minimum of effort on his part.[24]

By contrast, physical environmental conditions encouraging curiosity and exploration by less disadvantaged people include complexity and novelty of objects, spatial arrangements that allow for variety in behavior rather than sameness and routines, and differential feedback or responsiveness to one's explorations, as suggested below.

The first proposition on the three material conditions, that environmental complexity excites curiosity, is amply demonstrated in the research literature. In a study of two-, four-, and seven-year-olds exposed to polygon objects of varying degrees of complexity, the more complex the objects, the longer the older children explore them.[25] In a study of children's responses to pictures, the children visually explore all incongruous pictures longer than the banal ones, and the older children show a preference for the more incongruous pictures.[26] In still another study, one-year-olds, having access to two rooms with two toys in each, consistently choose the more novel stimulation.[27]

Space should, of course, be adequate to the exploratory activity of the children involved, and neither too confining nor overcrowded. Too cramped quarters, as any nursery school teacher knows, encourage combative behavior rather than inquiry. A living place in which the constant noise of family members, visitors, and a glowing television set obtrudes upon children's awareness allows little opportunity for the privacy which fosters elaborations of fantasy sequences.[28] In addition, in such milieus, there may be little responsive object feedback to the exploring child. In his monograph on infants' exploratory manipulation and play, Robert McCall finds the sounds which some toys make when they are manipulated, or their shape-changing plasticity when squeezed, foster more concentrated exploration, richer play, and increasingly longer sustained time spent with the toys if the feedback is appropriate to the child's level of development.[29] This important finding on object feedback, or responsiveness, as a condition fostering exploration—a physical parallel to the previously cited social condition of caretakers' concerned support and responsiveness—is reaffirmed by John Watson's work. He studied young infants, using mobiles that are responsive to the babies' head pressures on their pillows, which activate the colorful gadgets hanging over their cribs.[30] The principle is that even the very young become engaged by and extend their interest in what responds to their overtures.

Finally, children's explorable arenas are embedded in macrosocieties, some of which are economically more innovative, and/or structurally more flexible, and/or politically freer than other societies. There is limited understanding of how such gross macrosocietal forces affect small, boundaried arenas such as children's living places, group care, or school settings. Yet obviously the range of options, the variety of toys and other artifacts, and the novelty and complexity of handcrafted objects available for children's exploration and play depend on a society's inventiveness. Mass-produced sameness provides vast quantities of what must eventually become all too familiar. Such standardization affects a people's desire to create, to seek new methods, and to inquire, given the lack of models and the limitation of outlets for such innovation. Social contexts obviously influence children's areas of interests;

urban Nigerian children express more curiosity about technology and applied science than rural children who ask more questions about biological phenomena.[31] Admittedly, an economically noninnovative society may not restrict its children's interests in natural phenomena. How far children may pursue their science-based questions in any society, however, will obviously vary with the levels of technical inventiveness and knowledge in that society.

If macroproductivity affects options at the level of explorable arenas, so macrostructural flexibility influences access to options—the reachability of goals for the curious—depending on the children's group memberships. Black or Chicano children in poor families have fewer options and less privileged arenas for inquiry because of the rigidities of a society that excludes them from many opportunities which are accessible to economically more advantaged children. Even economically advantaged children whose parents are employed in routinizing, depersonalizing bureaucracies may not be rewarded by their parents for questioning and other evidences of curiosity. When people and families must maintain their status in societies in which mobility is relatively slight, children's explorations are not likely to be favorably viewed by adults. They must accept things as they are. Inquiry and quest are upsetting. Adrienne Rich remarks that many schools "reward conformity, passivity, and correct answers and penalize the troublesome question as 'trouble-making,' the lively independent active child as 'disruptive,' curiosity as misbehavior."[32]

Finally, macropolitical freedom seems essential for arenas to be fully explorable. "Modern liberal society is the parent of individuality. It could not develop in a society in which there is no freedom to explore . . ."[33] A political system that strongly curtails its citizens' freedom of inquiry quite probably also, via a chain of inhibitory communications passing ultimately through parents and teachers to young children, reduces the latters' sense of being able to reach what excited their curiosity. Observations by child development specialists, who are accustomed to young, curious, and hyperactive American children who are "into" everything, note the constrained behavior of nursery school children living outside of America's orbit—for example in China. Jerome Kagan remarks of the nursery school children he observed in China, "The children were quiet, affectively subdued, obedient, minimally restless and amazingly non-aggressive . . . Consistent restraint of excessive spontaneity was evident in the nursery environments."[34] William Kessen reports more fully as follows:

A vignette may measure our sense of contrast with children of other cultures. One of Peking's kindergartens admits the children of foreign diplomats as well as the children of Chinese officials. We watched as the teacher showed to all a fine new mechanical Ping Pong game that moved and made noises fascinating to the children. The Chinese children, most of them about four years old, gathered around the toy in a tight circle and watched the Ping Pong game, with no shoving and no reaching out. As soon as one of the non-Chinese children appeared, he lurched in a wild grab for the toy.

We talked a great deal to teachers about the control and restraint of Chinese children; we inquired about hyperactive and aggressive behavior; we tried, not very successfully, to describe some of the behavior problems of an American school. By and large, Chinese teachers did not understand what we were talking about; they testified that they had never seen a hyperactive or disruptive child—of course, some children were sometimes "naughty" but apparently not for long—and, truth to tell, neither did we among the thousands of Chinese children we saw. . . .[35]

Where formal political controls are firm, the likely message, even to the very young, is one of limited access, with no point in seeking.

In summary, for children's arenas to become optimally explorable, ten conditions have been proposed as conducive to children's inquiries. Four social climate conditions are openness, concern, demonstration of exploratory behavior, and children's biopsychosocial advantage. Three physical environmental conditions are complexity, appropriate space, and object responsiveness. Three macrosocietal conditions are economic inventiveness, structural flexibility (and nonbureaucratization), and political freedom. Most speculative and needing systematic empirical study are the last three, the macrosocietal conditions.

In the following excerpt from the book, *Why Nursery Schools?* Gwladys Mary Goldworthy, former supervisor of nursery school education for the London County Council schools, touches in her informal and discursive remarks on the previously discussed conducive social climate and material conditions that foster children's curiosity behavior.

OPENNESS, CONCERN, AND EXPLORATION IN A NURSERY SCHOOL (RECORD NO. 10)

The environment provided in a good nursery school is rich in opportunity for creative effort, while offering an endless succession of free choice. This freedom to create leads to joy and the richer the opportunities for creative expression the deeper is the joy. Where there is laughter and happiness springing from the joy of creation, there is little time for antisocial behaviour. In another chapter I have stressed the fact that the difficult child is usually a *bored* child.

An incident springs to my mind which illustrates this point extremely well, I think. A young, newly trained teacher was trying to cope with a four-year-old boy who spent his time rushing round the room worrying other children. When the opportunity arose, I asked him if it would not be more fun if he found something exciting in one of the cupboards—something which a boy of four would love to do. His quick reply was: "I can tell you, there ain't nothing in them cupboards which a boy of four would like to do." I followed this up with a joke and said: "Come on Reg. We will go together and look through those cupboards." After our combined investigation, I had to say: "You were quite right Reg. There isn't anything in these cupboards for a boy of four." He shouted at me: "I told you, didn't I?" and then rushed into the garden, where he continued to be a nuisance!

A supply of suitable equipment was soon sent to that nursery class and the young teacher was enabled to carry out the work for which she had recently been trained. Progression in types of activity which lead to a sense of achievement is essential if boredom is to be avoided. The truth of this was emphasized when I saw a small boy standing alone in a school playground watching an aeroplane flying overhead. While standing there the boy was approached by the schoolkeeper and for several minutes they were engrossed in exchanging information about the aeroplane—its name; the number of engines; the possible wing span and the skill of the pilot. At this point, an anxious teacher called out: "Please come in at once Tommy." The boy gave the schoolkeeper a look of thanks; shrugged his shoulders and said: "Ah well! I suppose I must go in now and *thread a few beads.*"[36]

In this record, emphases on opportunity and free choice reflect the need for "openness" and "options." Adult "concern" marks the supervisor's search with the child for suitable playthings. Adult "demonstration" or at least co-involvement appears in the schoolkeeper's and the child's examination together of the aeroplane. Materials which provide "a sense of achievement" are likely to show "object-responsiveness." Without such, as the record illustrates, boredom results. Exploration—and competence development—come to a standstill.

COPING, EFFECTIBLE ENVIRONMENTS, AND STRESSFUL SITUATIONS

Coping and the environments which successful coping affects have their developmental and conceptual antecedents in what has just been discussed in the previous section—curiosity, exploratory behavior, and responsive arenas. In what follows, attention is given not only to successful coping, which attains its goals in the surrounding world, but also to environments that drastically exceed in their demands and thus defeat individual and collective efforts. Such defeats or threats of defeat may become stressful situations, involving sequences of defensive behavior which in extremes, if overly prolonged, may result in participants' death.

Competence and its Contexts

Competence has at least two sets of context—those in which competence is developed and those from which competence aims to derive its rewards. Coping and competence are thus not simply personal behaviors and capacities; they are contextually embedded developments. Their residua include personal feelings of capacity to control. People are only as competent as their environments allow them to be, in all too many cases.

Children develop modes of coping to overcome problems in their environment. "Coping patterns are most easily seen when a child or an adult is confronting a new situation which cannot be handled by reflex, habitual, or other routine or automatic action,"[37] says Lois Barclay Murphy. Her illuminating booklength study of the "paths toward mastery" of thirty-two children, from about ages two-and-a-half years to five-and-a-half-years, documents the wide variability in coping strategies and styles not only of different children but also of the same children at different times. Such human variability must not be forgotten when generalizations like those that follow confine themselves to the narrow trails of averages and what is most frequent.

Coping and competence have biological beginnings. "If the embryo tiger did not develop claws, the grown tiger would not survive . . ."[38] Beyond such bodily and maturational fundamentals, competence has at least two psychosocial meanings. It refers, objectively, to the "behavior which has as its goal the attainment of an effect upon the environment that is contingent upon the organism's own action,"[39] or, one might add, action in concert with others. Subjectively, competence refers also to a self-regarding attitude, "the end result" of successful coping, "evidenced in an individual's approach to his milieu and characterized by the expectation of being an effective doer, capable of actualizing his goals and of finding gratification in his own potency."[40]

These two components of competence are what R. W. White sees as a capacity and "a sense of competence." The former he defines as "fitness or ability to carry on those transactions with the environment which result in its [an organism's] maintaining itself, growing, and flourishing," including homo sapiens' "ultimate ability to subdue and transform the environment to his own use."[41] (There are hints of rugged individualism and ecological exploitation in the implicit ideology of some of the competence literature, an issue to which I shall return in the next chapter.) The subjective sense of competence is also called by White a "feeling of efficacy."

Personality theorists concerned with the self, such as Harry Stack Sullivan, distinguish between one's self-esteem, growing out of the "reflected appraisals" of approval one gets from other persons, and "the feeling of ability or power" associated initially with such biological effectors of the environment as the infant's "mightiest tool," according to Sullivan, "the cry," the use of which enables infants to make others respond to their needs and wants.[42] In effect, a strong sense of personal competence (efficacy, ability, or adequacy) locates the power of one's successes or failures of coping within one's self. By contrast, people with low self-adequacy perceive the "locus of control" for things that happen to them or that they want done as being external to themselves, in the hands of the fates or other forces or people. Psychologist J. B. Rotter's original studies of "locus of control"—and the subsequent work of others using his concepts and measures—indicate a stability in adults in their orientations to their own efficacy or external forces.[43] Herbert Lefcourt, who did a review of most of the early relevant studies, concludes "the sense of control, the illusion that one can exercise personal choice, has a definite and positive role in sustaining life."[44] Many of the studies on internal-external control find the "externals," by contrast with "internals," more aggressive and untrusting, and with lower self-confidence. None of these studies focus on the contextual constraints and inadequate material options "externals" often suffer.

Reducing such discovered associations to enduring personality characteristics seems to give a rather ludicrous or unreal air to the studied phenomena, because people "who are restricted by external barriers and feel subjected to limited material opportunities," such as the poor and the racially discriminated against, have obviously sound empirical grounds for developing "an externally oriented outlook on life." Under such circumstances, to become in Rotter's terms "internals," feeling themselves largely responsible for their miserable circumstances, merely adds guilt to their other pains and deprivations. Their frequently, but not immutably, low sense of competence or efficacy and their typically appropriate external blaming of "the system" are facts, however, that the human services must address in programs aimed to improve such conditions.

Children's development of a sense of competence occurs, by definition, with the expectation that a large measure of the locus of control is internal. Early acceptance of oneself as responsible for one's successes but not one's failures grows into an acceptance of one's failures too, at about ages eight to nine years, when normally a sense of self-responsibility first appears and begins to stabilize.[45] Failure may, of course, be a function of overwhelming environments, or a sense of failure may be pervasive in some children, rooted in the contexts and experiences they had to endure in the course of their earlier efforts to develop coping strategies. These developmental contexts, within which competence and a sense of competence have their origins and early growth, bear some scrutiny.

The profile of explorable arenas provided in the previous section of this chapter resembles in some ways the environments that seem to foster children's coping capacities. One carefully designed nine-month-long observational study of thirty-six nine- to eighteen-month-old firstborn infants in "poor" New Haven families yields findings relevant to questions about early contexts fostering competence.[46] Note that half the children in this study were black and half were white, with equal numbers of girls and boys. The picture emerging from the monograph report is as follows:

The kind of "optimal maternal care" described shows "a highly significant linear relation with children's competence." Maternal responsiveness is especially associated with the children's overall competence, including cognitive, language, and social capacities. Such "optimal maternal care" in this study includes "expression of affection, social stimulation, contingent responsiveness, acceptance of the child's behavior, stimulation and effectiveness with materials, and appropriateness of maternal behavior for the child's age and ability." As in the profile of conducive conditions in explorable arenas, the optimal context for competence development includes ample parental concern and parental demonstration of "effectiveness with materials."[47]

As to the issue of restrictiveness, more relevant to older children than to the nine- to eighteen-month-olds in the New Haven research, a comparative study of 183 nine- to fourteen-year-old Israeli children in six different kibbutzim reveals that the children who report having more control over their environments are the children who earlier in their lives were given more freedom and responsibility for their own affairs.[48] The interplay of a greater sense of competence with children's opportunities for age- and stage-appropriate autonomy is, however, optimally accompanied by adult concern and responsiveness. In fact, a series of studies by Diana Baumrind on the development of competence in children and adolescents indicates that neither parental "permissiveness" nor its antithesis, parental "authoritarianism," provides the optimal familial milieu. Rather, what she calls "authoritative" parenting, with its clear structures for the guidance of children, emerges as the most conducive milieu for childhood competence. She summarizes her three studies of preschool children and the home observations of their families as follows:

1. Parents of the children who were the most socially responsible and independent were themselves controlling and demanding; but they were also warm, rational, and receptive to the child's communication. This unique combination of high control and positive encouragement of the child's autonomous and independent strivings was called *authoritative* parental behavior.
2. Parents of children who, relative to the others, were discontent, withdrawn, and distrustful, were themselves detached and controlling, and somewhat less warm than other parents. They were called *authoritarian* parents.
3. Parents of the least socially responsible and independent children were themselves noncontrolling, nondemanding, and relatively warm. These were called *permissive* parents.[49]

In summary, Diana Baumrind says, "Authoritative discipline tends to foster in children a particular kind of social competence which is associated with success in Western society."[50] The contexts in which such children cope successfully are likely to be schools, neighborhood settings where they interact in networks of peers and functionary adults, and their own families. The range of environmental expectations and demands in such arenas normally does not extend beyond the developing capacities of relatively healthy children. Thus, they cope well.

But what happens when there is a breakdown in the interaction between environmental demands and personal capacities—when demands greatly exceed capacities? Breakdowns occur under a wide variety of circumstances, ranging from the extremes of natural catastrophes with which no one can cope, at least initially, to losses of personal competence due, for example, to a sudden illness or, by contrast, long-term deprivations. Such situations are likely to be stressful to the persons involved because they feel they are helpless and unable to cope. Since the human services are engaged in both the avoidance or prevention of frequently occurring stressful situations and the restoration of competence after overwhelming experiences, the last part of this chapter examines the topic of coping under stress by drawing on two illustrations.

Coping with Stress

Situations become stressful when environments fail to respond to extensive or, under threat, intensive efforts, in ways that people need and expect them to respond. If the situation lasts without change and one's coping resources are thus proved ineffectual, feelings of helplessness result. Human service workers have to be aware of the dynamics of stressful situations for many reasons, but ultimately so that people can be helped, whenever possible, to regain their sense of competence.

Stressful situations are overwhelming because they involve people so totally, challenging their psychological, social, and bodily capacities and proving the ineffectualness of their other resources. A central dimension in such situations is time, making crisis centers and emergency services so crucial for the following reasons.

Stressful situations may begin suddenly or emerge gradually. They may pass quickly or endure for long periods of time. Adaptations people make to stressful situations tend to depend, in part, on the pace of onset and the duration of the situation. A temporal sequence of events and responses can be described, from the outset of earliest cues, through the first failed efforts to cope, to some resolution of the situation and partial or total recovery, or, instead, the continuance of threatening and uncoped with pressures and eventual fatigue, exhaustion, and even death. Crisis interventions provide emotional supports—since people under stress may feel abandoned—and coping assistance, thus cutting short the period of threat so that exhaustion and possible irreversible damage do not occur.

Typically, stressful situations start with ambiguous or unfamiliar cues, as in the following record of the onset of a child's illness. Norma Jean's puzzling early physical symptoms were not immediately familiar to her parents, and then, when partially recognized, were so upsetting to them that they denied or minimized them. Consequently, they put off appropriate coping action, such as calling in medical help. Cognitive distortions, misperceptions, and denial are frequent onset responses to situations that are life-threatening. Human service workers can provide early accurate information and give people the reassurance they need to take effective steps. Note, however, that clarification of the meaning of ambiguous or unfamiliar signs may require more than merely informing people of facts they do not want to recognize or accept. Norma Jean's father at first engaged in habitual modes of coping when his daughter seemed ill, and even following the doctor's upsetting diagnosis, "for two or three days after I was still, you know, feeling that, well, maybe they was wrong." Cognitive as well as emotional resources are at work here, including relevant understandings and beliefs and preparation from prior similar situations—which sometimes strengthen people's abilities to cope a second time if they emerged from the first situation relatively unscathed.

Once a threatening situation is accurately defined, people may remain unable to cope by themselves. At such times, their informal networks or formal human services must be called on, although some extremely independent people may find the need for help from others troublesome and resist its use. More typically, survival needs overcome such resistances. In fact, trying to cope under stress usually narrows people's awareness to the present and their own self-centered concerns. Nothing beyond the immediate stressfulness of the situation occupies their attention. Such behavior is, of course, highly appropriate or adaptive. When seriously ill, one must mobilize one's energies to recover one's health and capacities. In a situation in which threat is communitywide, involving all people equally, as in the flood situation described in the next chapter, an intense kind of emergency or collaborative community may arise, aimed at the group's survival, in which the narrowed here and now focus is present but, in a sense, the boundaries of the self seem to extend to include all others in the same crisis situation.

What happens when the acute phase of a stressful situation ends? Former habitual ways of doing things may no longer be possible; radical and irreversible changes may have occurred during the crisis. For example, because of her residual physical handicaps, Norma Jean's peer relations and play activities must change when she returns from the hospital. Her parents' emotional support during the transitional period were undoubtedly important in helping their ten-year-old daughter to cope with her new physical limitations and the resultant changes in her social network. Lacking such a supportive family, Norma Jean should have had access, perhaps by a referral through a hospital social worker, to human services aftercare in the community. At least her parents should have had adequately knowledgeable and emotionally responsive professional resources to draw upon for their own coping efforts.

When stressful conditions persist unabated over long periods—as in the situation in the second and final record in this chapter, "Improving Access of Low-income People"—families like the Kahns may surrender to their feelings of incompetence and hopelessness. Then, long-term programs of intervention may be necessary. To keep such families afloat, constant and very specifically targeted services may be needed, in addition to ongoing financial assistance; the focus of the school–community worker's intervention in her quoted record is an example of a kind of service which may have to be given repeatedly for such overwhelmed families. When the failed interaction between a family's limited capacities and an unresponsive environment continues over a very long period—and sometimes a lifetime—the damages to people may become irreversible. Surviving then depends on a steady and patient input from workers who are not themselves easily worn down by people who seem unable to develop abilities for adequate self-maintenance. Human services in families where there is serious child neglect ideally offer long-term work with "damaged parents" who need parenting themselves because they never had a childhood.[51] This may be Mrs. Kahn's background. One justification for long-term help for her and her family is that it will reduce the likelihood that her children will continue, into still another generation, ineffectual coping with a world that seems too much for them.

But first, I present a record of the Mason family and the father's recollections of the onset of Norma Jean's illness.[52] Note how early efforts to cope change as perceptions of the situation change, and how persistent denial may be. And in the posthospital or second part of the record, consider the importance of the mother's support for her daughter in her loss of former friends and gaining of new ones. Norma Jean's ability to cope may largely spring from her mother's softening the blows of peer rejection and providing opportunities for her to engage in new kinds of play activities with other handicapped girls as at least a transitional arrangement.

STRESS, ILLNESS, AND PHYSICAL
HANDICAP: ONSET AND SOME
CONSEQUENCES OF LOSS
OF COMPETENCE (RECORD NO. 11)

The onset of nine-year-old Norma Jean's illness is movingly described by her father, a foreman in a lumber mill, as he noticed, tried to make sense of, and was threatened by his daughter's changing behavior and apparent symptoms. Many months later, after Norma Jean had turned ten, there are observations of some of the social–psychological consequences of her residual physical handicap; these are the second part of this record, illustrative of an enduring stressful situation, involving a loss of competence—with which stress is almost always associated. Recalling the onset of Norma Jean's illness, her father said:

"Well, [Norma Jean] had a little, slight cold that week. . . . But that week, all that week, why, she went to school. We even asked her one morning, I believe, if she wanted to stay home. She said no. . . . She didn't want to lose any time, she said. She didn't seem sick. And Saturday is when we noticed that—you know, she felt worse. But of course she's—Lord, I mean—years previous she's been sicker than that and went to school. We never noticed anything, never given anything like polio a thought. And then Saturday I was working daylight shift and when I came home from work she was out in the lady's yard next door. . . . She said, 'Hi, Dad.' She acted all right to me, and I didn't even give it a thought about her being sick. Then when she come in, why she started laying around and she acted to me maybe more like she had an upset stomach than she had a cold. . . . And that night . . . I give her a dose of milk of magnesia, just a small dose. And the next morning, why her bowels hadn't moved, and I give her another small dose, and still thinking that it was more of a upset stomach than it was a cold—see, because you could have took it either way. Well, she just laid here on the sofa all day. She watched television. That day some time she started complaining about her leg feeling heavy. And she went upstairs to the bathroom two or three times, without any assistance. I didn't give it a thought, and that Saturday night [the previous evening], though, I told my wife, not giving a thought in the world that anything could happen to us, I said, 'You know, I'm always scared about polio.' I didn't give it a thought in the world she had it—I'm just thinking, you know. . . . But I didn't think it'd happen to us. And so she laid around all Sunday, and we put a pad on her leg, and I rubbed her leg some. . . . Couple of times I started to rub it, you know, and she told me to stop. And she went to bed, I guess about 9:30 or 10 o'clock, something like that. . . . She ate a good supper and, well, you know, we figured she was eating and all, she was just feeling punk. . . . I told my wife that night, I said, 'Well, if she don't feel too good in the morning, call Dr. S.' So the next morning she seemed to have a temperature. . . . A little later on her temperature dropped and my wife told her that if her temperature come back again she was going to call Dr. S. And it come back. She called Dr. S. and I don't—I just forget what the temperature was. It was a little high—wasn't even too high, I mean, but it was a little along. And Dr. S. come. She [Norma Jean] didn't want him to come, you know. Now that's one reason my wife was holding off, because she was afraid he was going to give her a needle, see! And my wife was just trying to please her. . . . So after she saw that the temperature did come back . . . she got a little more worried, and then she called Dr. S. and he come, I guess around 2:00 to 3:00, somewhere in around there. I was working. My wife tells me that he closed the bedroom door and come down and started calling right away trying to get an ambulance. He said he—it looked like polio to him. He was going to send her to Eastern Hospital [the receiving center for all polio cases in the area] for sure. Then he called me, and I come home and I rushed her right up to Eastern. . . . Dr. S. called some doctor up there . . . and we took her in the little waiting room there—examination room, I guess you'd call it. This doctor came down in about ten to fifteen minutes. . . . He examined her all over, testing the reflexes and the muscles, you know. So then they put her on a stretcher and took her to the children's ward. And then Dr. R. come in. We was in a waiting room there. He come in and he told us that she definitely had polio. And I was so in doubt, you know. . . . I said, 'Well, ain't you going to take a spinal test? How do you know she's got it?' He said, 'Well, all the symptoms are there.' He said, 'We're so sure she's got it that we're not going to put her through that misery.' So then they told us how often we could see her and all, and how long she'd have to stay there [before being transferred to a convalescent hospital]. We went in to see her, and that was it. And I—for two or three days after I was still, you know, feeling that, well, maybe they was wrong. But they wasn't."[53]

Of the several neighborhood friends with whom Norma Jean played before her illness, Sally and Eleanor were by far the closest. All during the time Norma Jean was in the hospital, these two were extremely attentive and solicitous, writing her frequently, sending gifts, and inquiring almost daily of Mrs. Mason how Norma Jean was progressing. On the weekend visits home that Norma Jean made prior to her discharge, Sally and Eleanor spent almost all their free time with her and often accompanied her back to the hospital in the Mason family car.

Less than two months after her discharge, changes were already evident in Norma Jean's relationship with these and other neighborhood children. According to Mrs. Mason, Eleanor had more or less completely "drifted away," while Sally came to play with Norma Jean much less frequently than she had previously. This hurt Norma Jean, and she would often ask Mrs. Mason why Sally did not visit when she expected her to. Wishing to protect Norma Jean's feelings, Mrs. Mason would tell her, "Well, maybe her mother has something for her to do. She has a small brother and she might have to mind him. Why don't you call her up to see if she can come over?" When Norma Jean would call, as often as not Sally would have some excuse for not being able to come—homework, an errand to run for her mother, babysitting with her little brother. Sally never reciprocated by calling Norma Jean and inviting her to her house. At about this time, Norma Jean began to play dodgeball in front of the Mason home with several of the younger children in the neighborhood, who were apparently flattered by the unaccustomed attentions of an older child.

In the months that followed, Norma Jean saw less and less of Sally and instead became very friendly with a somewhat older (12 years) neighborhood girl named Gloria. Norma Jean had known Gloria before her illness but she, Eleanor, and Sally did not especially like Gloria and frequently excluded her from their favorite activities. Now Norma Jean and Gloria were fast friends, Gloria accompanying her almost everywhere, helping her with her wheelchair, and doing whatever she could to make things easier for Norma Jean. As Mrs. Mason described the relationship, "She's like a mother to Norma Jean." According to Mrs. Mason, Norma Jean knew this and took advantage of it by having Gloria do many things for her that she could easily do for herself.

The close friendship between the two girls lasted through the summer, but with the arrival of fall Gloria's visits became much less frequent. Mrs. Mason attributed this to Gloria's growing interest in boys and her corresponding loss of interest in female companionship. On occasion Gloria still would swoop down on Norma Jean, suddenly and unannounced, and try to inject their relationship with some of its former enthusiasm. After several such attempts Gloria ceased trying to make amends and thereafter the two girls saw each other only rarely.

Throughout this period, however, Norma Jean slowly—and, at first, very cautiously—began making friends at the school for handicapped children she attended. During her first semester there she joined the glee club and began having regular twice-a-week phone chats with one of her classmates. For some time, though, neither visited the other's house. In the fall of that year Norma Jean began inviting this girl and several others from her class to her home for weekend parties, garden picnics, and record-listening sessions.

The last time the family was seen, some sixteen months after Norma Jean's discharge, a somewhat mixed pattern obtained with respect to her friendship pattern. During the school week she still on occasion played dodgeball or some other game with several of the neighborhood children, but in a much more casual and disinterested way than before. Her important recreations were more and more reserved for weekends, when she would gather with her girl friends from the school for handicapped children. Moreover, her two friendship circles remained strictly segregated; apart from herself, no child who belonged to one also belonged to the other. This did not mean, however, that Norma Jean had lost interest in her neighborhood friends. Increasingly, though, when she made overtures in their direction, she discovered that they were going off on activities in which she could not participate. As Mrs. Mason reported, "She still sees the girls going off, or she'll call them up and ask if they're going to the show today, or what are they going to do, and they'll say, 'Well, we're going ice skating.' Well, I imagine she's bound to feel hurt inside in some way."[54]

Although preventive medicine has removed poliomyelitis from the list of scourges that afflict children and their elders, other illnesses still attack and reduce the competence of people like Norma Jean. These days, however, handicapped children are likely to attend schools with other children who lack handicaps. Normalization programs bring together people of diverse capacities; the nonhandicapped learn from handicapped peers, and potentially everyone gains in situations where help can be given informally as well as received. Normalization arrangements at school increase within manageable limits the situations with which everyone should learn to cope. Both the handicapped and the unhandicapped increase their competence and decrease the likelihood of finding interaction stressful when otherwise strange or unfamiliar encounters become daily experience.

Workers in the human services help to build competence by making environments manageable and/or by counseling people in ways that increase their sense of mastery. Psychiatrist Jerome D. Frank sees demoralization as the central psychological problem besetting most patients and strengthening their coping abilities as the major therapeutic goal.

> . . . all schools of psychotherapy share certain features that combat a state of mind of almost all of their patients regardless of their specific symptoms. This state may be termed demoralization, which manifests itself directly by such common symptoms as anxiety and depression and interacts with symptoms that have other causes . . . . symptoms wax and wane with the severity of demoralization, and by crippling the patients' coping abilities predispose to demoralizing failure experiences. All schools of psychotherapy combat demoralization through a confiding, emotionally-charged relationship with a trusted help-giver. . . . all have the same morale-raising functions. These include strengthening the therapeutic relationship, inspiring the patients' hopes for relief, and increasing the sense of mastery.[55]

The demoralization, crippled coping abilities, and failure experiences just described characterize the Kahn family and especially the single mother in the record which follows. These are typical characteristics of people living under prolonged stressful conditions. In the record, the helper is not a psychotherapist but an advocate who makes material resources accessible. Is the effect of this approach also morale-raising? Does it increase clients' sense of mastery? The record is from a double-barreled human service program of the 1960s when the "War on Poverty" was being fought.[56]

IMPROVING ACCESS
OF LOW-INCOME PEOPLE:
A WELFARE RECIPIENT
BECOMES A SCHOOL-COMMUNITY
WORKER AND HELPS "A FAMILY
REACHED IN TIME OF NEEDS"
(RECORD NO. 12)

The "double-barreled" aspect of this program is that both the helpers and the people they help are or have been income assistance clients. The introduction to the report states:

. . . a group of low-income persons, recruited and trained by the Richmond Community Development Demonstration Project, began their salaried, experimental assignments as School Community Workers with the Richmond Unified School District. These assignments grew out of the School District's continuing search for ways to improve its services, and the Project's interest in demonstrating that the employment of persons drawn from the low-income community was a long overlooked, but potent, means to produce the desired, but elusive, service improvements. . . .

Of the five black school-community workers in the first phase of the project, two give the following information about themselves. One woman is aged thirty-three, mother of six children, and a welfare recipient most of her married life. Having had to leave high school in her senior year, she has worked as café waitress, car wash helper, domestic worker, baby sitter, supervisor of nurses' aides on the midnight shift of a convalescent hospital, and as volunteer in a cooperative nursery school and den mother for both cub and boy scouts. Regarding the future, she says, "I would like to be a professional social worker, since our society only recognizes professionals as helpers in the social work field. I would like to devote my time to serving poor people like myself and not forget from whence I came." One of the men, aged thirty-two and father of five children, completed grade ten while in the Air Force where, at age nineteen, he married. His prior jobs include construction work as cement finisher, pipe layer, jack hammer man, and dynamite man as well as odd jobs in a car lot and as recreational worker with teenage boys in a neighborhood center. He says, "My future plans are to be in a position to help myself and others. I think this would entail having the unlimited power and knowledge to be most helpful to myself, my family and the community."

What follows is a case record by one of the five workers—a record called "A Family Reached in Time of Needs."

This case was referred to me August of 1966, Saul Kahn. Several things were wrong at this time, including too many absent days during the school year. So then I made a home visit to the Kahn family. I talked to Mrs. Kahn about the days of absence that Saul had. What would this year be like? She told me that she hoped that he would not have as many absent days as he had and we talked and we brushed around the bush. So then she told me that there were reasons for some of the days and there were no reasons for other days. For example, she gave me this reason, some days he was sick, some days he was not. I asked her did she do anything about those days he wasn't sick. She said no, it was not too much she could do. Being his mother I thought there was something maybe she could do. But she said that there wasn't anything. So then I chewed the fat. I came on back and told her, well, the reason I really made this home visit today is that I wanted them to know that I was the new School Community Worker. And that I was at Holmes this year and that I would like for them to feel free to call me on anything that they feel that I could be of some kind of help to them. Then I left and I went back to the office and I sat down and began to look over Saul's records.

Saul had taken some type of test by some professional. The test showed that Saul was slightly retarded and slow learning and had a very low achievement. Then I began to think about that. I went out the next day, August of 1966, what day I just don't remember. But I talked with Saul about this. Saul I said how's things going today? He said, "great." So I began to talk to his mother about him. Has she had any problems out of Saul. She said no, he is the only one that she had that has never been in trouble.

Then Saul sat down and listened to me very nicely. Then I began to ask him did he understand me. Saul then began to quote some of the things that I had said. He said yes I heard you. Then he sat there with very normal manners, I began to wonder. I said to myself Saul's not retarded. Because if he can sit here and listen and quote some of the things that I say then I think that it is only because of his surroundings that he is not proficient. I began to look at his home, it was not adequate for any child to be in. House was not clean, no decent place to sit, no place for him to even eat or lay, no bed, no dinette set. So he could not help but feel highly emotionally and disturbed. When he goes out he has no clothes on to look sufficient. He always thinks someone is going to kid him. So he feels very emotionally when someone says something.

So then I went back to the office and I sat down to decide what I could do in this case. They have not asked for any help, but what can I do. I concentrated on the Kahn family all that afternoon. The next day I made another visit, I went by and talked to Mrs. Kahn. She told me that she had been in the hospital and that she had been sick. So I looked around at the furniture which was in poor condition. So Mrs. Kahn began to explain to me the condition of the house and why it looked like it did. She said that the kids tore up the stuff, that it had worn out and all that didn't wear out they tore up. So I asked her what can I do to help you in some way or try to get some type of furniture or something. Well she told me that there wasn't too much she thought I could do about it at the time. She said that she had called the social worker and talked to her about it, and the social worker told her that they didn't have enough funds to buy furniture for anybody. That a dinette set and a bed wasn't really a necessity. A bed was something you must have but they didn't have the money to allow.

I told Mrs. Kahn to give me the social worker's number and name. She gave it to me, and I did not tell her anything about what I was going to do. I just told her that I would like to have it. I said that I might call her up and she said that it would not do any good. She replied these words to me that the social worker said, "They could not give her any money for furniture." I said that was okay I would like to talk to her anyway. I left and went back to the office.

That same evening I got on the phone and called the social worker. I made contact with her and she asked me, "Who are you?" I said the school community worker at Holmes School and I was calling her concerning the Kahn family. She was not cooperative. Then she began to ask me about Saul. I told her that Saul needed clothes and that I didn't think that he would be able to enter school without clothes. She told me that there was not anything she could do about it. I mentioned to her that the furniture in their home was not adequate for a family. I talked to her about the bed and also the dinette set. She told me that she thought that the only thing that they would allow would be $30 for a bedroom suite if they needed it. She was a new social worker and she had never made a visit to the Kahn family home. I told her to go out there and look and see; those people need help, they need something to eat on and sleep on and she began to set a date.

She went out there the next day. She looked and then contacted me and told me that I was right that something had to be done. So we began to try to work together on some of these things such as furniture and clothes. She explained what had to be done to get these things. After she checked into it she told me that her supervisor will not okay any money for clothes or furniture. I began to tell her if there is a need for a bed then you can get that okayed. She tells me no she doesn't think so. She asked me to give her 3 or 4 days, which I did. She looked into it and she called me up and tells me that they only allow $30 for a bed and $30 for a dinette set. She said that I would have to get an estimate on what this cost and I got an estimate at two or three used furniture stores. They were for $119, $108 and $64. Then she tells me that is too much money at every place. I asked her, what can you buy with $60 that is adequate? She said nothing. She said that she checked the records and found out that Mrs. Kahn had received money for furniture before and it had been possessed. We cannot do anymore. I told her that something else can be done. She told me that she would see what she could do and she would call me back.

I waited on her for two weeks; she did not call. The third week I called her and she wasn't in. I took one day and went down and talked to her supervisor. I knew of the supervisor from the time I worked for the Welfare Department. She told me that she would see what she could do, she would okay it. She would have to get it approved from Martinez (the central office of the County Welfare Dept.). I asked her who do you see in Martinez. She told me and I took off and went to Martinez. I talked to the supervisor who was over the head supervisor in Richmond. She said that when the request came in she would okay it and she did. She okayed the request for the furniture and not that for the clothes. We did get that one thing solved, the furniture.

I began to wonder how I could help her get some clothes. I needed help from one of the school community workers working in another school. I talked to Helen Simms, Newel School Community Worker. She asked me what is your trouble. I told her that I needed clothes for a family, and I wanted to know where I could get some. She said that there is a Welfare Room only at Newel and it only gives clothes to Welfare recipients. I began to look into that. I found out that I needed a letter from the Principal of Holmes School where I work. I told the Principal what the necessary things that had to be done for me to get clothes for this family. The guidance supervisor wrote a letter for me. So that this was done.

Then I made another visit to the family after I had done all of this. With contacting these different agencies and getting supporting help from the Welfare Department, Probation Department and the School Community Worker, we solved this one thing. Some of the things we solved were:

1. Furniture for the house; dinette set and bedroom set
2. Clothes for Saul and Alice and Daniel and David; three are in school.

Mrs. Kahn and also the children are very happy and pleased. This case will remain open. But right at the time it has been closed. These are some of the things that have been accomplished by the School Community Worker.

Is this a record of familial incompetence or of bureaucratic nonresponsiveness? Or both? When Mrs. Kahn says of Saul's school absences, "it was not too much she could do" but the School Community Worker "thought there was something maybe she could do," one sees a difference between a woman who probably feels helpless, if not overwhelmed and demoralized, and another woman who feels a sense of power and competence. Evidence of the latter is clear in the way the School Community Worker goes about getting from the welfare department what she feels the Kahn family rightfully should have. The bureaucratic environment is responsive, apparently, only to the determined and strong thrusts of a woman who knows her way—as a former welfare recipient, perhaps—through its hierarchical structures.

This kind of advocacy on behalf of the poor and disabled is a human service some professional workers in bygone days might have questioned. They would have argued that the family's own incompetence is only reaffirmed by their seeing someone else able to do for them what they have in the past failed to do for themselves. But perhaps the Kahn family, and specifically Saul, become better able to cope after such an experience is modeled for them. And is Saul more likely to attend school with adequate clothing, and is he more likely to do school work and feel better about himself in a home that is decently furnished? The evidence in this chapter on the covariance of supportive environments, feelings of competence, actual coping, and even curiosity behavior would lead to an affirmative reply.

Finally, to contrast this chapter's two records on coping under stress, note that they call for quite different modes of intervention. The first difference is in the temporal nature of the two stressful situations. The onset of Norma Jean's illness is sudden, making of the situation a crisis, with residua or convalescence and aftercare life style changes to be worked on. By comparison, Mrs. Kahn's reference to her hospitalization and illness suggests that difficulties besetting this family began gradually and have been of long duration. Secondly, the families' emotional and coping resources in the two situations differ markedly. In the rather sparse one-parent Kahn family record, there is no evidence of sharing or group support among the four children and their mother or of the latter's providing the kind of emotional sustenance and sympathetic understanding the Masons give their daughter, Norma Jean. Mrs. Kahn just does not have the energy or, as an apparently socially isolated single parent, the social network supports to be able to cope. The long-term stress seems to have worn her down to a point of helplessness and surrender. Under such circumstances, the ombudsman-like efforts of the School Community Worker, acting on the family's behalf, seem essential if the Kahn family's home environment is to be bettered at all. But beyond such a one-time windfall, the Kahns probably need ongoing support and neighborly concern for many years if they are to keep their heads above water. Coping often requires such cooperative activities when environmental odds are too much for individual personal capacities. The following chapter, on reciprocity and caring communities, moves us from competence for purely personal gain to its collaborative uses and advantages.

NOTES

[1] Mary D. S. Ainsworth and Sylvia M. Bell, "Attachment, Exploration, and Separation: Illustrated by the Behavior of One-Year-Olds in a Strange Situation," *Child Development,* 41 (1970), p. 53. Quoted with the permission of the Society for Research in Child Development.

[2] Ibid., pp. 60–61 and 64.

[3] J. M. Arsenian, "Young Children in an Insecure Situation," *Journal of Abnormal and Social Psychology,* 38 (1943), 225–49.

[4] Harriet L. Rheingold, "The Effect of a Strange Environment on the Behavior of Infants," in B. M. Foss, ed., *Determinants of Infant Behavior, IV* (London: Methuen, 1969), pp. 165–66.

[5] Jean Piaget, *The Origins of Intelligence in Children* (New York: Norton, 1963), p. 258.

[6] Eleanor E. Maccoby and S. Shirley Feldman, "Mother-Attachment and Stranger-Reactions in the Third Year of Life," *Monograph of the Society for Research in Child Development,* 37 no. 1 (Serial no. 146) 1972, pp. 58–59.

[7] Ibid., p. 1.

[8] Kato Van Leewen and June Tuma, "Attachment and Exploration: a Systematic Approach to the study of Separation-adaptation Phenomena in Response to Nursery School Entry," *Journal of the American Academy of Child Psychiatry,* 11 (1972) 314–40. See also Leah Matas, Richard A. Arend, and L. Alan Sroufe, "Continuity of Adaptation in the Second Year: The Relationship between Quality of Attachment and Later Competence," *Child Development,* 49 (1978), 547–56.

[9] Maccoby and Feldman, "Mother-Attachment," p. 53.

[10] Kenneth Keniston, "Foreword," in Alison Clarke-Stewart, *Child Care in the Family: A Review of Research and Some Propositions for Policy* (New York: Academic Press, 1977), pp. ix–x.

[11] Robert M. Saxe and Gary F. Stollak, "Curiosity and the Parent–Child Relationship," *Child Development,* 42 (1971), 373–84.

[12] Roberta R. Collard, "Exploratory and Play Behaviors of Infants Reared in an Institution and in Lower- and Middle-class Homes," *Child Development,* 42 (1971), 1003–15.

[13] N. Jane Gershaw and J. Conrad Schwarz, "The Effects of a Familiar Toy and Mother's Presence on Exploratory and Attachment Behaviors in Young Children," *Child Development,* 42 (1971) 1662–66.

[14] Charles D. Smock and Bess Gene Holt, "Children's Reactions to Novelty: An Experimental Study of 'Curiosity Motivation'," *Child Development,* 33 (1962), 631–42.

[15] Richard C. Endsley, M. Ann Hutcherson, Anita P. Garner, and Michael J. Martin, "Interrelationships among Selected Maternal Behavior, Authoritarianism, and Preschool Children's Verbal and Nonverbal Curiosity," *Child Development,* 50 (1979), 331-39.

[16] Theodor W. Adorno, Else Frenkel–Brunswik, Daniel J. Levinson, and R. Nevitt Sanford, *The Authoritarian Personality* (New York: Harper, 1950). See also Else Frenkel-Brunswik, "A Study of Prejudice in Children," *Human Relations,* 1 (1948) 295–306, and "Intolerance of Ambiguity as an Emotional and Perceptual Variable," *Journal of Personality,* 18 (1949), 108–43.

[17] Wallace H. Maw and Ethel W. Maw, "Social Adjustment and Curiosity of Fifth-Grade Children," *Journal of Psychology,* 90 (1975), 137–45.

[18] Craig T. Ramey and Vera Piper, "Creativity in Open and Traditional Classrooms," *Child Development,* 45 (1974) 557–60, p. 558.

[19] Ibid., p. 558.

[20]Patricia Minuchin, "Correlates of Curiosity and Exploratory Behavior in Preschool Disadvantaged Children," *Child Development,* 42 (1971), 939–50.

[21]Collard, "Exploratory and Play Behaviors."

[22]Marian Seligman, "Early Development of Preterm and Full-Term Infants: Exploratory Behavior in Eight-month-olds," *Child Development,* 47 (1976), 606–12.

[23]Kurt Goldstein, *Human Nature in the Light of Psychopathology* (Cambridge: Harvard University Press, 1940, reprinted by Schocken Books, New York, 1963), p. 100.

[24]Ibid., pp. 101–2.

[25]Harvey N. Switzky, H. Carl Haywood, and Robert Isett, "Exploration, Curiosity, and Play in Young Children: Effects of Complexity," *Developmental Psychology,* 10 (1974), 321–29. The dimensions of object-complexity are themselves many and complex. See, for example, the use of incongruous and unexpected phenomena in a study by a pioneer student of curiosity, Daniel E. Berlyne, "Conflict and Information-Theory Variables as Determinants of Human Perceptual Curiosity," in Harry Fowler, *Curiosity and Exploratory Behavior* (New York: Macmillan, 1965). See also, Daniel E. Berlyne, "The Influence of Albedo and Complexity of Stimuli on Visual Fixation in the Human Infant," in David Lester, ed., *Explorations in Exploration: Stimulation Seeking* (New York: Van Nostrand Reinhold, 1969) and J. C. Nunnally, "Explorations of Exploration" in H. I. Day, ed., *Advances in Intrinsic Motivation and Aesthetics* (New York: Plenum Press, 1981).

[26]Terry T. Faw and Joseph A. Wingard, "Relation between Conceptual Development and Visual Exploration of Incongruity," *Developmental Psychology,* 13 (1977), 137–42.

[27]Hildy Ross, Harriet L. Rheingold, and Carol O. Eckerman, "Approach and Exploration of a Novel Alternative by 12-month-old Infants," *Journal of Experimental Child Psychology,* 13 (1977), 85–93.

[28]*Perspectives on Human Deprivation: Biological, Psychological, and Sociological* (Washington, D.C.: Public Health Service, National Institutes of Health, 1968), pp. 10–11.

[29]Robert B. McCall, "Exploratory Manipulation and Play in the Human Infant," *Monograph of the Society for Research in Child Development,* 39, no. 2 (Serial no. 155), 1974.

[30]John S. Watson and Craig T. Ramey, "Reactions to Response-Contingent Stimulation in Early Infancy," Paper read, in part, at the 1969 meeting of the Society for Research in Child Development, Santa Monica, California, and, in part, at the Institute of Human Development's Fortieth Anniversary Symposium, University of California, Berkeley, April, 1969; and John S. Watson "Cognitive–Perceptual Development in Infancy: Setting for the Seventies," Paper presented at the Merrill-Palmer Conference on Research and Teaching of Infant Development, Detroit, Michigan, February, 1970.

[31]Ebele Josephine Nwokolo Madnewesi, "Children's Interests and Concerns: A Study of Anambra (Nigeria) Elementary School Pupils," Ph.D. dissertation, Michigan State University, 1978.

[32]Adrienne Rich, *On Lies, Secrets, and Silence: Selected Prose 1966-1978* (New York: Norton, 1979), p. 63.

[33]Edward A. Shils, "Social Inquiry and the Autonomy of the Individual," in Daniel Lerner, ed., *The Human Meaning of the Social Sciences* (New York: Meridian Books, 1959), p. 120.

[34]Jerome Kagan, "The Nursery Age Infant in China," *Newsletter,* Society for Research in Child Development (Fall 1974), p. 6.

[35]William A. Kessen, "Children," *Items,* 33, no. 2 (June, 1979), p. 34.

[36]G. M. Goldsworthy, *Why Nursery Schools?* (Gerards Cross, Buckinghamshire: Colin Smythe, 1971), pp. 50–51. Reprinted with permission.

[37]Lois Barclay Murphy and collaborators, *The Widening World of Childhood: Paths toward Mastery* (New York: Basic Books, 1962), p. 8.

[38]Url Lanham, *Origins of Modern Biology* (New York: Columbia University Press, 1968), p. 11.

[39]Wanda C. Bronson, "The Growth of Competence: Issues of Conceptualization and Measurement," in H. R. Schaffer, ed., *The Origins of Human Social Relations* (London: Academic Press, 1971), p. 270.

[40] Ibid.

[41] Robert W. White, "Competence and the Psychosexual Stages of Development," in Marshall R. Jones, ed., *Nebraska Symposium on Motivation 1960,* vol. 8 in series in *Current Theory and Research in Motivation* (Lincoln: University of Nebraska Press, 1960), p. 100.

[42] Harry Stack Sullivan, *Conceptions of Modern Psychiatry* (New York: Norton, 1953).

[43] J. B. Rotter, "Generalized Expectancies for Internal versus External Control of Reinforcement," *Psychological Monographs,* 80, Whole no. 609, 1966.

[44] Herbert M. Lefcourt, "The Function of the Illusions of Control and Freedom," *American Psychologist,* 28 (1973), 417–25.

[45] Virginia C. Crandall, Walter Katkovsky, and Vaughan J. Crandall, "Children's Belief in their Own Control of Reinforcements in Intellectual-academic Achievement Situations," *Child Development,* 36 (1965), 91–109.

[46] K. Allison Clarke-Stewart, "Interactions between Mothers and their Young Children: Characteristics and Consequences," *Monographs of the Society for Research in Child Development,* 38, nos. 6–7 Serial no. 153, 1973.

[47] Ibid.

[48] A. Nadler and others, "Giving in the Kibbutz: Prosocial Behavior of City and Kibbutz Children as Affected by Social Responsibility and Social Pressure," *Journal of Cross-Cultural Psychology,* 10 (1979), 57–72.

[49] Diana Baumrind, "Parental Disciplinary Patterns and Social Competence in Children," *Youth and Society,* 9 (1978) 239–76, pp. 244–45. See also Diana Baumrind, "Authoritarian versus Authoritative Parental Control," *Adolescence,* 3 (1968) 255–72; "Current Patterns of Parental Authority," *Developmental Psychology Monograph* 4, 1, Part 2 (1971), 1–103.

[50] Ibid.

[51] Norman A. Polansky and others, *Damaged Parents: An Anatomy of Child Neglect* (Chicago: University of Chicago Press, 1981).

[52] Fred Davis, *Passage through Crisis: Polio Victims and their Families.* (Indianapolis, Bobbs-Merrill, 1963). Reprinted with the permission of the author and Bobbs-Merrill Co., Inc.

[53] Ibid., pp. 15–17.

[54] Ibid., pp. 146–147.

[55] Jerome D. Frank, "Mental Health in a Fragmented Society: The Shattered Crystal Ball," *American Journal of Orthopsychiatry,* 49 (1979) 397–408, p. 403.

[56] Richmond Community Development Demonstration Project, *New Careerist Casebook Number One: School Community Workers* (Walnut Creek, California: Contra Costa Council of Community Services, 1967), pp. 7, 9, 13, and 37–41.

Chapter 5
RECIPROCITY
AND CARING
COMMUNITIES

INTRODUCTION

School-aged Children and Young Teens Learn to Share in Caring Communities

In the playground at the nursery school, a child falls off a tricycle and cries loudly, more with outrage at what the vehicle has done to her than with physical pain. Two children playing in the sandbox look up, then continue their digging. Another child climbs down from the top of the jungle gym and runs over to the fallen tricyclist, strokes her head, and stooping down, looks her full in the face with concern and pats away a tear from her cheek. What in this situation evokes a sympathetic response from one child but not from others?

In a third-grade classroom, a red-haired girl leans over slowly and looks at the test paper her neighbor is writing. Her neighbor slides the paper closer to the redhead so she can read it more easily. The teacher sees this interchange, comes down the aisle, takes both test papers away, and says in a soft, controlled voice, "See me after class." The two girls look at each other wide-eyed, and first one, then the other, shrugs her shoulders with a so-that's-how-it-goes air of resignation. Why does one child share her answers, accepting the cost to herself when caught, while another might shield her paper from the eyes of a classmate? Does the latter believe that tests are intended to be primarily competitive, rather than to promote learning, and that each child should try independently to do better than her neighbor? Or, more simply, is the risk of being caught and punished by teacher unpleasant and to be avoided? Or is "cheating" morally wrong and not to be engaged in? Why the differences among children's beliefs and behavior in such situations?

The tenants in a large housing project are starting a mimeographed newspaper for all residents. Happening to drop into the organization meeting, two fourteen-year-olds say they would like to write a teens column for the paper. Three other young teens appear in the recreation room, and one says he would like to cover sports news at the community center. The two others volunteer to do some of the stencil typing and distribution of the first issue. One of the adult tenants expresses reservations about "kids" participation—"You can't count on them." The housing project recreation worker proposes that the teenagers be given a chance, and if they fail, they can be replaced. He reminds the people in the recreation room how helpful some of the teens were at the last election, distributing leaflets encouraging tenants to get out and vote, and baby-sitting for parents while they went to the polls. "In just a few years they'll be voting too." The woman who is the editor says, "Glad to have you with us. Plenty of work for all."

The development of caring, sharing, and other kinds of prosocial behavior reaches a turning and stabilizing point in the lives of young children at about age eight and a half. It continues to be apparent in some cultural contexts but gives way to competitiveness in others. This chapter elaborates on these developments and on the cultures within which generosity and reciprocity flourish. Particular attention is given to caring communities and some of the conditions under which community caring arises.

RECIPROCITY'S DEVELOPMENT
AND CULTURAL CONTEXTS

In the last chapter, I focused on competence as people's ability to affect their environment. "By dint of *personal* effort" or with "a capacity for *self*-direction" is sometimes tacked onto the idea of competence, thus individualizing it as though the doer were always a lone actor. In effect, the successful exercise of competence often occurs with societal tools or supports or within a group, team, or community, without which individual attempts to cope would often fail.

The individualistic idea of "competence" thus becomes entangled with its etymological cousin, "competition," both from the same Latin origin, but only Western society values join them conceptually. In this chapter, I move from competence, as contextually based personal capacity, to collaboration—the opposite of competition—as a social matrix for the use of competence. Much of the research on the development of children's collaboration and other prosocial behavior is focused on the developmental increase of their cooperation with agemates. For example, James Bryan's review of research on the growth of prosocial tendencies in childhood is called "Children's Cooperation and Helping Behaviors."[1]

Secondly, in Chapter Three, on attachments, I discuss the idea of "synchrony," or the pacing of social interaction to accommodate the rhythms of one or more other persons with whom one is trying to communicate. In Chapter Three, synchrony in early infant-mother interaction is alluded to as the beginning of "reciprocity." This chapter carries the story of reciprocity a few stages further. But first, what is meant by reciprocity?

Unfortunately, it has a few different but related meanings. Reciprocity differs when seen from the vantage points of a psychologist and of a sociologist. The sociologist observes from a base in society and is primarily concerned about what happens to human dyads and larger collectives. The sociologist stresses the equal and mutual obligations to one another of any twosome involved in "a mutually gratifying pattern of exchanging goods and services."[2] Furthermore, sociologist Alvin Gouldner refers to "reciprocity" as a norm, or set of societal expectations, involving both rights and duties for the donor and the recipient in any interchange; the norm obligates the recipient to become a donor and the donor a recipient in some immediate or future exchange. I shall return to Gouldner's ideas on reciprocity in the second half of this chapter. In this section, I will discuss some psychological perspectives on reciprocity.

Representing the psychologist's more personal and interior views, H. R. Schaffer remarks sweepingly, "The basic characteristic of all interpersonal behavior is reciprocity." He continues, "Reciprocity involves the building up of chains of coordinated interaction sequences, during which each partner participates in a process of stimulus interchange, the nature of which is affected both by the signals received and by the structural characteristics of the receiver."[3] Among the "structural characteristics of the receiver" must be a capacity for reciprocity. This capacity allows for a self-regulating approach to social interaction, whereby I can temper my behavior with you to accommodate my perception of your rhythms and tolerances. And you must do the same with me if our interaction is to continue, or at least not become discordant. To be able to do so, each of us must observe the other relatively undistortedly, and from such cues, I, for example, must be able to imagine how you feel as you interact with me. This occurs only at an advanced level of both cognitive and emotional development. Such reciprocity normally first becomes possible, cognitively, at about age eight or nine. It marks a totally different interpersonal orientation from the use of another person as an inanimate object or pivot for one's own desires. The use of peers as objects occurs frequently among three- or four-year-olds at play. It continues to occur sometimes among adults when they are under stress, or more typically and frequently if they have been stunted in their own social development.

Finally, this chapter addresses reciprocity as a personal capacity which underpins all prosocial behavior of a nonaccidental kind. The somewhat unfortunate or awkward term, "prosocial behavior," has won widespread use in recent years as the opposite of the long familiar term "antisocial behavior." The latter is associated in extremes with delinquent or criminal assaults on persons, property, or the smooth running of social institutions. Prosocial behavior, psychologist Paul Mussen explains:

> ... refers to actions that are intended to aid or benefit another person or group of people without the actor's anticipation of external rewards. Such actions often entail some cost, self-sacrifice, or risk on the part of the actor. A wide variety of behaviors is encompassed by this rubric, including generosity, altruism, sympathy, helping people in distress by giving material or psychological assistance, sharing possessions, donating to charity, and participating in activities designed to improve the general welfare by reducing social injustices, inequalities, and brutality.[4]

The unanswered question is whether prosocioal behavior is always or ever "altruistic"—that is, unselfishly concerned with the welfare of others and in no sense egoistic. Can a giver give with no throught of approval or reward from others, or even of self-approval for doing and being "good"? The nature of altruism has provoked a long and unresolved debate. Some psychologists have become reconciled that a "diversity of definitions is still with us."[5] Reciprocity and collaboration, as the central developmental ideas of this chapter, suffer less definitional ambiguity.

Development of Prosocial Behavior

Six orphaned children, aged three years to three years and ten months, arrived together in 1945 at an English wartime residential nursery under Anna Freud's direction. There she and Sophie Dann observed the six children for seven months. The children had had a harrowing earlier life. Before their first birthdays, they had all lost their parents and thereafter survived, following some moving about, in a Nazi concentration camp under the care of "undernourished and overworked" inmates. After they were liberated from the concentration camp, they were sent as a sixsome to Anna Freud's Hampstead Nursery where, subsequently, they were described as showing typically

> ... almost complete absence of jealousy, rivalry, and competition, such as normally develop between brothers and sisters or in a group of contemporaries who come from normal families. There was no occasion to urge the children to 'take turns'; they did it spontaneously since they were eager that everybody should have his share. Since the adults played no part in their emotional lives at the time, they did not compete with each other for favors or for recognition. They did not tell on each other and they stood up for each other automatically whenever they felt that a member of the group was unjustly treated or otherwise threatened by an outsider. They were extremely considerate of each other's feelings. They did not grudge each other their possessions . . . , on the contrary lending them to each other with pleasure. When one of them received a present from a shopkeeper, they demanded the same for each of the other children, even in their absence. On walks they were concerned for each other's safety in traffic, looked after children who lagged behind, helped each other over ditches, turned aside branches for each other to clear the passage in the woods, and carried each other's coats. In the nursery they picked up each other's toys. After they had learned to play, they assisted each other silently in building and admired each other's productions. At mealtimes handing food to the neighbour was of greater importance than eating oneself.[6]

This is most unusual caring behavior for three- to four-year-olds. If not for the human catastrophe which had thrust these orphaned children together in a concentration camp, it seems unlikely that their mutual sharing and caring relationships would have developed, at least so early in their lives. One wonders whether human catastrophes are needed to foster widespread reciprocity. In the second part of this chapter, I review some ideas on how an "altruistic community" may arise when disaster strikes an inhabited region.

In order for people to provide help to one another or any persons in need, the helpers must be able to put themselves in the needy person's shoes and feel vicariously the pain the others are suffering. They must also be willing to suffer the costs of giving aid, or at least be satisfied with the possibility of no reward for themselves. Young children are normally not cognitively able to take the role of the other until about age eight. Nursery school-aged children are, as one group of experimental child psychologists put it, "primarily own-gain oriented." These researchers find no increase in cooperative behavior among nursery school children, even when the task they are engaged in calls for coordination of their activities—although there is a sharp growth of competitive behavior in situations fostering such interaction.[7] In another study of preschool children, in a day care center, a construction task is given for them to perform singly and then in same-sex twosomes. Not until the children are six-year-olds does their paired interaction begin to be facilitative of their efforts, the experimenters observe.[8] In still another study, the idea that preschool children do *not* understand or accept the norms of reciprocity—for example, that people should help and not harm those who have helped them[9]—is confirmed by their reactions to cartoons showing reciprocal or nonreciprocal behavior.[10] Generally, preschoolers lack the capacities that consistent or lasting reciprocity requires.

There are anecdotal reports of some preschool children, and even infants, responding sympathetically to one another, as in Anna Freud's record of the six children, quoted above. Other observations appear in the books of Lois Barclay Murphy,[11] Susan Isaacs,[12] and Anna Freud and Dorothy Burlingham.[13] There are also many observations of young children using each other unfeelingly as objects. For example, "Freda (20 months) pushed four children over in succession and tried to sit and rock on them," or, as targets for aggression and counteraggression, "Carol (3½ years) tried to snatch a doll from Jessie (2 years). Jessie bit her so she had to let the doll go."[14] The likelihood that such behavior is largely influenced by children's situations at the preschool level is suggested by Murphy's evidence on different contexts; she concludes from an analysis of observers' ratings that "a child may be extremely sympathetic one day in one group and very aggressive the next day with a different combination of children."[15] The environmental influences on the children's behavior which Murphy's analyses include are the "culture pattern," or social climate, of each children's group, the children's social class background, and the specific activity in which they are engaged, e.g., swinging, which encourages cooperative behavior "since few of the children could 'pump' themselves in the swing adequately without being pushed."[16]

Children's prosocial behavior seems to become less unstable or situationally determined when the children are about eight or so years of age. Then there occurs what Piaget calls "a transition from initial egocentrism," by which time the child is cognitively capable of, among other things, "substituting for the egocentrism of the earlier years a game involving rules and team spirit."[17] To play team games, the child must be able not only to recognize the responsibilities inherent in his or her own role on the team; the child must be able also to anticipate what teammates will do. Team games like baseball call for teammates' cooperating toward the shared goal of winning the game. In their nine positions, each with its own obligations, baseball teammates play together against the other team's batter and members in the field on bases, striving to get "home."

Team games are much more complex than earlier played "it" games like hide-and-seek. In the gross structure of "it" games, the child who is "it" opposes alone all the other unrelated hiding children. There are no teams, only crude rules for the behavior of "it," and no cooperation is expected among players. Thus, typically, younger children play "it" games rather than team games. Younger still than the players of "it" games, with their modicum of rules which the very young cannot understand or conform to, is the "make-believe" or fantasy play of nursery school or kindergarten children. In such play, children merely use one another as pivots to act out their spontaneous imaginings: "You be the baby, and I'll be the mother," or

"I'll be the storekeeper, and you come to buy some milk." No prescribed and shared rules or structures must be learned and followed; once the make-believe scene is set, the children's spontaneous imitations of grown-ups provide a *commedia dell' arte* type of scenario.

The foregoing description is an elaboration of ideas and illustrations presented by George Herbert Mead in his sociological classic, *Mind, Self and Society*. Mead contrasts imaginative play with teamwork in order to clarify the conditions under which the "self," as object to itself, and "the generalized other," or community, represented also by one's teammates, come into a person's awareness. Mead writes:

> If we contrast play with the situation in an organized game, we note the essential difference that the child who plays in a game must be ready to take the attitude of everyone else involved in that game, and that these different roles must have a definite relationship to each other. . . . The organized community or social group which gives to the individual his unity of self may be called "the generalized other." The attitude of the generalized other is the attitude of the whole community. Thus, for example, in the case of such a social group as a ball team, the team is the generalized other in so far as it enters—as an organized process or social activity—into the experience of any one of the individual members of it.[18]

In Piaget's terms, young children, still engaged in "egocentric play," lack the cognitive capacities to participate in "collective symbolic games." Not until between seven or eight and eleven or twelve, does Piaget think, "an ever-increasing coordination of roles" and the necessary socialization can occur, to make reciprocal relationships possible.[19] For George Herbert Mead, a "self" and responsiveness to "the generalized other" are essential for engagement in situations in which one takes on the attitudes or roles of other persons, as in team games or other situations calling for reciprocity. While "reciprocity" has a special meaning for Piaget in the stage of "operational thinking" and specifically "concrete operations," the details of which are not relevant here, note that the emergence of operational thinking and concrete operations occur, on Piaget's timetable, from about age seven to twelve years, during which period Piaget acknowledges the importance of the "interchange of thought . . . a coordination of viewpoints . . . and therefore a form of cooperation between several individuals."[20] As the child emerges from egocentrism, the dominance of his own viewpoints no longer prevents the consideration of the viewpoints of others. With the development of new cognitive structures, there can be give-and-take reciprocal relationships between peers or equals.

Thus, on the issue of reciprocity, the independent thinking of a world renowned psychologist and a seminal sociologist converge. Growing out of observations and theories of different academic disciplines, such convergence or shared meanings suggest the validity of their interpretations.

This convergence of thought is not limited to George Herbert Mead and Jean Piaget. Psychologists with a psychoanalytic perspective, a student of Piaget's who studied Norwegian children in the classroom and the psychiatrist Harry Stack

Sullivan with his interpersonal orientation, all, from their theoretically very different positions, agree that at about age eight young children become able to form and sustain reciprocal relationships with agemates. This diverse literature has been reviewed and summed up as follows:

> From a psychoanalytic perspective, Isaacs discusses the postoedipal child's turning "from his parents to other children for emotional satisfactions. . . . This is not, of course, a sudden change but covers the space of a year or two or even longer." More specifically, she writes: "In the strictest sense of organized group reciprocity, there is little truly social behavior among children under seven or eight years. . . . Not until the middle years of childhood does one see that ability in the child to identify himself with his equals, and to maintain a positive attitude to them in spite of minor differences of individual interest, which underlies stable group relations."[21a] Bornstein divides the latency period into two periods, "the first from five and one half to eight years, and the second from eight years until about ten years. . . . In the second period of latency . . . the superego has become less rigid. The ego now can devote itself to a greater extent to coping with reality. The average eight-year-old is ready to be influenced by the children around him. . . ."[21b]
>
> The beginnings of the child's capacity for social reciprocity, at about age seven or eight, are documented by a student of Piaget's, Ruth Fröyland Nielsen. On the basis of her own experimental work with children in Oslo, she distinguishes between a second stage of social development, the egocentric or presocial stage, from about three or four years of age to seven or eight, and a third stage, the stage of reciprocal relations, from seven or eight to thirteen or fourteen. "If the second stage represents the development of the simple desire to communicate with others, which we have called 'la socialité de l'enfant,' the third stage is characterized by the development of a progressive, reciprocal adaptation, of 'la sociabilité'."[21c]
>
> From still another theoretical perspective, Sullivan discusses the chum, an intimate relationship which first becomes possible at about age eight-and-a-half. He describes preadolescence as "marked by the coming of the integrating tendencies which, when they are completely developed, we call love, or, to say it another way, by the manifestation of the need for interpersonal intimacy. . . . Intimacy is the type of situation involving two people which permits validation of all components of personal worth. Validation of personal worth requires a type of relationship which I call collaboration, by which I mean clearly formulated adjustments of one's behavior to the expressed needs of the other person in the pursuit of increasingly identical—that is, more and more nearly mutual—satisfactions. . . ." Sullivan distinguishes between the juvenile era, with its "need of similar people as playmates," and preadolescence, with its "specific new type of interest in a *particular* member of the same sex who becomes a chum or a close friend. . . . somewhere between eight-and-a-half and ten. . . ." He adds, ". . . nothing remotely like this appears before the age of, say, eight-and-a-half, and sometimes it appears decidedly later."[21d]
>
> Thus, diverse theories converge on the appearance of a capacity for reciprocal, mutual, or collaborative relations among children starting at about age eight.[21]

Having traced and documented the development of capacities for reciprocal interaction and relationships in children, I must move on to a consideration of the cultural bases for collaborative behavior and other evidence of reciprocity. I remarked at the outset of this chapter that too often professional as well as popular thinking about coping neglects the collaborative nature of much human environment management, especially in the complexities of present-day Western society. Within this sociocultural milieu, the emphasis is on individual achievement to the neglect of its social and collaborative context. For human service workers, such neglect is dysfunctional. The undeveloped prosocial capacities of young children should be fostered in programs set up, for example, for child care in crèches, nurseries, and kindergartens, and for older children in schools and community centers. The design of such physical and social contexts which are growth promoting—or, at the least, not growth stunting—depends on relevant knowledge of both developing people and their changing and changeable environments.

Culture Contexts of Collaborative Children

School-aged children's behavior reflects simultaneously the levels of competence reached in their development and the mores and values of the culture in which the children are being socialized. No child can do what he or she is not physically or psychologically capable of doing, but there is more likelihood of capacities in later childhood expressing culturally approved than disapproved behavior. Children's sometimes volatile feelings also influence their behavior, of course, and situational factors, such as the rules of a game, may foster or constrain competitiveness or collaboration. Still, when the values of both adults and childhood peers concur, intergenerationally agreed upon norms are likely to be followed by seven- to eleven-year-olds. To illustrate this thesis, in this section I offer some relevant observations on Native Indian, Mexican, and Israeli kibbutzim children.

Seven- to eleven-year-olds, with an average age of eight years, were engaged in an experimental game. About fifty Blackfoot Indian children, with equal numbers of girls and boys, and an equal number and distribution of urban, middle-class, nonIndian Canadian children in Alberta participated. The experimental game they played is Millard Madsen's ingenious Cooperation Board. It calls for four children playing at one time to try to draw lines with a remotely controlled pen through a set of circles. The pen is manipulated by strings and cannot reach a circle if any other children are simultaneously pulling the strings toward circles in their own direction. High scores, consisting of many crossed circles, are obtainable only when the foursomes collaborate. The experimenters comment, "Observations of the children while they were playing indicate that the Indian children developed verbal strategies for cooperation . . . Competitive behavior, when it occurred, was typically reprimanded by the other players." By contrast, among the nonIndian children, "Much effort was expended in keeping other players from gaining an 'advantage' . . . even though they often realized that this strategy would result in greatly decreased earnings."[22] The authors conclude:

> . . . there is a marked tendency for Blackfoot children to cooperate with each other when it is adaptive to do so. They seem better able to inhibit competi-

tive responses than are nonIndian children. While the intervening steps are unclear at this time, it is tempting to relate these differences to differences in the cultural backgrounds of the two groups. Certainly the Blackfoot traditions of sharing material wealth within the family and the sharing of child raising and housekeeping duties seem implicated. . . .[23]

Earlier in their report, the authors describe more fully the living places of the Indian children and the nonIndian children, the latter coming from an elementary school in Lethbridge, Alberta, "a small southern Alberta city," and the children in the sample being "a good cross section of middle-class urban Canadian society." By contrast:

> The Blood Indians of Alberta, members of the Blackfoot nation, reside on the largest Indian reserve in Canada. Its 360-square-mile area is made up of prairie and foothills and is used extensively for grain farming and cattle grazing. The Blood have recently established a manufacturing plant for the construction of prefabricated houses. While the population is scattered throughout the reserve, most of the people reside in several small communities. The traditional Plains Indian culture is of course no longer present in its complete form among these people, but certain aspects of family life, particularly the sharing of labor and child-rearing duties among members of the extended family, bear resemblance to earlier cultural forms. Material achievement is viewed as highly desirable, but strong social pressures exist for sharing wealth among family members.
>   While Blood Indian parents have the choice of educating their children in integrated schools in neighboring communities, many children attend one of several schools located on the reserve which are administered by the federal government. The children attending these schools are almost exclusively Indian, and while the teachers attempt to provide the children with experience in the larger society surrounding the reserve, the large distances and difficult travel conditions keep off-reserve contacts to a minimum. By contrast, urban Canadian children are raised within the general North American cultural milieu with its support of individual competition and achievement.[24]

Thus, in segregated rural communities, in a culture in which adults are expected to share their wealth within extended families, the school-aged children behave more collaboratively than do urban, middle-class agemates.

A second native people's context ideally suited for collaboration has been vividly documented among the Hopi. The Hopi Indians in northern Arizona consider themselves the oldest settlement in what is now called the United States of America. These quite homogeneous people were still considered in the early 1940s to have "probably preserved more of their ancestral heritage than any other tribe in the United States."[25] Their beliefs, underlying "the whole Hopi world view with its emphasis on interdependence and reciprocity," provide a model cultural context for the propagation of collaborative behavior. Their views are described by anthropologist Laura Thompson and Indian Service staff physician Alice Joseph in a University of Chicago study done under Committee on Human Development auspices:

> Theoretically all phenomena, natural and supernatural, living and dead—including man, animals, plants, the earth, sun, moon and clouds, the ancestors

and the spirits—are interrelated and mutually dependent through the underlying dynamic principle of the universe—which we shall call the law of universal reciprocity. This law implies the concept of immanent or cosmic justice. The emphasis is not, however, on the idea of rewards and punishments or on punishments alone (retribution), but on the mutual exchange of essentially equivalent but not identical values according to fixed traditional patterns, in the interests of the common weal. Man, the elements, animals, plants and the supernatural cooperate in an orderly fashion, by means of a complex set of correlative interrelationships, for the good of all.

This concept of the universe is not "mechanistic" in the usual sense of the term, on account of the special role played by man in the scheme of things. Whereas, according to Hopi theory, the non-human universe is controlled *automatically* by the reciprocity principle, man is an active agent who may or may not acquiesce in it. While the world of nature is *compelled* to respond in certain prescribed ways to certain stimuli, man not only responds but also *elicits* response. Hence, man, in the measure that he obeys the rules, may exercise a certain limited control over the universe.

Hopi philosophy, therefore, ascribes to man an element of choice—which, it seems, is dependent on his *will*. And this element of choice, this concept of a free-will-within-the-law, we may expect to be reflected in Hopi social sanctions and in Hopi personality. In fact it is crucial to an understanding of the dynamics of Hopi society.

To show how the law of universal reciprocity operates, we shall first touch on another basic tenet of Hopi thought. All phenomena, living and dead, which are important, either positively or negatively, to the Hopi in their struggle for existence, are grouped into mutually interrelated orders or classes and these orders are combined into overall, interdependent categories. This web of categorized orders of phenomena gives basic form to the cosmos. . . .

Such basic categories and their subdivisions form the framework within which the law of universal reciprocity operates. For it is between orders and categories of phenomena rather than between individuals that correlative exchange takes place. Individuals usually interact reciprocally not on their own, but in behalf of a group. For instance, a man functions in a reciprocal exchange of goods or services not as an individual but as a representative of his household, clan or secret society. In similar fashion, the leader of a ceremony theoretically correlates with orders of natural and supernatural phenomena in behalf of his clan, secret society and village, and also, in major ceremonials at least, for the good of the whole tribe and all mankind.[26]

Nor is it only observable behavior that reflects Hopi beliefs about interdependence and reciprocity. Thoughts are assumed to cross the highly permeable boundaries between persons and plants. "Unlike ourselves, whose thinking is tied in with concepts of imaginary space, the Hopi supposes that his thinking, say of a corn plant, has actual contact or interaction with it. 'The thought should then leave some trace of itself with the plant in the field. If it is a good thought, one about health and growth, it is good for the plant; if a bad thought, the reverse.' "[27]

Had these early '40s and '50s analyses of Hopi culture by anthropologists Laura Thompson, Harry Hoijer, and Richard Whorf been published at a time when interest in cross-cultural comparisons of children's prosocial behavior was as high as it became three decades later, researchers would have beelined to the Hopi villages of Moencopi, Shungopovi, and Old Oraibi in the hopes of being able to observe the children's degree of collaborativeness. As Western society values impinge upon such cultures, the people and their children tend to lose their commitments to sharing. They become more individualistic, and in moral terms, selfish, as a sizable number of studies—some of which I shall now discuss—make clear.

Cooperativeness characterizes not only some native peoples in North America but also in Australia. Research "results clearly support the contention that cooperative behavior is a salient aspect of interpersonal relationships among Aborigines"; such Aboriginal behavior is "culturally determined," the authors maintain, as they observe 13- to 15-year-olds reprove a peer for seeming to be competitive with a "typical remark" like " 'Come on . . . you're just greedy for money.' "[28] With acculturation to Western ways, Arab village children give less credence to the values of sharing with extended family members.[29] A series of studies, using Millard Madsen's "Cooperation Board" game, reveals that Mexican village children tend to be more cooperative and less competitively individualistic than Mexican–American (Los Angeles) children. Moreover, the latter are more cooperative and less competitive than Anglo–American children in Los Angeles. In one of Madsen's reports, observations are made of thirty-six Mexican village children in Nuevo San Vincente, fifty-four miles south of Ensenada in the State of Mexicali. The number of circles they cross on four trials—the higher scores indicative of greater cooperativeness—is contrasted with the parallel performances of forty-eight Anglo–American children in Los Angeles, given in averages in the following table:

Mean Circles Crossed per Trial[30]

	1	2	3	4
Anglo–American	1.5	.4	.8	.4
Mexican village	1.8	3.6	5.4	6.5

Beyond the quantitative evidence, psychologists Madsen and Ariella Shapira remark:

> Even though the tabled results are nonoverlapping, they do not present the vividly contrasting behavior as observed by the experimenters. The often aggressive, wild, shouting matches among the children in the United States, who were desperately but unsuccessfully trying to cross their circles, was in total contrast to the rather slow, quiet, and deliberately cooperative behavior of the Mexican village children.[31]

Two other researchers, in a 1977 report, contrasted two lower socioeconomic status groups of American children and also found the Mexican–American children to be more prosocial, the Anglo–American children more competitive.[32]

Children growing up in Israel on farm cooperatives, some of which have expanded their rural economics to include on-site communal workshops or small factories, have become subjects of great interest, especially to anthropologists and psychologists. Different kibbutzim are oriented toward different ideologies, but most provide residential group care for their very young children and thus "natural experiments" for social scientists interested in the effects of different child-rearing and socialization programs.

In one study of Israeli children, twenty boys and twenty girls between six and ten years of age, with an average age of eight years, were drawn from three different kibbutzim, two with a radical socialist and very spartan or puritanical way of life and one somewhat more moderate in its ideology. These forty children were contrasted in the experiment with forty city children, of similar age, from "Mount Carmel, an upper middle-class community in which most people have a relatively high income."[33] "The hypothesis that kibbutz children would show more cooperative behavior than city children in Israel was confirmed."[34] But beyond this expected finding were the observations of peer group pressures to cooperate among kibbutz children and their competitiveness as a group against other groups. By contrast with the city children:

> Among the kibbutz groups the picture was entirely different. When individual reward instructions were introduced, the first response of most of the groups was to set up rules for cooperation. Some examples of these responses were: "OK gang, let's go in turns," or "Let's help each other," or "We'll start here, then here," etc. Some groups asked E [Experimenter] if they were allowed to help each other or whether they could go in rounds like before. When E said they could do as they wished, they always decided upon cooperation. These children were very organized in their performance. They usually had decided the order before the trial began. During the game they were also very active in directing one another.
>
> The kibbutz children were very eager to do well as a group and tried their best to improve their performance on every subsequent trial. Some of the groups asked to compare their results with other groups and wanted to know what the best score had ever been. Such responses indicate that a desire to achieve and to do well characterizes these children, who do compete with other groups on the kibbutz but not within their group. At the group level, they cooperate and work together as a team.
>
> In most of the kibbutz groups there was a great concern about equality in prizes ("Every one should get the same"). They were so concerned about this that, in many cases, they rotated the starting point so that if they were stopped before a round was completed a different child would get the extra prize on each trial. When, in some isolated cases, one of the children tried to compete against the others, the group usually restrained him.[35]

The authors' general comments about the kinds of milieu from which the children in this experiment come contribute to an understanding of the sociocultural contexts generating cooperative and other kinds of prosocial behavior in children. They write:

> Children in an Israeli urban middle-class community are encouraged by parents and teachers to achieve and succeed. Competition is an acceptable means of arriving at this goal. In the kibbutz, on the other hand, children are

prepared from an early age to cooperate and work as a group, in keeping with the objectives of communal living. Spiro (1965)[36a] found, through questionnaires given to parents in the kibbutz, that generosity and cooperation were the most frequently rewarded behaviors, while selfishness and failure to cooperate were among the behaviors most frequently punished.

The formal teaching methods in the kibbutz are also noted for their minimal emphasis on competitive goals and techniques. Grades and examinations are viewed as unnecessary or even undesirable. Competition, with all its punitive aspects, is far less intense in the classroom of the kibbutz than in that of the city. Not only do the agents of socialization avoid inducing a favorable set toward competition, but also the children themselves develop an attitude against competition. Spiro found that only one out of 28 students saw himself or his peers as being competitively motivated. By far the majority of the students said that their desire was primarily to become equal to their peers or, as Rabin (1965)[36b] observed, to raise the achievement level of their group as a whole. Generally, kibbutz children do not accept competition as a socially desirable norm and dislike those who try to excel over members of their own group. This anti-competition attitude is so strong that, according to some teachers, students are ashamed of being consistently at the top of the class. Spiro also found that these cooperative attitudes and behaviors increase with age concomitant with a decrease in competitive motivation.[36]

Note that in the study just quoted, as well as in previously cited reports in this section, the contrasted groups of children differ by social class as well as by whether their living places are rural or urban. In the Israeli study, for example, the cooperative kibbutz children are also rural, and the competitive "upper middle-class" children are also urban. Similarly, the cooperative Blackfoot Indian children are rural and matched with "middle-class urban Canadian" children, who are less cooperative and more competitive. Fortunately, other studies use social class as an unconfounded independent variable, so that the influences of economic constraints or comforts and their attendant values bearing upon children's prosocial behavior may be considered more clearly.

In brief, these studies find school-aged children of lower socioeconomic status more sharing, cooperative, and otherwise prosocial than their middle-class agemates. For example, among the Anglo–American children in the study by Knight and Kagan, those of lower socioeconomic status are more prosocial than their upper middle-class counterparts. Among the five-year-olds in Jerusalem kindergartens, who were asked to give candy to classmates who had none, the middle-class boys were less generous when the recipient did not know who the giver was. Lower-class children did not respond this way, but were apparently more likely to explain their giving in terms of "altruism" (e.g., "I gave so he'll be happy") rather than, like the middle-class boys, in terms of "reciprocity" (under obligation to give because of past, immediate, or anticipated services rendered by the other).[37] Still other researchers generalize that "competitive behavior is not a universal value in Western society, but is more characteristic of the middle class, while culturally and economically deprived children are more cooperative and group-oriented."[38] Why this association between economic deprivation and children's sharing?

Group orientation rather than individualism characterizes geographically stable, traditional families, by contrast with the free-to-be-mobile nucleated middle-class family. In the latter, each person's pursuits and achievements tend to take precedence over any total family concern. In the traditional family, children are expected to contribute their earnings to the group's limited, pooled, economic resources, to take care of younger siblings, and to do chores which economically better off middle-class families, with their greater number of options, may pay baby sitters or cleaning ladies to do. Expectations in a traditional family, which is often an extended family, are not, of course, always or even perhaps often realized; values and behavior are frequently not in accord. In the larger traditional family, with more siblings and remotely related and multigenerational members under one roof than in the parent–child households of nuclear middle-class families, there are likely to be more candidates for every job to be done, and where money and other resources are more limited, there has to be more sharing, if only for survival's sake. This juxtaposition of the styles of traditional and nuclear families—the former group-oriented, the latter individual-oriented—is paralleled by lower-class and middle-class family styles, and even more closely by rural, in contrast with urban, ways of family and community living. I shall return to these issues in the last part of this section.

On the rural–urban dimension, rural life encourages, and at times demands, cooperation within families and among neighbors more than does urban living, with its network of specialists and formal services available on call, usually for pay. The pace and multiple options of city life seem to foster individualism and rivalry among its more affluent residents, who can choose among and acquire many of the city's material offerings. In a study of 168 Colombian first-grade children with an equal number of boys and girls from an urban neighborhood or a rural town, "the place of residence variable significantly influenced the [children's] cooperative behavior . . .; rural children cooperated more than urban children," and the writers conclude that their study "further validates a concept that urban living promotes competition even at such an early age as that of the subjects in this study."[39] In the previously cited report on the Mexican village children of Nuevo San Vicente, most of the adult males in that village are agricultural workers. Thus, these cooperative children are growing up in a rural setting, as are the Israeli children on kibbutzim, which are essentially agricultural communes. The association of children's cooperativeness with rural living places must be reconsidered in the face of study findings that both rural and urban poor children in Mexico are dramatically more cooperative than Mexican urban middle-class children.[40] Apparently being poor and/or rural induces children to share.

Why does city life interfere with children's and other people's sharing, helpfulness, and, more generally, reciprocity and collaboration? The research clearly supports but fails to explain adequately "urban unhelpfulness." One proposed explanation is that it is "an adaptation to overly demanding environmental conditions" in cities. People become excessively pressed and consequently self-preoccupied in a buzzing city. Reviewing studies on the low levels of urban helpfulness,

Charles Korte reports that in Turkey researchers found "the crowded, busy, noisy squatter settlements to be the most helpful areas," by contrast, for example, with "the quiet, sedate, suburban neighborhoods" which were "the least helpful areas."[41] He therefore questions the urban overload proposition, suggesting that responsiveness to the needs of other people comes from long valued, prosocial traditions among poor neighbors.

Having seen squatter or shantytown areas in developing nations, and especially what are called *gejiconda* in Turkey, I must make clear that, despite the residents' helpfulness, these poverty blighted living places are not fit for human habitation. Evidence of greater reciprocity and collaboration in poor neighborhoods should not contribute to a romantic view of poverty, one element in the antimaterialistic values of the counterculture in the 1960s. The repeatedly found association between being poor and sharing does, however, make one wonder how, under improved material conditions, this same prosocial behavior can be maintained.

Finally, children's chronological age enters the cultural scene as a component to be reckoned with. In the search for sociocultural contexts that seem to foster children's prosocial behavior, note that as children age from infancy through preadolescence—from their first to about their twelfth year—they not only develop new competencies and learn new social behaviors but they also normally become more and more broadly socialized into ways of living which their sociocultural milieus approve of and reward. The research in which children's age is a major variable suggests that their learning of prosocial behavior is patternable as follows:

Infants engage in more giving with parents or other adults during their second year of life than their first, but they do not accept or understand the value of reciprocity as preschoolers nor become stably prosocial until they are about six to eight years old.[42] After this, as they approach their teens in Western society, and especially in urban, middle-class milieus, they become increasingly less generous, less helpful to others, or generally less prosocial—a disturbing commentary on what contemporary society does to its young in view of its central values regarding acquisitiveness and, more broadly, individualism. The evidence for this decrement follows.

In his review of the research on children's cooperation and helping behavior, published in 1975, James H. Bryan notes:

> Children appear to learn, by middle childhood years, that one should help another. . . . But there is evidence, from studies within the laboratory and naturalistic settings, that children may well learn attitudes, as they age, that mitigate against self-sacrificing activities. Thus, some children will not sacrifice a reward that they deserve; others well trained in competition or exposed to a competitive situation, will be disinclined to help a needy other or to cooperate. Finally, there is some evidence which leads to the inference that within some naturalistic settings mental and chronological age may be negatively related to aiding peers.[43]

Madsen, drawing on his own research and others' work, says, "An age trend toward increased competition with age in the United States is . . . at least under some conditions, quite well established."[44] For example, Ervin Staub's study of 232 children's helping behavior in grades one, two, four, and six arrives at the "unexpected" finding that helping at first increases and then decreases with age "after second grade," or as ten-year-olds become more involved in their own peer groups.[45] In one study of two age groups, Kagan and Madsen found their four- and five-year-olds more cooperative then the seven- to nine-year-olds.[46]

Assuming children to be teachable and ready by the five- to seven-year-old period, quite diverse cultures first assign children of this age group to new roles and responsibilities in their society, according to a review of fifty ethnographic studies with good coverage of childhood.[47] In effect, this means that extrafamilial adults begin to educate the children, in formal schools and elsewhere, in appropriate or approved, socially contributory behavior. The more closely adults supervise the children's behavior—as in a Head Start preschool program—the less the children engage in prosocial behavior with peers, and at the same time, the less aggression they express as well as the less imaginative play.[48] The importance of adult modeling prosocial behavior for children is repeatedly supported by studies. High school seniors, selected for intensive study because they are judged to be likely to "get ahead" in the world, would counterbalance their individualism by aiding people in difficulty if they themselves experienced help in their own efforts to rise.[49]

The least completely acculturated members of an individualistically oriented society may be the most helpful; mentally handicapped children have been found to be more helpful than their normal agemates—the former probably having learned less about the norms for personal advancement and also receiving more help from others, and thus experiencing the modeling of prosocial behavior.[50] In a cooperative setting, those least in touch may also be least cooperative. In rural Appalachia, the members of forty-six families who were least helpful or most neglectful of one another also, by contrast with seventy-two nonneglectful families, were least connected with helping networks and more isolated from other kinds of social participation in their communities. They were thus subject to fewer rural pressures to help others or themselves.[51]

In summary, prosocial behavior in children is fostered among more geographically stable and more slowly paced or less thoroughly urbanized people. The reciprocal help needing and help modeling found in working-class neighborhoods contribute to the children's socialization into mutually helpful ways with their peers. Their lives are likely to be traditionally oriented, their families group-structured rather than being attuned primarily to individual wants and personal independence. In such contexts, young people live very interdependently and learn from adults and peers who suffer and share daily adversities. Taking the role of others in troubled circumstances is not difficult; they have all been through them. By contrast with more affluent people who can buy their own way through obstacles, the less affluent learn to cope by sharing, collaboratively. Acquisitions are functional, not a central purpose of living.

In a world of decreasing natural resources, reduction in overconsumption by a relatively small segment of the world's peoples is a necessity. Human service workers are typically committed to such a conservationist perspective and engage in programs to this end. At the higher levels of government, they press for policy developments that address the problems of the maldistribution and depletion of resources. At the level of neighborhoods and other living places, they participate in the organization and ongoing development of locally shared and reciprocal services. These vary from community to community. They include collaborative child care and cooperative housing and house repair programs, and other neighborhood improvement efforts. They involve remedial programs, such as short-term crisis intervention, transition houses for abused family members, widow-to-widow counseling, and comparable approaches to personal and family emergencies.

At the very least, human service workers model prosocial behavior in the living places where they work. It is well documented that, from middle childhood on, people understand the principle that we should all help one another. More than verbal repetition of this dictum is needed, however. For children and others to follow it, it must be demonstrated, accepted with commitment, and lived. Prosocial behavior begets prosocial behavior, especially in communities where caring is part of the daily way of life.

CARING COMMUNITIES

Reciprocity as a part of normal community life is illustrated in Chapter Three under the heading of living place networks—to a limited extent when I quoted observations of sociability in a Boston Italo-American neighborhood, and much more explicitly in the record of twosomes and threesomes of neighbors helping each other in a working-class English housing development outside London. For more formalized and widespread examples involving all the people living in a region, I turn first to a rural and then to a village example. There people are strongly identified with and committed to the traditions of their culture, arising in part from the deprivations they have suffered. In such settings, one can see clearly the force of their cultural expectations upon all the people, as well as how the helpers are themselves helped in return.

Expectations for collaborative efforts and other prosocial behavior forcefully impinge on a community when their living place is beset by a natural disaster or some other assault upon all residents. Typically, communities have no prearranged organization or well-defined roles for responding to sudden, and fortunately infrequent, disasters. The development of an "emergency social system" to cope with common needs may occur when a tornado or fire or flood overwhelms a region. For such a collaborative organization to arise, *all* the people—that is, all segments of the community—must feel themselves to be in great danger. This feeling unifies them. Such a common threat is what bonds together the warring factions in a children's camp when the water supply for the whole camp goes dry, as in Muzafer Sherif's "Robber's Cave Experiment."[52] This chapter ends with descriptions of a caring community which arose after the dykes had broken and towns were flooded in the Netherlands. When one considers how reciprocity, caring, and other kinds of prosocial behavior appear in living places under serious threat, one wonders about the need for such external stressors as preconditions.

Yet the two illustrations that follow describe prosocial behavior as part of normal community life—among Irish farmers and eastern European Jewish villagers—under no stress. Or rather no extreme stress. For as the threat of famine has constantly goaded Irish farmers, so persecution and pogroms constantly endangered the lives of Jews. Perhaps, if we all were sufficiently aware of the increasingly grave depletion of natural resources and the holocaust dangers of another war, no community today would live without a sense of common threats to life. In sharing these, all people are under stress, and mutual care might then arise among all of us.

Community Sharing and Coherence

I start with two illustrations of reciprocity in normal community life. The first brief description is of farmers' practice in Ireland in a book written by an Irish folklorist. The second is an analysis of the place of charity in the no longer existent Eastern European Jewish village called a shtetl. The source of the second quotation is a book deriving from a Columbia University library and seminar study, which involved anthropologists Ruth Benedict and Margaret Mead, and, as seminar leader, Conrad Arensberg. For Arensberg, as Margaret Mead writes in her foreword to the book, "the Jewish shtetl community merged against his field study of the Irish countryman and his wide sociological acquaintance with traditional rural and peasant cultures . . ."[53] Thus, there are links between these two illustrations of community reciprocity.

RURAL AND VILLAGE SHARING:
TWO EXAMPLES (RECORD NO. 13)

First, from Seán Ó Súilleabháin's *Irish Folk Custom and Belief:*

One of the most pleasant customs in rural Ireland was that termed *combar na gcombarsan* (mutual help given by neighbours). This help was always forthcoming whenever needed. Individual farmers "gave a hand" to one another in times of urgent need, and the compliment was repaid as occasion arose. An extension of this kind of mutual help was the *meitbeal,* where a number of neighbours joined together for a day or two in helping, free of charge, someone who had a special type of work to be done: turf-cutting, harvesting and so on. The work was thus done more quickly, and the only charge on the person who received the help was the provision of food and, perhaps, some entertainment, when the task was completed. This man would on later occasions join other *meitbleacha* in return, and thus a great spirit of cooperation existed in country districts.[54]

Rural community reciprocity is in all likelihood universal where relatively small farm holdings exist. When agriculture becomes industrialized and depersonalized on huge ranches, money pays for whatever is needed. Neighborly sharing and caring are likely to disappear.

In a chapter called "Charity Saves from Death," in Mark Zborowski's and Elizabeth Herzog's *Life is with People: the Culture of the Shtetl*, they explain that the Hebrew word *tsdokeh* signifies "charity" but really means "social justice," and they continue as follows:

Tsdokeh covers all acts of giving, from *ndoveh,* the alms given to the beggar, to *gmilus khassodim,* a form of benefice in which mere material help is combined with "bestowing of loving kindness," and which is therefore of a higher quality.

Life on the shtetl begins and ends with tsdokeh. When a child is born, the father pledges a certain amount of money for distribution to the poor. At a funeral the mourners distribute coins to the beggars who swarm the cemetery, chanting "Tsdokeh will save from death."

At every turn during one's life, the reminder to give is present. At the circumcision ceremony, the boy consecrated to the Covenant is specifically dedicated to good deeds. Every celebration, every holiday is accompanied by gifts to the needy. Each house has its round tin box into which coins are dropped for the support of various good works. A home that is not very poor will have a series of such boxes, one for the synagogue, one for a yeshiva in some distant city, one for "clothing the naked," one for "tending the sick," and so on. If something good or something bad happens, one puts a coin into a box. Before lighting the Sabbath candles, the housewife drops a coin into one of the boxes. . . .

Children are trained to the habit of giving. A father will let his son give alms to the beggar instead of handing them over directly. A child is very often put in charge of the weekly dole at home, when the beggars make their customary rounds. The gesture of giving becomes almost a reflex. When anything out of the ordinary happens, one says a blessing and one drops a coin into the box.

The "social justice" of the shtetl is not wholly voluntary and not wholly individual. Much of it is, and there is wide latitude for individual performance. Nevertheless, it is firmly woven into the organization of the community—or rather, it provides the central mechanism by which the community functions. The interweaving of individual benefaction with collective community service, of the voluntary with the compulsory, of religious injunction with civic obligation is essential to the organization and the flavor of the shtetl. . . .

The patterns of giving and receiving represent a key mechanism in the shtetl, basic to individual relations and community functions, and paramount in the ethical system to which all relations and all functions are referred. Giving is both a duty and a joy; it is a source of heavenly approval and also a source of earthly prestige. The fortunate man is the one who is in a position to give. The unfortunate is the one who is under pressure to accept. Granted the correct situation, accepting is not necessarily painful—but under any circumstances, giving is counted among the great gratifications of life. . . .

. . . Giving, however, is not an act of simple altruism, for the donor profits far more than the receiver.

The rewards for benefaction are manifold and are to be reaped both in this life and in the life to come. . . .

A popular legend tells that when a man dies and his soul enters Heaven, it is received by his good deeds and bad deeds, and according to the amount of each the soul remains in Heaven or is sent to hell. A popular wish that may be used either as a blessing or as a curse is, "May this rise up to meet you," that is, when your soul enters Heaven may it be judged by this that you have done to me.[55]

Both the Irish farmers' and the Jewish villagers' exchange of services and goods illustrate many of sociologist Alvin Gouldner's observations on the workings of the norm of reciprocity. The kinds of behavior described in both illustrations make for interdependent relationships among residents and thus stronger integration, or coherence, of their community. The ties between donors and recipients, although of a different nature in the two examples, are nonetheless bonds that express the mutual needs of all participants.

Secondly, note that although the social statuses of the Jewish beggars and their more economically comfortable benefactors differ markedly, their mutual needs for each other equalize their power. Later in the chapter from which I quoted, there are vivid descriptions of the arrogance and demanding approaches of many beggars, knowing that those who give to them are dependent on the beggars for an afterlife place in Heaven. Similarly, the Irish farmer who receives help realizes that he will shortly be helping, and probably feels less "put down" and more on a par with those who aided him, since their tradition calls for equal give-and-take or reciprocity.

Alluding to potlatch ceremonies in which extensive gift giving occurs, Marcel Mauss remarks that between givers and receivers, a "hierarchy is established . . . To give is to show one's superiority . . . To accept without returning or repaying more is to face subordination, to become a client and subservient . . ."[56] Also, the more powerful may exploit the less powerful, extorting from the weak whatever is wanted without giving anything in return. Thus, reciprocity must be linked with equality of relationships.

One undesirable aspect of the association between equality and reciprocity is that "the norm may lead individuals to establish relations only or primarily with those who can reciprocate, thus inducing neglect of the needs of those unable to do so"—for example, "children, old people, or those who are mentally or physically handicapped . . ."[57] Hopefully there are other norms or a moral code to promote care for a society's disadvantaged.

Third, reciprocity generates stability and continuity in community life, beyond what the interdependence and equality of residents tend to foster. Reciprocity, as Gouldner remarks, is a "starting mechanism" for social interaction, but it also perpetuates it in that future obligations are invoked by the receipt of service or goods, and such obligations tend to keep a community going, donors having vested interests in their future receipt of returns from their earlier giving. Community continuity may seem irrelevant in an age of such rapid social change. Yet there seem to be many losses for personal development in present-day societal discontinuities, a few of them well expressed by psychiatrist Jerome D. Frank as follows:

> From the standpoint of the individual, loss of temporal continuity undermines features of character that provide the basis for personal meaning and significance. These include formation of long-term goals and enduring values and persistence in their pursuit, as well as such characteristics as responsibility, commitment, and integrity, all of which require time to develop and be tested. In an instantaneous society the only virtue is sincerity, an admirable quality to be sure, but only if it is modified by consideration of its long-term consequences. Members of encounter groups, for example, can afford to "let it all hang out" because they know they will never see each other again.[58]

Reciprocity contributes to continuity of community life as creditors await the repayment of indebtedness. Without such continuity—that is, in a highly mobile world—people who owe you a returned favor may have left the region, and next time round you may seek immediate repayment in money for neighborly services rather than expecting some form of barter at a later date. Without community stability, the norms of reciprocity described in the illustrations of rural Ireland and Eastern European Jewish village life could not have been woven into these people's cultures.

Fourth and last, in the course of the development and sustaining of community cohesion, equality of relationships, and stability and continuity, reciprocity may well engender—if it does not originate with—a kind of mutual caring, and even love, among some of those who live and work together, cooperatively. Distinction is made in the book on the shtetl between an impersonal giving of alms to the poor and "a form of benefice in which mere material help is combined with 'bestowing of loving kindness,' and which is therefore of a higher quality."[59] Mauss repeatedly refers in his cross-cultural study of gift giving to the circulation of goods in some enlightened societies for other than utilitarian purposes.[60] And Richard Titmuss, in his book on blood donations as commodity or gift in the United States, Japan, the Soviet Union, and the United Kingdom, generalizes as follows:

> . . . examples drawn from both complex and traditional societies indicate that the personal gift and counter-gift, in which givers and receivers are known to each other, and personally communicate with each other, is characterized by a great variety of sentiments and purposes. At one end of the spectrum, economic purposes may be dominant as in some forms of first-gifts, which aim to achieve a material gain or to enhance prestige or to bring about ma-

terial gain in the future. At the other end are those gifts whose purposes are predominantly social and moral in that as 'total social facts'[61a] they aim to serve friendly relationships, affection and harmony between known individuals and social groups.[61]

The distinction being made is between giving in accordance with the norm of reciprocity, with an anticipation of a return, and giving because one *cares* for others—whether for a person, a group of persons, an entire people, or *homo sapiens* and all living organisms. The distinction Titmuss makes need not, in its second part, be confined to "known individuals and social groups." One can be loving, as the great religions suggest, without "knowing." If one truly cares, there may be no thought of return in kind.

Community Collaboration under Stress

I have made repeated references earlier in this book to the ways in which, under a shared threat such as a natural disaster, the people in a community will unite and collaborate, although the community may have been rife with conflict prior to the common danger. A sharing culture, like those described previously in this chapter, may arise quite suddenly following a catastrophe. After World War II and into the 1950s, studies of communities under stress were made as contributions to Civil Defense planning; such studies were of interest also to students of social change.[62] Might a collaborative "emergency community" effect changes in a community that lasted beyond the emergency's restoration period?

Among observations and analyses of community crises are four volumes on the Holland flood disaster of 1953. The excerpt that follows comes from that report by social researchers in the Netherlands. Following the observations of what happened in Kortgene directly after the flood, I shall discuss some of the questions the record raises for the human services.

THE RISE OF AN "EMERGENCY COMMUNITY" AFTER A DISASTER (RECORD NO. 14)

In one single night the world of the Kortgener had simply been swept away by the water. A village community no longer existed. Normal family-life had become impossible. One situation dominated the scene, the fact of having received a personal blow and the subsequent action. The people who were evacuated from the village entered into a different world which had not been struck; moreover they lived there more or less isolated with regard to one another. The ones who stayed behind, on the other hand, were together in the dry places. Their world at that moment was occupied by only one thing—the disaster and its consequences. Within the framework of the spontaneous and mainly informal activities . . . , a center came into being where all sorts of people were driven towards one another. In a very close relationship they formed such a remarkable group, that the disaster in Kortgene and its consequences cannot be understood without a closer examination of this community which was created by the battle against the flood-water and its consequences, and to which we, therefore, will refer as an "emergency community." . . .

The men who stayed behind were in the first place those who had been active during the initial emergency situation, for instance the families in the "Graaf van Buren" and the "Bierhuis" opposite, the truckdriver who had done so much to warn the people, the agricultural laborer and a few others who had taken an active part in the rescue-work on the "Torendyke" and elsewhere, and finally several hurriedly formed teams which could be of service anywhere in the present situation. . . .

These people who remained took up three posts, as it were. In the most obvious position here was the cafe-restaurant, "Graaf van Buren," which became the center. During the night of the catastrophe, this building had already had a central function as one of the few places in the village where the water had not caused destruction. One could go by boat into the village directly from this cafe. During the night of the disaster the mill, on the other side of the village, was also a rallying point, but only as a provisional rescue-center. As soon as the evacuation was under way, that is early Sunday morning, this point lost any further function.

At the premises of the Cooperative Society and the "Bierhuis" the circumstances were different. They became "subsidiary centers" for the inn. The latter, having been a rescue-center, immediately assumed the character of an evacuation center as well, and later in many respects the focal point through the leadership of the cafe-owner. The "Bierhuis," also, was used as a clearing-house for the evacuation, and later a medical post was established there. Under the leadership of the manager of the Cooperative Society, the company's buildings were used as an accommodation center for all sorts of people, and later also for the many helpers who had come from other parts of the Netherlands (such as Arnhem) and other countries (Germany, France) to render assistance.

It is hardly possible to visualize the pitiful condition of Kortgene and the surrounding district when, on Monday afternoon, the evacuation was complete.

People were confused and dejected by this situation—a real leader with prestige and an accepted authority position was missing. A considerable number of people were slightly wounded and one or two had sustained serious injuries. Communications with the outside world were broken. There was doubt as to the adequacy of the food and water supply for the next few days. The threat of the water continued. There were breaches in the dykes. Weakened culverts which connect the Stadspolder Kortgene with other flooded polders were on the verge of collapse. Their destruction might delay the draining of the Stadspolder for weeks. Hardly a start had been made on the recovery of the dead people and animals. People who still clearly remember the situation around the "Graaf van Buren" on Sunday and Monday, speak of a "hopeless," a "confusing" situation. This, however, was soon amended in certain respects; by Monday the energetic efforts of those who had remained behind had begun to show results.

Food supply soon ceased to be a problem. At the request of the cafe-owner of the "Graaf van Buren" the bakers in Wissekerke had begun immediately to bake bread on Sunday. In the afternoon, a little boat went around the village to take some food to the people who had not yet been evacuated from their homes. A skipper from Katsveer who had collected his parents from the village on Sunday night returned early in the morning with crates of porridge and milk. On Tuesday foodwaders, etc., were dropped from planes. All the food thus received was taken to the inn, where it was prepared and distributed to all comers. This "airlift" set up strong associations with the last World War. It gave the people the feeling of impending liberation. "They are helping us. They know about us." Another striking point in this connection is that almost every person interviewed said, ". . . and on Sunday a plane flew over." The mere fact of this gave the people strength. . . .

At Colijnsplaat the decision was taken first to drain the Stadspolder and not to use it as a drainage reservoir for the other polders. No pumps were required for this reclamation, as the water could be disposed of by means of sluices. The culverts through which the water from the other polders is normally drained via the Stadspolder were closed, strengthened, and guarded. In part it was thanks to the activity of the innkeeper and a grain dealer who on Sunday afternoon, assisted by others, strengthened a collapsing culvert, that this fast reclamation of Kortgene was possible. When the village was finally cleared of water on Wednesday, the damage and destruction were overwhelming. The streets were filled with furniture, straw, wood, barrels, pieces of barns, etc., all covered with soft, slimy ooze. A start was quickly made on the wreckage clearance. . . .

The care of the wounded was the service organized the most quickly and efficiently. After the Burgomaster's telephone call to Goes, a Red Cross column started from there on Sunday morning. It could, however, not go further than Wolphaartsdyke, which was also flooded. Assistance was given by the doctor of Wissekerke who had received an early warning (at 6 a.m. on Sunday). He called in the district-nurse of Wissekerke and requisitioned the "emergency depot" at Geersdyke which had been established some years ago and contained stretchers, blankets, etc. From 7 a.m. onwards he was in the "Bierhuis" taking charge of the wounded and, when necessary, their transport. Under the directions of this doctor and of the secretary of the First Aid Society (who, as the local representative, knew the situation and the people), great activity was displayed here. On Wednesday, the secretary had it broadcasted that anybody with even the slightest wound, incurred during salvage or repair work, must come to the "Bierhuis" to have it bandaged. In the course of the weeks over 2,000 cases were treated, toward the end with the assistance of a Red Cross team from Goes.

Another activity which had become urgent in the emergency was the recovery of the dead, of whom only a few had been retrieved from the ruins on the "Torendyke." It was mainly Kortgeners, simply working people (often Calvinists) who volunteered for this work at the request of the innkeeper. The bodies were identified by the police with the aid of the active manager of the Cooperative Society. Following identification, the victims were interred at the cemetery in Colijnsplaat.

In order to prevent the spreading of infection as much as possible, an animal "cadaver-team" was formed on Tuesday, under the direction of the two butchers in Kortgene. The dead animals were removed in ships.

It was not easy to acquire ships for this purpose. The majority of the skippers did not like this type of load at all. On Tuesday morning a Belgian ship entered the harbor to inquire after relatives. A grain dealer from Kortgene, who told the skipper that all were well, said, "We need your ship," and before the skipper realized what was happening, his ship was filled with dead animals.

Thus we see that while there was confusion during the first few days and weeks, there was also organized activity centering in the "Graaf van Buren." In the sections that follow we will deal further with the question of the mode of living of the people in and around that inn. . . . Not only the world of the people, but also, as it were, the village community, was forced back to a more primitive level. In a sense, this "emergency community" replaced the village community. As a group, the "emergency community" was primitive to such an extent that the actions of its members could not have taken place outside the actions of the group. That is why the tradespeople who remained in the village only to guard their own possessions, were not a part of the "emergency community." The people had been struck, and acted accordingly. Anyone who did not act from this standpoint did not exist for the "emergency community." He became a stranger, even an enemy, so that the people outside this group were almost regarded as "enemies."

Hence, the group-behavior in Kortgene assumed a most peculiar character. On the one hand there were all sorts of modern aids with which the emergency situation was met. On the other hand, we see the more primitive and non-rational factors which intermingled with these modern aids, and which also characterized the group-behavior of the "emergency community." This behaviour was primitive because the ramifications of the village community into different groups such as family, club, party and class, was replaced by one "unramified" group, the "emergency community." Non-rational due to the group-consciousness which now sprang up. The common struggle created a strong tie. This was apparent in regard, for instance, to the economic structure of the "emergency community."

Unlike the normal village community the economic structure of the emergency community was no longer based on a monetary economy, but on the "non-rationalism" of a primitive communal community. This economy was made possible by the most modern means, e.g., materials from planes.

By "communal" we mean that the people owned everything in common and nothing privately. Even those few people who had not lost everything no longer regarded the remainder of their own possessions as their private property.

A man who had lost his family, his home and all his possessions, went to Colijnsplaat to ask the municipal authorities for an advance in order that he might evacuate to his relatives in Amersfoort. He received, however, only three guilders, which was not sufficient for his fare, and he contemplated suicide. The daughter of the cafe-owner gave him 30 guilders, her savings toward a new coat.

Thus it is demonstrated that economic behaviour without its social background cannot be explained. The "non-rationalism" of the communal community is based on a group behaviour of a particularly intensive and exclusive character. That is why within this emergency community there was no thought of buying and selling. On the other hand, a certain form of barter-economy arose among the tradespeople who had remained and who possessed goods. Afterwards they were supplied with dropped goods, distributed through the inn.

Another cafe-owner who had stayed behind, like those tradespeople, had become envious of his colleague of the "Graaf van Buren." While the latter was distributing everything, regardless of whether it belonged to himself or whether it had come by "airlift," the former complained to the municipal authorities at Colijnsplaat that the cafe-owner of the "Graaf van Buren" was, if you please, too sparing with his distributions.

Money no longer had any value. It might even be found among the mess in the streets, but it was left there. What was the use of money in this emergency?

At this time, there was hardly any evidence of stealing in Kortgene. Most remarkably and characteristically, at a certain moment, the rumor arose that the fishermen from Arnemuiden who were lying in the harbor had been stealing. This was, however, merely a rumor. The fishermen apparently did not belong to the "emergency community."

The communal economy, of course, could not last. Gradually there came economic tendencies which were most inclined towards the "rational," but they did not spring from the emergency community itself. The latter was rather characterized by the acquisition of a certain measure of self-reliance and autonomy. This tendency was fostered from . . . the outsiders who came in contact with the emergency community. . . .

Moreover, strengthened by war-reminiscenses—which played an important role in the people's present experience—the people adopted a decidedly hostile attitude towards a party of Germans who had come to help. It was whispered that they were spies.

From these psychological phenomena, a contrast was created, forming one of the backgrounds against which the antithesis between the people who had remained at Kortgene, and the municipal authorities temporarily established at Colijnsplaat, would be viewed. The contrast between "non-rational" group forces and rational action taken outside the group—albeit for the sake of that group—is one of the factors which determined this sharp conflict. Those in Kortgene knew only what was happening there. It was the necessary limitation by the grace of which all intensive group-life existed. Identification with behavior and interests of the "in-group" led of necessity to its antithesis whenever the behavior of those who did not belong to that "in-group" was concerned. . . . Within the community the people only saw what was happening there, and nothing else. The worlds of the people coincided and had the same horizon, viz. the common struggle. The ramified village community was reduced to one unramified group.

Some men who lost their whole families through the disaster not only established themselves in the "Graaf van Buren" (one of them stayed there for months), but the very maintenance function of the family was taken over there. Anybody could sleep and eat there whenever he wished. An occasional individual, more adventurous and poetic, who found the family tie to be oppressive, was heard to say, in spite of all the horror, "We will never have such a fine time again!"

While an occasional individual felt the common struggle and its consequences as a liberation, nearly everyone experienced it as a unifying force, previously unknown, whose later disappearance was experienced with a sense of loss.[63]

Many issues and questions relevant to the human services arise from a record such as this. I shall comment on three major aspects: the immediate effects of a shared threat to survival, the community's mobilization, and social change following a community's successful collaboration under stress.

When a threat to survival is shared by the members of a community, the situation is very different from stressful situations involving only one person. The nine-year-old girl, Norma Jean (Record No. 11 in Chapter Four) suffers the onset of her life-threatening illness alone—that is, as an individual person. So far as she knows, no one else is similarly threatened at the same time. Feelings of isolation and abandonment contribute to feelings of incompetence or utter helplessness. The emotional support of Norma Jean's parents must have nourished her capacity to deal more effectively with her crisis, but the parents were not themselves, like her, being assaulted by the same physical threat. Similarly, Mrs. Kahn (Record No. 12) feels helpless and hopeless in her social isolation. She has no awareness that she is part of a sizable population of single parents heading families with young children and living in poverty. By contrast with these stressful situations involving isolated individuals, when the dykes break in Kortgene, people of all social and economic positions and different church memberships are equally under attack and may be washed away and drowned. Following the flood's impact, and during the emergency conditions immediately thereafter, the survivors realize that they have suffered a threat to life together. A community disaster not only evokes basic survival responses but it also is a great social equalizer. In the record of the Holland flood, several people are reported to have escaped to such safe shelters as the upper stories of a building in the company of other villagers with whom they had never before shared such close quarters. In such quarters, social status differences seem to vanish. "Now we were lying in the same bed with Mrs. B., who always used to be too genteel even to look at us."[64] Shared threats to survival have such immediate effects.

How does a community mobilize itself? The brief period of warning and the possibility of people misinterpreting or denying its significance make the impact of a natural disaster all the more difficult for a community to cope with since people are not prepared. Information dissemination is often made more difficult by the breakdown of normal means of communication. Formal and established government controls and customary social organization, including official leadership, may prove inappropriate and incompetent to deal with the novel problems of a disaster. The ongoing structures of community life may disintegrate. A whole new set of priorities arises with human survival at the top of the list. All other former daily concerns give way to this one. In Kortgene, after the initial crisis seemed to have passed, needs for food and shelter, medical care for the injured and physical care for the still endangered, and the threat to public health of the dead bodies of people and animals became the central focuses for action. Lost and damaged property was secondary.

With Kortgene's mayor and councilmen evacuated to another village, natural leaders emerged from among the able-bodied people remaining. The manager of the Cooperative Society provided shelter in the Society's buildings. The Graaf van Buren cafe owner organized the distribution of food. Others supervised and participated in the reclaiming of the land by sluicing and draining off the water. Money lost its value. Emergency giving and barter became modes of exchange. During such "primitive" and "nonrational" social interaction, as the observers categorize it, a new caring and sharing culture appeared. It is the result of and it further generates some of the kinds of prosocial behavior which is the focus of this chapter.

The emergence of prosocial behavior within a community under stress is a remarkable phenomenon. It occurs repeatedly, and with a unifying effect in community social relationships, bringing together people from different and sometimes formerly conflicting segments into "one unramified group." But when the flood waters completely subside, the debris is removed, and the evacuees have returned, does social life revert to its accustomed, predisaster ways?

There are no across-the-board answers to this question, but there are some hints of conditions that make a difference. Systematic studies have not been carried on for a long enough time in postdisaster communities, but there are anecdotal reports and general observations. One observer remarks on "long-run changes initiated by disasters" that "present evidence indicates that disasters induce changes wherein the resultant social structure differs considerably from the pre-disaster forms," but he cites only macrosocietal evidence—what happened to nations after they were defeated in wars or hit by the 1930s Great Depression and the social movements that arose as a result.[65]

Allen Barton speculates as follows:

For a community to maintain permanently the extreme generosity and mutual concern of the first days after a disaster is probably impossible without extraordinary indoctrination and commitment to utopian goals. But the maintenance of communications about the suffering of others, of social intimacy between people in different positions, and of ideologies and beliefs that emphasize collective responsibility for the welfare of all members of the community might make it possible to achieve permanently higher levels of community solidarity and mutual helpfulness than are normal in most modern societies. Whether this loss of social differentiation and individual responsibility would cause a decline in economic or intellectual productivity is another question, which experience in the kibbutzim of Israel and future experimental communities may ultimately answer.[66]

Beyond such speculations by American sociologists comes a report of dramatic postdisaster social change in a village in Africa, two years after a typhoon had flattened and devastated the community. The special administrative arrangements for self-help in the village in the "Food for Work" program seems an essential element in the change reported. The record should be of special interest to human service workers engaged in disaster work or others concerned with social change of this kind. The observations were made and reported by Gilles Latour, Head of Projects in Lesotho for the Unitarian Service Committee of Canada.

COMMUNITY COOPERATION
TWO YEARS FOLLOWING
A CATASTROPHE (RECORD NO. 15)

Two years ago, Ramoroke was a small village like so many others in this district of Qacha's Nek in southern Lesotho. Subsistence agriculture on small plots of terraced land, and free-grazing mountain herds of scrawny cattle, sheep and goats were the mainstay of its survival. Here, as elsewhere in Lesotho, most of the farming was done by the women. Young boys took over from absent fathers and older brothers in driving their animals to isolated and dismal cattle posts in the high mountains, from December to May, keeping them out of school. This may explain, in part, why the very low literacy rate of 25 percent is still significantly higher among females, who usually manage to receive a few years of primary schooling.

As in many villages and towns, community life was rife with petty conflicts, self-defeating individualism and distrust of any change or development initiated by one particular group or family.

Ramoroke was a particularly poor, tradition-bound, Basotho village, on the edge of isolated survival, with barely a footpath leading to it. Then, with no warning, exactly two years ago, disaster struck in mid-afternoon. A violent typhoon tore down from the mountain, sweeping all in its path in a few terrifying minutes. It left a dust-clouded and narrow corridor of absolute destruction. Ramoroke was in the middle of this path and it was literally blown away. By what many here still see as a miracle, all members of the twenty-nine resident families threw themselves, as one, facedown on the ground. As their thatched huts, animals and crops were swept into the countryside; as their once sleepy village disintegrated in a whirl above their prostrated bodies, they prayed and hung on for dear life. They lost everything but their lives and, incredibly, only a few of them suffered injuries from flying debris. Nothing was left—not a blanket, not a cooking pot, not a bench to sit on. They rose and, in utter shock, surveyed the ruins: uprooted trees, piles of rubble, flattened crops and dead animals lying around. Little did they realize that, far from being the

end of Ramoroke, it was the beginning. Indeed, the slate had been \
their whole life as a community had to be rewritten.

After the initial shock of the swiftness and violence of the cata\
bouring villagers came to their rescue. But their means were poor, an\
they could share was not enough to clothe, shelter, and feed the stunn\
of Ramoroke. The local district administration of nearby Qacha's Nek or\
on-the-spot relief operation, and two blankets per person were provided b\
Cross to keep out the penetrating chill of the Southern African summer nigh\

The district coordinator, who is the chief government officer in the lo\
ministration, was quick to see in this desperate situation, the making of a m\
construction and development effort. For some time, he had been striving to \
about some collective awareness of needs in villages throughout his district a\
generate cooperative efforts to improve life, introduce simple but more effic\
farming methods, and generally, to stimulate initiative and progress. His efforts had
been frustrated by the prevailing conservative attachment to things past and, sup-
posedly, proven, the stubborn refusal to change, the fear of the new and of the
unknown. But he had also been defeated by the paralyzing individualism and suspicion that had prevented the development of any form of cooperative work among
villagers dominated by self-interest and lack of motivation. He now sensed that the
cruelly distressed refugees of Ramoroke would instinctively pull together as one,
having nothing left to fall back on, and that they would surely reach out eagerly
and take any proffered help, even if it meant altering radically some long-held
concepts of community life and personal responsibility.

His first rule, from the very beginning, was that they should do everything
themselves, for themselves, however long and painful the organization of this effort
might prove to be. Consequently, as tents were issued, the village chief and his
people were told that local authorities could provide the equipment, but would not
order or organize the method by which they should be distributed, where they
should be set up, and by whom occupied, or how they should be maintained. It
was up to the people themselves to devise their own leadership, structures, discipline. They had to do this to their best advantage and had to find ways to satisfy
everyone fairly.

As the government Food Management Unit rushed in food relief, they were
once again warned that there would be no handouts, no welfare assistance for the
next few weeks or months. They were not only to take responsibility for distribution of foodstuffs but also were to agree among themselves very rapidly on a short
list of community projects which would enlist the support and labour of all, under
a Food for Work program. This, in fact, meant that the reconstruction of their village, and the subtle fabric of social functions and responsibilities that govern community life everywhere would have to be evolved within a general consensus, with
each and everyone contributing his and her share of thinking, feeling, and work,
rather than left at the mercy of personal whim, self-interest or sloth.

And it worked! Under the Food for Work program, they quickly started construction on a road, from Qacha's Nek to their village, which is still in use and

us, bumping and groaning but in a reasonably short time, on our visit
two years later. And as we arrived in the village, we saw a group, made
f women, with shovels and picks, working away on this same road which
g continued on to the next village. This is a very significant development
the past, all materials and goods had to be brought up by horse, mule or
acks of the villagers themselves. As new crops were planted, the villagers,
der a Food for Work program, installed a water system and went on to de-
community vegetable gardens and the beginning of what could become a large
d. Houses were rebuilt and life began again, not where it had been interrupted
e typhoon, but with a new attitude of collective effort and spirit.

The new Ramoroke is a place where people have become aware of the fact
t the prosperity and health of one depends on the progress and work of all.
Disaster has brought them together in a cooperative way, and the local administration wants to take advantage of this to conduct a series of model pilot projects
in small-scale development which will set an example for surrounding villages and
eventually for the whole district. They wish to continue the work already started
and have plans to develop a piggery, orchards for apples and peaches, all of these in
a cooperative way, using the ideas and labour of the whole community.[67]

Why two years after the disaster did this village retain the collaborative ways
which first arose as an emergency community response, during the restoration
phase, following the impact of the typhoon from which everyone in the village had
suffered? The crisis brought on an enduring social change, perhaps because new and
effective rules for village life were proposed by a local government officer who was
sophisticated about community development procedures and the administration of
human services, and the people found the new ways got them what they needed.
They thus learned more effective coping measures than they had used in the past.
Much more was involved than merely "indoctrination," as Barton previously suggested. There was group practice in prosocial behavior in a time of critical need, and
the new ways worked. When mutual concern and reciprocity are found to bring
desired results—with an emotional "plus" of good feelings about one's group and
one's self as a member—the impulse to prosocial behavior apparently can be sustained for years beyond the stressful situation that suddenly brought about the
change.

NOTES

[1] James H. Bryan, "Children's Cooperation and Helping Behavior," in E. Mavis Hethering-
ton, ed., *Review of Child Development Research*, vol. 5 (Chicago: University of Chicago Press,
1975).

[2] Alvin W. Gouldner, "The Norm of Reciprocity in Preliminary Statement," *American
Sociological Review*, 25 (1960), p. 170.

[3] H. R. Schaffer, *The Growth of Sociability* (Harmondsworth, Middlesex, England:
Penguin Books, 1971), p. 172.

[4] Paul Mussen and Nancy Eisenberg-Berg, *Roots of Caring, Sharing, and Helping: the Development of Prosocial Behavior in Children* (San Francisco: Freeman, 1977), pp. 3-4.

[5] J. Philippe Rushton and Richard M. Sorrentino, eds., *Altruism and Helping Behavior: Social, Personality, and Developmental Perspectives* (Hillsdale, New Jersey: Lawrence Erlbaum Associates, 1981).

[6] Anna Freud and Sophie Dann, "An Experiment in Group Upbringing," pp. 127-168 in Ruth Eissler *et al.*, (eds.) *Psychoanalytic Study of the Child*, vol. 6 (New York: International Universities Press, 1951), pp. 133-134.

[7] Charles G. McClintock, Joel M. Moskowitz, and Evie McClintock, "Variations in Preferences for Individualistic, Competitive, and Cooperative Outcomes as a Function of Age, Game Class, and Task in Nursery School Children," *Child Development*, 48 (1977), 1080-85.

[8] Roger W. Peters and E. Paul Torrance, "Dyadic Interaction of Preschool Children and Performance on a Construction Task," *Psychological Reports*, 30 (1972), 747-50.

[9] Alvin W. Gouldner, "The Norm of Reciprocity," p. 171.

[10] Thomas J. Berndt, "Lack of Acceptance of Reciprocity Norms in Preschool Children," *Developmental Psychology*, 15 (1979), 662-63.

[11] Lois Barclay Murphy, *Social Behavior and Child Personality: An Exploratory Study of Some Roots of Sympathy* (New York: Columbia University Press, 1937).

[12] Susan Isaacs, *Social Development in Young Children: A Study of Beginnings* (New York: Harcourt Brace, 1937).

[13] Dorothy Burlingham and Anna Freud, *Infants without Families* (London: George Allen and Unwin, 1944).

[14] Ibid., p. 25.

[15] Lois Barclay Murphy, "Social Behavior and Child Personality," in Roger G. Barker, Jacob S. Kounin, and Herbert F. Wright, eds., *Child Behavior and Development* (New York: McGraw-Hill, 1943), p. 357.

[16] Ibid., p. 351.

[17] Jean Piaget, *Play, Dreams and Imitation in Childhood* (New York: Norton, 1962), pp. 139-40.

[18] George Herbert Mead, *Mind, Self and Society* (Chicago: University of Chicago Press, 1934), pp. 151 and 154.

[19] Piaget, *Play*, p. 140.

[20] Ibid., p. 164.

[21a] Isaacs, *Social Development*, pp. 397 and 11.

[21b] Berta Bornstein, "On Latency," in *Psychoanalytic Study of the Child*, vol. 6 (New York: International Universities Press, 1950), p. 280.

[21c] Ruth Fröyland Nielsen, *Le developpement de la sociabilité chez l'enfant: Étude experimentale* (Neuchatel, Switzerland: Delachaux and Niestle, 1951), p. 158.

[21d] Harry Stack Sullivan, *The Interpersonal Theory of Psychiatry* (New York: Norton, 1953), pp. 245-46.

[21] Henry S. Maas, "Preadolescent Peer Relations and Adult Intimacy," *Psychiatry*, 31 (1968), pp. 161-62.

[22] Anthony G. Miller and Ron Thomas, "Cooperation and Competition among Blackfoot Indian and Urban Canadian Children," *Child Development*, 43 (1972), p. 1109. Quoted with the permission of the Society for Research in Child Development.

[23] Ibid., pp. 1109-10.

[24] Ibid., pp. 1104-05.

[25] Laura Thompson and Alice Josephs, *The Hopi Way* (Chicago: University of Chicago Press, 1947), p. 11.

[26] Ibid., pp. 37-38.

[27] Harry Hoijer, "The Relation of Language to Culture," in Alfred L. Kroeber, ed., *Anthropology Today* (Chicago: University of Chicago Press, 1953), p. 565. Citing Benjamin L. Whorf, *Four Articles on Metalinguistics* (Foreign Service Institute, Department of State, 1949).

[28] Elizabeth A. Sommerlad and W. P. Bellingham, "Cooperation–Competition: A Comparison of Australian, European, and Aboriginal School Children," *Journal of Cross-Cultural Psychology*, 3 (1972), p. 153.

[29] Ariella Shapira and Jacob Lomranz, "Cooperative and Competitive Behavior of Rural Arab Children in Israel," *Journal of Cross-Cultural Psychology*, 3 (1972), 353–59. Quoted with the permission of the Society for Research in Child Development.

[30] Millard C. Madsen and Ariella Shapira, "Cooperative and Competitive Behavior of Urban Afro-American, Anglo-American, Mexican-American, and Mexican Village Children," *Developmental Psychology*, 3 (1970), Table 2, p. 18.

[31] Ibid., p. 20.

[32] George P. Knight and Spencer Kagan, "Development of Prosocial and Competitive Behaviors in Anglo-American and Mexican-American Children," *Child Development*, 48 (1977), 1385–94.

[33] Ariella Shapira and Millard C. Madsen, "Cooperative and Competitive Behavior of Kibbutz and Urban Children in Israel," *Child Development*, 40 (1969), p. 611. Quoted with permission of the Society for Research and Child Development.

[34] Ibid., p. 616.

[35] Ibid., p. 617.

[36] Ibid., p. 610.

[36a] M. E. Spiro, *Children of the Kibbutz* (Cambridge, Mass.: Harvard University Press, 1965).

[36b] A. I. Rabin, *Growing up in the Kibbutz* (New York: Springer, 1965).

[37] S. B. Dreman and Charles W. Greenbaum, "Altruism or Reciprocity: Sharing Behavior in Israeli Kindergarten Children," *Child Development*, 44 (1973), 61–68.

[38] Sommerlad and Bellingham, "Cooperation–Competition," p. 149.

[39] Gerardo Marin, Beatriz Mejia, and Claudia de Oberle, "Cooperation as a Function of Place of Residence in Columbian Children," *Journal of Social Psychology*, 95 (1975), 127–28, p. 128.

[40] Millard C. Madsen, "Cooperative and Competitive Motivation of Children in Three Mexican Subcultures," *Psychological Reports*, 20 (1967), 1307–20.

[41] Charles Korte, "Constraints on Helping Behavior in an Urban Environment," in J. P. Rushton and R. M. Sorrentino, eds., *Altruism*, p. 327.

[42] Ervin Staub, "A Child in Distress: The Influence of Age and Number of Witnesses on Children's Attempt to Help," *Journal of Personality and Social Psychology*, 14 (1970), 130–40; Roger W. Peters and E. Paul Torrance, "Dyadic Interaction."

[43] Bryan, "Children's Cooperation," p. 173.

[44] Millard C. Madsen, "Developmental and Cross-Cultural Differences in the Cooperative and Competitive Behavior of Young Children," *Journal of Cross-Cultural Psychology*, 2 (1971), 365–71, p. 369.

[45] Staub, "Influence of Age." See also, Dal F. Hay, "Cooperative Interactions and Sharing between Very Young Children and their Parents," *Developmental Psychology*, 15 (1979), 647–53.

[46] Spencer Kagan and Millard C. Madsen, "Cooperation and Competition of Mexican, Mexican-American, and Anglo-American Children of 2 Ages under 4 Instructional Sets," *Developmental Psychology*, 5 (1971), 32–39.

[47] B. Rogoff, M. J. Sellers, S. Pirrotta, N. Fox, and S. H. White, "Age of Assignment of Roles and Responsibilities to Children," *Human Development*, 18 (1975), 353–69.

[48] Aletha Huston-Stein, Lynette Friedrich-Coffer, and Elizabeth J. Sussman, "The Relation of Classroom Structure to Social Behavior, Imaginative Play, and Self-regulation of Economically Disadvantaged Children," *Child Development*, 48 (1977), 908–16.

[49] Victoria Steinmetz, "People Need Help but People Take Advantage: The Dilemma of Social Responsibility for Upward Mobile Youth," *Youth and Society*, 7 (1976), 399–438.

[50] Lawrence J. Severy and Keith E. Davis, "Helping Behavior among Normal and Retarded Children," *Child Development*, 42 (1971), 1017–31.

[51] Norman A. Polansky, Mary A. Chalmers, Elizabeth Buttenweiser, and David P. William, "Isolation and the Neglectful Family," *American Journal of Orthopsychiatry,* 49 (1979), 149-52.

[52] Muzafer Sherif and others, *Intergroup Conflict and Cooperation: The Robbers Cave Experiment* (Norman, Oklahoma: University of Oklahoma Book Exchange, 1961).

[53] Margaret Mead, "Foreword," in Mark Zborowski and Elizabeth Herzog, *Life is with People: The Culture of the Shtetl.* (New York: Schocken Books, 1962), p. 16. Copyright 1952 by International Universities Press.

[54] Seán Ó Súilleabháin, *Irish Folk Custom and Belief, Nósanna agus Piseoga na nGael.* (Dublin: Three Candles, 1967), p. 34.

[55] Zborowski and Herzog, *Life is with People,* pp. 193-95.

[56] Marcel Mauss, *The Gift: Forms and Functions of Exchange in Archaic Societies* (London: Routledge and Kegan Paul, 1970), p. 72.

[57] Gouldner, "The Norm of Reciprocity," p. 178.

[58] Jerome D. Frank, "Mental Health in a Fragmented Society: The Shattered Crystal Ball," *American Journal of Orthopsychiatry,* 49 (1979), p. 399.

[59] Zborowski and Herzog, *Life is with People,* p. 193.

[60] Mauss, *The Gift.*

[61] Richard Titmuss, *The Gift Relationship: from Human Blood Supply to Social Policy* (London: George Allen and Unwin, 1970), p. 210.

[61a] A term used by Marcel Mauss to signify "an event which . . .is at once social and religious, magic and economic, utilitarian and sentimental, jural and moral"—and not, for example, merely economic. From Titmuss, *The Gift Relationship,* p. 210.

[62] George W. Baker and Dwight W. Chapman, eds., *Man and Society in Disaster* (New York: Basic Books, 1962).

[63] Excerpts from L. W. Nauta and P. J. van Strien, Chapter IV, "Group-life at Kortgene during the First Few Weeks after the Disaster," *Studies in Holland Flood Disaster 1953, Vol. III* (Amsterdam: Instituut Voor Social Onderzock Van Het Nederlandse Volk, 1955), pp. 40-49. Quoted with permission the Netherlands Universities' Joint Social Research Center.

[64] *Holland Flood Disaster,* III, p. 102.

[65] Gideon Sjoberg, "Disasters and Social Change" in Baker and Chapman, *Disaster,* pp. 373-77. Quoted with permission.

[66] Allen H. Barton, *Communities in Disaster: A Sociological Analysis of Collective Stress Situations* (Garden City, New York: Anchor Books, Doubleday, 1970), p. 305.

[67] Gilles Latour, "Letter from Lesotho," Unitarian Service Committee (USC), Ottawa, Canada, April, 1982, pp. 2-4.

Chapter 6
JOBS, INTIMACY, AND SELF ESTEEM
YOUTH SEARCHING

INTRODUCTION

Youth Develop in Productive Work and Intimate Peer Partnerships

The period of life called youth extends from early or mid-teens through early or mid-twenties, over roughly a ten-year span which may begin somewhat earlier or later. Youth is a peak period for the pursuit of curiosity, especially about one's own relationships with peers and how one can cope in adult roles. In the search and test processes, awareness of one's own body, one's self as a separate being, and one's society's complexities expands.

Two arenas are of particular concern, the worlds of work and of new, intimate personal relationships, especially those with sexual involvements. There is much to be explored and discovered, but the search does not always go easily. For most youth, there are at least occasional failures, and for some youth the failures are extensive and devastating—only dirty jobs if any jobs at all, no lasting or trustworthy friendships, and no sexual connections with more than momentary meaning. The sad consequence may be a cessation of search and hope.

Availability and choice of work—especially work that is more than temporary wage earning—vary regionally and seasonally, as well as between poor and privileged youth. Patterns of friendship and the differences between sexual mating and sexual partnership seem to occur differentially among youth in different segments of society. Some of these differences and similarities are explored in this chapter. They may serve as a base for the development and functioning of human services attending to the optimization of life during youth and the subsequent years that build on the experiences of youth.

In current contexts youth seem quite different from the adolescents of former decades. Then, parents had answers and were committed to certainties, and distrusting or questioning teen-agers rebelled against them. Now uncertainties seem quite pervasive. Despite their rebellion, most adolescents in the past seemed to be successfully socialized by parental criteria, until about the mid-sixties. Since then, youth have been serving as models to some of their elders, some of whom are, like these youth, engaged in a searching style of life.

Moreover, new technologies—in industry, sex, and many other arenas of life—have generated new ways of behaving that people of all ages must learn, as well as new perceptions of time, space, and the whole life course. These new perspectives open life styles to change, especially the life styles of youth. There is a potential freedom in youth, for it just precedes whatever commitments are made to child bearing and rearing, to one's own family life, and to one's neighborhood—a context to which children indirectly, through their parents' protective concerns for them, give added coherence and constraining power.

Youth are of special concern to the human services for many reasons. How one begins work, or whether one is initially unable to find employment, may lastingly influence one's occupational life. In industry and other workplaces, in employment programs that place youth in jobs, there are increasing numbers of counselors

and other psychologists, social workers, and industrial sociologists. Effective vocational services—information giving, planning, training, counseling, job finding, and
job creating, etc.—grow out of society's enlightened labor policies which should
give youth high priority. Among today's apprentices are tomorrow's managers, and
among today's underemployed and out-of-work youth develop some of today's
enterprising thieves and alienated outsiders.

In conjunction with youth's friendships, sexual encounters, and partnerships—or, for some youth, interpersonal failures, loneliness, and suicide attempts—
there are both supportive and remedial human services. Their range extends from
community recreational programs and church-affiliated groups for singles to sexual
counseling, urban street work, and crisis center or suicide prevention services. This
chapter aims to provide perspectives useful to people who work with and on behalf
of youth.

YOUTH ENTER THE LABOR MARKET

Pathways to work vary among societies and subsocieties within complex human
collectivities.

> When I am a man, then I shall be a hunter
> When I am a man, then I shall be a harpooner
> When I am a man, then I shall be a canoe-builder
> When I am a man, then I shall be a carpenter
> When I am a man, then I shall be an artisan
> Oh father! ya ha ha ha[1]

So once spoke young Kwakiutl males, living along the Pacific Coast of British
Columbia. Similar words may have been spoken by young Kwakiutl females. With
such early clarity about life course direction and the future and with a limited range
of occupational choices, there was likely also to be little anticipatory concern
among Kwakiutl youth in their settling on meaningful work. With it came an occupational identity, locating and integrating them in their community. This important
part of youth's double query, "Who am I? Who am I to become?" seems readily
answerable in such a context because Kwakiutl society was then a slowly changing
one, with clear intergenerational continuities. In Margaret Mead's terms, the culture
was "postfigurative"—that is, the young could learn appropriate and applicable behavior primarily from their parents and other elders.[2] In more rapidly changing
worlds, agemates become the instructors of choice, and parents may have to turn to
their children and other youth, as in present-day Western society, to understand
some of what is going on. Children can no longer be apprenticed to their parents'
generation to learn occupations that are radically retooled or becoming extinct.

Still, a continuous pathway from school into full-time work existed for some
youth as late as the 1950s in the French village of Peyrane, as the following quo-

tation makes clear. Note also the vivid description given of the period called youth, through which the transition to work occurs. That period was considered by the people of Peyrane "the happiest years of one's existence."

> For the children who are not sufficiently intelligent or ambitious to go away to school, life suddenly becomes enjoyable and simple after they have reached the age of fourteen. They are no longer children. They are young people, and only two things are expected of the young people of Peyrane: to support themselves and to have a good time. They will have no other obligations until they become sufficiently *sérieux* to settle down and establish a household of their own. The five or ten years between school and marriage are relatively free, free of the harsh discipline of school which the young people have left behind them, free of the family responsibilities they will eventually have thrust upon them. This is the period of life which the people of Peyrane call "the happiest years of one's existence."
>
> How to earn a living is no problem for the average child like Jules Marchal. The day after the Prize Program, which ended his schooling, he went to work on the farm of his father. There was no sudden break between school and work, for Jules had always worked with his father when he was not in school. Now he worked with him all the time, just as he had expected to do when he finished school.[3]

In marked contrast to this idyllic picture of rural France in the 1950s, youth in North America in the 1980s face a very different employment scene. The most recent U.S. federal information (for 1981) is that while total unemployment is 8.2 percent of the work force, 22.4 of sixteen to nineteen year olds and 24 percent of twenty to twenty-four year olds wanting work cannot find jobs. Among just white youth, about 17 percent are out of work, but among minority youth—mostly blacks and Hispanics—the unemployment rate is over 35 percent or twice the rate for white youth. Though figures fluctuate somewhat seasonally and otherwise, there is long-standing and constant evidence that youth is heavily overrepresented among those available members of the labor force who have no work. What happens to young people who have left school but cannot find work is the focus of the second part of this segment of Chapter Six. First, I shall discuss the situations of the young who do find jobs and some special components of workplaces which make initiation into the work force a more or less involving experience.

Beginning Jobs and Workplaces

Youth's approach to work follows a variety of routes, depending in large measure on the socioeconomic level of the family and neighborhood in which youth have grown up. For example, on how working-class youth obtain working-class jobs, Paul E. Willis observes:

> On its side, the marketplace is highly selective in the access to jobs it affords the youth of different social groups. The young who have spent their school years in battle with educational authorities and a curriculum they felt irrele-

vant to their lives now face a world which has only unskilled jobs—if any jobs at all—to offer them.[4]

In addition, at least some decades ago, working-class youth had economic obligations to their parents; the expectation that they contribute to the family income did not change until the youth were themselves married.[5]

The composite picture of young workers and their workplaces presented in this section derives from studies in several publications,[6] credited by footnotes in the following text only when direct quotations are made. My plan is to sketch the pathways followed by present-day youth into the labor market and to provide a set of lenses for examining and comparing youth's workplaces and their human components.

Most young people's crossing into the world of paid work occurs gradually, almost imperceptibly, through small jobs, usually neighborhood-based—for example, babysitting, running errands, backyard work, newspaper delivering, or helping out in owner-managed local stores where such still exist. Whether pressed by economic need or wanting primarily to establish some independence from family subsidies, the quite young are often eager to make some pocket money. They do so mostly by serving familiar or nearby people for a minimum compensation.

Some youth, especially those in poorer or economically marginal families, but also increasingly youth in middle income homes, move into more regular part-time employment, concurrent with school but after classes, weekends, or during school holidays. These are part- or full-time jobs or short-term jobs during the summers, in public eating places or other workplaces where there is frequent turnover of unskilled employees. Such seasonal, or sporadic, work has a tentative quality to it—a kind of reciprocal trying out by employers and youthful employees, an exploration with no long-term commitments or serious intentions. For employers, youth cost only a minimum wage; for youth, self-testing and learning to accommodate to new time schedules and other job requirements are part of the small compensation in these noncareer jobs. Some unskilled youth, often after having suffered through years of low achievement at school, continue in a series of such jobs well into their later adult years. This is the only kind of work they can get or feel comfortable doing.

When most youth leave school, serious full-time job seeking begins. Those without job-finding connections in their own personal networks follow the "want ads" and go on interviews. This is likely to be a period of great tension. There are the pressures of self-discipline and self-evaluation that previous school days, even at their worst, rarely occasioned. In bad times of low employment, hunting for work may continue for a long and anxious stretch, broken only by odd jobs or short-term relief jobs. To understand the experience of those who do locate and enter a first job with prospects of continuity, one must consider simultaneously the relevant orientations and expectations of youth, as well as what workplaces offer by way of a reception for their new workers. In addition, specific jobs within workplaces differ on dimensions that deserve review, both generally and in regard to the qualifications and hopes of the individuals starting work in these jobs.

In Chapter Two of this book, I discussed human variability and three related societal dimensions: options, access, and controls. These three dimensions are equally relevant to workplaces, the range of jobs youth enter, and youth's job satisfactions.

Options mean choices—what one study of youth at work calls "variety" and "freedom" on the job.[7] A survey of youth's desired job characteristics tapped the options idea through the statement, "You don't have to do the same thing all the time."[8] Young workers are "bothered" by the lack of variety or options on their jobs.[9] In a survey of youth's work attitudes, Simon found:

> Supervisors who appeared to make a positive effort to allocate interesting or varied jobs were well thought of, even if they could not always do so. This was very much more important for apprentices . . . , who were keen to gain a varied experience . . . Operatives, in general, accepted that they would be doing one job or working one machine. Those supervisors who made little effort to vary work contributed to ratings of dissatisfaction with the job as a whole . . .[10]

Discussing "the social character of young workers today" by contrast with their seniors, Sheppard sees "a greater emphasis among young workers to do interesting and enjoyable work" and improve the quality of their work ("51% stress quality of work") more than improving their pay ("38% cite more pay")—all as part of their "overall rating of the need to make work more interesting."[11]

Interest and variety are typically found in professional work or in the work of craftsmen, who are involved in the design, execution, and completion of a piece of pottery or another handmade object. For interest and variety to be found in entry level jobs of the kind most youth are likely to be employed in, the human factor in the workplace must be balanced against the need for efficient production. Job satisfaction must be valued or, perhaps, found to covary with the turning out of a better product. In settings where workers feel committed to a workplace, they may share chores by rotating from job to job to provide some variety for all co-workers. Generally, the most routine jobs can be kept to a minimum or combined with other kinds of work so that what is most tedious is time-limited for any one worker. There are many ways to structure a job for greater variety.

Access on jobs has multiple referents, but perhaps its clearest is the access to advancement young workers have as their skills increase. In the survey data David Gottlieb draws on, of over 4,000 low income high-school-aged youth in three different Eastern U.S. cities, about 40 percent of the respondents being black youth, 90 percent wanted jobs in which "If you work hard, you can get ahead."[12]

Career advancement also provides, of course, another kind of option or variety. In Sheppard's study of young as compared with older workers, youth are more concerned "about promotion opportunities and their chances to 'get ahead' in their current jobs" and tend to be "responsive to any educational or training opportunities that might be offered which would get them a better job."[13] The young are also readier to change jobs, being less committed to an organization than their elders. Opportunities for promotion are likely to keep young workers in a given workplace.

The exercise of controls at work includes opportunities for workers to participate in some of the decision making. In Gottlieb's large survey of poor urban youth, "opportunity to use own ideas" was desired by 70 to 74 percent of black youth and by 66 to 70 percent of white youth.[14] Sheppard reports, "Contrary to many popular images about the new, young workers, our interviews draw a portrait of them as feeling their jobs offer them little chance to exert a sense of responsibility" and thus "a large majority of these young workers rate their jobs as having little importance."[15]

In smaller work units than those that occupy the employees in Shepherd's study, such as the "human-scale technologies" and miniplants about which E. F. Schumacher writes, there are opportunities for involved and responsible worker performance.[16] Anthropologist Sandra Wallman sums up the issue of worker responsibility on the job with the following observation: "Degrees of alienation are greatest where the worker has negligible control over the value and the disposition of his product, least where he initiates the work effort, organizes time, place, person—all the elements of the work process, and can identify with the product and the values of the product."[17] Between these extremes lies a broad stretch of alternative arrangements employable in different workplaces that decentralize authority so that workers may experience some degree of responsibility for the goods they make or the services they provide.

In addition to options, access, and controls, the interpersonal component of jobs is important. "In some occupations the most crucial relations are those with one's fellow-workers. It is they who can do most to make life sweet or sour," writes Everett C. Hughes in his early essays on the sociology of work and occupations, adding that the interpersonal aspect of work may include "the consumers of one's work or services." He cites as definable roles that bring people together "the janitor and the tenant" or "the musician and the listener," to which a long list of paired roles, such as sales person–customer or worker–foreman, could be appended.[18] For some youth, contact with people is more important than a job's pay.

Young workers entering a first job depend heavily, in many ways, on the other people in their new workplace. One British survey of youth who had just made the transition from school to work contributes the following findings. In reply to the question, "Thinking back before you started work, what were you looking forward to?" about a quarter of the respondents—twice as many young women as young men—said "interest in meeting new people," and among the major worries was "getting on with people at work."[19] High among the items given in response to queries about what people should be told when they first come to work is "comments about the people at work," and when asked "What stands out about the first days at work in this job?" memories of "the kindness and helpfulness of the people at work" were reported by 31 percent of all females and 20 percent of all males as of the time they first became full-time workers.[20] As another researcher remarks, ". . . the period immediately following school-leaving is a particularly crucial time. The school situation does provide some kind of supportive structure, and often no adequate replacement is available to the school-leaver on entering the work environment."[21] Human service workers, interested in facilitating the transition to a work setting for newcomers, should apparently be sure that the orientation to the job includes introductions to experienced workers who participate in the initiation and welcoming of incoming youth.

While employment still seems an important part of life, it may not have the same intense personal significance for today's youth as it once had. A few decades ago, Everett Hughes referred to "work" as "one of the more important parts of . . . social identify." He discussed people's developing "pretensions to give their work, and consequently themselves, value in the eyes of each other and outsiders" by giving fancy titles to relatively menial jobs or "dirty work" because "an occupation carries with it a self-conception."[22] But youthful workers of the eighties may be less committed to *an* occupation, less likely than some of their parents to be workaholics, and more likely to have a diversity of extra-work involvements to which they may have equally little permanent attachment. In a very complex and constantly changing world, which television beams into children's and young people's expanding lives, choices seem infinite. For such reasons, the Kwakiutl boy's chant, quoted earlier in this chapter, "When I am a man, then I shall be a hunter . . ." is a voice not only out of another culture but also another era. The uncertainties of youth's early occupational choices is matched by the tentativeness of many occupations themselves. And, concurrently, the most appropriate and serviceable self, in such transient times as the present, may be a "protean" or constantly adapting self-process, as psychiatrist Robert Jay Lifton proposes.[23] The proposition by Erik Erikson that "identity" formation, as a major task of adolescence, includes "beginnings of a work identity" and "sense of workmanship" seems now a historically and culturally rooted view, more relevant to the first half or two thirds of this century than to the present.[24]

A first full-time job can be a vital experience for youth. It involves, as I said before, self-evaluations and self-discipline. Given the ephemeral nature of many early jobs, however, the linkage between at least entry level jobs and the self is likely to be weaker than was true for the stably occupied young apprentice of former times. Commenting about the under-thirty workers he surveyed in the 1970s, Sheppard says, " . . . we cannot ignore the contention that young workers of today play it 'loose,' and, in the job world, this means a lower identity of self with a particular occupation."[25]

Advocates speaking on behalf of youth and spokesmen for the humanizing of work share a common language. Simplifying what he had earlier elaborated as part of "Buddhist economics," E. F. Schumacher proposes as "the three purposes of human work":

> First, to provide necessary and useful goods and services. Second, to enable every one of us to use and thereby perfect our gifts like good stewards. Third, to do so in service to, and in cooperation with, others, so as to liberate ourselves from our inborn egocentricity.[26]

Through employment, which has a collaborative component to it, youth may develop their own capacities, and, at the same time, integrate themselves with others in the societies for which the "necessary and useful goods and services" are being provided in part through their own work.

One statement of policy on youth begins as follows:

> If youth are to be valued, they must be *of* the society—participants, not recipients. That is the crux of any theory valuing youth. . . . Young people must be allowed and encouraged to produce things, perform services, and create art forms . . . Perhaps of equal importance, these activities must have a logical continuation; that is, there must be "career" possibilities in youth commitments and activities. . . . A theory that values youth must bring together individual needs and societal needs."[27]

As the first of the identified individual needs, "Young people need *security*. As society finds fewer roles for youth, youth problems will increase. Youth cannot be financially secure if they cannot find work."[28]

Youth without Work

Concern about finding work is top priority among youth. In a region where there are mostly unskilled jobs and a high level of unemployment, one survey of school leavers concludes that the young men are "despairing" and the young women "only slightly less so."[29] How do youth manage without money or an income? What are the sources of their economic dependencies, and how do they feel about and cope with these supports? For how long can they continue to be economically dependent? How does a young person explain to others in a personal network how it is that he or she is jobless? Is it easiest to quiet one's own self-doubts by moving into a peer group in which joblessness is the norm? And what then? How are their days structured without prescribed hours of work or other employment obligations? The young person who is attached to others is likely also to be a curious being, with a range of competencies. How and where are these capacities put to work? If a sense of incompetence is fostered by an inability to find work, what may youth do to prove that they are not incompetent, useless, helpless? How are youth's relationships in a family and in a neighborhood affected by joblessness? I shall not offer speculative answers to these questions in this section; I have been unable to find adequate studies of these problems. I can, however, provide some descriptive details suggesting the scope of the problem, who is most extensively affected, and a few of the effects. I shall also review some of the underlying conditions for youth unemployment, which offer keys to what should be done to change the situation.

There are many reasons to view youth unemployment as a major social problem. Concern about it does not signify merely an overzealous commitment to the work ethic, which presumes that only hard toiling people are worthy. There are other and perhaps related moralities, more social than individual in their orientations and prejudices. They conceive of work not only as an economic means of providing for one's own food, shelter, and other provisions but also as a desirable integrative or linking force between working people and other aspects of their society. To be unemployed is, in many realms, to be out of touch. There is also the contributory aspect of work; in light of the norm of reciprocity, discussed in Chapter Five, competent people who are fed and sheltered through the labors of others owe those others some, at least indirect, returns through their own efforts. Whether in a money or a barter economy, young people need something of value to exchange. Finally, from a personal developmental perspective, there is evidence that unemployment during youth affects later occupational chances and the pathways that adult careers follow. There are some questions among experts in this field about the long-term effects of unemployment in youth, but I shall shortly present relevant conclusions of at least one group of economists. First, however, what is the picture of youth unemployment in the U.S.A.?—not too different, incidentally, from the picture elsewhere in the industrialized and nonsocialist parts of the world.

All the United States' facts on unemployment suggest that youth are by far overrepresented among the unemployed, and that those most often without jobs are minority group members living in families with the lowest incomes and housed in the poverty neighborhoods of inner cities. National data on age groups, race, and ethnicity in the United States, as of the late 1970s, tell us "Nearly one-half of all unemployed persons in the United States today are between the ages of 16 and 24, even though that age group accounts for only one-fourth of the total labor force" and "unemployment rates for nonwhite youths . . . are more than double those for white youths" and "The unemployment rate for Spanish-origin youths tends to be higher than that for all youths but much lower than the rate for black youths." Further, among the ranks of Hispanic youth, using data for October 1976, "the unemployment rate for Puerto Rican youths tends to be quite close to that for black youths" but "the unemployment rate for Mexican–American youths is much closer to the average for all youths."[30]

I shall return later in this section to a few of the social conditions underlying these inequities, but since the transition from school to work is a major issue in this chapter, I begin here with how prior schooling is associated with young people's employment. The educational backgrounds of youth aged sixteen to twenty-four are related to their chances of being *un*employed as follows:

Nonwhite college graduates	1 in 14
College graduates	1 in 14
High school graduates (no college)	1 in 8
Nonwhite high school graduates (no college)	1 in 4
School dropouts	1 in 4
Nonwhite school dropouts	1 in 3

These Congressional Budget Office computations[31] from federal agency data give a depressing picture of especially black youth's employment chances. Starting from the bottom of the list, note first that the nonwhite dropouts are in the least advantageous position. Moving up, note secondly that nonwhite high school graduates seem no better off in regard to employment during their youth—that is, from sixteen to twenty-four years of age—than all youth who have dropped out of school. Both groups suffer a one in four chance of unemployment. This is not to say that later in their adult lives there may not be employment advantages for blacks who complete high school, but in youth graduation does not improve their employment chances. Finally, note that college graduation does equalize the chances of employment for nonwhites and other college graduates. At this level, education does seem to have practical payoffs, but one ought not consider college graduation alone the cause for employment benefits because most of the nonwhite youth who are able to make it through college probably have other things going for them too. With the rare exception of the unusually talented and very highly motivated full scholarship students, most young black men and women who finish a four-year college program must, like their white classmates, have part-time jobs or other economic resources, drawn possibly from their relatively advantaged families or somewhere else in their social networks. Although a very important factor in occupational success, education—and changes in educational policies—must be combined with other programs if the high rate of youth's unemployment is to be reduced, as discussed later.

What are some effects of unemployment among youth? One group of economists at the University of Utah, in a publication of the W. E. Upjohn Institute for Employment Research in Michigan, present some impressive data and conclusions. Drawing on longitudinal studies, covering seven years and following the same persons over time (in 1968, 1972, and 1975), they report that "being without a job while out of school seems to have an adverse effect on subsequent earnings." More specifically

> The impact is more pronounced when the experience occurs between the ages of 20 and 24, but teenage labor force status is also related to subsequent wage and salary earnings. Whether for young men or young women, black or white, time spent out of school and out of the labor force represents a loss of experience that is associated with a clear earnings disadvantage later on . . . The differences by race and sex are also pronounced. Among young men, out-of-school black youth are more seriously affected by adverse early labor market experiences. Among young women, however, no differences by race are apparent. Young women, black and white, however, are more seriously affected by early labor market experiences than young men. The findings presented here contradict the thesis that unemployment is a phase through which every youth passes with no long term adverse consequences. Clearly, it is never possible to control for all differences in personal characteristics, background, and experience. Nonetheless, the fact that early labor market status continues to be related to subsequent earnings after adjusting for those factors which are consistently found related to labor market experiences does provide some strong evidence of long term effects.[32]

Longitudinal data give one a sense of pathway and suggest direction into the future, always somewhat modifiable, but also always starting from a given position in the past. The idea of continuity in work career is supported by the finding: "By the time these cohorts [that is, all persons studied] of young men and young women have reached the ages of 23 to 26, the employment patterns reflect fairly consistently those observed among adult workers. There will continue to be some movement out of unskilled and semiskilled jobs into the professions and other positions of greater responsibility, but as a group, adult work patterns are becoming well defined. It is at this point that the transition into primary jobs is under way. The characteristics of these jobs are well known. They tend to be stable and well paid, with opportunities for future growth and advancement." Given this pattern for career success, one can understand its obverse among the youthful unemployed: "For the young, this loss of valuable work experience results in relative disadvantage later on."[33]

In addition to education and early work experience itself, there are many other conditions related to unemployment among youth. There is the changing nature of work itself and the poor fit that inexperienced youth can make with that world. For example, some of the repetitive jobs which decades ago provided youth with an entry into the occupational arena are now automated and no longer available. Youth, and especially teenagers, have long been given lowest preference as workers, below the increasing numbers of older women now in the labor market. And women are second choice to men of the same age except when they will work for less pay! As the last to be chosen, youth suffer a fluctuating employment rate as the labor market draws on or exhausts other segments of the population.

The mobility of both youth and workplaces is still another issue. The flight of young people from rural areas and mechanized farms to urban centers is being matched by the flight of factories and their semiskilled jobs from central urban centers, where black youth, in particular, seek employment. Also, the pathway from leaving school to full-time work reveals the disjunctions between educational and even vocational training, and the changing nature of the jobs themselves. Such disjunction reflects the more general and widespread chasm between adults and the young in North American society. Children and adolescents are kept from meaningful participation in so many aspects of their society—not only economic, but also political and social, as though youth threatened their elders, their power, their jobs.

There is, though, some growing interest in youth's social integration.[34] In some European nations, for example, teenagers spend part of their school days visiting workplaces in which they try their hands at entry level jobs. In such programs, youth's growing familiarization with work in the process of production is found, in a series of surveys, to be a most important orientation not only to employment, but also to broader social activities.[35]

What explains the high unemployment rates among minority group youth? Access-denying barriers keep black and Hispanic youth, especially, out of jobs. The barriers include racial prejudice and discrimination; the separateness of racially defined ghettos and similar living places with their locally limited networks and communication channels, and their sometimes less adequate educational programs; and the rapid population growth and youth-heavy distribution of the populations, which increase the competition for available jobs.[36] All the conditions that contribute to the high unemployment of minority youth must be considered when corrective programs are being planned. But the basic problem remains a macro-societal, structural one. In view of the material lacks and deficits of people all around the world–the illclothed, inadequately nourished, and indecently housed–it would seem that greater productivity and more producers or workers are required. In addition, so many human services are insufficiently staffed, from infant health care and early education programs for the very young to social supports for the fragile elderly who want to continue living in their home neighborhoods and might be able to do so with a modicum of the kinds of service youth could provide so easily. On the one hand are youth wanting employment, and on the other are societies in urgent need of workers. But the issue of auspices for job creation and the question of who pays for newly created jobs–the public sector or the private?–hang in mid-air while youth remain out of work.

What happens then when youth are unemployed? In time, personal demoralization and alienation from an unresponsive society seem inevitable, coupled with personal self-doubts and lowered self-esteem that may give way to a consuming and all-pervasive anger. Unemployment keeps youth a "they" in the "we" world of working and societally integrated adults. "They" have both less public social regard and less social power than "we." "They" have fewer social options, much less access not only to jobs but also to the goods of society, and clearly less control of their own lives. As a consequence, some young people who cannot find legitimate ways of earning money slide into illegal work. One extensive review of the literature on youth unemployment, delinquency, and crime concludes that youthful crime is directly attributable to lack of legitimate work.[37] Although one may understand why unemployed youth might resort to crime nowhere is it considered the equivalent of regular employment, even in high-crime neighborhoods.

In ghettos, as elsewhere, a steady job is likely to confer upon the employed the high regard of peers and thus feed the worker's self-esteem. Although there may be occasional, self-defensive sneering at the Joe who has to work for a living, the advantages of a steady income are recognized. For example, in Southside Chicago, the corner pub provides an important meeting place for socializing among those whom Elijah Anderson calls "the regulars," "wineheads," and "hoodlums." People who frequent "a Place on the Corner" include a group of petty criminals and men with low-level jobs, and here the status rating gives top ranking to the regularly employed who have a stake in the established system.[38]

The relations between legitimate youth unemployment and illegal work in which some youth engage are predictable. In W. Gordon West's year-long participant observational study of forty "lower-class males" who were "serious thieves" between the ages of fifteen and twenty-three, finding a job or the commitment to a sexual partner were associated with quitting their illegal activities:

> Twenty-one of my interviewees "went straight" by the summer of 1973. Most became involved with a woman: this required that they support their partner and any children and necessitated a larger income than serious theft provides. Most have sought and obtained better jobs, partly from having gained more experience, being older, and having contacts pay off. A few are on welfare or

job-training programs which provide at least partial support. Only 3 have re-formed without a spouse or good job.[39]

Such findings give another side to the linkage between employment and the social integration of youth.

The background conditions of the forty youth in West's study blend imperceptibly into the social background conditions of youth who run the highest risk of joblessness. They are described as growing up in lower- or working-class, urban, high density neighborhoods, where the families tend to be large, frequently female-headed, and with a majority of household heads themselves out of work. Of the forty youth, average schooling was only 8.4 years; almost all were dropouts from nonacademic school programs. Thirty-five of the forty had juvenile records. Their prior work histories are most relevant, and I quote:

> The thieves who had left school had spent an average of 40–45% of their time unemployed by the time of the interviews, and 91% of them were unemployed at least 20% of this time. The jobs they obtained were low-paying . . . and low status menial ones, such as printers' helpers, delivery-boys, etc. They had difficulty maintaining employment, averaging 7.5 months per first job, and 3.9 jobs in the average time of 3 years between school-leaving and interviewing. In sum, they all had economic problems.[40]

One must, of course, add, as does sociologist West, "Not all persons who come from the same background as the sample become thieves."[41] Nor is it my intent to suggest that even most unemployed youth turn to thieving. But unemployed youth inevitably become restless, and unrest may take on many forms. I have not yet addressed the issue of the growing number of college graduates and more highly educated youth who are having difficulties in a nonexpanding economy in finding education-related jobs or any jobs at all. The need for job creation, specifically for youth, and other societal efforts is apparent.

Much of what is needed is implicit in the prior discussion of what underlies youth unemployment and the special conditions of minority youth. Both the public and private sectors of society, in coordinated fashion, must generate the kinds of jobs that youth can do. They should be jobs that offer a future. In addition, school programs can bring youth closer and in more continually involving ways to the worlds of work. Some of the basic problems involve urban decay and a totally demoralizing way of life. Inner city social redevelopment planning and programs should not only improve the chances for youth employment, but also provide jobs for youth.

For human service workers, an understanding of the strains and plights of the young entering the full-time labor market after their formal schooling is over should generate an array of supportive services. These include ongoing group meetings of youth during this transitional period which focus on how to find work, how to make it through the first weeks of a new job, how to use one's time constructively while awaiting employment, how to cope with family and other adult reactions to unemployment, how to help advocates of full employment for youth, how to exert pressure on those able to create jobs, how to present a visibly united front of youth wanting work, and, generally, how to exercise one's competencies collaboratively on an environment which must be made more responsive to a major human need.

FROM PEER GROUP TO
PARTNERSHIP—OR LONELINESS

Having found unequal access to jobs for youth in different social strata, I propose also that intimate relationships in which sexual partners share concerns for one another's happiness and well-being are an option more readily available in some youth groups in our society than in others. When equality between the sexes is not valued, genuine partnerships and intimacy are less likely. When intimate relationships are absent, loneliness—even in the midst of a group of peers—may be experienced.

The sections that follow explore how peer group orientations to sex and intimacy lead to reciprocity between sexual partners who share some commitment to each other, or, instead, to a series of sexual matings. Sometimes, in the latter situation, male dominance and social pressures for repeated conquests are overriding orientations precluding intimacy. The "other" is an object, not a person.

Secondly, thoughts about loneliness and its concomitant, a devalued self, are presented. This section also touches upon the self's dependence during youth on peer relations and friendships. The ultimate in protracted loneliness, coupled with feelings of gross inadequacy and unlovability, is depression, and, as in the report on sixteen-year-old "Retep Reklaw" in the final section of this chapter, suicide. The past few decades' increase in the rate of suicides among youth—to say nothing of the many times greater rate of unsuccessful suicide attempts—make this another important facet of the youth scene. Youth's suicides reflect on the larger troubled society in which youth's ideals, and movements for world peace, ecological conservation, and related goals seem so remote from the way world affairs are moving. In an unresponsive environment, the self suffers, and without the mutual supports of an intimate relationship, loneliness becomes almost inevitable, and, at its worst, unbearable.

The Interplay of Work and Intimate
Relationships

Before I turn from youth's jobs to youth's sexual and loving relationships or their absence, however, reciprocal connections between these two arenas of love and work warrant some attention. Both work careers and shared intimate relations visibly begin during the period called youth. The interplay between the two, for most individuals, is more complex than the following introductory sketch can suggest. It is important, however, for counselors to realize that their efforts to deal only with problems of sexuality or interpersonal closeness may become nonpro-

ductive—or more involved than they had expected—because of the extensive interaction of love and work in people's, especially young people's, lives. Since earliest
searching for both goes on simultaneously in youth, successes or failures in one
arena inevitably affect what happens in the other.

The power of a commitment to a sexual partner can regularize youth's occupational life, as suggested by West's previously cited evidence of how thieves "went
straight" when they married.[42] The influence of intimate relationships on youth's
work performance and careers—and vice versa, the effect of work on youth's intimate relationships—extends far, of course, beyond West's evidence. For example,
emotional ties may geographically limit where youth look or train for work, what
hours are given to work, what kinds of personal alliances are made at work, and
how totally involved in a job a young worker becomes.

The linking of intimate relationships to participation in the labor market
is generalized by Ann Swidler in a provocative essay on changing ideas about love
in the U.S.A. She writes

> One of the great justifications for conformity to the world of work, for ac-
> ceptance of social limitations, for "settling down" and "toeing the line" is
> love. Women are told that washing socks, cooking, and cleaning are morally
> fulfilling because they express love. Men feel that going off to work every
> day is meaningful because it supports the wives and children they love. Love
> elevates and transforms the mundane activities of life, but in doing so it
> also binds people to that life.[43]

This is part of the binding, or commitment, that is alien especially to many contemporary youth and that influences and makes conflictful their earliest searching
for intimate relationships and even their first sexual encounters—how to get close
without getting stuck. It is, in a sense, a supportive social context for the psychological process of ambivalence, in which both attraction, or love, and repulsion, or
hate, invade the same relationship. Work's influences on partners vary, moreover
lifelong. For example, later in life when couples have connected with more or less a
sense of permanence, their connection may be weakened by the demands—or
attractions—of a job. Synchronization and equilibration between work investments
and interpersonal commitments can be very difficult in the modern, mobile world.
The balancing act increases in complexity with marriage and the birth of children,
especially as women also engage in jobs at all levels of skill, responsibility, and power. Mates of both sexes are expected to work overtime or go away to training sessions and meetings. The complications for dual career or two-income couples in
professional and managerial jobs as well as for spouses in blue collar vocations are
manifold.[44]

The problem for intimate relationships is that work may impinge on couples'
relationships more extensively than couples' relationships impose on work. Adjustments are made in couples' expectations of one another rather than in the market
place's requirements for the job. The degree of partners' conflicts today tends to

vary with the extent of the male's adaptability to the female's changing status and diminishing responsibilities at home. By contrast, in the decades ahead, in demo-cratic, postindustrial societies, adjustments should more often be made in work roles and other aspects of the occupational arena to accommodate more adequately the needs of people in their intimate relationships and responsibilities rather than the reverse. There should, for example, be more part-time and shared jobs, synchro-nized with couples' child-rearing schedules. Generally, we should expect a more equitable articulation of the needs of people in their living places and in their work-places.

But such ideas advance our story beyond the life-span period of youth. The interplay of youth's search for meaningful work and for significant intimate re-lationships is itself in an arena of complex associations, in which changes of one kind may bring about changes of another kind. For example, working youth and unemployed youth have more or less money to spend on or share with sexual partners. What they can do together, where they can go together, and even the na-ture of their sexual experiences are influenced more or less directly by their po-sitions in—or absence from—the world of work. In Michael Schofield's large-scale study of the sexual behavior of over 1,800 English fifteen-through-nineteen-year-olds, he reports:

> The teenagers were asked how much was in their pay packet last week. . . . There is an association between the level of sex activity and the weekly wages for boys ($p = 0.01$) and for girls ($p = 0.02$). A special effort was made during the interview to get an estimate of the amount of money each individual had left to spend. . . . There is a very strong association between spending money and the level of sex activity. Boys who have a lot of money to spend are much more likely to be sexually experienced ($p = 0.001$); and this is also true of girls ($p = 0.02$).[45]

Similarly, earnings, the nature of one's employment, and the kind of living place one resides in are all interrelated. Income determines where one can afford to live, and the social networks in one's living place often steer one to certain jobs or kinds of job. These same social networks, and especially one's peers and closest friends, orient young people to sex as part of the experience of youth's relation-ships with agemates. Attachments within peer groups often include earliest mates and partners. Attitudes toward others—for example, seeing others as persons rather than objects—range widely across the spectrum of youth groups. And the extent to which loneliness within a peer society is expected, tolerated, or actively reduced by concerned friends varies significantly from group to group. Different groups, also depending on their cultural values and idiosyncratic histories as well as societal con-texts, order priorities regarding private behavior in intimate relationships and public performance in the labor market in quite different but essentially interrelated ways. Youth service workers should be informed about these priorities for the young peo-ple whose job and relationship problems their services address, however obliquely.

Orientations to Sex and Intimacy

Basic to the structure and mores of any society are norms for relationships between the sexes. Through popular mythologies and historical records, the diverse and changing distributions of power and respect between females and males have been portrayed and thus implicitly defined and redefined. Central to these narratives has been the theme of domination versus shared power.

Domination reduces sexual relationships to mating. The "other" person is seen as object—more or less attractive, but still merely an object, mortar or pestle, vessel or phallus. A sharing orientation promotes partnerships in intimate relationships of which sex is an important part. In relationships in which partnership is valued, giving pleasure is as important as one's own enjoyment, and concern for one's partner may at times reduce one's own immediate satisfactions, constraints exercised in the interests of the "other's" welfare.

In their earliest explorations of sex, youth approach each other with expectations learned in their families and their living places, and most typically and recently among their youthful, same-sexed peers. So oriented, sexual overtures are likely to be made to other locals; "propinquity"—or living close by—is repeatedly and not surprisingly found to be a precondition for early attractions and adventures.[46] School- or classmates become young teenagers' earliest "crushes."

Neighborhoods and peer groups in which male dominance, or machismo, overrides an appreciation of mutuality emphasize the contest or conquest aspect of the first adolescent sexual encounters. When the female is reduced to object, such initial explorations are likely to be reduced to power trips for the boys. Such mating, rather than partnership, fulfills some of the young teenager's needs, psychological as well as biological. The self-centeredness of a young and uncertain self may find such mating "ego-syntonic"—that is, befitting and satisfying a youthful person's expectations and psychic needs. The experience, if biologically gratifying, may be self-aggrandizing. But if among the boy's psychological quests is a simultaneous search for genuine closeness in a cross-sex relationship, to the extent that the girl is reduced to object, to that same extent the boy's sense of incompleteness or loneliness is likely to prevail. Note that while these processes have been described in a social context of male dominance, the same consequences appear for girls who reduce their mates to objects.

Objectification of the "other" and loneliness go hand in hand. There is no person of any depth perceived in the "other." While the ultimate in objectification occurs during periods of serious emotional disturbance such as depression and is sometimes a precondition for suicide, objectification is basically a learned orientation, fostered in social groups whose members perceive all nonmembers or "they's" as nonpersons or objects. Powerfully cohesive one-sexed groups of early adolescents may thus objectify nonmembers or members of the other sex.

Within neighborhoods where machismo is strongly valued, for the girls to be integrated in their own peer groups—to be "in" with their agemates—alliance with a boy may be essential. As the price for such an alliance, sexual favors are likely to be equally essential. Such archaic language seems appropriate to describe early teen-age traditional rites, admitting participants into what was once called "adult sexuality," and, at the same time, into full-fledged membership and closeness, not with their sexual mates but with their same-sexed agemates.

The crucial part played by peer groups in such initiation only begins with the stipulation of sexual expectations and, through its network alliances and extensions, the provision of a mate. Once chosen, the girl is evaluated by the boy's peers, and the boy by the girl's peers. Such evaluation contributes to either the continuation or rupturing of the sexual relationship.[47] Only rarely may the strength of the new relationship overpower and survive the disapproval of peers. Nor is such an early relationship likely to remain a secret one for boys who belong to boys' groups or girls who belong to girls' groups. Part of the private pleasure is the public review of the experience, if only with a same-sexed confidant in the group. Since twosomes who have been together are almost always seen together, these rare participants who may want to remain private will be exposed by gossip sooner or later. For much early sexual pleasure is verbal, visual, and vicarious—both among same-sex peers talking separately with one or the other of a sexually linked twosome, or among peers who may guess (or fantasize) about a relationship.

Out of such peer discussions, orientations to sexual behavior and sexual relationships are formed. The findings in Ira Reiss's study of premarital sexual permissiveness are not surprising. In his student sample of over 800 males and females, both whites and blacks, he found that ". . . 89 percent of the respondents saw themselves as similar in standards of sexual permissiveness to their very close friends. This is considerably higher than the 63 percent who saw themselves as similar to their mothers and the 77 percent who saw themselves as similar to their peers, and is further evidence for the position that peers, and close friends in particular, are crucial in shaping the individual's sexual standards."[48] More recently, Joseph Hornick's study, an investigation of over 800 youth, also indicates the importance of peers in determining individuals' sexual attitudes and behavior.[49] And Ulf Hannerz concludes his qualitative study of the roots of black manhood:

> Groups of one's friends give some stability and social sanction to the meanings that streetcorner men attach to their experiences—meanings that may themselves have been learned in the same or preceding peer groups. They, probably more than families, are information storage units for the ghetto-specific male role. At the same time, they are self-perpetuating because they provide the most satisfactory contexts for legitimizing the realities involved.[50]

In the English study of teen-agers, Schofield found a significant association between level of sexual behavior and group membership. That is, for both boys and girls, those who were group members were also much more likely to have had sexual intercourse, while the inexperienced of both genders were "less likely to go round in groups." Moreover, teen-agers who were "in mixed groups were most likely to be sexually experienced," an especially important context for the girls, since those girls who remained in single-gender groups were less often sexually involved with boys.

Such findings are not evidence only of opportunity or of access but also of shared values, and of other kinds of pressures, more often felt than verbally communicated. For example, Schofield reports the following: "Boys who are non-experienced tend to think that their friends have more sex than they do ($p = 0.05$); this combined with the strong pressures towards conformity in teenage groups, must be one of the influences that lead a boy on to sexual experimentation."[51]

From such studies, we are reminded of the pathway youth follow from peer group membership to early sexual encounters and mating to, ideally, partnership with another in a relationship as a couple. Hopefully, the couple relationship provides the kind of shared intimacy that youth seek. This includes the exchange of notes about some of the darker sides of the self and sympathetic responses to such feared revelations. It includes sexual gratification from both the giving and receiving of pleasures unknown in any other kind of communication between people. It precludes or remarkably diminishes feelings of loneliness and contributes to higher valuations of youth's developing self, but may in time rupture and provoke some of the deepest despair youth can experience. Sometimes, however, such partnerships survive as marriages and shared parenting and as such carry us into the arenas of early family life which are the focus of the next chapter.

Before I move that far, however, I must first introduce some antecedent issues. This section has dealt with orientations to sexual intimacy during youth without attention to earlier developmental processes. Children's understanding of gender and sex-stereotyped behavior, as well as their classification of themselves as girls or boys, begins in the preschool years.[52] If sharing and equality are to mark youth's heterosexual relationships, the early play and school experience of young children should avoid sexist discrimination. For example, the use by both boys and girls of toys which traditionally have been considered only male or only female is part of an androgynous socialization which aims ultimately to develop collaborative relations with agemates regardless of gender.

All that has been said about sexual partnerships, as contrasted with objectification of one's mate as a non-person, applies equally to homosexual and heterosexual relationships. A consequence of seeing and using one's mate as an object is ultimate loneliness, no matter what the sexual orientation of the people involved. Loneliness is, of course, a special concern among lesbians and gay men because fear of discrimination and reprisals keeps many homosexuals closeted and avoidant of any intimate friendships. In addition, this kind of secrecy puts a severe strain on youth who are searching for jobs, gratifying peer relations, and sustaining meanings in life. But the difficulties for homosexual youth during the transition period of coming out, in view of public prejudices, cannot be underestimated either. Most metropolitan human service systems include, in family service agencies or elsewhere, counselors who specialize in helping homosexuals with the dilemmas they face.

Loneliness and some of its ramifications in youth are the focus of the following section. Loneliness may be the root of a plethora of more readily recognized problems which visibly occupy the public's concern, such as teenage promiscuity, teenage pregnancies, and the teenage use of drugs and alcohol. Loneliness and boredom are experienced as an emptiness in life which must somehow be filled. The alternative of suicide has increased in the U.S.A. over the past few decades two or three hundredfold among adolescents.[53] Yet underlying loneliness among youth has received scant systematic attention.

Loneliness and the Devalued Self

Before a young person finds an intimate partner, a gnawing loneliness may invade his or her life. Because so few lonely people realize how widespread their problem is—and that it grips almost everybody at some time—they talk about it shamefully, if at all, in terms that conceal the depth of their feelings. Those who express such discomfort openly in our society may be seen as personally deficient or be overly belittled or blamed for their troubled condition. Thus, a thirteen-year-old girl moderately describes her loneliness, being sure to ascribe the cause to others:

> . . . I don't have many friends because people who call themselves your friends are really your enemies, sweet in front of your face and gossips behind your back. If you call those kind of people your friends, then I guess I have as many as anybody else if not more. But it would be nice to have a real friend, one to tell all your problems to. All I have to tell my problems to is my diary.[54]

Her yearning for "a real friend" is an honestly stated wish. Also evident is the fact that the objective, social context for loneliness may belie its inner presence; teen-agers seem to be part of a "crowd" and still feel terribly lonely. On the other hand, the rare creative "loner" may not experience such sometimes crippling feelings.

Loneliness may be understood in a variety of conceptual contexts. One such view is that loneliness arises from extended communication failure, especially if one's most personal messages are not received or responded to in ways suggesting they have truly been listened to. This is another instance of a nonresponsive environment that inhibits social development. The clue for youth workers is that their genuine and sensitively responsive listening may enable them to become bridges to a less lonely existence for some of the youth they serve. There are other facets to the complex and desolating emotion of loneliness, and thus also to relevant professional efforts. Loneliness has many associated feelings and possible sequelae. In the five short essays by "preadolescent youngsters" which Clark Moustakas includes in his first book on loneliness, the range of reported feelings are described by the five boys and girls as follows:

> 1. Empty, that's how it feels to be lonely. A sense of being in a deep dark pit, with nothing in sight, and no way out. 2. . . . thoroughly abandoned. To me, loneliness seems to have different stages. At first I usually feel mad, even a little bitter. 3. . . . not wanted. 4. I was beginning to hope that the world would come to an end.—I didn't care. 5. . . . longing for someone, anyone.[55]

Note that at least five different feelings make up the composite portrait of loneliness which these preadolescents describe. First, solitariness which is more than being a person alone; it includes a sense of remoteness from life and thus emptiness. Second, the feeling that other people cause one's loneliness by rejection and abandonment. Third, feelings of severe constraint that one cannot modify oneself, that one is locked away "in a deep dark pit . . . no way out." Fourth, feelings of anger, the target of which may become the self in depression. Fifth, utter hopelessness and futility: " . . . the world would come to an and.—I didn't care."

I am not proposing that all these feelings are part of every person's loneliness. Moreover, loneliness takes on other aspects too. But it is interesting that in the more thoroughly studied condition of personal adaptation to stress—when one's personal competencies, social network, and other resources are insufficient for one to be able to cope with the demands of a strange and pressing situation—the previously reviewed feelings associated with loneliness occur. Faced with an unmanageable, serious problem threatening one's life or continued well-being, one may feel all alone, abandoned, angry, and ultimately hopeless with "no way out." One is at such times prone to join up or pair with *any* other person who appears on the scene—anything to avoid continuing isolation, "longing for someone, anyone." Following a long and unrelieved period of such separateness—whether one is in solitary confinement or internally constrained from forming a responsive relationship—the prospect of death may seem a release.

Youth will pay almost any price to reduce loneliness, although they are trapped in it by an accompanying sense of distrust of peers who seem rivalrous and bitchy. Without access to a sympathetic ear or effective counseling services, the young may feel their continued loneliness give way to its depressive undercurrents, then to a sense of futility, and ultimately to suicidal impulses. Crisis center telephone lines are often engaged by lonely youth. So also are staff members in many other social agencies and psychological or psychiatric facilities.

Developmentally, severe loneliness may have its origins in the inadequacies of child–parent or other early attachment; the deficiencies may lie in the absence of an early, supportive network. At that time, the very young child may first learn of his or her own value, her lovability—or fail to. In the latter case, shyness may develop and contribute to loneliness, a fear of being rejected, of not being loved or liked, and thus a reluctance to risk extending oneself in relations with others. Or, after early network and attachment deficits there may follow an inability to reach out and pursue curiosities, which results in boredom, lack of interest in the novel or strange, and a concurrent personal dullness that puts off other people, keeps them uninterested and avoidant. In such a no-win matrix, there is little opportunity to develop any social competencies. When one is rarely given to by others, one does not learn reciprocity. Those who must repeatedly receive but cannot reciprocate usually do not long remain a "friend." Lack of capacity for mutuality guarantees ultimate loneliness. Thus, to becoming a lonely youth the pathway may be a long one, with many developmental junctures or transitions at which turning toward more personally gratifying routes might be encouraged by sensitive family members, concerned neighbors, or astute community workers in schools and health or social services. Awareness of conditions contributing to painful loneliness allows for preventive as well as remedial efforts. There are also macrosocietal or structural and cultural contributants to the problems of youth's loneliness.

Many social observers have ascribed to America's excessive individualism and competitiveness the widespread consequence of loneliness. For example, sociologist Philip Slater states early in his book, "The competitive life is a lonely one, and its satisfactions are very short-lived indeed, for each race leads only to a new one."[56] Toward the end of his text, where he considers corrective action, he proposes to break the pattern by "establishing communities in which"—among other things, but first of all—"children are not socialized exclusively by their parents. . . ."[57] In my earlier chapter on networks and attachment and in the next chapter on young families and their neighborhood and other supports, similar theses are proposed as necessary, not only for the healthy social development of children but also for the continuing healthy social development of their otherwise possibly quite lonely parents.

Preceding Slater by a generation, British anthropologist Geoffrey Gorer, generalizing from his observations on *The American People,* had the following to say about the needs of American children and youth. The American young, Gorer claims, need almost constantly to have other people present.

> If nobody is there, if one is alone, how can one still the gnawing doubts that maybe one is not a success, not lovable, not worthy of love? It is these feelings which make loneliness intolerable to well-adjusted Americans, and account for the numerous social features which are designed to obviate it. . . .
>
> The presence, the attention, the admiration of other people thus becomes for Americans a necessary component to their self-esteem, demanded with a feeling of far greater psychological urgency than is usual in other countries. This gives a special tone to the social relationships of Americans with their fellows . . . , they are, in the first instance, devices by which a person's self-esteem is maintained and enhanced.[58]

Gorer's observations, though dramatically overextended, seem relatively valid at least for some teenagers and their cliques as well as for some one-sexed or double-dating groups of young people in their early twenties. To the extent that youth, from early adolescence on, are engaged in clarifying, redefining, or shoring up an amorphous sense of self, with its uncertain boundaries, the "crowd" becomes especially important at this period of life. Without membership in a crowd, the lonely sufferer is relatively as well as absolutely deprived. The outsider to such a crowd cannot answer the frequent question, "Who am I?" at even the most superficial level of self-inquiry, with such replies as "one of Amy's crowd" or "a member of the Dux A.C."

Yet such membership is no guarantee against loneliness. In fact, membership in some such groups may ensure the continuation of one's loneliness, and by doing so, provide for the continued life of the group itself. Males in streetcorner crowds and other one-sexed groups are often unwittingly engaged in this kind of process, heckling the member who seems to be getting "hooked." And yet they sanction mate collection as a valued sport. In the group's perspectives, sexual "objects" are valued to the extent that (and as long as) they participate satisfyingly in the game, but the development of a partnership between persons in an intimate relationship is strongly discouraged. And thus feelings of loneliness are sustained.

It probably takes a genuinely intimate relationship in youth for the crystallization at a deeper than surface level of a sense of self and self-acceptance. Less than intimate relationships call for too much "front" or "face," the kinds of publicly acceptable behavior which teenagers recognize in their elders as "masks" but simultaneously feel themselves compelled to put on, so their nonintimate peers or the crowd will not disapprove of them. Only in intimate relationships can youth be self-revealing, "warts and all," in the mutuality of respect and love. Such relationships sometimes miraculously flourish in the teen years and early twenties. This is not to say they may not flourish also later in life. But in youth, given the special interplay of self-development and intimacy, intimate relations have a unique value for persons on the verge of young adulthood and their first responsibilities in family life and concurrent occupational involvements.

Without an intimate relationship as a context for youth's inquiries about self, the lonely person has only archaic memories out of the past and current superficial peer reflections to answer the "Who am I, really?" question. These are unlikely, without even the quasi-intimacy of a professional helping relationship to equip a person to enter into a close, loving liaison. The circularity in youth of self-devaluation and loneliness, and loneliness and self-devaluation, is essentially a downward spiral or at best a kind of static, no-growth situation. Calls for help sometimes are made as suicide attempts, or in the kinds of warning statements written by "Retep Reklaw" and quoted and discussed in the following and final section of this chapter.

THE SEARCH FOR MEANINGS

Adolescents' calls for help are often inaudible and oblique signals to their parents (or other adults) who may not, for many reasons, be listening or respond. So often, as Chapter Eight on the middle adult years makes clear, parents and their agemates are undergoing their own self-preoccupying transitions just as their children are in adolescence. Other facets of the situation also warrant brief review.

In the years prior to adolescence, children's explorations and play may not always be painless, but they focus on externals—on the physical, on action, and sometimes on social status. This looking outward gives a stability to childhood's developing self which parents typically find easy to live with. By contrast, adolescence introduces a consciousness of self—or self-consciousness—which destabilizes behavior and relationships in ways often upsetting to whole families. The life transition of youth is a major one because so many aspects of living are simultaneously under question. As previously indicated in this chapter, concerns involve jobs and schooling, peers and intimate relationships, sexual behavior and one's body, sometimes social injustice and always self-image and one's family. The questions, previously addressed to how the world works, shift to the self-preoccupied "Where am I going?" and by extension, to the purposes and meanings of life. Judgments about elders become increasingly critical, as the locus of self-knowledge interiorizes in the growing introspection of the maturing person.[59] Such processes tend to shut out parents at a time when their sympathetic support could be so helpful. Peers do not completely replace parents. It is no surprise that research on adolescent runaways and suicides uniformly reveals the presence of excessive parent–child conflict.[60]

Consider the self-reports of a teen-aged minister's son who, in the two years before he killed himself, wrote the following "story" and letter. In his critical search for meanings and his conflicts with his parents, his wanting to turn everything upside down is perhaps symbolized by his spelling his own name, Peter Walker, backwards as "Retep Reklaw."

ADOLESCENT SUICIDE—A SIXTEEN-YEAR-OLD'S "STORY" AND "FAREWELL LETTER" (RECORD NO. 16)

The Story of Retep Reklaw

Retep Reklaw was in constant search of peace and freedom. Freedom from his problems, freedom from his sisters and parents, freedom from the whole world. He wanted a solution, a relaxant, to make him forget all of life's problems. As the days passed Retep found life more and more tense and increased his search for serenity. Retep found part of his solution at school. He was in grade ten in the local high school and faring well. And to make things even better there were many pretty girls at school. But Retep found problems at school. He was not athletically developed. His skill and coordination in many sports was lacking. Retep found himself being heckled constantly by classmates.

Retep worked hard to get his good marks and therefore was often very tired after a day of schoolwork. He searched for a badly needed means of relaxation but his search was in vain. Therefore he found some pleasures but more problems at school.

Retep stepped off the bus and headed home. The week had been a terrible one and the effects were showing on Retep. Retep had made an error of judgment in the volleyball game which had cost his team the victory. His teammates threw insult after insult at him. He felt relieved to get away from that group of "friends." Retep had received during the week four hard tests as the mid-term report card was coming up. Retep was worried about the results of the tests. Arriving home, he was confronted with a note telling him to shovel off the walk. He cursed, but finished it in fifteen minutes. As he stepped in the door his mother confronted him again. "Don't take off your coat. Here's a list of things I need from the store. I forgot to go this morning when I had the car." "It must be twenty below outside. I'm not going to freeze my behind because of your mistake. You can go yourself."

"Now don't talk back to me, son. You do as you're told. On your way you can make an appointment with the barber. Your hair's a mess. It looks disgraceful."

She had ignited him to a point where his flame could not be doused. He flew into a rage and, doing something he never would have done lest he hurt her, struck her with his fist. He stared at his hand for a moment as they both stood stonefaced. The room became silent and the air became dessicated as the intensity of the situation developed. He turned and fled upstairs to his room. He quickly locked the door and collapsed on the bed.

Resting for a few minutes, his mind was a kaleidoscope of a thousand thoughts. His mother screaming at him, his "friends" screaming at him, the whole world screaming at him. Retep dropped off to sleep. Waking half an hour later his head had stopped spinning. Everything was stark and silent. He sank back and observed his room. It was small, and its appearance seemed to make him feel safe, beckoning him to continue resting. Retep was now isolated from the outside world, that dirty world which he despised. He was safe from reality. Here was his answer.

Retep found a stick of incense and, lighting it, placed it in a cup. The sweet oriental smell then filled the room. He found his cassette recorder and shoved in a tape. The Beatles started singing. "He's a real nowhere man, sitting in his nowhere land, making all his nowhere plans for nobody. Knows not where he's going to, isn't he a bit like you and me." Disgusting, he thought. Angrily he flipped the forward button wildly. He stopped it as he cooled down and set the machine on "play." The Beatles were still singing. He was about to change it when something made his hand stop. The music was strangely relaxing. "Let me take you down 'cause I'm going to strawberry fields." He started going off into a dream as the incense drifted about the room. His body was completely relaxed and his body floated above the bed. His glasses slid from his nose and dropped to the floor. He did not try to pick them up. Although he could not see anything, he found the darkness better without them. They were a symbol of that world, and he felt better without them. His mind was a total blank and he found it to be a pleasant feeling. "Nothing is real, and nothing to get hung up about, strawberry fields forever."

Retep felt a sensation he had never experienced before. The music and incense filled his body, and for the first time Retep Reklaw was not at war with the world. "Living is easy with eyes closed, misunderstanding all you see." The music called him further in, as he lit one incense cone after another. When he lit them all he was more relaxed than ever. He was in his own world where he was king. "It's getting hard to be someone, but it should work, it doesn't matter much to me."

Retep's mind became hazy and his thinking unclear. He was not afraid, however, because there was nothing to be afraid of. There was nothing but peace, beauty and tranquillity. And nothing to get hung up about. "Strawberry fields forever."

When the police broke the door down the music had stopped and the incense was no longer burning, but Retep Reklaw, laying on the bed, was finally at peace.

Farewell Letter (Written over a Year before His Suicide), Dec. 6, 1975

To everybody:

Please don't misinterpret what I have done. I want no one person to take the blame. It was my decision, and I am not sad that I did what I did. There are very many reasons why I did this. First, and this may seem strange, I am very curious as to what happens after death. Sorry, Mom, but I can't take what the Bible says as the Gospel Truth (heh!) I really am an agnostic.

Secondly, everyone will die sooner or later by old age or an atomic war, so why not sooner.

Thirdly, the pressure of schoolwork and homework were just too much. With six big projects going at the same time I knew I just couldn't take it. And if it's this bad now it sure won't get any better in university.

Fourthly, sorry Mom and Dad, but you must admit we didn't have very good relationships. You drove me nuts sometimes, Mom, and I probably did the same to you.

Fifthly, I see the world turning into an evil place. There is too much corruption, exploitation, misery, and pain. If people say, "Oh, it's too bad he's dead, and I'm happy to be alive and living and well," then the situation might change. I am hopeful.

Sixthly, I am really screwed up in so many areas. I have so many questions about life and no answers. It really got to me. I think I really said this in my poems. My poems and my short story will tell you everything you want to know. The Beatles played the biggest part in my "life." They really helped to relax me. They really did more for me than anything else. Oh, how they would make my body and soul float in the air. And I always cried when I realized that they are no longer producing music together.

I believe that pure Marxism is the best possible society. No class distinction. Everybody at the same level. That's beautiful. So I guess I am like Joan and Craig and am dying for peace and love.

I thought having a religion was important. Mine was a mixture of Buddhism and Christianity, but I could not take all the stuff in the Bible about miracles, etc., which don't seem to be possible. Buddhism tries to eliminate the thought of "I." It appeals to me because it stresses the finding of truth within your own mind.

Dad, I thought you were an okay person. You really tried to get things right for the Indian. I hope you continue and that you are successful. You really amazed me in that you always had a joke for the situation. I think you have come up short this time. You treated me well and I thank you for what you have done for me.

Mother, I know you will rest most of the blame on yourself. Don't. It was my decision. We did argue a lot. I really didn't understand you and I know you didn't understand me. Although I bothered you a lot and vice versa, I realize that you have gone through a lot, and I thank you for the help that you have given me.

Arlene, you were a beautiful person and I hope you continue in that path. You were very close to me and I know this will affect you in many ways. I thought you would answer my poems and was very disappointed when you didn't. I really felt a love between us and it was nice. I loved you in many ways. You always amazed me with your strict belief in God. I will remember you and my mind will think of you often. Remember me. Love, Peter.

Jim, you were a very close friend and I enjoyed your companionship. Try to remember what I have taught you. Try to pick up where I left off. Above all, keep going and fight for betterment. Remember me, Peter.

I want to say thank you to all my teachers over the years. I'm sorry it did not work out better.

"Many times I've been alone and many times I've cried; anyway you'll never know the many ways I've tried." (Beatles)

"Living is easy with eyes closed, misunderstanding all you see. It's getting hard to be someone but it all works out. No one I think is in my treee. I mean it must be high or low." (Beatles)

"All the lonely people, where do they all come from? All the lonely people, where do they all belong?" (Beatles)

Please don't hassle my friends about this. They knew all right, but they sure tried to talk me out of it. My last request is to play Strawberry Fields Forever, and A Day in the Life, in that order, at my funeral. Please don't deny me that much. Keep trying for peace and love.

Peter Walker[61]

One might speculate on why Peter's search for meanings ended in his suicide. The two documents provide many suggestions, but the remarkable aspect of these writings is that they state concerns and themes that are the typical preoccupations of many youth for whom suicide is never seriously considered a solution. Perhaps the central difference is that Peter experiences no sense of deeply supportive relationships, from family or peers, with whom to share—and recognize the comparative nonuniqueness of—his feelings of despair.

Peter's serious misunderstandings and conflicts with his parents come through most dramatically in his fantasized striking of his mother. Elsewhere in the book from which this record comes, Peter's sister remarks about their father's never expressing how he feels and about their mother's stating her opinions but not listening enough or understanding others. Regarding peers, Peter was not a part of any of the school groups—"He just couldn't fit in"—and "I don't think he knew the right way to act around girls."[62] Peter's remarks about peer disapproval—constant heckling and throwing "insult after insult"—are coupled with his concerns about his body—"not athletically developed" and the glasses, left dropped on the floor, because in the darkness, he was "better without them." In addition, school pressures and the long road ahead through university were high among experiences he wanted "peace and freedom" from. All of this becomes generalized into a sense of isolation and alienation from "that dirty world which he despised" and for which only the Beatles gave sympathetic response—"a nowhere man" and "nothing is real" except "all the lonely people."

Peter is one of many. The high incidence of suicide attempts, especially among youth in the fifteen to twenty-four age bracket, has led the human services into specialized suicide prevention programs as part of the mental health network. Such programs may call for mandatory reporting of self-inflicted injuries, temporary care homes, community supports and follow-up aftercare (the latter sometimes provided by volunteers), the mobilization of suicide attempters' personal networks, and relevant professionals, such as school counselors. Outreach efforts and preventive training can sensitize teachers and others to the symptoms of depression, publicize local mental health resources, and review what can be done when a "story" like Retep Reklaw's comes to one's attention.[63] After his death, Peter's sister said that if only they had known, they might have helped.

Perhaps the problems of youth, tragically dramatized by a Peter Walker, might be more extensively prevented by youth's meaningful and useful involvement in their communities' affairs. Many adolescents suffer a keen awareness of injustices in society—for example, Peter's concerns about Native Indians and class distinctions—but youth lack avenues for the expression of their concerns in collaboration with agemates and others. Youth are probably so responsive because of their psychological vulnerabilities, as their unquestioned childhood beliefs about the world collapse. Also, there is the discrimination they themselves face in the job market and under the petty tyrannies of autocratic teachers or the distrust of some adults in key positions. For many reasons, youth feel alienated from a society in which they are provided no significant places. They are approved of only as students or apprentices. But might not youth's ideals be profitably kept alive for both themselves and their societies? Neighborhood and human service programs[64] should engage more young people than currently participate in useful community work.

Without meaningful roles, their underlying alienation and fears continue, whether youth act out antisocially or withdraw, rarely directly expressing their sentiments. Literate high school seniors can put into words what their less verbal agemates also feel. One need not be suicidal like Peter Walker to suffer the strains of the major life transitions young people experience. I end this chapter with two poems by high school seniors, written in the early 1980s, and expressing some of the same concerns that Peter expressed. In "A Change," a university-bound male high school senior portrays his sense of loss in moving on from "where a young boy was" to the dangerous and frightening world of adulthood. In "The Life and Times of People," a popular female high school student editor confesses to similar concerns about leaving "my youth behind" but adds a clear statement about her feelings of alienation "in someone elses [sic] world."[65] Both these young people, who at times feel the moods of their poems, at other times, from what I know of them, are deeply invested in life and "this crazy world."

TWO POEMS BY YOUTH
(RECORD NO. 17)

A Change

Like a deserted house,
The man is changing.

Broken glass on the driveway,
And wild, uncut branches coming in
To hang upon the rocks.

Walk with care,
The rain has left it slippery here

Old pilings, rotted, broken like teeth.
Where a young boy was

The man changing
is like this.

The Life and Times of People

Travelling down the road of life
Encountering all the casual conformities
of life in the masses
me just another person who doesn't understand
what this crazy world is all about
Another kid, acquaintance, daughter
(and possibly reincarnation of a prehistoric slug)

No, we are just people now
and no use pretending.
Clear-cut victims of biology
Disillusioned with life
and certainly unwilling to be connected with the process
in any way whatsoever
Just growing older in someone elses world
Going through all the motions
Living until I die
I am just a survivor
Experiencing the surface emotions
and the weakness of humanity
Just living on.

Once close to youth
Whose infectious euphoria invades regions unknown
but permeating all the same.
I feel lost when far away: a vague feeling of forgottenness

But in front of me
years of adulthood stretch like infinity
I reach out
and when I grasp I must drop and leave
my youth behind
amid other memories.

NOTES

[1] Quoted, source uncited, in *The Family of Man* (New York: The Museum of Modern Art, 1955), p. 50.

[2] Margaret Mead, *Culture and Commitment: A Study of the Generation Gap* (Garden City, New York: Doubleday, 1970).

[3] Laurence Wylie, *Village in the Vaucluse,* 3rd ed. (Cambridge, Mass.: Harvard University Press, 1974) p. 99.

[4] Paul E. Willis, *Learning to Labour: How Working Class Kids Get Working Class Jobs* (Farnsborough, England: Saxon House, 1977) p. 96.

[5] Jane Synge, "The Transition from School to Work: Growing Up Working Class in Early Twentieth Century Hamilton, Ontario," pp. 249–69 in K. Ishwaran, ed., *Childhood and Adolescence in Canada* (Toronto: McGraw–Hill Ryerson, 1979).

[6] In addition to single, cited papers, these include two American anthologies, one British collection, and the Canadian reader cited in footnote 5: David Gottlieb, ed., *Youth in Contemporary Society* (Beverly Hills: Sage, 1973); Arthur Pearl, Douglas Grant, and Ernst Wenk, eds., *The Value of Youth: a Call for a National Youth Policy* (Davis, California: Responsible Action, 1978); Christopher Murray, ed., *Youth in Contemporary Society: Theoretical and Research Perspectives* (Windsor, Berks.: NFER Publishing Co., 1978).

[7] Harold L. Sheppard, "Youth Discontent and the Nature of Work," pp. 99–112, in Gottlieb, ed., *Youth.*

[8] David Gottlieb, "Poor Youth: A Study in Forced Alienation," *Journal of Social Issues* 25 (1969) 91–120.

[9] Sheppard, p. 103.

[10] M. Simon, "Young People's Attitudes to Work," pp. 134–57, in Murray, ed., *Youth,* pp. 146–47.

[11] Sheppard, p. 106.

[12] Gottlieb, Table 5.

[13] Sheppard, p. 106.

[14] Gottlieb, Table 5.

[15] Sheppard, p. 103.

[16] E. F. Schumacher, *Small is Beautiful: Economics as if People Mattered* (New York: Harper and Row, 1973/1975), and *Good Work* (New York: Harper and Row, 1979).

[17] Sandra Wallman, "Social Anthropology of Work," *Current Anthropology* 21 (1980) 299–314, p. 306.

[18] Everett C. Hughes, *The Sociological Eye: Selected Papers on Work, Self, and the Study of Society* (Chicago: Aldine-Atherton, 1971), p. 345.

[19] T. Keil, "Managers and Young Workers," pp. 107–133 in Murray, ed., *Youth,* p. 119.

[20] Keil, p. 124.

[21] C. Murray and D. Haran, "Youth, Education and Training," pp. 85–106 in Murray, ed., *Youth,* p. 103.

[22] Hughes, *Sociological Eye. . . ,* p. 343.

[23] Robert Jay Lifton, "Protean Man" in *History and Human Survival* (New York: Random House, 1970), pp. 316–31.

[24] Erik Erikson, "Identity and the Life Cycle," *Psychological Issues,* 1 (1959) 94, 127–28.

[25] Sheppard, p. 105.

[26] Schumacher, *Good Work,* pp. 3–4; also *see Small,* pp. 54–55, "The Buddhist point of view takes the function of work to be at least threefold: to give a man a chance to utilize and develop his faculties; to enable him to overcome his egocentredness by joining with other people in a common task; and to bring forth the goods and services needed for a becoming existence."

[27] Pearl, *Value of Youth,* p. 24.

[28] Ibid.

[29] R. E. Pahl, "Living without a Job: How School Leavers See the Future," *New Society* 46/839 (November 2, 1978) 259–62.

[30] Congressional Budget Office, Congress of the United States, *Youth Unemployment: The Outlook and Some Policy Strategies—Budget Issue Paper for Fiscal Year 1979* (Washington, D.C.: U.S. Government Printing Office, 1978), pp. xiii, 22, 23.

[31] Ibid., from Summary Table, p. xvi.

[32] Arvil V. Adams and Garth L. Mangum with Wayne Stevenson, Stephen F. Seninger, and Stephen L. Mangum, *The Lingering Crisis of Youth Unemployment* (Kalamazoo, Michigan: W. E. Upjohn Institute for Employment Research, 1978), pp. 114–15. Quoted with the permission of the W. E. Upjohn Institute for Employment Research.

[33] Ibid., pp. 98, 102.

[34] Henry S. Maas, "The Child's Responsibility to Society," in David S. Freeman, ed., *Perspectives on Family Therapy* (Vancouver: Butterworth, 1980).

[35] Mikk Titma, "Formation of Young People's Orientation towards Work," *Acta Sociologica* 22 (1979) 345–59.

[36] Congressional Budget Office, *Youth Unemployment,* pp. 15–16.

[37] Daniel Glaser, "Economic and Sociocultural Variables Affecting Rates of Youth Unemployment, Delinquency and Crime," *Youth and Society* 11 (1979) 53–82.

[38] Elijah Anderson, *A Place on the Corner* (Chicago: University of Chicago Press, 1978).

[39] W. Gordon West, "Serious Thieves: Working Class Adolescent Males in a Short-term Deviant Occupation," in Ishwaran, ed., *Childhood and Adolescence,* p. 333.

[40] Ibid., pp. 325–26.

[41] Ibid., p. 331.

[42] Ibid., p. 333.

[43] Ann Swidler, "Love and Adulthood in American Culture," in Neil J. Smelser and Erik Erikson, eds., *Themes of Work and Love in Adulthood* (Cambridge, Massachusetts: Harvard University Press, 1980), p. 131.

[44] Rhona Rapoport and Robert Rapoport, *Dual-Career Families Re-examined: New Integrations of Work and Family* (New York: Harper, 1977); David G. Rice, *Dual-Career Marriage: Conflict and Treatment,* (New York: Free Press, 1979); see also, Chapter 9, "Work and Its Meaning," in Lillian Rubin, *Worlds of Pain: Life in the Working-Class Family* (New York: Basic Books, 1976.)

[45] Michael Schofield, *The Sexual Behaviours of Young People* (London: Longman's Green and Co., 1965.)

[46] Bert N. Adams, "Mate Selection in the United States: A Theoretical Summarization," in Wesley R. Burr, et al., eds., *Contemporary Theories about The Family: Research-Based Theories* (New York: Free Press, 1979).

[47] Adams, "Mate Selection."

[48] Ira L. Reiss, *The Social Context of Premarital Sexual Permissiveness* (New York: Holt, Rinehart, and Winston, 1967), p. 136.

[49] Joseph P. Hornick, "Premarital Sexual Attitudes and Behavior," *Sociological Quarterly* 19 (1978) 534-44.

[50] Ulf Hannerz, "Roots of Black Manhood," *Transaction* 6 (October, 1960) 12-21, p. 19.

[51] Schofield, *Sexual Behavior . . .* , pp. 160, 167.

[52] See Aletha Huston, "Sex-typing," in Paul Mussen, ed., *Carmichael's Manual of Child Psychology,* 4th ed. (in press).

[53] Arthur L. Rosenkrantz, "A Note on Adolescent Suicide: Incidence, Dynamics and Some Suggestions for Treatment, *Adolescence* 13 (Summer 1978) 209-14.

[54] Jules Henry, *Culture against Man* (New York: Vintage Books, 1965), p. 151.

[55] Clark E. Moustakas, *Loneliness* (Englewood Cliffs, New Jersey: Prentice-Hall 1961), pp. 40-42. On loneliness in its most extreme form, leading "ultimately to the development of psychotic states," see Frieda Fromm-Reichmann, "Loneliness," *Psychiatry: Journal for the Study of Interpersonal Processes,* 22, (February, 1959) 1-15. See also L. A. Peplae and D. Perlman, eds., *Loneliness: A Sourcebook of Current Theory, Research and Therapy* (New York: John Wiley & Sons, 1982).

[56] Philip Slater, *The Pursuit of Loneliness: American Culture at the Breaking Point* (Boston: Beacon Press, 1970), p. 6.

[57] Slater, *The Pursuit,* p. 142.

[58] Geoffrey Gorer, *The American People: A Study in National Character* (New York: Norton, 1948), pp. 107-108.

[59] Morris Rosenberg, *Conceiving the Self* (New York: Basic Books, 1979).

[60] B. F. Corder, W. Shorr, and R. F. Corder, "A Study of Social and Psychological Characteristics of Adolescent Suicide Attempters in an Urban Disadvantaged Area," *Adolescence* 9 (Spring 1974) 1-6; E. A. Grollman, *Suicide: Prevention, Intervention, Postvention* (Boston: Beacon Press, 1971); P. A. Marks and D. L. Haller, "Now I Lay me Down for Keeps: A Study of Adolescent Suicide Attempts," *Journal of Clinical Psychology* 33 (1977), 390-400; J. D. Teicher and J. Jacobs, "Adolescents who Attempt Suicide: Preliminary Findings," *American Journal of Psychiatry* 122 (1966) 1248-57; T. Brennan, D. Huizinga, and D. S. Elliott, *The Social Psychology of Runaways* (Lexington, Massachusetts: D. C. Heath, 1978).

[61] From *Growing Up Dead,* by Brenda Rabkin. Reprinted by permission of the Canadian publishers, McClelland and Stewart, Limited, Toronto, 1978, pp. 121-25.

[62] Ibid., pp. 134 and 135.

[63] N. L. Farberow, *Bibliography on Suicide and Suicide Prevention* (Washington, D.C.: National Clearinghouse for Mental Health, U.S. Public Health Service, 1979); N. L. Farberow, *The Many Faces of Suicide* (New York: McGraw-Hill, 1980); M. Boldt, "A Model for Suicide Prevention, Intervention and Postvention," *Canada's Mental Health* 30 (March 1982), 12-15.

[64] Maas, "The Child's Responsibility."

[65] The poems are by Stephen Steele and Patty Moore, with whose permission they are printed here.

Chapter 7
YOUNG FAMILIES AND SOCIAL SUPPORTS

Introduction: New parents need social supports.

Macrocontexts, Family Interaction, and Social Development
    A Young Three-generation Family (Record No. 18)

Dimensions and Variants of Family Life
    Chicano families in barrios
    Young middle-class families and their social supports
    Poor black families in urban neighborhoods

Changes in Family Life over Time
    Starting family life
    Ending family life young
        The Hoover Family (Record No. 19)

INTRODUCTION

New Parents Need Social Supports

Young families are especially responsive and vulnerable to the influences of their societies, particularly economic and political conditions and the society's cultural contexts. The ways of life in local neighborhoods and their options for family life also exert a powerful influence on how family members interact with one another and with the people beyond the family's boundaries.

Since families are the primary context for all their members' social development, the extrafamilial supports available and accessible to them in their societies and living places are of great importance. For beginning families, the opportunities for sharing the young child's care seem crucial. Child care supports may take the form of informal local network exchanges or formal facilities provided through the human services. This chapter examines the nature of and reasons for family supports and how they in turn affect family interaction and the social development of members.

Couples who become parents enter a radically different mode of life. How they spend their time—whether with each other, with friends and relatives, at work and in leisure pursuits—undergoes sizable and qualitative changes from the patterns of their childless days as a couple. Prior to and after the birth of a child, working mothers typically—and fathers sometimes—take time off from their jobs for various periods. Thus poorer families' incomes are seriously reduced in countries that have no income maintenance programs to replace lost earnings or no subsidies for child care if parents go back to work.[1] Moreover, supplying an infant's needs, particularly when there are health or related special problems, and there is no national health program or other medical coverage, can be costly and tip the fragile balance of a poor family's budget. For both poor and materially comfortable parents, a firstborn curtails the former sense of freedom and privacy of a childless couple. The network supports of extended family, friends, and neighbors, as well as societal family policy, become of paramount importance in the launching of family life.

The birth of a first child also offers couples a chance to strengthen their own attachments to each other. If a newborn reduces a couple's former freedom and privacy, the baby also offers them a common focus for their love and concerns for another person and an opportunity for shared care giving and planning for their future lives. In cultural milieus in which tradition provides no models for men to share with women in directly caring for their own children—where parents' roles are clearly and firmly differentiated by gender—there may arise, in the context of worldwide changes in women's statuses, new dissatisfactions and conflicts between parents. Thus, the availability of outside help for the young family again becomes an issue.

Conceptual approaches to understanding and working with families have proliferated in the past few decades. The approach used in this book is consistent with the framework of social development. The family is seen as the primary context for all its members' social development, and thus variants in family life are of special concern. Beyond the conventional, nuclear two-parent family, families range in size and composition from single-parent one-child units to large rural communal families, some committed to Eastern philosophies or other creeds and sharing not only a living place but domestic chores and child care as well. These are the kinds of families psychologist Bernice Eiduson and her colleagues at the University of California at Los Angeles have been studying longitudinally since the mid-1970s.[2] Obviously single-parent families and communal families are likely to need different kinds of extrafamilial supports and to generate quite different contexts for their members' social development.

In this chapter I provide a framework for understanding and serving families seen primarily as contexts for members' social development. Young families in different macrocontexts and living places are described to illustrate some uses of the family framework. How young families may change over time is considered in the last part of this chapter, which is focused on the early years of family life, while children are no more than preschoolers. Chapter Eight, on the middle years of adulthood, and Chapter Nine on old age include sections on the later stages of family life. The social supports families need change over time. In this chapter on the young family, help with child care is a primary issue.

MACROCONTEXTS, FAMILY INTERACTION, AND SOCIAL DEVELOPMENT

Family interaction affecting the social development of parents and their young children depends in large measure on the contexts within which the family lives— both its immediate living place and the larger society. To provide some points of reference for a later conceptual discussion of young families, I start with a brief description of a family living under very different circumstances from most, if not all, of the readers of this book. A group of American psychologists interested in young children arranged in the mid-1970s to visit the People's Republic of China to discover what they could, in a short visit, about the development and early childhood education of preschool children. In the course of their government-approved and guided tour, they visited a small number of families that included preschool children.

The following record of the research team's observations in one family is quoted in full from the team's book-length report called *Childhood in China*. The writers stress elsewhere in their text the serious limitations of observations based on very short visits and carried out always in the presence of an official guide and translator. For present purposes, this vignette seems to me an ideal document to introduce some ideas about relationships between a family's social and physical environment and the family's patterns of social interaction, both within the family and beyond its boundaries. The great differences between the political–social contexts of this family and the contextual counterparts of family life known to most of the readers of this book help to highlight the extrafamilial impingements ultimately on the ongoing social development of all family members. In reading the observations on the three-generation family living in Shanghai in the People's Republic of China, consider which aspects of the social environment, as well as the family's physical living place, seem to affect the family's way of life. How then are all these influences likely to make a difference in the social development of each family member and especially the young children? To answer the latter question, with such inadequate evidence available to us, we can only be speculative. Following the record, I offer some observations and speculations of my own.

A YOUNG THREE-GENERATIONS FAMILY (RECORD NO. 18)

We were in a workers' village in Shanghai; it was mid-morning on a weekday, and our two local hosts ran ahead to inquire where there might be a family with young children and mother at home. There were two circumstances in our favor; a substantial number of workers in China have their regular days off on weekdays instead of on Sunday, and many others work on late or night shifts, thus they might be at home and available at this morning hour. Our escort returned with good news; she had found a family with young children in which not only the mother, but also the father was home.

We were welcomed warmly into a bedroom–living room now filled to capacity, for in addition to the visitors there were four smiling adults, all greeting us at once, and two children, a three-year-old boy and a six-month-old girl. The father and mother appeared to be in their early thirties. Both parents were at home because neither worked on a morning shift: the wife was employed in a medicine factory from two forty-five in the afternoon til ten-thirty at night; the husband worked on the night shift at a dyeing plant. Although he was up and around in the late morning and early afternoon, it quickly became apparent that major responsibility for the care of the older child was taken by the maternal grandmother, a genial woman who beamed on the entire gathering and exchanged side-talk with an age-mate who turned out to be the next-door neighbor, also a grandmother.

What happened yesterday? We asked the parents to give us a picture of one day's life in their family; they told us about the previous day.

Grandmother got up at six, went to market for milk, and returned about an hour later to help the three-year-old get dressed and to prepare breakfast. At about the same time, the father returned from his night shift. At eight, the mother woke, dressed and fed the baby, and put her back in bed for three hours. The family had breakfast (the boy ate porridge with milk), and afterward grandmother took her grandson for a walk in the park. By nine, the father had gone to bed, mother was busy with housework and knitting, and when grandmother and grandson returned from their walk, the grandmother washed the dishes and began to prepare the midday meal. While the adults were busy, the grandson looked at children's books, then went out to play with other children on the block. At eleven-thirty the baby awoke and was tended by mother. At noon, the family, except for sleeping father, ate their midday meal.

In the early afternoon the grandson took a nap and mother left by bus for her factory, taking the baby with her. When the boy woke up at three, grandmother gave him a snack, after which he went out in the neighborhood to play for about an hour. When he returned, grandmother, who is illiterate, told him stories from a picture book. At four-thirty father woke up, washed the boy's quilt, and played with his son for awhile.

We interrupted to ask what else the father did in the home, and were told that he often helped with the cooking, washed diapers, and sewed the children's clothes. Indeed, he had made the attractive shirt and pants that his son was wearing. As these were displayed we could see the six layers the child wore for warmth.

Relation between Adults and Children within the Family

Throughout the interview, there was much attention given to the two children by all three adult members of the family. During the visit, the baby remained in her mother's arms; she did not cry once for the entire hour and a half we were together (including the subsequent visits to other apartments, and the picture taking outdoors). The mother's manner was assured and affectionate. Occasionally, she would look at the baby, cuddle her closer, or amuse her with a soft rubber animal toy. The three-year-old boy alternated between periods of activity with toys and furniture and periods of being held, first by the grandmother, and then by the father. In his play, the boy improvised with an empty chair he carried about, placing it sideways on the floor as a kind of stable for the toy horse he pulled about on a string. All three adults spoke to the boy frequently and were very affectionate with him; the father, at one point, took him upon his knee and gave him the baby's pink-faced rubber animal.

By contrast, no one except the mother paid much attention to the baby, and even she seemed to be more concerned with keeping the baby comfortable than with engaging her attention, a pattern we often observed in the treatment of infants in China and consistent with the view we heard expressed on several occasions by nursery-school personnel that in the first year of life "children can't do very much."

Next-door Neighbors

We never heard what the family had done on the evening of the previous day because of the arrival of more next-door neighbors. It turned out that there were three families living on the second floor—two retired couples, each in a single room, and the family we were visiting, which occupied two rooms. All shared the use of a centrally located communal kitchen and toilet. The three families were clearly on intimate terms, and there was so much joking and laughter that our interpreter smilingly threw up her hands. We could not leave without visiting everyone's apartment in turn. When we asked to take a picture, they came together as a group, placing the young parents and the two children in the middle. They stayed together as they said good-bye with waves and good wishes.

We were told later that the retired workers in this and other housing projects took special responsibility for the children of the neighborood. We were told, for example, that as the children walked to and from kindergarten and school, the oldsters would greet them on their way, look after the smallest ones, and strike up conversations with older ones to ask about their work at school and to talk about their own experience in the "time of bitterness."[3]

The significant contexts for this family cover a sizable range of environments. They start with the state-controlled economy and, through Western eyes, what seems like a very intrusive political system. The contexts include the mores of such a society, based on expectations that everyone—from the oldest members on down—contribute to the realization of societal goals. Thus, the grandmother has an essential part to play in the family's self-maintenance while both parents work. The contexts also include the neighborly village life, manifest in visits from the old people from next-door and their joining in the photograph. Important too for their effects on social interaction are the physical arrangements of the family's living place—their own two-room unit for the five persons, plus the kitchen and bathroom shared with their neighbors living in one-room units on the same floor. All these contexts conjointly add to the pressures toward a collaborative style of life, all persons doing for and with others in ways that, contrasted with Western individualism and privatism, might seem excessive. Social interaction in this family clearly emphasizes reciprocity and collaboration.

Constraints upon interaction as a total family three-generational unit are imposed by the father's night shift work and the mother's early afternoon until evening absence at the medicine factory. Father and mother are awake together in their apartment on working days only at breakfast time and the late evening between mother's return and father's setting out for the dyeing plant. Still, note that all three adults participate in meal preparations, the major share of this work done probably by the grandmother, and all three adults care for, play with, and apparently maintain affectionate relations with the children. Grandmother walks the three-year-old boy through the park and tells him stories, father plays with him too, while mother, giving some attention to her son, focuses most of her affection and caring on the six-month-old daughter, taking her along to work in the early afternoon where there is probably a crèche for infants attached to the factory. Thus, working mothers may continue to nurse and drop in on their infants periodically during their working hours. At the same time, even the very young are exposed to agemates and the care of adults outside their own families from their early days on. In a society that stresses collective relationships, such infant care facilities fit in well with the society's goals.

Three additional aspects of family members' behavior, associated simultaneously with their social contexts and their social development as persons, warrant observation. First, although the grandmother has a busy schedule within the family, she apparently enjoys the neighbors who are agemates and provide an opportunity for extrafamilial relationships. Recall Chapter Three's proposition on the need for parents' own peer relations so that they do not invest themselves completely in intrafamily living to the detriment especially of the development of the children in their care. Secondly, note the lack of sex-stereotyped involvements of the father who helps to cook, washes diapers, and sews clothes, showing to the American visitors, possibly with some pride, the clothes he had sewn for his son. When mother works and has an infant to care for, and grandmother shops and cooks and cares for the three-year-old son, father's household contributions are undoubtedly necessary as well as welcome. In the course of such behavior, he models for his son what men can do. Finally, note that the three-year-old son engaged in play with peers out on the road at least twice during the previous day with no indication that a designated adult supervises on such occasions, so that the autonomy of the young children is not curtailed. On the other hand, in village life style, "retired workers in this and other housing projects took special responsibility for the children of the neighborhood" and "look after the smallest ones. . . ."

What kind of social development is encouraged by family life of this kind in its relatively thinly bounded arena, readily exposed to strong extrafamilial contextual influences? Clearly, socialization aims for socially responsible participation in a society that stresses such societal involvement for all. Yet, note that despite such social pressures, the three-year-old son is also able to engage himself in private play in the midst of a crowded room. In terms of special relevance to the framework of this book, I see that "In his play, the boy improvised with an empty chair he carried about, placing it sideways on the floor as a kind of stable for the toy horse he pulled about on a string." In such imaginative play, the family setting itself becomes a comfortably explorable arena. A family that has the kinds of social supports available to this family—together with a host of obligations and constraints which are only implicitly indicated in this very brief report—is likely to become a strongly sustaining emotional and social support for all its members and particularly the young, who have multiple caretakers.

Regarding the social development of such young children in China, observations suggest that they are, by Western standards, extremely "well behaved" or self-contained, like the baby and her brother in the quoted family vignette, never interrupting adult talk or calling attention to themselves, but remaining apparently contented in the background. It must be remembered, however, that the baby in this family probably spends many hours daily in a nursery attached to the factory where her mother works. As *Childhood in China* and other reports make clear, there are extensive group care and educational facilities for young children, allowing almost all parents to work.

As a result, the family is only one of a few parallel contexts in which young children are socialized. Children are apparently recognized and appreciated everywhere as a national resource, and seen as "perfectible" creatures and assumed to be "docile."[4] Since the society has a strong interest in their being "perfected," there are many community agencies working in concert to provide for children's education. One visitor remarks, "On these long trips, as in almost every social setting in China, children are the center of everyone's attention. Yet for the most part they seem much less obtrusive and unmanageable than their Western cousins—perhaps because of their early exposure to socialization in nurseries, kindergartens, and a general communal environment."[5] Yale psychologist William Kessen provides additional observations to contrast "children of other cultures" with Chinese children; of the thousands of the latter whom the visiting American team of child development specialists saw, no child ever seemed hyperactive or disruptive, and, by way of an example of cultural differences in children's behavior, Kessen writes, as I have previously noted in Chapter Four:

> One of Peking's kindergartens admits the children of foreign diplomats as well as the children of Chinese officials. We watched as the teacher showed to all a fine new mechanized Ping Pong game that moved and made noises fascinating to the children. The Chinese children, most of them about four years old, gathered around the boy in a tight circle and watched the Ping Pong game, with no shoving and no reaching out. As soon as one of the non-Chinese children appeared, he lurched in a wild grab for the toy.[6]

Kessen adds that "Chinese children can be understood only when it is recognized that they exist in an ideological ocean."[7]

Such a statement characterizes nations in which the range of options and degrees of personal autonomy are smaller by far than in Western democracies. Yet the statement reminds us that families and their children in any society are subject to many surrounding forces. Unquestionably, of all the contextual influences on personal development, family is the most powerful, if only because it mediates and reflects intimately and at close range all other contexts. Any view of family's role in human development, however, must conceive of it not only as an "intimate environment," in Arlene Skolnick's phrase,[8] but also as an environment within the very powerful environments which surround all families. In short, family should be seen both *as* context and *in* context.

DIMENSIONS AND VARIANTS OF FAMILY LIFE

In the previous observations of the young Chinese family, an implicit framework guided the comments I made. The framework should now be made explicit. It is used throughout this chapter and subsequently when family life and the reciprocal influences of family on its members and of members on their family are discussed. The framework for observing and serving families grows out of the developmental schema that organizes this book. To start with, I list the ten dimensions of the family framework, although in this chapter I shall develop and illustrate just the first eight, leaving to the next two chapters on middle age and old age dimensions nine and ten. The family dimensions are sequenced to coincide with personal development. Within this framework, moreover, I shall consider some of the multiple variations of these themes of family life by drawing on studies of blacks. Chicanos, and middle-class urbanites whose ethnicity pales in a middle-class world.

Note that family is both an important context for its members as well as having contextual fields itself, as dimensions one and two indicate.

FAMILY IN CONTEXTS:

1. Family as a socioeconomic and cultural unit.
2. Family as core of its living place (and networks).

FAMILY AS CONTEXTS:

3. Family as mini-network (for members' primary attachments).
4. Family as explorable arena (for members' curiosity expression and development of interests and involvements).
5. Family as responsive environs (for members' development of competence and special capacities).
6. Family as collaborative group or subculture (for members' development of reciprocity and mutuality).
7. Family as evaluator, source of reflected appraisals (for members' changing self-images).
8. Family as parenting/partnership unit (for child rearing).
9. Family as community participant (for the practice of members' social responsibility beyond family boundaries).
10. Family as diverse, flexible social space (adapting to and supporting the changes of aging members).

As will be seen from the discussion of each of the first eight dimensions in the following paragraphs, no components of this orientation seem incompatible with major theoretical perspectives on family: the structural–functional approach, theory on family development, interaction theory and family seen as social system, exchange theory, or family crisis theory. These essentially sociological theories view the family in its totality, as an organism in which individual members and their personal development are *not* central focuses.[9] In the framework presented here, personal social development is the central concern, and family is considered primarily as a mediating and crucial context between members and their surrounding environments. The latter are the families' contexts, which give form to the first and second dimensions in the previous listing and provide the starting point for elaboration and discussion.

1. For all the protective strengths that families have in sheltering their members from the buffeting of the extrafamilial world, families themselves are inevitably vulnerable to major forces in their society—its economy, its political forms and changes, and its cultural heritages, seen against the cultural identifications of given families. For example, as cited earlier, the Chinese village family's work schedule and political meeting obligations reflect the state-managed economy and the communist government of their nation. It is obvious that family life is affected by these macrosocietal pressures. Similarly, the composition of the three-generation household, with its respect for and involvements of old people, is indicative of long-standing Chinese cultural values and practices. The economy and management of the household and the collaborative interaction of family members reflect simultaneously the forces of government, culture, and national economy. Thus, this Chinese family is initially understood as a socioeconomic and cultural unit of its macro-

society. Moreover, an understanding of any family's forms and processes rests upon assessing its social position or status within its macrosociety. The visited Chinese family is parented by factory workers. Were the family headed by a bureaucrat in the upper reaches of government, we might expect family processes to differ in many ways from the workers' family. In North America as elsewhere, a family's socioeconomic position determines some of the pressures to which its members are subject and the societal options which are more or less accessible to the family. A family's cultural heritage and identifications indicate some of the norms and values that guide family life, and thus also some of the ways in which a family may differ from others who share life in a multicultural society. Seeing a family as a socio-economic and cultural unit is a good starting place for understanding a family as a context for its members' social development.

2. A family's contextual options depend also on its residential location or living place. Living place includes home and immediate environs, the neighborhood or rural setting. In the vignette on the Chinese family, the first sentence locates the family's living place: "We were in a workers' village in Shanghai." Had the living place been an agricultural commune in the countryside, where parents went off to the fields early in the morning and returned home perhaps at sundown, varying with the seasons and the weather, a family would not have to adjust to the difficulties that spouses as factory workers have in an uncoordinated work schedule. But living place, as both physical and social space, affects a family's life style and especially its interaction both internally and in interplay with its neighbors. The spatial arrangements of the Chinese family's living unit as well as the building in which it is housed, with kitchen and toilet shared with neighbors, shape much of the family behavior. Opportunities for privacy, either being alone or together with only one or another member of the nuclear family, are constrained by housing space. Personal social development—for example, in regard to sharing and reciprocity—are inevitably affected. Family, as the core of the living place, has also various local network options, differing with housing arrangements and neighborhood patterns. These networks may provide supports or substitutes for family and thus profoundly influence attachments and other social developments of family members.

3. Family as mini-network is part of the larger networks of informal attachments and formal linkages which may at times support and at other times constrain family members. Within this mini-network, primary attachments are formed and change over time throughout life. The earliest attachments are bases for further social development; well-grounded attachments supply affective relationships, feelings of personal security, and bases for the reaching out that curiosity impels. Beyond family as mini-network and the changing opportunities it provides for supportive, nonsupportive, under- or overattachments (see Chapter Three), human service workers assess the additional supports available to family members through extrafamilial networks. Through the latter, family members can find additional or substitute attachments that foster emotional development and opportunities for cognitive growth as curiosity and new interests are pursued.

4. Parents themselves may express their curiosities openly, as ideal models of people interested in novelty, change, and complexity. As such, their family house-

hold and the adventures the family pursues beyond its boundaries serve as arenas in which the young and all members can explore. Exploration is often playful and creative. It typically has, also, a problem-solving element to it. It begins with questions and continues as special interests and involvements emerge. It sharpens cognitive processes as what, how, why, and other questions arise. Family serves as an explorable arena for the three-year-old son in the Chinese village family who "improvised with an empty chair he carried about, placing it sideways on the floor as a kind of stable for the toy horse he pulled about on a string." None of his three adult family caretakers inhibit his engagement in such activity. In fact the relationship between attachment and exploration is graphically clear in the observation that the boy "alternated between periods of activity with toys and furniture and periods of being held, first by the grandmother, and then by the father"—as though each adult provided temporarily a home base from which, reassured ın the midst of strangers from North America, the child could venture forth again to explore. The time or freedom the adult members of this family had to explore and question their own world is not suggested by the record. One senses that both lack of time and political constraints prohibited many kinds of inquiry. When the government of a macrosociety advocates unquestionable judgments and dogma, and if parents govern their families in a similar fashion, the natural, autonomous explorations of young children are likely to be constrained. Compare the range of these English mothers' comments about their four-year-olds' play and their own participation in it as bits of evidence of family in a more or less explorable arena:

> "He had a box of paints at Christmas; well, everywhere was covered and he was in it as well. He didn't actually *colour* anything, he just scribbled over the whole page. Well, to me, I didn't think he was getting much out of that; I put them out of the way; I thought, well, he's just that bit young to appreciate them."[10]

Or,

> "If he's happy and healthy, he's usually dirty. If he kept clean I should think there's something wrong with him."[11]

Or,

> "I don't like her to have water—she's inclined to make herself wet through."[12]

Or,

> "Well, just now, his father has made him a sword, like Robin Hood's, and he's got a piece of wood, and he pushes it in his belt, and then we have to fight, and I'm the Sheriff of Nottingham and he's Robin Hood."[13]

There are developmental gains to be had from such explorations. The Newsons, from whose study these observations come, remark that children learn through playing Robin Hood and other roles to extend their social understandings of other persons's feelings and needs, beyond the self-centeredness of early childhood.[14] Moreover, families able to explore widely, in fantasy and along other routes, may be less likely to be so overwhelmed by stressors which are unfamiliar and bind them to the here and now. Of course, family interests in the new, the changing, and the complex can be developed only after basic biological survival needs have been adequately met.

5. The Shanghai village father who is apparently proud of making his son's clothes also demonstrates many other competencies. In fact, the entire family seems well able to cope with its daily imperatives. In this familial context there is evidence for family members to assume that the world—or at least the family's immediate environs—is usually manageable. In addition to demonstration, however, the family's essential role in the development of its members' competence is its own responsiveness, in so far as it is able, to the coping efforts of its members. Do other family members react appreciatively when one in their group prepares a meal for them all to enjoy? Are the cook's capacities appropriately and supportively appraised in ways that further culinary efforts and increase competence? Competence involves energy output and a feeling of power; members' ineffectual efforts to contribute to the family welfare reduce their sense of efficacy or self-adequacy. Put-downs of developing capacities can, of course, be devastating. The family as a sensitively responsive environment may need to engage outside resources to further the capacities of members to enable them to develop and use new strengths. Human service workers may provide supports for family life, which in turn enable a family to become more responsive to the growing effectiveness of its own members. As with curiosity, which is difficult to pursue in families where basic needs are too meagerly met, so the development of capacities and of a sense of competence is not fostered in families suffering poverty, serious illness, or other stressful conditions which spawn feelings of helplessness or incompetence.

6. Families may be ideal contexts for the development of capacities used collaboratively, or they may encourage, directly or obliquely, each person's going it alone. The vignette of the Chinese family suggests coordinated teamwork in child care and home maintenance which involves the three adults in many kinds of reciprocal and sharing interchanges. In such a milieu, children are socialized for cooperative participation in a macrosociety which, with its huge population and relatively limited resources, demands much sharing. Societies and families differ, of course, in the degree to which working together is valued. Family as a collaborative subcultural group models and otherwise encourages its members to be concerned about the well-being of people other than themselves.

7. In the course of all such processes, families serve, openly or only by indirect communication, as the evaluators of their members. Old-time prescriptions in books on parenting which advocated that parents be "nonjudgmental"—when near total permissiveness was the order of the day—proposed the impossible. (Permissiveness is itself a value on which those urging nonjudgmentalism were themselves judging others.) Socialized human beings are value-oriented creatures. Know-

ing in most situations "right" from "wrong," they invariably approve, merely tolerate, or disapprove of not only their own self-evaluated feelings and behavior but also the same of other people and especially those close to them, their families. In the course of such appraisals, often unspoken but nonetheless communicated, family members contribute to the self-images of their kin. As "self" develops, in large measure from the reflected appraisals of significant others, who is more significant, particularly in early life, than one's own family members? Later in early adolescence and youth, self-images are likely to go through important changes. Then, efforts at productivity on the job or at school and one's first important extra-familial intimate relationships are made. At that time, family evaluations of members as youthful workers or lovers inevitably affect reorientations in identity—feelings about one's work competence or lovability. Whether families approve or disapprove of their youthful members' earliest job or sexual experience may affect how these family members subsequently, in their own nuclear families, undertake their responsibilities of parenting a first child and living with a spouse.

This brief overview takes us to the eighth dimension in the family framework. Together with the seven earlier dimensions, number eight is elaborated upon subsequently in this chapter. But the nuclear family whose parents are at midlife (dimension number nine) is discussed in the next chapter, and the tenth dimension on the family of diverse and flexible forms necessary to accommodate the continuities and changes of old people is one of the focuses of Chapter Nine on old age.

Having proposed that understanding family life begins with seeing it as a socioeconomic and cultural unit, I turn now to some variations in such units and the related differences in family forms and processes, starting with networks and attachments, and their consequences for members' social development.

Chicano Families in Barrios

In the United States, one of the fastest growing segments of the population are Spanish-speaking families who are of Mexican descent. Most such families inhabit Spanish-speaking neighborhoods or *barrios,* not only in the Southwest but also stretching to Chicago and Detroit and further east where they begin to link up with other Spanish-speaking Americans from Puerto Rico. Although Chicano families today live at every socioeconomic level in American society, they are preponderantly working class and poor. As long ago as the early 1940s, an anthropological study of a settlement or *colonia* of Mexican–Americans in a California city thumbnail-sketched families at four different social class levels. The richest were the *señores grandes* (big people) who were also "a liaison group with the Anglo–American world," but the poor were the "numerical bulk" of families like Juan and Lola Perez's stable family or the one-parent family of eight children and their deserted mother, Cuca Garces.[15]

In such gross terms, the families could be seen to differ in socioeconomic status, but they still shared many cultural values which were expressed differently but nonetheless reflected in their family lives. These included traditional expectations for male and female family members which clearly distinguish sex roles. The females were considered primarily the keepers of the home, and especially when young, in need of protection or chaperoning by brothers and fathers. The males were the family's prime representatives and protectors outside the home, and its sources of first authority within the family, according to many studies of Chicano family life.[16] Such standards are, of course, in the broadest sense, indicative of traditional family life in many parts of the world. Even middle-class Anglo parents and especially fathers still tend to approach their daughters more protectively than their sons, although their practices may be less ritualized than in Hispanic families. Moreover, the portrait of father as lord and master may, as a much vaunted public image, serve merely to mask the fact that mother more than father is the real power within the family. Mother may permit the father's image of *machismo* to go unchallenged as part of her own private strength.

The descriptions of a "modern" wife and mother are revealing, as long ago as the 1940s study. The Cerna family is moderately well off; Linda Cerna grew up in a carefully protected family environment, essentially respecting the values of her parents. Nevertheless, when interviewed as the mother of teenage children, she said that "she considers herself her husband's partner," and she will not bring up her daughters the way she was brought up. At the time, she was giving little parties at home for her fourteen-year-old daughter, aware that her neighbors might be considering her an *alcahueta* (panderer), but she still was clear that when her daughter turned sixteen, "none of this running around all night with one boy, the way those American girls up on Tenth do. There is a lot to be said for the Mexican way of keeping an eye on your girls, if it isn't overdone."[17] The workings of the internal mini-network of family are suggested by these observations. But thus far the family's living place and extrafamilial network, so central to Chicano family life, have not been noted.

In the *barrio* of today at least poorer Chicano families' emotional and social supports derive from their culturally defined and identified living place. Boundaries between family and the surrounding barrio, often peopled by extended kin, are thinner or far more permeable than the typical middle-class Anglo–American family's boundaries. Of the barrio as source of symbolic and united identification for Chicanos, Felipe de Ortego y Gasca writes:

de donde vine?	Where am I from?
pues del barrio, como tu	Why from the barrio, like you
dime, cual Chicano no ha nacido ahi	tell me, which Chicano was not born there
cual Chicano no sabe de esa vida?	which Chicano doesn't know that life?
No me cuentes del barrio tuyo	Don't tell me about your barrio
porque el mio fue igual:	for mine was the same:
el tuyo y el mio	yours and mine
es el mismo barrio	are the same barrio
aunque el mio esta por alla en el destierro	though mine is over there in the diaspora
y el tuyo mas aea.	and yours over here.
Que no sabes, carnalito,	Don't you know, kinsman,
que dondequiera que vive un Chicano	that wherever a Chicano lives
alla hay tambien un barrio?[18]	there too is a barrio?

The poet's sense of what Marta Sotomayor calls a "feeling of belonging and co-hesion" engendered by barrio life must be counterbalanced, however, by Soto-mayor's observations on "the negative aspect of the barrio" in the "almost total lack of resources coming into the confined community to meet the needs of the residents."[19] These must be primarily large-scale material needs among poor barrio families, for basic emotional needs seem typically to be met in barrio life, where extended family members also reside.

Characteristically, Chicano nuclear families are embedded in their extended families. Daily life is spent with extended kin and daily problems tend to be shared with them. Especially in barrios where extended kin often live close by, daily stresses are reduced by participation in reciprocal aid arrangements. Moreover, major crises may be experienced as somewhat less stressful because one rarely, in such family contexts, has to face them alone. If feelings of abandonment increase the feelings of helplessness one suffers in catastrophic circumstances, the nearby availability of extended kin can reduce such suffering.

Particular help is given to female-headed households by extended kin, al-though, as warned in one study report from the Spanish-Speaking Mental Health Research Center in Los Angeles, it is "an idealistic view that all Mexican–Americans have an immediate source of emotional and material help in any and all kin."[20] Obviously, for extended family help to be exchanged, members must live nearby, be available, and have the resources to share. Still, it seems important that when the extended family can help a family in need, "The head of the household does not lose face," as Sotomayor observes, because "the extended family pattern couches his feelings of failure."[21] If one is helped by one's own, one may not experience the shame one feels when strangers give "charity." The entire dynamic, under such circumstances, is different, when one has grown up in a culture that fosters group membership and reciprocity. There are feelings of belonging, in a much larger net-work than typifies the identifications of a middle-class Anglo–American family member who is socialized for independent achievement.

The sense of personal identity developed within the barrio and the extended family makes a difference to family members not only when material help is needed. The boundaries of extended family pertain also when personal weakness or other problems are discussed and emotional supports are needed. As one Mexican–American remarks,

> [Mexicans] are proud people. They're the type of people that would rather stay together in a little circle within their own family and try to work out their problems themselves than go outside—even to discuss it with, say, [a] friend. We would really have to be very close in order for a person to tell me what was happening, as far as their child was concerned, or their husband, or themselves. Because they keep that to themselves.[22]

The cultural beliefs and values that foster the development of such pride simultane-ously strengthen the bonds of the family within which—primarily, or only, within which—a proud people may reveal what their pride conceals everywhere else. Thus, it is no surprise that in this world wives and mothers limit their discussions of their family problems to women kin and then typically to the one confidante within the extended family whom they feel closest to and trust most completely. Human service workers, and especially those who are not Spanish-speaking, are unlikely without difficulty to establish a self-revealing relationship with such women. In addition to pride, constraints may include the kinds of suspicion or fear of strangers, and, under crisis conditions, anxiety about *el ojo* or the evil eye—concerns which are sympathetically understood within the extended family.

Given such norms, Mexican–Americans who lack a close, supportive kinship circle may feel very deprived. Comparing herself to her cousin, one woman remarked:

> I always used to think how lucky she is. Why can't I have a mother like that? Or why can't I have a sister like that? And it used to hurt me. . . . I think a family should be close to where—*not* to share your problems or for them to say "We'll pay your rent, don't worry"—not that kind of closeness. But closeness to know they're there to help if I need anything. To have affection, that *confianza,* I don't know how to say it in English. Confidence, like to go to my sister's and feel at home—like it was my home. And for them to come over here and feel this is their home. But it's not that way.[23]

Thus, the norms for family attachments and behavior may evoke pain or disappointments as well as pleasure and supports.

What, now, may be the effects upon Chicano personal social development of families providing and embedded in such a way of life? The discussion has touched on Chicano families as socioeconomic and cultural units, as the core of their barrios as living places, as mini-networks in the larger networks of extended family, as arenas somewhat closed to outside exploration, as responsive environments engaged in mutual aid arrangements and reciprocity so that competence is shared, and as sources of social identities in *la raza,* or symbolically, the barrio, as the quoted poem suggests. Readers may recall that in Chapter Five I cited a series of studies on reciprocity or sharing among school-aged children in various cultures, and that repeatedly among the most collaborative groups were the Mexican or Mexican-American children. This chapter elaborates on the socialization context for such social development, with its emphasis on mutual help and sharing of material resources.

Young Middle-class Families
and their Social Supports

Having just read about Chicano family life in the barrio, how does one react as sociologist Alice Rossi elaborates on "the social deprivation of both women and children in the isolated contemporary household" in the following statement?

> . . . women are deprived of the social support system of other women, which in the past helped to lighten the burdens associated with the rearing of children, and children are deprived of easy access to peers and adults other than their parents during the important early years of growth and development. It

is likely that the child-growth centers can become a means of compensating for the isolation of children that results from the residential and work patterns typical of urban industrial society.[24]

The "residential and work patterns" alluded to have not yet visibly invaded barrio life. Women's isolation is far from being a general problem for poor Spanish-speaking families. Nor, as I illustrate in the section following this one, is women's isolation from one another and a support system to help with child rearing a common problem among many of the poor black families in the United States. What Rossi refers to is, however, an issue in middle-class urban families. To understand this problem, which touches on all the dimensions of family life presented earlier in this chapter, one must start with a consideration of family as the core of its living place and as a socioeconomic and cultural unit before moving on to the matter of networks and other aspects of family life.

New, young, middle-class families are often inadequately attached to urban neighbors or closeby kin and long-term friends. There are many reasons for this. Getting married and having a first child in middle-class homes frequently entail setting up a new household in a place far removed from parental families and former homes. This is because of the likely differences in economic statuses between parents who are at the peak of their incomes and their married children who are just starting out in their careers. The latter cannot afford to live in the same area in which the former have long made their home.

Such geographic displacement happens less often in the working class. Poor middle-aged parents and their just-married children are more likely to be in similar economic straits and may even share a domicile to ease their mutual constraints. In addition, there are more often interdependencies of other kinds in the kinship ties of working-class mothers and their married daughters, as studies have made clear.[25] In fact, in a San Francisco Bay Area inquiry into working-class family life, Lillian Rubin observes not only that "relationships with extended family—parents and siblings" are "at the heart of working class social life," but also that "this close involvement with extended family inhibits joint friendships with outsiders since it fills both the time available and the need for social relationships."[26] Still, working-class wives and husbands are likely to retain more of their premarital same-sexed close ties than can middle-class wives and husbands, in new neighborhoods and under new pressures, especially with the birth of the first child.

In a review of studies of friendships over the life span, B. Bradford Brown says, "At marriage, many of a middle-class person's individual friendships are terminated, and those that survive generally become less intense, joint friendships of the conjugal pair . . . These joint relationships often evolve into 'couple co-ordinate friendships'" forming "the basic unit of middle-class social life."[27] Such young wives and mothers may become connected primarily with other young wives and mothers of similar ages, economic and social aspirations, and lack of freedom because of their child-care obligations. They thus feel rarely able to help each other on a regular basis when out-of-home employment requires scheduled child care. It is then especially that Rossi's observations on "the isolated contemporary household" make sense. Husbands and fathers working on as inflexible a work schedule as their young wives are of little help. The young middle-class family's neighborhood ideally includes some kind of formal child-care arrangement which is within the family's budgetary limits.

A family's living place and a family's socioeconomic status may combine to determine the kinds of social support parents need and the uses they make of their networks. In a study done in Gothenburg, Sweden, "single mothers . . . made greater use of their personal social networks than did married mothers, particularly for assistance in emergencies and for emotional support," but further analysis revealed that the single mothers were also less well off economically than the married mothers, and this fact was "partly responsible" for the greater or more multiplex involvement of single mothers with their personal networks. "Apparently the economic hardships associated with single parenthood contribute to greater dependence on friends (than is true of married mothers)."[28] In this same study, neighborhoods varied in the accessibility of their formal services. When the economically better off married mothers lived in high-access neighborhoods and used the services extensively, they were also found to be engaged in large personal networks in numerous activities. But in similar high-access neighborhoods where the poorer single mothers lived, those who made extensive use of formal services tended to have small personal networks and engage in few social activities with network members.[29] It seemed as though only the poorer mothers who lacked adequate personal networks used the formal services. This occurred in Sweden, a nation in which any sense of stigma about the use of public services has long disappeared. Poorer families everywhere seem to prefer personal relationships and personal services over formal ones. Middle-class families seem to have no such preferences. Although over the years they may develop large networks of middle-class friends, they still use accessible formal services.

Generally, it seems clear that the friends of young middle-class parents do not provide an exchange of the kinds of services which are available from formal agencies. The informal reciprocity prevalent among the studied poorer Swedish single mothers and their friends, as well as in Chicano and poor black families, is normally less frequent in middle-class family networks. Perhaps having the money to pay for some services, which are handled on a personal barter basis among poor families, makes the difference. But the difference does not end there.

The young family's needs for social supports of many kinds, and especially for child care, involve—in the terms of our framework for observing and serving families—much more than only the family as a socioeconomic and cultural unit, family as core of living place (with its services and other resources), or family as itself a mini-network. The issue of social supports takes us beyond attachments to the development of family members' reciprocity or sharing of competence and personal resources. To return, for purposes of comparison, to Chicanos, research psychiatrist Robert Coles in volume IV of his series of reports on "children of crisis" generalizes on the basis of his extensive field interviews and observations in the Southwest:

> Quite early on, when six or seven, Chicano children begin to develop a sense of loyalty to their people, to their *fate,* that distinguishes them from Anglo boys and girls of the same age. They become less and less, rather than more and more individualistic. They renounce personal ambition . . . [30]

They become, in short, more and more collaborative, deferential to one another, and, simultaneously, less personally achievement oriented. Perhaps they lower their sights and personal expectations in light of their awareness of limited chances for their getting ahead in a society that discriminates against them. Perhaps they line up their own goals on a level with what they perceive to be the low level of expectations for their attainments by those in power around them. Low-level aspirations are a hedge against personal disappointments in low-level achievements. Perhaps they are committed to the cultural sanctions, shared by many native people in North America, that to surpass one's peers is to show little respect for them. Whatever the meanings of such behavior, Chicano family and barrio life demonstrate and support such orientations daily. By comparison, middle-class mothers and fathers, who are often interested in careers and advancements more than in merely adequately paying jobs, may build a major part of their lives and the parenting and socialization of their children around the values of personal achievement. These may run counter to a collaborative way of life. Time out to help another family is time lost in one's own race. Paying for formal services rather than participation in neighborly reciprocal exchanges, which make one indebted and obliged for future repayments, fits into an independent familial style.

Intensive sharing and working together occur among middle-class families, however, in times of crisis, i.e., in a natural disaster. When in early 1982 in Inverness, California, water flooded down the hillside toward Tomales Bay, inundating homes with mud and debris and damaging the community's fresh water supply, electrical power, and communications with the outside world, the largely professional and middle-class family residents banded together and worked effectively for several days during the emergency to meet their joint survival needs. When the emergency had passed, one commuter resident about to return to work in San Francisco remarked of the collaborative experience:

> "It's been exhilarating. . . . It was good teamwork. . . . It's sad to leave. I feel really let down. It's kind of like the feeling after an ocean passage, you know, where the eleven people and a 50-foot boat is your whole world for a couple of weeks." Meszaros [local man in charge of the emergency work] accompanies him out to the schoolyard. They hug each other. . . . Ruth Thorsen [another community resident] prepares to leave her post in the information and volunteer service room to clean out her house in Second Valley. "We'll revaluate on Monday to see what's needed. . . . It's been incredible how everyone pulled together."[31]

When the degree of interdependence among families in a community is dramatically heightened by such a crisis, they can "pull together," and in the process, experience an emotional high in their sense of closeness and shared identity with one another.

Normally, the needs for social supports in middle-class neighborhoods exert no such unifying, centripetal pressures. Each family has its separate paths to follow, as an "isolated household."

With so large a proportion of women in the labor force during hours that overlap with their husbands' work times, the issue of child care remains a central concern in young middle-class families. Two alternate approaches to this dilemma, beyond formal group care which in most neighborhoods remains in short supply, should be mentioned. Both these approaches reflect again on the interaction of family friendships and human services, or how family needs for social supports and emotional supports intertwine.

The first approach was an effort to develop child-care help in a relatively informal but nonetheless formal program. In Portland, Oregon, social worker Arthur Emlen and his colleagues set up and studied a neighborhood child-care service which linked working mothers with typically older, "empty nest" women who offered themselves, at home, as brokers for child caretakers. The service provided consultation and brokerage, or linking, of the mothers who needed child-care help with the women available for such service. One finding was that in the source of such service, emotional support between the working mother and the caregiver sometimes entered into what had begun as a quasi-formal service relationship. Thus, the Portland study illustrates the interplay between formal and informal family networks as well as between emotional support and the provision of services in the following ways:

> The degree of friendship or social distance maintained between mothers and caregiver was a critical dimension of family day care. An optimal social distance appears to be maintained in which friends become more distant and strangers become closer. . . . Those arrangements started between friends . . . tended to be used only temporarily. The task of renegotiating a prior relationship from one of friendship to one involving exchange of money for services proved to be hazardous either to the friendship or the child-care arrangement: the arrangement was terminated to save the friendship or the friendship was lost. However, a well-negotiated contractual relationship between strangers was consistent with friendly relations, in which mutual satisfaction bred a special friendship that contributed to an enduring arrangement.[32]

Such evidence suggests that informal and formal or paid for and friendship linkages must be carefully worked out if network attachments and services are both to survive. When barter rather than money is exchanged in family networks—in short, when reciprocity is at work—the outcome may be very different from what the Portland study indicates. In a book called *Helping Ourselves: Families and the Human Network,* the physician–author Mary C. Howell—who advocates the use of informal resources rather than professionals whenever possible—proposes:

> We can institute regular and equitable arrangements to share child care within our social networks. In some cases the most workable arrangement will be an exchange of child care for child care: if you take care of our children on

Monday, Wednesday, and Friday mornings, we shall take care of your children on Tuesday, Thursday, and Saturday afternoons. Or a group of parents in a neighborhood may pool resources so that a dozen children may spend time together in the care of three adults. . . . In other cases, child care may be exchanged for entirely different services . . . meals prepared, lawns mowed, or housecleaning services. . . . When a child stays in the home of another family, and when the arrangement proves to be a compatible contact of family and childcare styles, the two families involved can grow to be very close. The family daycare arrangements of my own family have created relationships very like kinship.[33]

Clearly, young middle-class families need social supports, especially in regard to their young children. The provision of such services sometimes seems to involve also an emotional support component. Rossi's observations about "social deprivation" and "the isolated contemporary household" are appropriately considered by planners of services for young middle-class families. For example, along with child care, women's groups that discuss the special issues related to the changed status of women might fill a gap in the lives of some busy middle-class mothers.

Poor Black Families in Urban Neighborhoods

In black ghettos, families' efforts to cope in order to stay alive and avoid depression or desperate behavior require sharing and cooperation from extended family and close friends. Whether supported by earnings from a low-skilled and often irregular job or by welfare payments, such black families must depend on others in their community to help out when they run out, just as somehow the poorest of them manage to help others when they need help. "Sometimes I don't have a damn dime in my pocket, not a crying penny to get a box of paper diapers, milk, a loaf of bread. But you have to have help from everybody and anybody, so don't turn no one down when they come round for help."[34] Whether called mutual aid, reciprocity, or "swapping," the process is essential for families on a mere subsistence income. Such processes are ingrained in the population, the ethnic social identification, and the solidarity of poor black families in white America.[35]

One can never be sure when one will run out of money. The slightest unexpected expense may empty the purse prematurely. Even normally, there is rarely enough for a family's rent, food, and other essentials. Being able to count on kin and others to provide something gives some reassurance that one will not become totally destitute and have to resort to desperate means. Still, the efforts that obligations entail may be draining in many ways, emotionally as well as materially. Old women in a network may discourage a younger woman's marriage so they can continue to count on her help without a husband's counterexpectations. Strains may develop from nonreciprocation: "If someone who takes things from me ain't giving me anything in return, she can't get nothing else."[36]

Among poor American blacks, taking care of others begins early in a child's life. For example, a firstborn woman remembers as a three-year-old caring for her newborn brother:

> Most of my recollection is looking after the baby. I remember mother carried me to a rocking chair to hold the baby. To keep the baby she'd tie me in the rocking chair and that's the way she would do her work.[37]

Starting so early in this kind of caretaking relationship is likely to increase one's feelings of competence in such roles. Thus, the long-learned capacities of a young woman described in "Coming Up as a Girl in the Ghetto" fall right into place when she brings her three children to live with her mother and her mother's six children. Not yet age twenty-one, this young mother remarks about looking after nine children:

> All the kids and us got along fine. I would buy clothes for *her kids,* and she would buy for mine. When she would go out I would keep the kids. They was just like they was mine, 'cause I kept them. While they (the mother and stepfather) was at work I kept the kids. So they didn't have no problem; they could work and stay on the place.[38]

The history of black families' collaborative coping is reported to have begun in the United States during slavery days when the survival of blacks repeatedly depended on their working together. The poverty of most blacks since then has perpetuated "the mutual aid system" of black extended families.[39] Collaborative coping is thus part of a long cultural heritage. As such, it remains entwined in black families' assumptions about living and essential social practices. Collaboration becomes basic to family socialization. Such behavior is both modeled and preached. In addition, the multiple advantages of an extended family's sharing ensure its continuation by persons reared in such families. For example, receiving help may be accompanied by little if any sense of the stigma or shame that middle-class families' members may feel when helped, since the latter assume that coping independently and making one's own way on one's own is the right way. Such a family's having to be helped is indicative of the personal failure of the breadwinner and, by diffusion, other family members.

Of course, as with almost any set of social expectations, problems may arise in their realization. It seems ironic that families in poverty, with the slimmest resources, are expected to give to others in their extended kinship network, and there are undoubtedly times when, in the course of sharing, a donor family's members must severely tighten their own belts to do so. In addition, there may be an unwillingness to share, or demands from many sources may be excessive, and resources may be inappropriately given away. A daughter's earned money, turned over for five years to her mother's safekeeping for the daughter's college education, may be given to an older sister who is in a crisis situation.[40] Moving geographically far away from the kinship network may save an aspiring member who wants (selfishly?) to get ahead. Rupturing attachments adds seriously to the strains of upwardly mobile family members who try to make it on their own.

Coping in black communities does not always, of course, involve sharing. Much of the physical environment in black ghettos is unyieldingly unresponsive to family efforts at local improvement. And jobs—when jobs are available for unskilled or semiskilled workers—are likely to be tedious, menial, and poorly paid, only rarely exciting curiosity or personal interest and involvement. Competence required on such jobs is low-level, activity often repetitive. Returning home daily after such routines may not inspire more than relief from drudgery. The family living place may be both dismal and resistant to any efforts at improvement, a condition which further reduces feelings of competence. For example, home maintenance skills are understandably challenged and overwhelmed in the house of a young couple, both employed, with two children, whose housing unit is described as follows:

> This apartment, like all the apartments in this complex, was poorly built. The electrical system was faulty, and fires had broken out as a result. Johnny said there had already been two small fires in his apartment. The walls were so thin you could hear people who lived in the apartments next door, as well as those above. The roof leaked; water stains could be seen on the ceiling as well as the walls. The screens were torn off the windows and doors; Johnny said he had replaced them several times and wasn't going to again. The doors didn't lock and his front door has a hole in it. . . .[41]

This family's plans to save enough to move to better quarters had been defeated by Johnny's wife having to take time off from work, being "in and out of the hospital" with a variety of somatic problems. Johnny's two sisters' children were often in the house, playing with their cousins while Johnny tried to watch TV. To modify the sense of entrapment such circumstances induced, Johnny is reported to have become involved in gambling. When there is little in one's environment that one can control through one's own or one's family's coping efforts, letting chance take over at a gaming table makes some kind of sense. But what can children in this family and its immediate milieu learn about the value of developing special capacities, about their applicability, and about the environment's responsiveness to personal efforts? Perhaps they learn primarily the difficulties of trying to make it on one's own and the importance of family relationships. Writing of "the elasticity of residence patterns," Carol Stack notes, "That one can repeatedly join the households of kin is a great source of security among those living in poverty, and they come to depend on it. The loyalties toward kinsmen offset to some degree, the self-defeating ordeal of unemployment and poverty."[42]

Because racism so reduces the economic and social opportunities of American blacks, the black family network becomes an essential support and buffer for its members. Considered as socioeconomic and cultural units, poor black families cope cooperatively with amazing power against strong odds. Thus, well-informed human service workers see black families potentially and typically as a powerful resource—and not in a context of deviance or pathology.

Most blacks themselves, in a study done in Dayton, Ohio, recognize the superiority of their own families over economically comparable white families in at least certain respects—for example, providing shelter for their own dependent members, whether they are children or the aged, and valuing education and wanting their children to attend college. Knowing how the society works, they want better access to its opportunities. In addition, black families are seen to encourage industriousness, "teach their children to be happy, even when times are hard," emphasize the importance of religion, and "stress cooperation within the family."[43] Such values in black family life are sometimes not given their due by workers in human service agencies, set up to intervene remedially in family problems—whether of serious illness or other crises—rather than to help prevent problems by supplementing supports and family strengths.

The Michigan Survey Research Center's longitudinal panel study of a representative sample of the same 20,000 American men, women, and children over more than a decade examines, among other issues, "the question of the stability over time of the status of being poor."[44] Considering what has just been noted about the fluidity of the black family household, sharing its quarters with needy extended kin and others on an open come-and-go basis, I note the Michigan study finds "a considerable amount of variation in family income from year to year" and that "changes in family composition are the most important factor producing change in family income relative to needs."[45] Moreover, the Michigan researchers find that "wage advantages enjoyed by white men cannot be explained solely or even primarily by superior qualifications or more attachment to the labor force"; they conclude that "those who claim that the labor market treats workers fairly in the sense that equally productive workers are paid equally are likely to be wrong."[46] (Similar differences are found in the wage gap between men and women.) Finally, regarding black families, "compared to the sometimes poor, the persistently poor were disproportionately black and in female-headed families." As reviewers Lee Rainwater and Martin Rein conclude, "Clearly it is the persistently poor who should be the primary object of antipoverty policy."[47] Seeing the victims of racism and other consequent gross disadvantages in terms of social deviance and pathology confuses cause and effect. Such perspectives are likely to decrease rather than increase black family members' optimal opportunities for their own development.

CHANGES IN FAMILY LIFE
OVER TIME

In this chapter thus far, dimensions of family life have been examined in terms of families' economic situations, ethnicity, and living places. The dimension of time has, however, been ignored. Over time, especially during families' earliest years together, individual family members grow and develop at different rates, modifying relationships within the mini-network of family. In addition, the events in the family's external milieus, as well as internally, are likely to bring about significant changes in the ways families live. In this last part of Chapter Seven, I shall focus on a few of the changes which may be triggered by the very start of family life with the birth of the first child, and then, finally, by the removal of children and termination of a young family's life. The latter situation occurs when a child welfare agency apprehends and tries to make permanent plans for the children in a Native Indian family.

Starting Family Life

When a couple says, "We are starting a family," they mean that a first child is either planned or on the way. In the latter case, the couple who has previously related primarily to each other as a dyad, will now, as a pregnant mother and expectant father, cease to be a twosome. Awareness of the coming baby modifies the nature of their interaction with one another in many ways. They have either a common concern which brings them closer together or a sense of intrusion which separates them from each other, and sometimes they experience both sets of feelings ambivalently at various times during the nine-month gestation period. In addition, a new orientation to the future influences much of what they do; prospective parents get involved in matters that will shape their world tomorrow—factors with which their child will have to cope and about which childless or unattached people may have much less concern. Use of the family framework (presented earlier in this chapter) makes clear how a couple's lives are altered, probably more dramatically and totally than at any earlier time in their lives, with the birth of a first baby.

Specifically, their household becomes a different kind of economic unit, money resources shrinking as the wife takes leave from her employment or as family income is allocated to new kinds of expenses for the neonate. Living place—both neighborhood and domicile—have new demands imposed upon them as, for example, a protected place for baby to sleep or quick advice in what seems like a crisis is needed. Ready accessibility to the couple's social network becomes crucial as a resource for information, brief substitute infant care, or emotional support during the sometimes strained and draining parenting of an infant. Most important perhaps, as illustrated below, are the changed relationships of the parental couple with one another, when the household's composition and daily preoccupations are so radically changed by an infant's presence.

For many parents, curiosities and shared interests and involvements peak with the arrival of a new creature, so fascinating to observe as growth and behavior changes occur visibly almost daily. So many young parents have had inadequate preparation for the care of a newborn, and especially one who may require special attention, that parents may feel their personal competence challenged in ways that devastate their sense of self-adequacy. Ideally, their social supports can provide emotional props, too. Between the parents, issues of reciprocity—of partnership—arise as they probably never have before the baby's birth. How much and what parts of a newborn's care can a father share with a mother? Collaboration between spouses is expected to vary with differences in cultural norms regarding male and female roles in the household. Still, when a parent is feeling overwhelmed and helpless, a sympathetic spouse is not constrained by cultural sanctions but somehow manages to provide assistance, directly or indirectly. Although philosophies and social behavior differ among cultural groups, "people everywhere share basic human sentiments that transcend all cultural differences."[48]

Finally, families communicate their values to all members, if only by evaluating their members' behavior and thus contributing to the development of their self-images. With the arrival of first child the newly formed family adds the identity of "parent" to the spouses' self-images, an identity quickly qualified as "good" or "bad," "happy" or "troubled," as a host of factors and the parents' perceptions of them define their new roles. In brief, each of the dimensions of family and its influences on members' development is changed with the birth of an infant.

Since the keystone in the arch of family life is the strength of the marital relationship, it is important to recognize that the quality of that relationship has been found frequently to decline when the first child is born.[49] In a Knoxville, Tennessee study of couples located through prenatal classes, four kinds of negative themes regarding becoming a parent were identified and documented:

1. "the physical demands of caring for the child,"
2. "strains on the husband–wife relationship ... caused by less time spent together as a couple, changes in the sexual relationship, and the belief that the child's needs are more important than the needs of the husband and wife,"
3. "emotional costs experienced by the new parents" related to their feelings of "total responsibility" and "uncertainty about their competence,"
4. "opportunity costs and restrictions" regarding such matters as their social lives and recreation, money, and careers."[50]

Mothers, in other studies, made such remarks as the following:

"He didn't like the time and affection I gave the baby instead of him. He kept referring to the child as 'your baby.' "[51]

"One day I woke up and there I was, married and with a baby. And I thought, 'I can't stand it! I can't stand to have my life over when I'm so young.' "[52]

This working class woman's husband remarked some years later:

"I had just turned twenty and, all of a sudden, I had a wife and kid. You couldn't just go out anymore when you felt like it. If you wanted to go anyplace, you had to take the kid, and that meant carrying the milk and stuff wherever you went. By the time you got him all together and ready to go, it wasn't worth going.

"We used to run around a lot before he was born, and then we couldn't anymore. I guess it wasn't all his fault; we didn't have the money to go places and do things anyway. But I still used to get mad at him, and at her, too—my wife, I mean—because I felt like it was on account of them I was stuck."[53]

At no time, of course, does being poor help when one becomes a new parent! For this reason, family allowances of various kinds have been provided in Austria, Canada, Czechoslovakia, Denmark, West Germany, Finland, France, Hungary, Israel, Norway, Poland, and the United Kingdom,[54] and the need for at least a family *starting* allowance has been urged, to offset the economic dislocations caused by childbirth in economically marginal families, particularly.[55]

In addition to economic constraints, the transition to parenthood brings on many other kinds of social and personal change. In contemporary society, prenatal *and* postnatal group meetings for parents offer a forum for the sharing of concerns and experiences regarding changes which a new child brings to a couple's existence. The health and social services conjointly should routinely provide early parenting programs for all adults who are starting a family.

It is likely in the next few decades that the transition to parenthood will become a less problematic process than it seems today. This is in part because fewer and fewer couples who do not want to become parents are likely to find themselves with newborns. Demographic evidence of the 1970s in the United States indicates that more couples chose to have fewer children and to have them later in life when they felt readier.[56] Despite inferences made from such data (and from those on divorce) that "the family" is in decline, it is equally plausible to argue that the increase in variations on traditional family forms gives support to the remarkable adaptability and survival of family life. Moreover, steps on the pathway to parenting may very well change. For example, the practice of husbands attending the deliveries of their children, giving emotional support to their wives and otherwise sharing in the birth process, may prove to have lasting effects on the bonding and involvement of fathers with their neonates.[57] Most important perhaps is the acceptance of a less romanticized and more realistic set of expectations regarding parenthood. Young couples will then be better prepared to take the difficult with the good aspects of caring for their progeny. Writing of the beginnings of family life in a French village in the 1950s, anthropologist Laurence Wylie remarked, "As young people settle down to raise a family they find their freedom is gone, and their work, their responsibilities, and their worries have increased many times. They accept the situation, since nothing can be done about it: but they join in the general chorus of adults complaining about it."[58] Perhaps such a chorus will in time become more acceptable in the New World as in the Old, where pain is recognized as an integral part of life and material comforts are less available and less expected.

Ending Family Life Young

There are limits, of course, to how much pain and deprivation a family can take and remain intact—or at least remain effective in its child care roles. The professional literature on family conflict and divorce stresses the communication problems of spouses upon whose relationship continuing family life depends. In these times, most divorces occur within the first six years of marriage or while families are still young. But the causes of young family termination are less easily summated than the demographic data suggests. What lies behind the painful feelings leading up to, during, and following the ultimate ruptures? Vague terms such as *incompatibility* are not illuminating. Once divorce is decided on, such issues as child custody, the stages of spouses' adaptations to loss, economic arrangements, and available support networks are among the multiple matters of concern to both separated parents and human service workers who do family work. Little special attention, however, has been given to family disruption among the very poor and especially among such minorities as Native Indian families where the pains of family dismemberment are part of a larger context of social and personal disorganization.

I have chosen this route because I believe that societal pressures of economic and cultural kinds actively influence the termination of family life at all social class levels. With a primarily middle-class orientation, interpersonal and intrafamilial focuses currently guide family work in the human services. The extrafamilial situations of poor Native Indians are, however, too blatant as causes for their family problems for anyone to ignore them. Less obvious, but nonetheless influential, are money matters and other societal, religious, and cultural pressures that affect marriages and their termination in skilled blue collar families and the broad range of white collar families.

Native men and women migrating to towns and cities from the poverty of their villages or reserves often find the increased pace, the impersonality, and their exclusion from any but the drinking community very strange and depressing. Problems and dilemmas of "child neglect" bring unfamiliar officials such as the police, social workers, and judges into their lives. Such interventions sometimes result in their loss of their child(ren) and the exacerbation of their "problems of alcoholism, unemployment, and emotional duress," as Renate Andres writes about Native people: "Family breakup following the removal of a child increased the likelihood that remaining children will be removed."[59]

The Hoover family, a Native Indian family living in the northwestern United States, came to my attention through a demonstration project on permanent planning for children in foster care. Permanent planning aims to prevent children's multiple replacements in foster care, from one foster home to another. Permanent planning seeks, from the moment a child enters care, to contract with the child's parent(s), on a time-limited basis, for the child to be returned home, under specifiable conditions, or for the child to be relinquished for either adoption or a long-term foster home placement if the child's own parent(s) cannot be helped to care for the child in a relatively stable way. Permanent planning seems well-rooted theoretically in what is known about children's developmental needs for a sense of permanence and security in their family lives. It seeks to avoid or reduce the attenuation of reciprocal relations between child and parent when children enter foster care.

There are painful dilemmas, however, in this as well as other child welfare programs when one considers the cultural contexts out of which Native Indian parents and their children come and against which their "child neglect" must be considered. The following observations on Native Indian ways are especially germane to an understanding of families like the Hoovers, out of what their apparent demoralization grows, and the kinds of macrosocietal economic and social policies which should be developed to prevent families from reaching the kind of deterioration and personal tragedy the record reports. Renate Andres, whose observations are supported by other Native Indian writers,[60] generalizes as follows:

> . . . Indian identity is derived from the relatedness to communal or tribal groups. Historically, the Indian child belonged not only to a specific family,

but also to the extended family which shared relatedness to other families in other communities, through blood lines and official ties. In this setting the child identified with his people and his tribe, and could expect care, protection and security in this cohesive kinship system. If a child's parents could not look after him he was accepted by a related family, thereby reinforcing his Indian identity.

. . . The introduction to new values and mores, the loss of traditional roles in kinship, the decline of importance in the male role, and social dependency due to the loss of an economic base, has lead to increased family strife. Alcoholism, drug addiction, delinquency, crime, physical and mental illness, as well as the abuse and neglect of children, are all behavioral symptoms of stress itself.

. . . Traditional Indian religions teach and practice a pantheistic view of life. This view holds to the basic truth that man is a part of a delicate balance in a universe in which all life forms and natural elements inter-relate and interact. No part is more or less important than another and man must live his life in such a manner that the balance be not upset. By contrast, most Caucasian religions subscribe to the belief that nature is to be mastered . . .

Indian parents pay high respect to the individuality of their children, allowing them great freedom to grow and develop in natural ways. Parents instruct their children about right and wrong, but allow them the decision. White parents tend to believe that it is the parents' responsibility to direct and control children until they have internalized the values of the parents, and have been prepared for their superior role in the scheme of things. Any child caught between these two sets of values will be confused, and find it difficult to internalize either code of behaviour.

. . . As the Indian child grows older, he is shown less overt expression of affection and learns by example not to display openly his own feelings. Fairly early after weaning the child has learned remarkable emotional self-control. He rarely indulges in emotional displays and appears to accept all occurrences without show of surprise. This characteristic has given Indian people a reputation for being a stoic people and it is often interpreted by Whites as "limited emotional response" or "lack of feeling."[61]

Perhaps the most pertinent observation is that the apprehension and removal of a child begins or contributes significantly to the downward cycle of family dissolution. The message that a young parent is not able to care adequately for his or her child(ren) is likely to be devastating. Communicated across a gap in cultural values, what is heard is likely to be interpreted with confused emotions of hostility and self-deprecation, or at least with the feelings of deprivation a study of Puerto Rican and other impoverished New York City mothers experienced when their children were removed and placed in foster care.[62]

The report on the Hoover family derives originally from child welfare records. It might be revealing to have a taped description by Lillian Hoover of what happened, from *her* perspective. The termination of family life is, of course, a stressful experience for the children, the parents, and in this kind of situation, the human service workers involved, probably contributing to the high rate of burn-out among caseworkers in child protective agencies.

THE HOOVER FAMILY
(RECORD NO. 19)

On October 3, 1975, two groups of people gathered in the lobby of Trask County Courthouse for the beginning of a two-day hearing which would decide whether or not Lillian Hoover's (names of clients and others have been changed) parental rights to her four children should be terminated. One group consisted of this mother, her sister, her court-appointed lawyer and a psychologist. In the second group were three social workers, among them Joyce Miller, assigned to the Permanent Planning Project, Dan Simons, an attorney from the Portland Public Defender's Office representing the interests of the children, the district attorney, another psychologist, and a former landlord of the mother.

Termination hearings, unlike other civil proceedings which involve the interests of only two parties, consider the interests of three parties; the parents, the state, and child. Each party may have legal representation. Lillian hoped the court would decide that she could be an adequate parent to her children. The child's attorney would argue that it was in the best interests of these four children that the mother's rights be terminated and they be placed in adoptive homes; and in this case the state agreed that Lillian's rights should be terminated.

It would be a difficult hearing for everyone. The pro-tem judge was faced with what another judge has called "one of the most drastic actions a state can take." State v. Jamison, 251 Or. 114, 117, 444 P. 2d. 15 (1968). Lawyers know that it is difficult to evaluate whether in any given case the grounds for termination can be proved or disproved. Joyce, the caseworker who had tried to help Lillian become an adequate mother, would now have to testify publicly and in detail about Lillian's repeated failures to make a home for her children. Lillian faced the possibility of permanent loss of her children and knowledge that she had been judged an inadequate mother by society.

Foster Care Placement
and Initial Assessment

The Hoover children's first experience with the Children's Services Division (CSD) took place on July 20, 1971, when they were picked up and placed in substitute care. At 10:30 a.m. on that day officials of the Trask County Health Department found the four children, ages five, three, two, and two months, at their home alone. The children were described as very dirty, and having various skin rashes and burns, and without adequate clothing. Of particular concern was the two-month old baby who had no bottle or diapers. The parents were believed to be at a drinking party. Three days later when the parents contacted CSD they did not deny that they had been involved in such parties, nor that they had left the children unsupervised during these times.

The condition of the house was described by the landlord as totally unlivable. The garbage consisted of "unused abundant foods, beer and wine bottles (some half full), and all kinds of junk and clothing. The upstairs rugs had to be discarded because they were hopelessly soiled with paint, ketchup, and syrup. All the mattresses . . . had to be taken to the dump because they were totally soiled with blood and urine. Dirty diapers were thrown all over the house and outside in the yard. They had plugged the toilets with clothing and used the whole house as a bathroom."

The children were made wards of the court with care, custody, and supervision awarded to CSD. They were placed in foster homes; the baby in one home and the three older children in another. The Hoovers agreed to foster care as a temporary plan and expressed a willingness to make the necessary changes so the children could be returned.

During the following year, the parents visited the children three times and would often miss appointments. In August of 1972 the Hoovers separated. After his separation from Lillian, Sam never saw his children again. Lillian disappeared until early in 1973, when she asked to visit the children and indicated she was going to divorce her husband and wanted to make a home for the family. Plans were made to accomplish this goal but Lillian's efforts to follow through were sporadic, and in July she disappeared again. She contacted the agency in December with the request that the children be released so she could take them to live with their grandmother in another state. An investigation of the grandparents' home led caseworkers to reject this as an unacceptable plan.

In December, 1973, the Hoover case was transferred to Joyce, the special permanent planning caseworker, as the children were considered likely candidates for adoption. They had been in foster care for more than two years and were thought likely to remain in foster care throughout their childhood if a permanent plan was not made for their future. Their own parents repeatedly failed in their efforts to be reunited with the children, but the children were young enough to be adopted by other parents.

The task of dealing with the court on issues related to child custody is complex, requiring special casework skills and astute supervision. Joyce was trained to handle court matters and other problems encountered in moving children into permanent homes. First, intensive services were provided to parents. If they could not demonstrate that they could provide an adequate home, voluntary relinquishment or court action to terminate parental rights was the goal.

Soon after Joyce had received the case the former caseworker took her to meet both of the foster families and the Hoover children. Caseworkers in this small county typically cooperate in this way to smooth the transition from one worker to another. Even though each worker is responsible for his caseload, consultation on cases and cooperation among workers is the rule.

Joyce relied on the local knowledge and the cooperative attitude of the other workers in her first task with the Hoover case—locating the parents. One of the caseworkers reported that she heard Mrs. Hoover was working at a nursing home and that Mr. Hoover was in jail. With these leads Joyce succeeded in finding Mr. Hoover but it took a month to locate Mrs. Hoover.

Casework with Father

By the time Joyce called the jail, Mr. Hoover had been released. Letters sent to his new address elicited no response. As active pursuit of elusive parents was a standard procedure for the project. Joyce visited the address she had been given by the jail and talked with Mr. Hoover who indicated an interest in having his children returned. When a month had gone by with no word from him, Joyce again wrote and asked what plans he had to visit and to achieve the other goals which would result in return of the children. Another month passed with no response, so she made a visit.

Even though transportation was available for Mr. Hoover, by August 1974, he had missed every opportunity to behave in a way that would result in the return of the children. Early in 1975, it became clear that a petition would be filed to terminate his parental rights.

Casework with Mother: Locating the Mother

Locating Mrs. Hoover was not easy. A check of all the nursing homes in the area determined that she was not employed at any of them. The next lead came from Lillian's sister whose children were also in foster care, and she reported to her caseworker that Lillian was living in a town nearby. Joyce wrote a letter and Lillian came immediately to the CSD office. She stated that she very much wanted her children back and was interested in a program for restoration. A plan was made for Lillian to visit the children regularly, to seek employment, and to obtain professional counseling. Counseling was considered essential because Lillian had continued to drink heavily and realized that she could not care for her children when she was frequently involved in drinking parties lasting several days.

Visits

For the first eight months of project activity Lillian kept half the scheduled visits with the children. When she came the visits were considered successful, as Lillian was affectionate and responded well to children. However, Jim, age two, screamed during part of each visit, and afterward became more obstinate and experienced some loss of appetitite. Richard, age five, wet the bed for several nights after the visits. Susan, age four, began clinging to her foster mother and asked if she did not "born" her, and Barbara, age eight, became hostile and overly assertive. Even though the children's behavior caused a problem for the foster parents, they were cooperative and seemed to understand that the outcome was uncertain and that visits were necessary. By this time the children had been in their foster homes for three years, and the three younger children hardly knew their mother.

Employment

Lillian's efforts to find employment were erratic, and the jobs she found were short-lived. She worked a few days as a babysitter and a couple of weeks in a tavern.

The caseworker referred Lillian to the Department of Vocational Rehabilitation, but she missed all appointments. She did see the DVR counselor once, however, when the CSD caseworker supervisor noted that both Lillian and the DVR counselor happened to be in the CSD office at the same time and asked him to interview Lillian then. The process of investigating the possibility of this service was speeded up by the helpfulness of Joyce's colleague.

Other Services

Lillian indicated an interest in parenting classes. In this small, rural county classes were conducted weekly and a newcomer could only enter at the beginning of the session. Lillian was enrolled but did not attend.

Lillian also missed two appointments for counseling at the Mental Health Association, prompting the counselor to write a letter stating that no more appointments would be scheduled.

During the seven months of casework activity all efforts to help Lillian meet the minimum requirements to obtain the custody of the children had not been successful. Visits to the children had been sporadic, employment fitful, and appointments for counseling and parent education classes had been missed. Lillian continued to move frequently and her housekeeping was as unsatisfactory as when the children were originally placed in foster care.

Written Agreement

In June 1974, Lillian moved to the State of Washington to live with her parents and planned to enroll in a rehabilitation program through the Indian agency. She was part Indian and therefore qualified for help through the agency.

In September a contract was written and signed by CSD and Lillian as a last ditch effort to motivate her to make at least the minimum changes necessary. If she failed at this, Joyce planned to move ahead with a termination of parental rights petition. The contract listed what each party would do. Lillian Hoover would: (1) Actively seek employment, and once this was obtained she would budget money to provide adequate food, shelter, and clothing for herself and pay child support of $5 per child per month; (2) visit the children twice a month at the CSD office and notify the caseworker one day in advance if unable to come; (3) participate in family counseling and in the alcohol rehabilitation clinic; (4) participate in medical appointments for her children; (5) remain at one address; (6) maintain adequate housekeeping standards. CSD would: (1) Work with Lillian in any reasonable way to regain custody of the children; (2) arrange visitation every two weeks; (3) help Lillian get assistance from other agencies and arrange transportation.

During the weeks following the signing of this contract, Lillian's behavior did not change. Through the Indian program, she entered an alcoholic rehabilitation facility for an 18-day stay. Three days before she was to complete the program Lillian left abruptly. Through her frequent moves Joyce persisted in her efforts to keep track of Lillian and get her to fulfill the terms of the contract.

210 *YOUNG FAMILIES AND SOCIAL SUPPORTS*

Petition for Termination

The target date of December 1974, passed without progress made toward meeting the contract terms. Joyce decided to petition for termination of parental rights for both parents. She had discussed voluntarily relinquishment of their rights with them but they rejected it. The parental behaviors which had necessitated the children's foster care placement were not improved. In fact, during the years their children had been in foster care the chances of reuniting this family worsened.

The decision to pursue termination was made only after reviewing the details of the case carefully with colleagues and Trask County caseworkers who knew the family. Joyce began preparing the case for the court hearing. She had documented each step of the treatment program, including all efforts to contact the parents, to put them in touch with other agencies, and their repeated failure to respond. She found witnesses, helped them prepare their testimony, filed the termination petition drawn with the assistance of the Metropolitan Public Defender Attorney, and obtained a court date. Filing the termination petition was delayed several times; it was not filed until July.

With the filing of the petition, CSD's work with the court began. Trask County was seen by agency staff as presenting a high barrier to the termination of parental rights. The court rarely held either termination hearings or review hearings in the past. For the Hoover case, this was the first contact with the court since the custody hearing four years before.

Until the advent of the project, termination of parental rights cases were rare in many Oregon counties and this was true of Trask County. Agency staff believed that the court actively blocked such cases. The judge was rumored to resist termination of parental rights and so would appoint a pro-tem judge to hear such cases. Caseworkers saw the court as obstructive and uncooperative, the case was scrupulously prepared, and taken to court only when compelling evidence was available.

Termination of Mother's Rights

As the two groups were waiting for Lillian's hearing to start, Joyce left the group and went over to talk with Lillian. She had grown fond of Lillian after a year and a half of intensive work with her, but was convinced that she could not be an adequate mother to the children. The judge and lawyers found termination a radical and painful action, but for the caseworker it was doubly tormenting. She had to testify against a person with whom she had been intimately associated, whom she had encouraged and tried to help. Together they had worked toward a goal and failed.

Lillian's attorney argued that Lillian could care for her children with the help of services offered by the Indian agency. A psychologist for Lillian testified that if she had psychological counseling, money due her for Indian inheritance, and family support, she could care for the children.

The state and the Public Defender, representing the children, argued that since no progress had been made toward reuniting this family in the four years and three months the children were in foster care, enough time had been allowed and this mother's rights should be terminated.

A summary of Lillian's past behavior relevant to her ability to be a mother, including patterns of visiting, changes of residence, efforts to control drinking, attempts to find employment, attendance at parenting classes and counseling sessions and her level of ability to provide for the children's physical needs was presented. Lillian's former landlord testified to her poor housekeeping. A psychologist who had evaluated both the children and the mother testified for the state that it was his belief that Lillian could not be an adequate mother to the children.

A few days later a verdict was handed down terminating the parental rights of Lillian Hoover to her four children. Joyce heard the verdict and told the news to Lillian. She wept.

Termination of Father's Rights

In January, the termination hearing for Sam Hoover was held. The state and the children's attorney's position was that Sam's parental rights should be terminated since he had not made the changes necessary to permit the return of his children. The testimony included evidence that visits were infrequent, financial support to the children nonexistent, attempts to find employment irregular, and that little effort had been made to care for the children's needs. Sam's attorney argued that he had re-married, settled down, and would soon be able to care for the children.

His parental rights were terminated but Sam decided to appeal the decision. The termination decision was upheld in the appellate court.

The three older Hoover children were adopted by their foster parents. At the time this was written, the fate of Jim was in doubt. He has lived with his foster parents since he was taken into foster care at the age of two months and was five years old at the time this was written. Adoption by these parents is unlikely since they are an older couple. It is possible that he will be placed in an adoptive home where he can visit with his present foster parents.

Aftermath

On November 11, in an interview published in the County newspaper, Joyce accused the local court officials of delaying termination cases. Trask County, she said, has the worst record of the 36 counties in Oregon. "One ongoing case has been delayed for several months because the hearing dates have been continually rescheduled." In a letter to the editor the Juvenile Court Judge and the court director denied these charges and offered data to support their position. Before the dispute was over, several additional articles had been written. Thereafter, communication improved between the court and CSD. The county juvenile judge began to hear termination cases himself, instead of appointing a pro-tem judge. In conversations with Dan Simons, the public defender attorney, representing children's interests, the judge indicated an interest in terminations and in becoming more acquainted with case law in this area. In assessing the situation in Trask County, Dan Simons said, "The obstacles (to terminations) existed because they hadn't been tested."[63]

The sad dilemma in the history of the Hoover family is that in the effort to provide the children with a family context conducive to their development, the human services may have magnified the parents' feelings of incompetence and suffering. The separation of Lillian and Sam Hoover would probably have occurred even though the children were not removed, although it is possible that their apprehension hastened the marital rupture. At the late date at which child welfare workers intervened, moreover, there was probably no alternate route to take. Or was there? One always wonders what might have been done for a "happier ending."

On a macrosocietal scale, Native Indian society needs provisions that enable the people to regain a sense of dignity and the capacities and options to live either autonomously or in an integrated way within contemporary society. I know of one Native Indian reserve that manages its own child welfare as well as other human services; it has some of the economic and personnel resources to do so. Under such circumstances, couples seem less likely to live as Sam and Lillian Hoover did, and if they should become so demoralized, their people can offer some of the help needed, which may make its receipt more acceptable—and effective.

Generally, the introduction of "permanent planning" in child welfare has led to thinking about and approaching the whole family rather than only placing the children. Traditionally in child welfare, as David Fanshel remarks, "Once the children enter care, the parents are likely to be treated as discardable."[64] A new set of perspectives on the family as a unit of interacting members with needs for supports as a unit is beginning to permeate the human services. But this should not occur in ways that minimize the continuing importance of each member as a person or of the family's environments. In the dimensions and variants of family life presented in this chapter, family is seen both as a context for all its members' social development and in its living place and macrosocietal contexts.

NOTES

[1] Sheila B. Kamerman and Alfred J. Kahn, eds., *Family Policy: Government and Families in Fourteen Countries* (New York: Columbia University Press, 1978).

[2] Bernice T. Eiduson and others, "Comparative Socialization Practices in Traditional and Alternate Families," in Michael E. Lamb, ed., *Nontraditional Families: Parenting and Child Development* (Hillsdale, N.J.: Lawrence Erlbaum, 1982).

[3] William Kessen, *Childhood in China* (New Haven: Yale University Press, 1975), pp. 23–26. Quoted with permission.

[4] William Kessen, "Children," *Items* 33 (June 1979), p. 34.

[5] David Finkelstein, "When the Snow Thaws," *The New Yorker,* September 10, 1979, 127–150, pp. 138–39.

[6] Kessen, *Items,* p. 34.

[7] Ibid.

[8] Arlene Skolnick, *The Intimate Environment: Exploring Marriage and the Family* (Boston: Little, Brown and Company, 1978).

[9] Wesley R. Burr and others, eds., *Contemporary Theories about the Family, Vol. II: General Theories/Theoretical Orientations* (New York: The Free Press, 1979).

[10] John and Elizabeth Newson, *Four Years Old in an Urban Community* (London: George Allen and Unwin, 1968), p. 156.

[11] Ibid., p. 162.

[12] Ibid., p. 160.

[13] Ibid., p. 168.

[14] Ibid., p. 166.

[15] Ruth D. Tuck, *Not with the Fist: Mexican-Americans in a Southwest City* (New York: Harcourt, Brace and Co., 1946), pp. 122–35.

[16] Ramon Fernandez–Marina, Eduardo D. Maldonado–Sierra, and Richard D. Trent, "Three Basic Themes in Mexican and Puerto Rican Family Values," *Journal of Social Psychology*, 48 (1958) 167–81; Nathan Murillo, "The Mexican American Family," in Nathaniel N. Wagner and Marsha J. Haug, eds., *Chicanos: Social and Psychological Perspectives* (St. Louis: C. V. Mosby Co., 1971); Fernando Penalosa, "Mexican Family Roles," *Journal of Marriages and the Family*, 30 (1968) 680–89; Robert Staples, "The Mexican American Family: Its Modifications over Time and Space," *Phylon*, 32 (1971), 179–92.

[17] Tuck, *Not with the Fist*, pp. 126–27.

[18] Printed with the permission of the author, Dr. Felipe de Ortego y Gasca, Director, Institute for Intercultural Studies and Research, Our Lady of the Lake University, San Antonio, Texas.

[19] Marta Sotomayor, "Mexican-American Interaction with Social Systems," *Social Casework* 52 (1971) p. 322.

[20] Jean Gilbert, "Extended Family Integration among Second-Generation Mexican Americans," in J. Manuel Casas and Susan E. Keefe, eds., *Family and Mental Health in the Mexican American Community*, Monograph no. 7 (Los Angeles: Spanish Speaking Mental Health Research Center, University of California, 1978), p. 46.

[21] Sotomayor, *Social Casework*, p. 321.

[22] Susan E. Keefe, Amado M. Padilla, and Manuel L. Carlos, "The Family as an Emotional Support System," in Casas and Keefe, eds., *Family and Mental Health*, p. 58.

[23] Ibid., p. 66.

[24] Alice S. Rossi, "A Biosocial Perspective on Parenting," in "The Family," *Daedalus*, 106 (Spring 1977), p. 25.

[25] Elizabeth Bott, *Family and Social Network* (London: Tavistock, 1957); Michael Young and Peter Willmott, *Family and Kinship in East London* (Middlesex, England: Penguin Books, 1962); Peter Townsend, *The Family Life of Old People* (Middlesex, England: Penguin Books, 1963); Peter C. Pineo, "The Extended Family in a Working-class Area of Hamilton," in B. R. Blishen and others, eds., *Canadian Society* (Toronto: Macmillan of Canada, 1965); Jeremy Boissevain, "Family Kinship, and Marriage among Italians of Montreal," in S. P. Wakil, ed., *Marriage, Family and Society: Canadian Perspectives* (Toronto: Butterworth, 1975); Hope Jensen Leichter and William E. Mitchell, *Kinship and Casework* (New York: Russell Sage Foundation, 1967).

[26] Lillian Rubin, *Worlds of Pain: Life in the Working-Class Family* (New York: Basic Books, 1976), p. 197.

[27] B. Bradford Brown, "A Life-span Approach to Friendship: Age-related Dimensions of an Ageless Relationship," in H. Lopata and D. Maines, eds., *Research on the Interweave of Social Roles, Vol. 2: Friendship* (Greenwich, Connecticut: J. A. I. Press, 1981).

[28] Anne Marie Tietjen, "Integrating Formal and Informal Support Systems: The Swedish Experience," in James Garbarino and others, eds., *Protecting Children from Abuse and Neglect: Developing and Maintaining Effective Support Systems for Families* (San Francisco: Jossey-Bass, 1980), p. 27.

[29] Ibid., pp. 28–29.

[30] Robert Coles, *Eskimos, Chicanos, Indians: Volume IV of Children of Crisis* (Boston: Little, Brown, 1977), p. 380.

[31] Jane Carroll, "How a Community Pulled Together," *California Living Magazine of the San Francisco Sunday Examiner and Chronicle,* February 21, 1982, p. 24.

[32] Arthur C. Emlen and Joseph B. Perry, Jr., "Child-Care Arrangements," in Lois Hoffman and F. Ivan Nye, eds., *Working Mothers* (San Francisco: Jossey-Bass, 1974), pp. 116-17.

[33] Mary C. Howell, *Helping Ourselves: Families and the Human Network* (Boston: Beacon Press, 1975), pp. 142-43.

[34] Carol B. Stack, *All our Kin: Strategies for Survival in a Black Community* (New York: Harper & Row, 1974), p. 32.

[35] Andrew Billingsley, *Black Families in White America* (Englewood Cliffs, New Jersey: Prentice-Hall, 1968), pp. 10-12.

[36] Stack, *All our Kin,* p. 34.

[37] David A. Schulz, *Coming Up Black: Patterns of Ghetto Socialization* (Englewood Cliffs, New Jersey: Prentice-Hall, 1969), p. 23.

[38] Ibid., p. 26.

[39] Elmer P. Martin and Joanne Mitchell Martin, *The Black Extended Family* (Chicago: University of Chicago Press, 1978), p. 29.

[40] Ibid., p. 34.

[41] Theodore R. Kennedy, *You Gotta Deal with It: Black Families' Relations in a Southern Community* (New York: Oxford University Press, 1980), p. 179.

[42] Stack, *All our Kin,* p. 123.

[43] David D. Royse and Gladys T. Turner, "Strengths of Black Families: A Black Community's Perspectives," *Social Work* 25 (September 1980), 407-9.

[44] Lee Rainwater and Martin Rein, "Tracking Family Experience in the Seventies," *Contemporary Sociology,* 9 (November 1980), p. 780.

[45] Ibid., p. 783.

[46] Ibid.

[47] Ibid., p. 784.

[48] Statement by the Japanese film director, Akira Kurosawa, in Lillian Ross, "Profiles: Kurosawa Frames," *The New Yorker,* December 21, 1981, p. 58.

[49] Joan Aldous, *Family Careers: Developmental Changes in Families* (New York: Wiley, 1978), pp. 164-69; Robert A. Lewis and Graham B. Spanier, "Theorizing about the Quality and Stability of Marriage," in Wesley R. Burr and others, eds., *Contemporary Theories about the Family: Research-Based Theories,* Vol. I (New York: The Free Press, 1979).

[50] Donna L. Sollie and Brent C. Miller, "The Transition to Parenthood as a Critical Time for Building Family Strengths," in Nick Stinnet and others, eds., *Family Strengths: Positive Models for Family Life* (Lincoln: University of Nebraska Press, 1980), pp. 159-62.

[51] Warren B. Miller, "The Intendedness and Wantedness of the First Child," in Warren B. Miller and Lucile F. Newman, eds., *The First Child and Family Formation* (Chapel Hill: Carolina Population Center, The University of North Carolina at Chapel Hill, 1978), p. 219.

[52] Rubin, *Worlds of Pain,* p. 81.

[53] Ibid.

[54] Kamerman and Kahn, *Family Policy.*

[55] Henry S. Maas, "Children's Environments and Child Welfare," *Child Welfare,* 50 (March, 1971), 132-42.

[56] Andrew Hacker, "Farewell to the Family?" *The New York Review of Books,* 29 (March 18, 1982), 37-44.

[57] Robert A. Fein, "Consideration of Men's Experiences and the Birth of a First Child," in Miller and Newman, eds., *The First Child.*

[58] Laurence Wylie, *Village in the Vaucluse,* 3rd ed. (Cambridge, Massachusetts: Harvard University Press, 1974), p. 151.

[59] Renate Andres, "The Apprehension of Native Children," *Ontario Indian,* 4 (April 1981), p. 35.

[60] See, for example, John G. Red Horse, "Family Structure and Value Orientation in American Indians," *Social Casework,* 61 (1980) 462–67, and other articles in the same volume of *Social Casework* by Charlotte Tsoi Goodluck and Gerald Thomas Wilkinson on working with American Indian parents and other Native people.

[61] Andres, "Apprehension," pp. 36–37.

[62] Shirley Jenkins and Elaine Norman, *Filial Deprivation and Foster Care* (New York: Columbia University Press, 1972).

[63] This version of the "Hoover Family" record comes, with permission for its use here, from Janet Lahti, "Adoption of Children in Foster Care: A Comparison of Processes Leading to Adoption by Foster Parents and Adoption by Others," Doctoral Dissertation, Portland State University, June, 1979. Dr. Lahti was on the research staff of the Permanent Planning Project, Regional Research Institute for Human Services, Portland State University, Portland, Oregon, under the directorship of Arthur C. Emlen.

[64] David Fanshel, "Foreword," in Anthony N. Maluccio and Paula A. Sinanoglu, eds., *The Challenge of Partnership: Working with Parents of Children in Foster Care* (New York: Child Welfare League of America, 1981). The current human services approach to families is suggested, partially, by the word "partnership" in the title of this book.

Chapter 8
MIDLIFE TRANSITIONS AND SOCIAL RESPONSIBILITY

INTRODUCTION

Middle Age Allows for Socially
Responsible Involvements

Middle age is the transition period between young adulthood and old age. Midlife is marked by greater diversity among people in their patterns of living and development than at any earlier time of life.

Midlife has been likened to a second adolescence, but somewhat longer, more moderately paced, and based on more experience in living than adolescence. Midlife and adolescence resemble each other in that both periods involve many biological, psychological, and social changes. One's self-image undergoes major redefinitions at both these times of life. As contemporary adolescents typically experience little of the storm and stress that their agemates suffered early in this century, so the middle-aged are not found in any of the few systematic studies on midlife to undergo the "crisis" popular literature emphasizes. The changes of the middle years, although some appear decremental, are usually gradual and are sometimes seen as a relief from young adulthood's strains and constraints.

In middle age, women enter their postreproductive phase, allowing for sexual expression without fear of pregnancy. Men slowly become aware of their diminishing physical powers as body awareness and body monitoring increase. The parents of people in their forties and fifties may become seriously ill or die, reminding the middle-aged to think in terms of the limits to their own "time left."[1] This is an impetus for self-reappraisals and changes in life styles to less routinized and more satisfying ways of living.

The children of married adults leave home, permitting their parents after two or more decades of family life to live as a childless couple again. The consequences range from second honeymoons to the pains of marital ruptures. The latter are followed by adaptations to living single again or to remarriage. Thus, early adult forms of family living—or nonfamily living—repeat themselves. Responses to these second chances are inevitably affected by the choices and imperatives of the first chance.

In regard to jobs and careers, women without child-care obligations may now expand their work roles, reenter the labor market, or return to school. The options the second time around are many for those who choose to pursue them. Men in lower level blue collar or white collar jobs reach occupational plateaus, and in increasing numbers retire early, or in hard times become unemployed. Men in professional and managerial jobs by midlife have either "made it" or must come to terms with the fact that they will never rise further. Under any of these circumstances, the accompanying affective response, as when children leave home, may be feelings of release. The pleasures of child rearing inevitably have their strains, as does the most satisfying of work.

Coupled with the previously cited biological changes, simultaneous changes in work and family contexts are likely to induce reappraisals in midlife of the self. "Who am I now?" asks the postparental woman freed from the full-time responsibilities that had conflicted so long with her extrafamilial work and other interests.

"Who am I now?" asks the older male when occupational striving and money pressures are lessened. Somewhat like adolescents, the middle-aged ask, "What shall I do now? Who shall I become?" The questions may rarely be this clear-cut, but subliminally at least there is an awareness of major changes in life conditions which seem more liberating than constraining. Youth's search for meaningful work and the obligations of early family life entail more imperatives and anxieties regarding unknowns than do midlife's transitional choices for those people who are still actively curious and adventurous.

With midlife's releases, there may be a broadening of involvements and social responsibilities in arenas larger than the family and the work setting. Bernice Neugarten remarks, "Some of the issues of middle age relate not to the creation of biological heirs but to the creation of social heirs."[2] Thus, reproductive capacities may be transmuted into social concerns, ideally expressed in broad terms. Erik Erikson calls such concerns "generativity" and includes under this heading "Care for the creatures of this world."[3] The middle-aged who expand their interests in this way may pursue them through churches or political parties or special interest organizations, becoming active in movements of different stripes, putting what they have learned about life and the world to use, and in the process becoming involved in new kinds of experience.

An alternate route is what Erikson calls "stagnation" which occurs when "Individuals . . . begin to indulge themselves as if they were their own—or one another's—one and only child; and where conditions favor it, early invalidism, physical or psychological, becomes the vehicle of self-concern."[4] In terms of the language used in the framework of this book, under such circumstances, curiosity about what is novel and changing shrinks and self-centered preoccupations take over. Such preoccupations may be accompanied by boredom, meaninglessness, and alienation, and, as in youth, loneliness. In the extreme, such feelings are to be found in the rooming houses and cheap hotels on Skid Row which accommodate mostly middle-aged men. In this seventh of Erikson's eight life stages, characterized by "generativity versus stagnation," the men on Skid Row have succumbed to stagnation.

But Erikson's bipolar ego development options, like "generativity versus stagnation," are not intended to encompass the wide range of contexts, interactional modes, and social development possible at this time of life. Within the broad limits of three arenas—the family and intimate relations, the world of work, and contexts for the expression of social concerns—this chapter aims to provide a sense of the diversities of midlife development and its milieus. From a field of still limited studies, I offer evidence and ideas for understanding and serving people in middle age.

MIDDLE AGE AND FAMILY LIFE

The interaction between social contexts and personal development, as life moves into the middle years, becomes increasingly difficult to analyze in terms of causes and effects. Students of adult development during the "second half of life" agree that developmental changes continue. But they also agree about the lack of evidence of chronologically related "stages" or many predictable sequences in development. In early life, we have seen how attachments provide a base for the expression of curiosity, how curiosity accompanies the development of competence, and how subsequently competence may become collaborative. In the teens and twenties there are analogous sequences that relate youth's changed self-image and intimacy to young adult partnerships in parenting, as I have indicated in Chapters Six and Seven. By the middle years, life pathways turn in so many different directions that what is predictably antecedent and what is subsequent have remained largely unpatternable as age-related phenomena. What then occurs in such arenas as, for example, the family, seems as much a cause as an effect of people's ongoing development. Interactional explanations become increasingly appropriate.

It thus is necessary to consider social development during the middle years of adult life in relation to such contexts as the family (or the work setting, as I do later in this chapter). Some transitions in family life are concurrent with parents becoming middle-aged. Moreover, differences in midlife development covary with continuing and satisfying family relationships or with disrupted family relationships. I thus look separately in this section at maritally satisfying, ongoing families and at families in which spouses' or other key relationships have seriously suffered and disintegrated, with or without physical separation.

Midlife Changes in Families and Parents

Marked changes in the age composition of a family require adaptations by all family members. The birth of a first child drastically alters the relationship between the formerly childless twosome who are now a parental couple. So, when children become adults, whether or not they physically leave the family home, their new status either creates a new marital relationship for the parents or renews an old one.

Human service workers and developmentalists have tended to focus on the adolescent's or youth's emancipation from parents, neglecting the concomitant emancipation of parent from "child" at this time. As the children mature, further individuate, and withdraw from parental supervision, the parents in two-parent households inevitably modify their interaction with each other as a married couple. As the family context changes with members' social development, so does the pattern of their interaction change. But what, specifically, are some of the developmental changes middle-aged parents experience when their children become adult?

To illustrate and provide a common base for discussion of this midlife family transition, I present part of a family therapy transcript from David Freeman's practice, quoted in his *Techniques of Family Therapy*.[5] The record is from a terminating or evaluation session in which the parents make explicit some of what they saw occurring at home during their treatment. In the process, this middle-aged couple clarify changes contingent upon their realization that their younger daughter has become an adult. This is something they became aware of with the family therapist's help.

What normally or at least frequently occurs when parents reach midlife are changes in the expressions of attachment and competence by all family members. This is not a sudden but rather a gradual process, originating with the children's attaining the independence of youth or young adulthood. But some parents may retain no longer appropriate perceptions of their child(ren) out of habit or more likely a sense of efficacy which continuing parental supervision gives them. Moreover, a parent's significantly changing perceptions and modes of interaction with one child are likely to affect patterns of interaction among other family members; and the reluctance of others to modify their accustomed ways may keep a long-term and outmoded dyadic relationship unchanged. The interplay of marital and parental interaction is illustrated in the family therapy transcript, and I discuss this matter following the record. In addition, the record touches on changes in self-image in middle age, as family roles change, and this issue is also examined in my later comments.

MIDLIFE ROLE CHANGES
IN THE FAMILY–TERMINATING
STAGE IN FAMILY THERAPY
(RECORD NO. 20)

FREEMAN: How about the two of you and this whole process? What impact has it had?

FATHER: Well, I think probably Mary listens more to me and my opinions than she did before.

FREEMAN: You would see a change in that?

FATHER: Oh, yeah, not that I blamed her because she is a mother and I think that is the kind of reaction of any mother.

MOTHER: I have very strong motherly feelings, you know, I admit that.

FREEMAN: One change that you would see then with Mary is she would hear more?

FATHER: Un hmm, um hmm. Well, she might agree with me before, but she might take a different route, and of course there was enough uproar in the family that I didn't want to continue any more by disagreeing with her and forcing my opinion on her. But probably the process of coming to these sessions has something to do with it too. And the fact that what she was doing for Trudy, really wasn't working. Giving in to her as much as she did. She didn't always, of course, and if something doesn't work you have got to try something else. And I think that is why maybe she listens to me more. She is going to bop me one in the eye when I get out of here. (Laughter)

FREEMAN: Her listening to you more, does that in any way encourage you to be more involved?

FATHER: Oh, yes, oh, sure. I think mothers are wise and I think the children read your motives as wrong. When you do something that you think is for the good of the children, it may be something that you feel you should do in your heart. Because you have an emotional attachment to your children. It is really easy to say, Okay, come on, woman, here is the house, we will look after you, we've got a shelter here. But you just postpone the inevitable in doing that. You can do that to a thirteen- or fourteen-year old, but of course when they are eighteen or nineteen they are old enough to be making their own decisions, and doing something about their lives.

FREEMAN: Um hmm. How about you in terms of this process and just the two of you?

MOTHER: Yeah, well, I think I am listening a little more to him, but I think he is having a little more to say with the children, too. There were an awful lot of years there where I did the lion's share of everything with the kids, because I was there and because he was off golfing and things like that. So I think that you get into the habit of doing so much with them and for them and I think it is bad, I really do. I think more and more that the father should be taking a far greater part and it should start right from the cradle. I believe this so strongly, and I didn't when I was younger. If I had, it probably wouldn't have made much difference because I think we were pretty young to have a family and he was busy trying to get established. I just think that it would have been left to me. When I see how young girls now expect their husbands to do a lot more with the children, I say, boy, more power to them. I think it is better for the children and better for the mother. The mother can just keep more of herself to herself. I think on a mother's part there is too much giving. Well, probably trying to live their children's lives for them, 'cause they are so concerned and now I—the way things turned out, with our family—I see that is unhealthy. I really do. But he is taking a bigger part now, aren't you?

FATHER: Yes.

MOTHER: You're calmer. You used to get more upset, with less provocation.

FATHER: Well, you communicate better, when you don't lose your temper.

FREEMAN: You agree with that? That you're calmer?

FATHER: Oh, yes. Over a year ago when Trudy raised her voice I would raise mine one octave higher and now the situation is reversed.

FREEMAN: What do you think has made you calmer?

FATHER: Well, I think it is common sense, really. When you stay calm, you don't lose your temper and start saying things you shouldn't.

MOTHER: I think too that coming here has helped you to get your perspective and see the kids, the girls that is, in a different light. And I can say the same for myself—because I am, oh brother, the way I am. When Trudy first talked about the farm my first reaction was kind of negative because I thought she would be bored. I was thinking of it the way I would look at it myself but I didn't say too much. This is the way it felt inside myself. Then, when we got talking about it and I started to look at it from her viewpoint, I thought, it might be terrific for her. But I think that it is hard for a parent to do, especially when an adult, or whatever Trudy is, has been so dependent on us. It is very hard to respect her ideas as an individual. And it really came home to me when this happened, because I had thought, now she is right. It would be fantastic for her. Yet I was just looking at it

completely from my own personal point of view, which was completely different. It had nothing to do with her. So I think I have
derived something that way.[6]

How are changing family context and the ongoing development of these
middle-aged parents interconnected? A pivotal age-related change in this family is
that Trudy, the younger of the family's two "children," has become an adult. Conflict in the family among mother, daughter, and father arise from parental nonrecog-
nition of their daughter's coming of age. They had continued to exercise parental
controls as though she were still a younger person.

With advancing years, there must be readaptations in families in the nature of
their attachments, the recognition and sharing of competencies, and the ways in
which family members decide and do things collaboratively. There are concomitant
changes also in personal identity, or self-image. Though the mother of a twelve-year-
old still remains a mother when her child becomes a twenty-year-old, obviously
different kinds of interaction should go on between them. Concurrently, the father's
interaction as a husband with his newly identified wife (now mother of a twenty-
year-old) is also likely to change, as suggested in the record and elaborated below.

Such social and psychological developments in middle age seem less like the
genetically programmed and age-linked changes found with considerable uniformity
among two-year-olds or eight- or twelve-year-olds. Major midlife developmental
changes occur in social interaction with diverse family and other contexts. They are
thus only grossly based in chronological and age-linked sequences. Still, midlife
developments become familiar as repeated phenomena of the kind suggested by the
therapy record. What appears in this transcript that has general—that is, more than
single case—relevance?

Note first that the parents are becoming closer as a marital couple as active
parental involvements subside. The father's first two comments in the transcribed
excerpt suggest this: "Mary listens more to me . . ." and not listening is "the kind
of reaction of any mother." As she ceases to be so active a mother, she is better
able to hear her husband, he feels, and thus they are communicating better or becoming closer as wife and husband. She recognizes his reentering the family, instead
of withdrawing, as she said he used to do, to "golfing and things like that." Recall
that in the previous chapter (Chapter Seven on young families), I discussed the
distancing that may occur between couples with the birth of the first child. Then,
with the last child's coming of age, mothers and fathers may uninterruptedly
again—without an "uproar in the family"—become wives and husbands. An old
attachment may be renewed without interfering relationships. Note that Freeman
as therapist sees the father as now "more involved."

Secondly, with middle age comes an awareness of one's generational identity
and its differences from younger—as well as, perhaps, older—ones. The mother in
the therapy record is keenly aware, for example, that "young girls now expect their
husbands to do a lot more with the children. I say, boy, more power to them." In
this instance, she is describing generational differences in sex roles. Partnership in

parenting is distinct from a role-segregated parenting style, with father on the job and mother in the home, as was the case about two decades (or one generation) earlier when this family began its parenting.

The concept of generations has both societal and personal developmental implications. Note how awareness of generation difference helps to sharpen mid-life redefinitions of the self in this mother. Generally, identity grows in part through group memberships. Identification with a group and one's generational cohort helps to define who one is. Grandmother and grandfather may have been members of the Flapper Generation of the twenties or the Depression generation of the thirties. Parents may have had their most significant socializing in the postwar affluence of the fifties or the counterculture of the sixties. What transpires between parents and children who are products of the Depression thirties, on the one hand, and the affluent fifties, on the other, is in part influenced by the identities each generation acquired in their time. The transcript refers obliquely to changing sex roles and the liberation of women as symbols of the members of a generation that the mother envies. Such women identify themselves differently from the way the mother in the record has defined her own self and live accordingly.

Of course, merely within the family, as children become young adults and parents become middle-aged, whatever conflict arises between individuating and self-emancipating youth and their parents accentuates the "we" and the "they" distinctions which are generational. Such distinctions involve different values, behavior, allegiances, and, of course, self-definitions. As youth explore their social worlds for clues to their changing self-images, clarified at first by defining "who I am *not*," so midlife adults discover their recategorized and redefined selves in part through intrafamilial child–parent differences. What seems unique about this process in contemporary society, however, is that, as this record suggests, the elders are being resocialized by their juniors. "I think it is better for the children and better for the mother," says the middle-aged mother about the young families in which fathers are more actively engaged in child rearing than was her husband. "But he is taking a bigger part now, aren't you?" she adds approvingly to her husband. In terms of this book's framework—contextual, interactional, and developmental—competence is exercised more collaboratively within the family, and this is indeed, as the mother says, healthier for everyone. Among other things, women in such situations have a higher sense of self-esteem. In midlife, the mother in this record seems to be moving in this direction with the help of a family therapist.

Having discussed the greater closeness of the marital dyad and the modified self-image of the middle-aged parents, I turn now to a third midlife change. Possibly as a result of the greater clarity about family process emerging in the course of therapy, the father became "calmer." But there are also general developmental processes occurring as men and women age which are in accord with the observation that the father is now less dominating and agitated when his authority is challenged in the family. In becoming "calmer" he is also becoming less aggressive, and this diminution of assertiveness among males as they age appears as a normal developmental pattern in later adulthood. David L. Gutmann's research, extending over a few decades, reports diminished aggressiveness in older men not only among mid-westerners but also cross-culturally among the Druze in the Middle East, among Navajo Indians in the Southwest, and more recently cross-species in the literature on studies of such infrahuman primates as macaque and rhesus monkeys.[7] As aging males become less aggressive and more nurturant, aging females become more assertive. This reversal of traditional sex roles in the later years of life has been explained in various ways: changes in the composition and functions of the family as mothers enter their nonreproductive phase and children leave home are seen as a reduction of biological and social inducers of maternal nurturance. Similarly, in most societal contexts, "established" fathers are less pressed to employ aggression in the market place at the peak of their careers and as they approach retirement.

This formulation should not be seen as minimizing the effects of family therapy on the father's increased "calmness." When goals in therapy are allied with—or do not run counter to—expected developmental changes, the chances of success are obviously greater. Moreover, therapies usually aim to help suffering people stuck in ineffectual situations to return to the pathways of normal developmental processes. Within them, many kinds of affective and coping capacities grow and environments become more responsive in ways that enrich life and its satisfactions. This, apparently, is what happened to the middle-aged couple who entered family therapy when in a bind with their younger daughter, and as a result, also with their marital relationship.

The strength of the attachment between spouses is repeatedly found to be the keystone to continuing and successful family life, in the middle years as well as earlier and later. In the Berkeley longitudinal studies, in which cohorts of people have been followed and repeatedly interviewed and tested from infancy or adolescence into midlife (and beyond), Arlene Skolnick reports, "The most salient quality in the highly satisfactory marriages is a strong affective commitment to the spouse . . ."[8] She is quick to add that such emotional attachment is *not* necessarily "togetherness." Moreover, "Few of the happy marriages seem to be completely smooth and without dissatisfaction and irritations . . . (But) the positive aspects of the relationship clearly outweigh the negative. In short, the satisfied spouses did not expect perfection."[9] The general conclusion of this longitudinal investigation of families followed into their middle years is that there is "no support for the hypothesis that marriages invariably corrode, with spouses becoming disengaged or disenchanted." On the contrary, the evidence supports the proposition that marriages grow better as child-rearing burdens decrease. Thus, there is a "great potential for change in intimate relations."[10] Such change can, of course, also be decremental, as I report in the section on marital ruptures in midlife, which follows. I must first add to these family context findings some parallel social developmental findings by Berkeley psychologists in the Institute of Human Development, studying the same people as Arlene Skolnick did, but focusing on them as individual persons in their forties.

Psychologically, these middle-aged parents show no signs of developmental losses. For example, regarding intelligence, Dorothy Eichorn and colleagues write,

"Contrary to trends inferred from cross-sectional data, decrease in IQ by midlife was not the norm; in fact, modest to moderate increases (average of 6.2 points) were characteristic" from ages seventeen or eighteen to forty-eight years.[11] This retention of intellectual competence is matched by developmental gains on a wide array of personal capacities and other attributes betokening potentials for involvements in a highly socially responsible life in the middle years. For example, psychologist Norma Haan notes, that "with minor exceptions" these middle-aged people, compared with assessments of them in early adulthood, were "more cognitively invested, nurturant, self-confident, open and intraceptive than at younger ages. They were more self- and sexually-expressive than in earlier adulthood . . ."[12] Even more to the point of the growth of a sense of social responsibility in midlife, Haan remarks about their becoming more "tolerant," and in summary, "Our middle-aged had also become considerably more giving and self-extending . . . as well as interpersonally predictable and accountable to others—or generative, to use Erikson's term." Finally, there was no evidence of any sudden developmental changes and "no evidence . . . of undergoing a midlife crisis."[13] None of this is to suggest, however, that, as at any time of life, there are not people who experience serious and painful attachment losses, failures in competence, and diminutions in self-esteem, or, following ruptures in attachment, a second chance for a better life.

The Loss of Family Attachments
in Midlife

Not all families, of course, are able to weather the vagaries of early and middle adult life without serious damage to or total disintegration of their marital relationships. Some couples continue to share a home, but little else beyond a smoldering hostility which periodically erupts. Others separate and divorce, a process which is almost always a painful one, even though preceded by much pain in family life while the members are still together. And while the couples who continue to live together in serious disharmony and those who separate pursue obviously different pathways, under both sets of circumstances there is a loss in family attachments. I shall thus give some attention to both in this section.

Marital attachments have many components—emotional closeness, reciprocal concerns about each other's welfare, and mutual sexual attraction. The essence is enjoying being together much of the time and unhappiness at prolonged separations from one another, with the desire to be back together again. Couples who out of habit and convenience and without mutual concern continue to share a household, or who are held together by negative or deeply ambivalent feelings for each other, do not live in a relationship which fosters their social development. As Chapter Three made clear, underattachments, involving neglect, or overattachments, in which independent development is stifled in the extreme by symbiosis (or folie á deux), are the kinds of relationships that human services are called upon to supplement or otherwise assist with. And when married couples contemplate separation or proceed with divorce, human service counseling may help to sort out some of the complexities and options involved. A particularly important kind of counseling with couples and their children addresses the issues of child custody and post-divorce co-parenting.[14]

Marriages continuing into midlife after emotional closeness and mutually protective attachments have failed are described in the Berkeley longtitudinal studies. It is difficult to understand, however, why these unsatisfactory marriages continue. As Skolnick says, the differences between satisfying and unsatisfying marriages do not lie in the amount of clashes between marital partners but in the seriousness with which participants themselves rate their discord. Underlying painful "negative attachment" are often severe personality problems, including in about 25 percent of these Berkeley marriages, serious drinking problems.[15]

Partners with alcohol dependency, compared with other adults, tend to be more hostile and self-defeating, more brittly defended and undercontrolled, more moody and irritable—in short, more unpredictable. One can understand the inability of such spouses to respond to the needs of a marital partner. Moreover, Mary Cover Jones' analyses of the longitudinal records of these same people in adolescence indicate that they were then also "less dependable, giving, and sympathetic." In summary she says:

> Our data give support to the hypothesis that problems of alcohol abuse have roots in early socialization experiences, particularly in the family. During adolescence, future problem drinkers, especially males, regarded their families as less happy, less affectionate, and less accepting of the child's growth and independence than other families. Compared with their peers, they expressed less affection, admiration, and respect for their parents.[16]

In such findings, one sees a continuing cycle of troubled family life from generation to generation. Living and growing up at home as a young child and adolescent, a person not only experiences direct influences on current personal development but also learns models for future use on how to be a marital partner and a parent. Such learning probably affects more than this 25 percent of failed marriages which involve alcoholism in middle age.

Spouses are still in their twenties when most of America's divorces take place, but the break-up of a marriage when couples are in their middle adult years assumes some very special problems. One problem is the far smaller chance that former wives in their forties or older will remarry. This is not to imply that all women need marital partners, either in their later years or at any time; in fact, it is men who by many mental health indicators are found to be much worse off when unmarried. Men are far more likely to remarry after a midlife divorce, although primarily to younger women. The problems for women divorced in middle age have to do with adapting to a completely new way of life after a young adulthood with a long-term investment in family living. The drastic changes following divorce are likely to be social and interpersonal, economic and emotional. The normal self-identity transitions of middle age become complicated by a life-pervading status change. It is not too many decades ago that the now archaic term "divorcée" implied casual sexual availability and the need for a whole new social network, different from the former marital and coupled relationships. In middle age, such social network changes following divorce remain crucial to a new way of life. Yet forming new social relationships at this period may be difficult. Typically, also at this time children are leaving home. Such disconnections, accompanied by feelings of abandonment, are a major component of many acutely stressful situations. Midlife divorces are likely, at least initially, to be acutely stressful for all persons involved.

Divorces simultaneously attack not only one's attachments and sense of identity but also one's competence. Competence is in part contextual. In giving up one's living place, as typically happens in divorce, one separates from a familiar neighborhood, its friendships, its services, and formal networks. One must learn to cope in a new and strange home, often under economic reductions and pressures which exacerbate feelings of displacement. Women face having to expand their earnings or reenter the labor market at midlife after a long absence; personal capacities are sharply threatened by unresponsive employers. Men have added financial responsibilities which add to the strains on their coping abilities. The sequence of events in separation and divorce can be understood as an ongoing and multifaceted stressful situation, from the initial warning stage, to the impact of separation itself—which may seem more or less sudden—through the complexities of divorce proceedings and efforts to adjust, and a subsequent recovery stage. In the recovery period, efforts are made to build a new life. Central to the success of these stressful processes are feelings of competence. The more actively former marital partners can participate in all phases of the separation and divorce, the less stressful the multiple changes are likely to seem. Informal and formal network supports are essential—the help of grown children and other kin, old friends and new ones, lawyers and human service workers. Severed marital relationships, even the most negative ones, have a way of persisting. They challenge one's memories of what one did or failed to do in the past. To reduce a sense of failure and incompetence—and often feelings of depression—ex-spouses' membership in a professionally composed and led group of other adults in similar circumstances may at least clarify what is a "normal" and expectable response to distress.[17]

A second chance following divorce may be found in a new family. Divorce in midlife followed by remarriage may bring step-parents into "reconstituted families" where adolescent children still reside. It may not be easy to develop a new marital relationship and social identity in a home where teen-agers are struggling with their own relationships with parents as well as with their own changing self-images. Adolescents may resent the intrusion of a third parent.[18] Their divided loyalties between their divorced parents are likely to make new attachments difficult. And the ambiguities of the step-parent role, especially in regard to disciplinary responsibilities, require everyone to participate in trying to clarify and agree upon new family ground rules.

The divorced parent with whom the children do not live also contributes to the complexities of a four-parent situation. Who participates in family celebrations and other special events, such as the weddings of grown children, Christmas gather-

ings, and birthday parties? One can understand a woman's anger when her preschool grandchild receives a birthday card signed "Grandma" from her husband's
second wife. Lucile Duberman reports step-fathers saying "I don't think my step-
sons treat me like a real father," or "There will always be resentment between us."
Later studies support her findings that difficulties in the development of a second
marital relationship are primarily caused by problems of "child rearing" and "outsiders' influence," the latter including the ex-spouse's.[19] As Ahrons and others say,
successful co-parenting depends on clear distinctions between past marital relationships and present parenting responsibilities. Drawing such distinctions may
require the help of skillful counseling. Former and often unresolved attachments
between ex-spouses have to be set aside for the sake of adolescent children's welfare.
It is important to differentiate between agreements made as parents and the residua
of a former but now ruptured marital relationship.

Of course, separation and divorce are not the only immediate source of lost
or stressed family attachments in midlife. The serious illness and long-term hospitalization of a spouse may gravely attenuate a marital relationship. The high incidence
of withdrawal, feelings of helplessness and depression among middle-aged women
appears to be related to seriously strained marital attachments. Degenerative physical ailments such as multiple sclerosis may require a husband's institutionalization
in midlife. In the days before chlorpromazine therapy began to reduce the need for
hospitalization of persons afflicted with schizophrenia, a research report on *Schizophrenic Women*, subtitled *Studies in Marital Crisis*, described "Irene James," her
midlife hospitalization, and the course of her illness, apparently related to her middle age.

THE PSYCHOTIC BREAK
AND FAMILY CRISIS
OF A WOMAN IN HER FORTIES
(RECORD NO. 21)

Irene James was forty at the time of her hospitalization; her husband Ralph was
forty-six. They had been married for nine years and had a seven-year-old daughter.
It was Irene's second and Ralph's first marriage . . . When Irene decided to divorce
her [first] husband and give up her child, the daughter was five, Irene's own age
when her mother died.

Irene married Ralph when she was thirty. A reserved, sedate, and conscientious
man in his mid-thirties, Ralph had had very little to do with women and had not
really expected to marry. The Jameses took Irene's daughter [by her first marriage]
to live with them and two years later had a daughter of their own. Irene felt quite
weakened by childbirth and required substantial help from Ralph in caring for the
baby during its first year. They moved near Ralph's job so he could spend more
time at home. Our impression is that at this time Irene experienced a self-contained
emotional crisis precipitated by identifications with her own mother. Further

trouble developed when Irene was thirty-five, her mother's age when she was born. Irene experienced severe abdominal pains and menstrual irregularities. She left the Catholic church, fearing that its teachings about divorce and sin would disturb the younger daughter and perhaps "split the family apart." Soon after this Irene became involved in a series of squabbles with neighbors; this led to a decision to move. During her psychosis several years later, she interpreted the squabbles as part of a neighbor's complex plot to seduce her. It is not known whether she thought this at the time, but sexual fantasies might have been evoked by the onset of menses in the older daughter. In any event, this daughter chose to go to live with her father right after Irene's difficulties with the neighbors, and Irene's symptoms abated for several years.

Irene's episode began dramatically within a week of her fortieth birthday, which was her mother's age at the time of illness and death. Irene fainted, attributed this to menstrual difficulties, and became convinced that she was entering the change of life. She experienced several events which she interpreted as snubs by neighbors and which she related to the earlier quarrels as part of the seduction plot. She could not distract herself from preoccupations about the plot to break up her family, was unable to do her work, to respond to others, or to sleep. After hospitalization she spoke of plots to make people sick and break up families, she noted the frequency of heart attacks at forty, and she had a reassuring dream in which her mother appeared and told her that doctors now have ways of curing illnesses that used to be fatal.

Irene was released in partial remission after fifteen weeks of hospitalization. She still believed in the reality of the strange neighborhood events but was no longer preoccupied, could keep her ideas to herself, and felt cheerful again. After a few weeks she began to feel very weak and felt as though she was slipping back. A doctor gave her vitamin shots, and she improved dramatically for about a month. She then relapsed into a very withdrawn and autistic state with rambling paranoid delusions. She remained at home in this condition for well over a year. At the end of the twenty-seven months following her first release, she was in the hospital, had been rehospitalized twice, and was overtly psychotic.[20]

I include this record not because it is particularly enlightening in regard to the mysteries of schizophrenia but because it encapsulates in one fragment of a life history so many of the stressors of the middle-aged. The middle-aged in our times have sometimes been referred to as suffering an intergenerational squeeze. What is meant by this is that in midlife one may have simultaneous pressures from one's children as youth or young adults, on the one hand, and from one's aging parents, on the other. The crises and sometimes resultant dependencies of both generations may fall upon seemingly competent and still strong midlifers. In the record of Irene James, the situation is somewhat skewed from the more usual one. Her adolescent daughter's sexuality seems to have threatened this fragile mother on the threshold of her own postreproductive phase. Normally, the menopause is not a threat to healthy women.[21] However, for a woman whose own sexuality is apparently troubled, as suggested by her fantasies regarding a neighbor's "plot to secuce her," the emergence of her daughter as a sexual being symbolizes the sense of replacement parents may feel when their children mature. Fathers may respond similarly to their son's vitality, especially when adolescents challenge paternal authority. Intergenerational conflict is essentially over the power which the middle-aged exercise and seek to retain over youth.

Pressure from her own parent occurs, in the midlife of Irene James, not from her mother's becoming ill and dependent or dying then, but rather from Irene James' enduring overattachment to her mother—an inadequate sense of boundaries between them. Just as she had felt, it seems, that her mother's experience in childbirth at age thirty-five might induce parallel or related events in Irene James' own life at the same age (a kind of anniversary reaction), so Irene James' psychotic "episode began dramatically within a week of her fortieth birthday, which was her mother's age at the time of illness and death." This is not a direct stressor, like a parent's death upsetting a middle-aged adult, but rather a reaction to an overattached parent–child relationship which had long survived the death of the mother. Through the middle-aged daughter's experiences runs the repeated concern that events beyond her control would "split the family apart." In a section of the record I did not include here, it is explained that after the mother's death at age forty, "the family broke up" and Irene James who was then about six began growing up in a series of foster homes. A variant of the intergenerational squeeze of middle age is reflected in Irene James' life.

When in fact parents do die and children are in their middle adult years, it must be remembered that "the parent tie is generally the longest of life's relationships" and "the prototype of attachment."[22] Mourning for the loss is likely to be replete with mixed and complex emotions. Memories of long unremembered experiences arise as one tries to recapture the essence of the dead parent and one's relationship with him or her. Although family members may draw together for the last rites, each person's image of the dead parent has its own unique qualities, as shared reminiscences at such times reveal. The crucial issue is that feelings of attachment persist long after the person with whom one is linked has died or otherwise abandoned the relationship. After deaths, separations and divorces, or other ruptures in family relationships, the sense and influence of a significant person may be projected into other relationships in that a new spouse may be expected to behave as an ex-spouse did or a small grandchild may be encouraged to take on the attributes of a dead parent. The power of attachments to outlive their continuing, live, social interaction is suggested in the psychotic break which Irene James (Record No. 21) suffered at age forty. It was, in a sense, a memorial response to her mother's death—and her family's dismemberment—when Irene James was only about age five or six. The experience of loss of an attachment in middle age may have early origins and longterm consequences. The human services may provide supportive counseling to help with grieving and group programs in which substitute or compensatory relationships can be formed after the critical period of mourning.

CHANGING MEANINGS
AND CONTEXTS OF WORK

In an intensive study of forty men between the ages of thirty-five and forty-five, Yale psychologist Daniel J. Levinson sampled his "biographees" from four occupational groups: hourly workers in industry, business executives, university biologists, and novelists. He thus expected to include representatives from "diverse sectors of society" for his research on how men move on from young adulthood and enter middle age. Work is such a powerful determinant of how one lives the other parts of one's life that sampling by occupational status makes good sense in a stage-focused study of lives and their uniqueness as well as their patternable uniformities. Levinson concluded his study with the generalization that "the nature of a man's work changes appreciably in middle adulthood," but even among only forty men, the variability in the turns of their occupational careers was so great that no more illuminating generalization about males' "midlife change in style of work" could be made.[23]

More fully quoted, the last phrase from Levinson's book is: "Most men undergo a midlife change in style of work and living." The linkage of work and living styles suggests their close interaction; one may have hobbies which are quite peripheral to the rest of one's life, but what one works at, and how strongly, affect and are affected by most of the other arenas of one's existence. Thus, the family life changes previously discussed interact with changes in the meanings work has for a worker or changes in workplace. And work changes covary also with such other life course changes in middle age as its new "time left" perspective, midlife's diminutions in physical vitality, and the kinds of psychological development and self-reappraisal described in the previous section. By midlife, too, one has a work history which exercises its own influences on present and future. How may that history vary?

Earning a living may be that and nothing more. Or it may mean a sizable commitment of one's psychic energies and an expression of one's curiosities. Work may be accomplished in a place that serves as a base for friendships with like-minded others, a sequence of opportunities to learn and increase one's competence, and a chance to contribute to society while fostering one's self-development. By middle age, there may be marked differences in the self-images of people whose work history consists of unrelated jobs or, instead, of a persistent career, no matter how disjunctive that career may have been, in terms of changed workplaces. Wage earners who are uninvested in their job, by middle age, start counting the days until they can retire. People who have been fortunate enough to have been able to follow a vocation or calling are more likely by middle age to have an accumulated sense of satisfaction from their meaningful production. Thus, Levinson remarks, "At midlife, many talented scientists turn increasingly to managerial, consultative and teaching activities," as related but different work.[24] On this route, poet Robert Penn Warren observes, "A young man's ambition to get along in the world and make a place for himself—half your life goes by that way, till you're 45 or 50. Then, if you're lucky, you make terms with life, you get released."[25]

Release may occur through new attitudes toward work at midlife or second chances in the workplace or other contexts of work. This section ends with the record of Studs Terkel's interview with Mario Anichini who at age fifty-five gave up butchering and returned to a vocation he had learned and enjoyed in his youth. Before we get to that record, however, there are other dimensions of the place of work and its relation to development in middle age which must be considered.

Jobs and Careers in Middle Age

There is "a marked decline in job and career satisfaction from the early to the late forties for men in lower middle-class occupations and those who have not been upwardly mobile."[26] By contrast, middle-aged men who continue to find satisfaction in their work feel a personal interest in it, see it as utilizing their abilities and giving them freedom to develop their own ideas, and get from it an income which they consider adequate. Thus, the kinds of priorities that youth set for a desirable job on their entry into the labor market—as I reported in Chapter Six—do in fact continue to pay off in middle age. Youth's interest in variety and options or opportunities for choice on the job are reexpressed in later life as workers' freedom to pursue their own ideas. The chance to get ahead is rarely any longer an issue, especially among the lower middle-class men. Considering where they are and the time they have left, they tend to "make terms with life," as Robert Penn Warren suggests.

In fact, satisfaction for blue collar workers comes from their sense of job stability. They are not often interested in the job itself, nor do they see it as cutting into their family life or other interests. Job changing occurred primarily in their early adult years. Security and no change are what they value in middle age as they look forward to retirement, according to sociologist John Clausen's conclusions from the longitudinal data on the occupational experiences of men born in the 1920s in Berkeley and Oakland.[27]

The pervasive influence of men's work on other arenas of life is suggested by the Berkeley findings on work's key connection with family life in the middle adult years. "The strongest correlate of marital satisfaction in men is current occupational status $(r = .33)$."[28] High-level jobs tend to promote contentment through the enjoyment of work whereas low-level jobs seem to promote tensions, perhaps because by middle age there is relatively little personal investment in low-level work, and its many obligations rub against the grain. Inevitably, then, such irritations carry over into the family scene and especially into marital relationships, or so the Berkeley longitudinal data suggest.

Given the generation of the cohorts under study in Berkeley, however, some of whom were children of the Great Depression and perhaps as a result followed rather traditional or safe occupational careers, the findings on work and the middle years may have limited generalizability. Note moreover that the findings on occupations, whether satisfaction on the job or work's relationship to marriage, are limited to the men in the study. Women and the world of work (perhaps because of the study's insufficient numbers of employed women) do not jointly enter analyses in the Berkeley longitudinal reports on middle age. Levinson's research suffers a similar limitation; his "biographees" who live in the North Atlantic states are men only.

Elsewhere, married women, well into middle age, are reported to be gainfully employed and still do a major part of the running of the household. They thus share the financial responsibilities of family life, earning money in increasing numbers as their children grow older. About 70 percent of the married women in the forty- to fifty-nine-year-old age group, when they had no children under sixteen years of age at home, were working, at least part-time, according to a large London study.[29] This kind of marital partnership, in which both spouses work as well as sharing other aspects of life, is called the "symmetrical family" by sociologists Michael Young and Peter Willmott, who have a long-term interest in British working-class life. "Two-income marriages" is probably a more common designation. By contrast, "dual-career families" is the name given to upper middle-class couples when both work as, for example, architects or in managerial positions and still accommodate each other at home and in other life arenas.[30] In the latter study of middle-aged spouses by dual-career anthropologists Rhona and Robert Rapoport, it is clear that the wife's occupation is not secondary to the husband's nor is she engaged in it out of economic necessity, but rather because of personal involvement. In fact, all sixteen families were nominated for the research by their professional associations as being highly qualified and particularly successfull careerists, as well as being the married partners of an intact family.

When both spouses reach their forties or fifties, as have the dual-career couples in the Rapoports' research, there may still be strains at home caused by the composite overload of work, family, and other pressures. The stresses are likely to be less in midlife than they were in early adulthood, when careers were being established and children were being born and tended in a tightly coordinated sequencing of equally important events. By midlife, patterns of coping have been experimented with and become flexible enough to adapt to changing life conditions, and the best tested arrangements have survived. Midlife is thus a more gratifying time of life for such work-invested marital partners. There may be a relatively difficult compartmentalizing of work life and home life—for example, work only rarely being brought home at night and a conscious effort made to keep managerial attitudes out of the marital relationship. Physical contexts—such as a weekend cabin or a sailboat—may be especially useful to give boundaries to leisure unintruded upon by work. Moreover, social networks may include many of the wives' associates who support the dual-career style of life, but fewer kin who may have been traditional in their values and become lost, say the Rapoports, in the career-making of the spouses.

Central to middle age and occupational experience is, of course, the reappraisal of the self. For dual-career couples, the "dilemmas of personal identity and self-esteem" were:

> . . . whether the wife was being a good wife and mother, or more fundamental-
> ly a "good human being" when she chose to pursue her career involvements,
> and whether the husband was sacrificing his "manliness" in altering his
> domestic life to take on a more participative role . . . A wife's defensiveness
> about following her chosen career line may make her particularly sensitive to
> criticism or it may exacerbate periods of self-doubt and depression. The hus-
> band may make great personal career sacrifices to help achieve the dual-career
> structure for its value to both parties, but he may show irritation or resent-
> ment at having modified his own personal identity in order to incorporate a
> successful wife into his patterns, sometimes in place of a more successful
> self.[31]

Still, such wives are likely to have enriched identities and other resources by midlife,
and husbands may be happier for having more fulfilled wives.

Of course, for dual-career wives also, middle age typically brings modifications
in interests, and the many complexities of having schedules that fit, not only between the marital partners but among the multiple roles they share. For example, in
the Rapoports' case study of the Bensons, a husband and wife architecture team
who work together in their home and office, the wife decides in her forties that she
no longer wishes to attend the international conferences they formerly went to
together. This life cycle withdrawal is presented as a matter calling for adaptations
by both spouses in a few arenas. But somehow it seems much less a family problem
than is suggested by the London fitter's remark, "I think the wife's place is in the
home. My wife says she wants to go out to work and meet people, but I don't
think it right."[32] Or in northern California, a wife who "used to work down at the
bank and . . . enjoyed it" yields to her working-class husband who says:

> Dammit, no! A wife's got to learn to be number two. That's just the way it is
> and that's what she better learn. She's not going to work. She's going to stay
> home and take care of the family like a wife's supposed to do.[33]

In the middle years especially, when the children are grown up, many middle-aged
women want to return to paid employment outside the home, seeking new meanings and self-definitions, prompted sometimes by marital ruptures or merely the
need for new contexts and expanded horizons. Working husbands who at this time
of life still insist that their wives be in the home when the husbands leave for work
and when, at the end of the day, they return home from work, are a decreasing lot,
opposed by changing norms regarding the rights and roles of women. Still, such
male values continue in many pockets of society, coupled sometimes with wife
battering, other forms of violence in the family, and alcohol abuse.

Retained authority at home may become a midlife issue especially for some
working-class men as they near the end of their work days and see themselves
threatened or replaced on the job by incoming better trained and stronger young
men. At the same time, children move to their separate living places, and only husband and wife remain at home. With the power of father attenuated and work
becoming more negatively charged, men's capacities to engage in a new kind of

husband–wife relationship seem all the more important. Then, too, leisure interests and activities become essential for a satisfying life—carpentry, sports spectatorship, or neighborhood involvements. The last of these may help the middle-aged to retain a sense of mastery, of being able to support or modify their physical and social environments when investments in work and perhaps at home too are diminishing. The expansion of neighborhood and broader social concern among middle-aged men and women, which I consider social responsibility, I shall discuss in the final section of this chapter. Before doing so, however, I must call attention to another dimension of the world of work at middle age—specifically, the second chance occupation, or by contrast, dropping out.

Second Chances and Constraints

Everyone has heard or read about the affluent corporation lawyer who closed his big city office and went off with his second family to a farm, or the fifty-year-old airline executive who left the "rat race" and moved to a resort area where he bought a small motel and spent as much time as possible fishing. The seedbed for such midlife career switches was the 1960s with its double stream of antiestablishment social movements—on one shore, the radical forces flowing from the campuses like Berkeley's,[34] and on the other, the less militant and more self-centered hippie counterculture.[35] Both streams united in the anti-Vietnam war crusade, but in addition they conjointly flooded and partially washed away the constraints that a "bourgeois work ethos" laid on young and old alike. Beyond the changes in life styles of individuals, the push was antiorganizational, against any centralization of power and for local autonomy. Some saw this centrifugal movement as socially disintegrative, while others welcomed the hoped for return of community life—a desire shared, for different reasons, by the political "left" and the political "right."

It is thus interesting in the 1980s to see how Kenneth Keniston interprets the University of Michigan's nationwide survey research findings on *The Inner American* and *Mental Health in America*,[36] encapsulated in the "new investment in self-expression." This perspective includes a questioning of conventional roles, a change in temporal focus from the future to the here and now, and a high priority on close personal attachments and intimacy. By contrast with the Michigan group who interpret this change in America's values as a response to the growing complexities of society, Keniston argues that, beyond this fact, many Americans have lost faith in such traditional social institutions as big government and big business.[37]

It is consonant with "the mood of Americans today" for those who had been locked into traditional jobs to risk, in middle age, a second chance. This is not to suggest that this same mode of midlife change will be made by younger generations who never enter the "rat race" in their youth; their self-reappraisals in middle age may turn other aspects of their lives in new directions. However, contemporaneous midlife occupational changes are of interest as the behavioral expression of inner developments which reflect feelings about "time left" in middle age.

In this arena, the public is aware primarily of upper middle-class professionals or managers who have gone rural or slumming. In a book that gives a vivid picture of Americans at work at all social class levels and in all the rich diversity of America's ethnicity, Chicago writer Studs Terkel includes his interviews with forty-year-old Fred Ringley who moved with wife and five children to an Arkansas farm and the running of a dairy bar far from the North Shore suburbs of Chicago and his high-paying advertising job; a financially successful lawyer who moved to a ghetto and Legal Aid work on behalf of poor whites from the Deep South, poor blacks, and poor elderly people; a forty-six-year-old woman who left the big city television producing of commercials, moving off with her husband to live in a farmhouse and go into a totally new kind of job that she thoroughly enjoys, as a librarian in a small private school. About her former television work and her new life and "the kids" at school who are "great" she says: "There hasn't been a tense day since. A charmed life. Don't miss the city, don't miss the job, don't miss the expense account (laughs), don't miss any part of it."[38] Studs Terkel's fourth "second chance" portrait is of a butcher who at fifty-five gave up butchering for stone cutting. Here is that interview.

MARIO ANICHINI AND HIS
MIDLIFE JOB CHANGE
(RECORD NO. 22)

In the yard outside the shop are statues in marble and stone of saints, angels, and fountains. The spirit of Look Homeward, Angel *and W. O. Gant hovers tempestuously. Yet, M. Anichini, artisan, has never been more relaxed. His son and colleague, Bob, interjects a contemporary note: "We also work in foam, fiberglass, polyurethanes . . ."*

In Italy I was working in marble a little bit. I was a young kid. In Lucca, a young kid do this, do that. Little by little I learned. When I was about twenty I came to this country here. I couldn't do anything like that, because of here we had a Depression. From '27 year to '55 I was a butcher. For twenty-eight years . . .

I started to get a little ulcer in my stomach. I had sciatica. So I hadda quit. So I stay for one year, I don't do nothing. But after, I feel I could do something. The plaster business, the tomb business. As soon as I started it, I started to feel better.

Bob: *He was about fifty-five years old when he started this business again. My mother thought he was losing his mind. But he insisted. Everybody from the area where he came from in Tuscany has a relative or somebody in the art business. You have Florence . . .*

There's change a lot. We use rubber to make a mold now. We used to use some kind of glue. It was only good for about ten pieces. Now with a rubber mold we can make three hundred, four hundred pieces. In Italy you gotta go to school one year to make a mold. Before, I used to make one piece, stone or marble. Maybe you a millionaire and you want to make it your bust. Okay, how much you pay?

Now nobody want to spend that much money. Over here I don't see so much good stone to work with.

Bob: *We used to sell statuary and fountains: a nymph holding a jug, pouring water. All of a sudden, with the ecology bit, people want to hear water running. In the city they want to be close to the country. So there's a combination of art and nature. When we started, I was quite against it. Who's going to buy a fountain? We put 'em indoors now as humidifiers. People are putting statues in their yards. There is such a demand for it we built a factory.*

I remember when I quit the butcher business. I was sick. When I started this business, I became better and better and I feel good and enjoy myself.

Bob: *For grave sites people in the old days wanted a certain statue, St. Anthony or St. Anne or something like that. We don't have much call for saints these days, especially now with the Church . . .*

People will laugh. Every time they see me, they see me better and better. I used to work in the basement. They say, "You eat too much dust down there, and you getting better and better. Before you work in the butcher shop, very nice, very airy, everything, you used to be sick. How come?"

Bob: *My dad had another man that didn't feel too well at what he was doing. He worked with my father in this—what he did as a kid, too—and he got healthy and fat and stuff like that. (Laughs). My dad was an old man fifteen, twenty years ago. Today he's a young man.*[39]

Mario Anichini's second chance occupation, chosen at age fifty-five, has many meanings for him. It provides him with a new sense of personal fulfillment, economic success, and ultimate family support and collaboration. An option pursued by him ostensibly because of health problems, the job Mario Anichini returns to is one he learned in his youth. In this process of reconnection with his past, he becomes, as his son says, "a young man" again.

The kind of work a person does is an important part of the person's social identity—how others label him or her—and, consequently, of the person's image of self. Mario Anichini's developing self-image in midlife can encompass the creativity in his new work as well as his symbolic return to his native Tuscany through his work. Moreover, stone cutting is work he freely chose, with a strong desire and sense of commitment, even initially against the advice of both his wife and son. The job of butchering had been pressed on him by the economic and employment limitations of his status as a new immigrant in America on the brink of the Great Depression. In middle age, he has a new kind of autonomy and self-expression in his work. It is, moreover, a vehicle for his patrimony or legacy to his son who can carry on the business; so important especially in his cultural heritage, this kind of generativity also assures his own "continuity." Normally, illness, particularly in middle age, assaults one's sense of control over one's environs. Mario Anichini can only derive feelings of mastery from his new work, and with the approval of his family and his extended social network a renewed sense of self-esteem.

In Mario Anichini's and the other second chance situations alluded to earlier, personal competence and contextual supports have fitted together so beautifully that the midlife changes went well. Macrosocial and local economic conditions and opportunities were favorable. The people all had a cash reserve to start from. They also had access to the vocational options that were available.

Perhaps because they were middle-aged and had accumulated enough experience related to their new jobs, they could start out well. If the accounts seem, however, too rosy, it must be remembered that gains as well as losses or deprivations may be experienced relatively—that is, in relationship to the experiences of other people or of one's own past experience. Some of the happiness inherent in midlife's second chances may be feelings of release from early adult strains and conventional obligations.

Conventional obligations as well as second chances are minimally apparent in a middle-aged population whose way of life is the upsidedown of what has just been discussed. It is a segment of society in which the human services, beyond helping to sustain life, have been blatantly unsuccessful by almost any other criteria. I earlier noted that Skid Rows (or Roads), New York City's Bowery, and other deteriorating urban enclaves that provide a sleeping place for people with "no fixed address" accommodate primarily unattached, mostly male, very poor, and often handicapped people of middle age.[40] It is a rather transient living place for the midlife rejects of society who lack employment and good relations with family members. One student of these disaffiliated people and their milieu called Skid Row "an open asylum."[41] The trajectories of the prior lives of midlifers who drift into Skid Rows seem to have allowed them no alternatives.

Donald Bogue's Chicago studies give evidence that Skid Row shelters many people who had earlier enjoyed a better life. They slide, for a variety of reasons, into the Chicago loop's cubicle rooms, or "cages," so called because of the low wire screen ceilings that span the short partitions between the five by seven foot rooms.[42] Perhaps half the occupants are alcoholics, both solitary drinkers and those whose only sociability is over a shared bottle. Many are psychologically or physically damaged. Aside from the streets and the bars, there are few other meeting places. Rarely is there even a library or a social center in such neighborhoods, and then a doorkeeper can admit only the sober and the sane. The substandard hotel lobbies, the cheap lunch counters, the postservice free meal missions, and the bars are the only places, aside from the streets, to sit. Impoverished, often on public assistance, the local people are divided between those whose downward mobility is hardly the base for a rewarding second chance and other people who, from the days of their chaotic childhoods, never had a first chance.

Since a major development of midlife is a self-reappraisal, what is the experience of the middle-aged in Skid Rows and comparable places? I have written previously in this book about how living place, family members' ongoing evaluations, and one's work contribute to one's changing self-image. The alienated, societal rejects on Skid Row lack employment, interaction in the context of family attachments, or even a permanent living place and its stable social networks. As a participant observer of vagrants or wandering people, Philip O'Connor considers them "outside society" and remarks about them and himself while living among them, "having undressed socially, what was left? Not even identity. However meretricious and insecure one's social identity might be, there was no other" for "people apart from their work. Work identifies, unsuitable work misinterprets." He then goes on to describe "the nightmare of lack of identity from which vagrants generally suffer . . ." in terms of how his own bodily sensations were affected, particularly when, in England, he hit the roads and walked and walked:

> So in daylight I noticed my own voice becoming extremely weak to my own ears, extremely abstract, and my movements and thoughts felt the same; while the world, between its nebulous phases of decomposition, roared into an augmented power. The physical facts of the lorries and cars rushing by one contributed to this rendering away of the self; along the road, one is always being left behind. The hilarity of independence this periodically induced was near to hysteria; one was too liberated into great lightness.[43]

These impressions of the "rendering away of the self" as one is in every way "left behind" are subjective evidence of the state into which men who are "too liberated" may fall. The power of the outside world increases; the locus of control externalizes, as they grow more remote from actuality. Whether they wish to be so unattached or are, apart from their desires, pressed into this condition by a confluence of social, economic, and psychological constraints seems an unanswerable question.

I remember once working with a forty-year-old man in a psychiatric hospital who had had a series of schizophrenic breaks in the midst of an adult life punctuated by much wandering. When he said he wanted to leave the hospital and find a job as a night watchman in a lumber camp, I knew that he had a good grip on the real world and the limits of his own interpersonal competence; he could manage to help drunken loggers back to their bunk houses, but could tolerate no more human communication or relationships than this. And what of the self of such people?

There are psychological reports on the intelligence and projective test results of homeless men—the Wechsler Adult Intelligence Scales (WAIS), the Rorschach, and other projectives—given over a ten-year period to whites and blacks in various shelters and other settings where homeless men are to be found. Although the samples fall within the normal range for intelligence, they score higher on verbal than on performance scales and repeatedly show "the feeling of unworthiness or uselessness."[44] The self emerges as one of very low self-esteem and low self-adequacy. This devalued self is coupled with evidence of depression, hopelessness, passivity, goallessness, inadaptability, and few interests. The latter I see as an absence of curiosity, based on feelings of insecurity. Habit must enable these men to go on living from day to day.

In one Skid Row area, an old Carnegie Public Library building has been refurbished by the city as a social center and a reading place. The director works closely with the public welfare system and part-time employment agencies, but the center's most effective role, along with merely providing an indoor place to sit and read, is its active recreational program and its advocacy involvements. A Skid Row has only the minimum elements of a permanent community, and its visibility and representation among, for example, municipal authorities are typically very slight. If seen at all, it is with distaste, as a necessary evil. A well-staffed social center for a Skid Row area may provide some sense of permanence and adequate representation for its people. In a recent thrust, some of the local residents have been engaged in an effort to halt or modify a nearby urban redevelopment program which would push the local people out of some of their present territory and promote the up-grading of hotels far beyond prices they could afford. With such programs, some of the residents see the center as "a place to feel worthwhile and use their talents." How many then "ease back into the work force" remains to be seen. Meanwhile, the game rooms, the theatre, the lounge and lecture hall, the gymnasium, the kitchen, and the TV room for watching sporting events are heavily used every day and night of the week.[45] May there be some midlife second chances for some of these people too?

SOCIAL RESPONSIBILITY IN MIDLIFE

> Middle aged men and women, while they by no means regard themselves as being in command of all they survey, nevertheless recognize that they consti- tute the powerful age-group vis-a-vis other age groups; that they are the norm-bearers and the decision-makers; and they live in a society which, while it may be oriented towards youth, is controlled by the middle aged.[46]

So Bernice Neugarten sums up the findings from a series of studies of over 2,000 normal men and women in Midwestern metropolitan areas. By midlife, socially, some people have attained recognized positions of power in their society; psychologically, as Neugarten concludes, of "central importance" are "the executive processes of personality in middle age: self-awareness, selectivity, manipulation and control of the environment, mastery, competence, the wide array of cognitive strategies."[47]

In short, the understandings and capacities developed over more than four or five decades of living are now put to use in decision making which affects large seg- ments of younger and older people in a society. The ground work for intergener- ational conflict is thus laid. The crucial question is the extent to which the executive powers of middle age are guided by a sense of social responsibility, rooted in values extending beyond self-interest. The developmental issue that arose earlier in life, for eight- and nine-year-olds regarding reciprocity and prosocial behavior (see Chapter Five), begs for reconsideration regarding the middle-aged. Though there is no question at this time of life but that "reassessment of the self is a prevailing theme,"[48] to what extent is that self oriented by values that extend beyond self-interest?

Values and related social development vary by region and cultural groups. Remember that the research on prosocial behavior among school-aged children (reported in Chapter Five) indicated less competitiveness and selfishness and more collaboration or team work among Mexican and Mexican–American children, Native Indian and rural children, Israeli kibbutz and Arab village children than among richer and urban children or other comparison groups. It is thus significant that in middle age studies of adults from different regions of the United States come up with similar findings about their potentials for prosocial behavior. At least, the research on the Atlantic Coast in New England and New York and the research on the Pacific Coast in northern California seem to agree with the Chicago-based research done in the Midwest. The consensus is, essentially, that psychological development by or during the middle adult years is hospitable to socially responsible behavior.

What are the core psychological developments? Who were the adults being studied, on the basis of which the formulations on social responsibility in middle age were proposed? Specifically, Erik Erikson's previously discussed ideas on "generativity" and the "gradual expansion of ego-interests" and "concern in establishing and guiding the next generation"[49] were revised for the second edition of *Childhood and Society* while he was attached to a private psychoanalytically-oriented hospital for emotionally disturbed adults in Massachusetts; he was also about this time giving seminars at Harvard University. Some years later, Daniel Levinson at Yale, studying employed men in New England and elsewhere in the North Atlantic region, wrote, "Middle adulthood is a season" for the ripening of "wisdom, judiciousness, magnanimity, unsentimental compassion, breadth of perspective, the tragic sense."[50] What better psychological grounding for the practice of social responsibility? Across the continent in Berkeley men and women born in the San Francisco Bay Area and now middle-aged are reported by Norma Haan to have "become considerably more giving and self-extending . . . as well as interpersonally predictable and accountable to others, or generative, to use Erikson's term."[51] Thus, psychological predispositions apparently exist, at least among a variety of North Americans, for the growth of social concerns and the expression of social responsibility in the middle years of adulthood.

The essence of social responsibility, as used in this text, is twofold. First, it involves a person's sense of obligation. The obligation is to work on behalf of or otherwise contribute to the general welfare beyond self-interest. The obligation is based on a keen awareness of one's group memberships—ultimately, the human race—and of human interdependence in society. Having obtained by the middle adult years some of the advantages of such interdependence, a middle-aged person should be ready to make some repayments. Thus, the sense of obligation. One cannot be responsible, however, for somebody or something about or for which one cannot do anything. Thus, the second component of social responsibility involves, as the dictionary says, "capabilities of fulfilling an obligation or trust." Again, the idea of competence arises. At this time of life, the middle-aged become especially crucial links in responsive environments, in supportive networks needed for attachments or collaborative communities important not only in helping but also in modeling and developing reciprocity in others. Together with the competence is its contextual base in positions of power which the middle-aged have access to. Thus, social responsibility has a value or "should" component, experienced as obligation, and a capability or power component.

Social responsibility may be expressed in a variety of ways. The volunteer in the neighborhood or on other levels of society, the active member of voluntary organizations in church or political life, the "candy striper" in the hospital wards, the board member of a social agency, the foster parent for a handicapped child, the visitor to the infirm old or handicapped and house-confined, the volunteer editor of a housing project newspaper, the knowledgable advocate for tenants threatened with eviction, the county's representative to the state capital on a controversial environmental issue—these and so many other undertakings can express social responsibility. They are oriented by social concern and put personal talents to use for nonpersonal—or not merely personal—collective benefit.

There are some occupations through which the middle-aged can pursue a socially responsible course of action. The issue of payment for one's work may cast a shadow over the presumably altruistic aspect of social responsibility, but I do not want to try to argue this point; the problem involves questions similar to the issues of free will versus determinism in philosophical discussions of moral or legal responsibility. Even within paid positions one can exercise discretion or choose options without regard to self-interest. This is at the heart of most professional work. Decisions are made on the basis of the best available knowledge and for the welfare of the people who are being served by the profession—at no time primarily for the professional person's own advantage. Codes of ethics to which professionals subscribe—and the sanctions and controls of professional associations—aim to ensure that professions are performed with social responsibility.

Having these issues in mind, I end this chapter with field observations on two judges whose positions allow them to remove children from their families for the children's own safety or welfare. Such judges are seen by some people as giving child protection and by others as contributing to family dismemberment. I present this record because it illustrates so well, in the contrast offered by the two judges, how power and its use are differentially affected by differing values. The values reflect in these instances regional differences that these judges represent. It is unlikely they would remain in power if they were not representative of the "cultures" in which they work. Note that these "cultures" are the two rural North Central counties described in Record No. 3 at the end of Chapter One. A reading of Record No. 3 before or in conjunction with Record No. 23 on the two judges, which follows, might help to put their different orientations and decisions in context.

Both of these middle-aged judges seem to see themselves as engaged in socially responsible decision making. That is, they use their competence and power to make decisions for the welfare of specific others and for the community or society at large. They must do so in accordance with existing codes and statutes which foster impartiality. Such fairness is an essential facet of justice. But despite the codes and statutes affecting the placement of dependent children, there is still much latitude for interpretation and decision making by the judges. This is why the exercise of justice is a prime example of socially responsible involvement, as is the protection of children and families and the community from harmful behavior especially by others who are powerful. Yet, note with what different values Judge Farnham Walker in the more affluent of the two rural counties and Judge Will Swanson approach questions of whether children should be removed from their families. Is one more socially responsible than the other? And to whom?

TWO JUDGES: VALUES
AND POWER IN MIDDLE AGE
(RECORD NO. 23)

Judge Farnham Walker, a man in his early fifties, lived in a town somewhat smaller than Abbotsford and in a county adjacent to Norden. His home was a wooden structure, comfortably and attractively furnished. The melting snow still muddied the unpaved street in front of the house one winter evening as we looked in upon the judge to get his views on child dependency and parental neglect. He talked in an easy, pleasant manner which gave one the impression that he was expressing personal convictions rather than delivering a cut-and-dried judicial lecture.

"God gave the parents children; it would take something very strong to take them away," said Judge Walker, and one felt immediately that this man would not wish to challenge the Almighty on matters so grave. "Yes," he said, "I am quite reluctant to set myself up as judge of someone's fitness to raise children." Then he described the case which seemed to have set a precedent in this rural state on matters of the removal of children from their own parents for neglect. This case occurred some years ago and involved the removal of a group of children from their parents in a county father west. These children were placed for adoption after the rights of their parents had been terminated, but the State Supreme Court reversed the decision on removal for neglect and returned the children to their parents. Judge Walker felt that this decision made judges in the state reluctant to remove children from parents unless delinquency was involved, and his own practices reflected this situation. "In my three years on the bench," he said, "there have been no cases brought before me of children where the grounds were strictly neglect and dependency." There had been complaints not based on delinquency, he explained, but these were over feeble-minded children who were only technically neglected and dependent and were in court actually because of their mental condition.

Judge Walker was hard pressed to think of any situation which he would include in the "neglect" category. He felt that, perhaps, someone incompetent to earn a living and care for children might be called unfit—but Norden County did not have many, if any, such people. Once in a while there were situations of immorality or drunkenness arising in other types of cases, and the judge had felt at times that the children involved might be better off in another home. But these cases came to him for other kinds of decisions and presented no issue of "neglect" to be acted upon.

Our visit with Judge Walker left us with a clearer understanding, from a different vantage point, of the Norden community, in which, to our questions, local residents repeatedly replied, "We just don't have dependent families or children here." This key judicial personage was part of a system whose values had best been expressed in the previously cited State Supreme Court decision against releasing children for adoption solely on the grounds of parental neglect. Thus the judge was a part of a judicial process which, for our purpose, was more theoretical than actual. Of the seven children in our study who came from within Norden County, none had been removed by Norden County's court on the grounds of neglect. . . . Consequently, cases involving neglect situations in Norden had to wait until they might finally be handled as cases of delinquency.

Judge Will Swanson seemed close to the local scene in Granger. We walked up the three flights of stairs to the top floor of the county courthouse to meet him in his office on an afternoon when he could spare some time from court duties. The judge greeted us cordially, settled back somewhat expectantly in his swivel chair, and awaited our questions. He was a small man, with tanned and rather leathery skin which gave him the look of one who spent a good deal of time out-of-doors. He spoke softly. There was nothing dogmatic or defensive in his manner. It was soon obvious that he too, like Judge Walker, was more attuned to delinquency cases than to dependency situations. It was difficult for him to keep the two separate, but at least the dependent child was a part of his experience and not a completely alien figure.

"The major problems," remarked Judge Swanson, "are those involving children being out on their own at night. If parents are out in the tavern while the kids are on the streets at eleven, twelve, or one o'clock at night, then I consider the children are being neglected. And it's that kind of neglect that leads directly into delinquency." He paused, then plunged into a discussion of the type of youth problem that seemed closest to his heart. "You may have heard about that big fight in the meadow in which thirty-seven boys were involved. I put all thirty-seven of those boys on a ten o'clock curfew. If we can get the kids *home* at ten," and he slapped his desk for emphasis, "we'd be rid of juvenile delinquency."

We brought the discussion back to the dependent child, for we knew that of the twenty-six local Granger County children in our study well over half had gone through court procedures which resulted in a modification or termination of parental rights. The judge corroborated our impressions. "The younger kids, maybe six or seven years old, would be removed temporarily if parents leave them late at night and go running around," he said. "But I give parents a warning first. And sometimes when parents lose control of their children I place the children with relatives for a while."

Judge Swanson was a key person in the determination of placement for Granger County children. He emphasized his reluctance to remove children from parents, and this reluctance became even stronger, he said, where he was asked to remove children permanently. In such a situation there was no further chance for the parents to come back into the picture, and Judge Swanson, like his counterpart in Norden, was not anxious to sever ties of kinship in a court of human law. Still, there were dependent children in Granger County, children who had been so defined by the community culture and by its welfare agents, and he was called upon to make grave decisions.

Most of Granger's dependent children, it will be recalled, were living in foster families. In many such cases the children were in a legal situation wherein their parents' rights had been modified but not permanently terminated. Since the judge ordinarily had no further contact with these children, there being no provision for periodic review of their cases, they remained in a rather indeterminate status in which their parents retained some but not complete legal control. This seemed to be the situation with about one out of every three Granger County children—a situation probably frustrating to social workers in their efforts to make permanent plans for children like Gary Olsen once they had left their own homes, yet still reflecting an atmosphere in which dependent families were really "not too different from the rest of us." As Judge Swanson so clearly said: "These families whose kids appear before me are really not very different from any other families. All families have problems. It's just that some families let things slide rather than making the kids toe the line. Then someone has to step in to do something about it." At such times Judge Swanson felt it was his duty to move in, reluctantly, to arrange legally for substitute parental care for some of the community's children.[52]

The beliefs and values of these two judges differ markedly. They make very different assumptions about the sanctity of family attachments and the rights of children to protection from neglect and abuse. Yet both these middle-aged men are engaged in socially responsible activities. They are concerned about local families and their children. They thus address a central part of their community's life. Moreover, concern about children is concern for the future, and this latter concern is fundamental to socially responsible involvements. Judge Walker's reluctance to remove children from their families suggests a commitment to a future which, as much as possible, resembles the present. At least it follows a "natural" course of events without professional intervention. By contract, Judge Swanson, although also reluctant to separate children from their homes, still believes "some families let things slide" and then "someone has to step in and do something about it." Thus the judges exercise their power and social responsibilities in different ways. Nor does it seem surprising that in a politically liberal county Judge Swanson is an active intervener, and in the more conservative county Judge Farnham Walker appears to be more accepting of the *status quo*.

These differences between the two rural judges pale by comparison, however, with how they both differ, in regard to social responsibility, from the middle-aged men on Skid Row. What different present contexts they inhabit and what different developmental courses they must have followed! Consider the stable, small town social networks of which the judges are a part by comparison with the transient and remote relationships Skid Rows usually afford. The judges and the homeless men differ also in their capacities for coping with the conventional world's demands, in their self-images, and especially in the orbits of their assumed social responsibility.

A sense of obligation to one's community and the capacities to participate are basic to community service and many other kinds of contribution to the general welfare. But some life style changes and personal preoccupations in the middle adult years may limit broadly-based, socially responsible investments. Consider, for example, Mario Anichini who changed careers in his fifties, or Mary (no family name given) who has just recognized her daughter's transition into adulthood and who is entering a new phase of her marital relationship (in the family therapy record), or Irene James who suffered a psychotic breakdown at age forty. Under such circumstances people may have little of themselves to invest in community service.

Such biographical fragments suggest the many different turns that a person's life can take at middle age, but one should not overgeneralize from them. Few people, like Irene James, suffer the serious kinds of midlife crises which the popular literature dramatizes, or for that matter, relatively few people personify the equally popular but antithetical theme "life begins at forty"—the time for "starting over."[53] Still, generally, the middle-aged are the normsetters, the decision makers, and most socially powerful age group. Their controlling involvements should reflect widespread community concerns.

Thus, the human services should anticipate and plan for the expression of social responsibility in the middle adult years. Community organizations and community development offices should offer a wide range of options for the participation of middle-aged residents. Volunteer bureaus should be active in their recruitment programs for as varied opportunities to serve as possible. Beyond working on social agency boards, people at midlife (through churches and other local institutions) should be able to inaugurate new neighborhood programs and social policies. As people's social awareness and concerns expand to environments extending beyond their immediate communities, so may the causes to which the middle-aged attach themselves and contribute their efforts.

In the framework of this book, social responsibility is the efflorescense of the social development that has preceded it. It starts with early attachments and subsequent explorations in a responsive world. Primary attachments provide one foundation for later feelings of social responsibility to other, more remote people. The reaching out of the curious, exploring person must somewhere along the life course become patterned and desirable behavior for later socially responsible involvements. Typically, the collaborative use of one's capacities on teams and other joint ventures should have been well developed for effective midlife contributions. Social responsibility is most often expressed in collaborative efforts. These efforts are unlikely to begin easily in middle age without earlier, preparatory experiences. Social development is a lifelong process. Human services addressed to young families, children and youth, and single young adults should plan programs that anticipate and thus foster the expression of socially responsible participation in community life when people become middle-aged.

NOTES

[1] Bernice L. Neugarten, "Time, Age, and the Life Cycle," *American Journal of Psychiatry,* 136 (1979), p. 890.

[2] Ibid.

[3] Erik Erikson, *Childhood and Society,* 2nd ed., rev. (New York: Norton, 1963), pp. 267-68.

[4] Ibid., p. 267.

[5] David S. Freeman, *Techniques of Family Therapy* (New York: Jason Aronson, 1981).

[6] Ibid., pp. 256-58. Reprinted with the permission of the author and the publisher, Jason Aronson.

[7] David L. Gutmann, "An Exploration of Ego Configurations in Middle and Later Life," in Bernice L. Neugarten and Associates, *Personality in Middle and Later Life* (New York: Atherton Press, 1964); "Parenthood: Key to the Comparative Psychology of the Life Cycle?" in Nancy Datan and L. Ginsberg, eds., *Life Span Developmental Psychology: Normative Life Crises* (New York: Academic Press, 1975); "Powers of the Aged: A Developmental Perspective," unpublished paper presented at Celebration in Honor of Bernice Neugarten: Personality, Social Structure and Public Policy in the Second Half of Life, University of Chicago, April 30–May 1, 1982.

[8] Arlene Skolnick, "Married Lives: Longitudinal Perspectives in Marriage," in Dorothy H. Eichorn and others, eds., *Present and Past in Middle Life* (New York: Academic Press, 1981), p. 288.

[9] Ibid., p. 291.

[10] Ibid., p. 296.

[11] Dorothy H. Eichorn, Jane V. Hunt, and Marjorie P. Honzik, "Experience, Personality, and IQ: Adolescence to Middle Age," in Eichorn,... *Middle Life,* p. 114.

[12] Norma Haan, "Common Dimensions of Personality Development: Early Adolescence to Middle Life," in Eichorn,... *Middle Life,* p. 149.

[13] Ibid., pp. 150-51.

[14] Judith Wallerstein and Joan B. Kelly, "Children and Divorce: a Review," *Social Work,* 24 (1979) 468-75; Nadine Nehls and Mel Morgenbesser, "Joint Custody: An Exploration of the Issues," *Family Process,* 19 (1980), 117-24; Constance Ahrons, "Redefining the Divorced Family: A Conceptual Framework," *Social Work,* 25 (1980), 437-41; Rhona Rosen, "Children of Divorce," *Canadian Journal of Family Law,* 2 (1979), 403-15.

[15] Skolnick, "Married Lives," p. 191.

[16] Mary Cover Jones, "Midlife Drinking Patterns: Correlates and Antecedents," in Dorothy H. Eichorn and others, eds., *Present and Past in Middle Life,* pp. 241-42.

[17] George Levinger and Oliver C. Moles, eds., *Divorce and Separation: Context, Causes and Consequences* (New York: Basic Books, 1979); Leonard Pearlin and Joyce Johnson, "Marital Status, Life Strains, and Depression," *American Sociological Review,* 42 (1977), 704-15; Robert Weiss, *Marital Separation* (New York: Basic Books, 1975).

[18] Jill M. Thies, "Beyond Divorce: The Impact of Remarriage on Children," *Journal of Clinical Child Psychology,* 6 (1977), 59-61; Emily B. Visher and John S. Visher, *Step-families: A Guide to Working with Stepparents and Stepchildren* (Secaucus, New Jersey: Citadel Press, 1980), pp. 195-99.

[19] Lucile Duberman, *The Reconstituted Family: a Study of Remarried Couples and their Children* (Chicago: Nelson-Hall, 1975), pp. 108-9 and p. 19.

[20] Harold Sampson and others, *Schizophrenic Women: Studies in Marital Crisis* (New York: Atherton Press, 1964), pp. 135–37. Reprinted with permission.

[21] Bernice L. Neugarten and others, "Women's Attitudes toward the Menopause," in Bernice L. Neugarten, ed., *Middle Age and Aging* (Chicago: University of Chicago Press, 1968).

[22] Sidney Z. Moss and Miriam S. Moss, "Some Observations on the Intergenerational Impact of Parental Death." Paper presented at the 33rd Annual Meeting of the Gerontological Society of America, San Diego, November, 1980.

[23] Daniel J. Levinson and others, *The Seasons of a Man's Life* (New York: Alfred Knopf, 1978), pp. 339 and 25.

[24] Ibid., p. 26.

[25] Carey Winfrey, "Robert Penn Warren: A Poet Ruminates on Grants, Taxes, The Creative Impulse, Marriage, and Life and Death," *International Herald Tribune*, Friday, June 12, 1981.

[26] John A. Clausen, "Men's Occupational Careers in the Middle Years," in Dorothy H. Eichorn and others, eds., . . . *Middle Life*, p. 329.

[27] Ibid., pp. 330–51.

[28] Skolnick, "Married Lives" in . . . *Middle Life*, p. 270.

[29] Michael Young and Peter Willmott, *The Symmetrical Family: a Study of Work and Leisure in the London Region* (Middlesex, England: Penguin Books, 1975), p. 105, Table 12.

[30] Rhona and Robert Rapoport, *Dual-Career Families* (Middlesex, England: Penguin Books, 1971).

[31] Ibid., pp. 290–92.

[32] Young and Willmott, *Symmetrical Family*, p. 101.

[33] Lillian Rubin, *Worlds of Pain: Life in the Working-Class Family* (New York: Basic Books, 1976), pp. 181–83.

[34] Max Heirich, *The Beginning: Berkeley 1964* (New York: Columbia University Press, 1970); Charles Frankel, *Education and the Barricades* (New York: Norton, 1968).

[35] Theodore Roszak, *The Making of the Counter Culture: Reflections on the Technocratic Society and its Youthful Opposition* (Garden City, New York: Anchor Books, 1969).

[36] Joseph Veroff, Elizabeth Douvan, and Richard A. Kulka, *The Inner American: a Self-Portrait from 1957 to 1976* (New York: Basic Books, 1981); Joseph Veroff, Richard A. Kulka, and Elizabeth Douvan, *Mental Health in America: Patterns of Health-seeking from 1957 to 1976* (New York: Basic Books, 1981).

[37] Kenneth Keniston, "The Mood of Americans Today," *The New York Times Book Review*, Sunday, November 8, 1981, p. 44.

[38] Studs Terkel, *Working: People Talk about What They Do All Day and How They Feel about What They Do* (New York: Pantheon Books, 1974), p. 542.

[39] Ibid., pp. 543–44. Quoted with permission of Random House.

[40] Donald J. Bogue, *Skid Row in American Cities* (Chicago: Community and Family Study Center, University of Chicago, 1963), p. 91, Table 3–2; Philip O'Connor, *Britain in the Sixties: Vagrancy* (Baltimore, Maryland: Penguin Books, 1963), p. 80, for age breakdown of over 2,200 men in a reception center, of whom almost 60 percent were aged forty to sixty-four years old; Samuel E. Wallace, *Skid Row as a Way of Life* (Totowa, New Jersey: Bedminster Press, 1965); James R. Rooney, "Societal Forces and the Unattached Male: An Historical Review," in Howard M. Bahr, ed., *Disaffiliated Man: Essays and Bibliography on Skid Row, Vagrancy, and Outsiders* (Toronto: University of Toronto Press, 1970); Howard M. Bahr, *Skid Row: an Introduction to Disaffiliation* (New York: Oxford University Press, 1973); Leonard Blumberg, Thomas E. Shipley, Jr., and Irving W. Shandler, *Skid Row and its Alternatives* (Philadelphia: Temple University Press, 1973).

[41] Bahr, *Skid Row*, p. 37.

[42] Bogue, *Skid Row*, Chapter 14, "Social Mobility of Homeless Men: Rise then Fall."

[43] O'Connor, *Vagrancy*, pp. 138–39.

[44] Boris M. Levinson, "The 'Beat' Phenomenon in Wechsler Tests," *Journal of Clinical Psychology* 20 (1964), 118–20; "The Homeless Man: a Psychological Enigma," *Mental Hygiene*,

47 (1963) 590–601; "The Intelligence of Middle-aged White Homeless Men in Receipt of Public Assistance," *Psychological Reports,* 1 (1955), 35–36; "Some Aspects of the Personality of the Native-born White Homeless Man as Revealed by the Rorschach," *Psychiatric Quarterly Supplement,* 32 (Part 2, 1958), 278–86, all annotated references in Howard Bahr, *Disaffiliated Man,* pp. 112–16.

[45] "Library is Haven to Old and Poor," *The Vancouver Sun,* Saturday, May 15, 1982, p. B-1.

[46] Bernice L. Neugarten, "The Awareness of Middle Age," in Bernice L. Neugarten, ed., *Middle Age and Aging* (Chicago: University of Chicago Press, 1968), p. 93.

[47] Ibid., p. 98.

[48] Ibid., p. 93.

[49] Erikson, *Childhood and Society,* 2nd ed., p. 267.

[50] Levinson, *Seasons,* pp. 25–26.

[51] Haan, . . . *Middle Life,* p. 151.

[52] Henry S. Maas and Richard E. Engler, Jr., *Children in Need of Parents* (New York: Columbia University Press, 1959), pp. 30–35.

[53] For examples of popular views on midlife crises and second chances see, Gail Sheehy, *Passages: Predictable Crises of Adult Life* (New York: E. P. Dutton, 1976); Damon Stetson, *Starting Over* (New York: Macmillan, 1971); Blake Green, "Can I Really be Turning 40?" *San Francisco Chronicle,* Thursday, May 1, 1980, p. 41. A perhaps unusual version of midlife's second chance involves Bobby Seale, chairman of the Black Panthers in the 1960s. In the 1980s at age 46, living "on a quiet street in one of Denver's nicer suburbs," Bobby Seale talks about the cookbook he is writing and says, "A few years ago, I realized I was planning a college education for my kids. It dawned on me that all the time I was in the Black Panther Party, I had never planned more than a month in advance." Report by S. J. Guffey in *The Sunday Oregonian,* July 11, 1982, p. A21.

By contrast, increasing early retirements by people in their mid-fifties in France have led to their becoming "a driving force in the community"–for example, through election to municipal councils, volunteer work with unemployed youth, or other socially responsible second-chance involvements. Report of Marie-Claude Betbeder, "The Joys and Frustrations of Early Retirement," *Le Monde* section of The Manchester Guardian Weekly, July 17, 1983, p. 14.

Chapter 9
OLD PEOPLE
CONTINUITIES
AND TRANSFORMATIONS,
LOSSES AND LEGACIES

Introduction: Old age requires environmental options.

Developmental and Contextual Continuities, Changes, and Losses
  Living places in old age
  Attachments, networks, and widowhood
      Four Life Styles of Old People and their Early Adult Antecedents
      (Record No. 24)
  Curiosity, competence, and retirement
  Aging selves

Legacies before and after Death
  "A Personal Note" (Record No. 25)

INTRODUCTION

Old Age Requires Environmental
Options

The continuing capacities and potentials of old people vary widely. The chronological ages and rates at which development and other transformations occur cover a broad range in old age. Environmental options, including human services, should be wide-ranging and responsive to the diversity of old people in their somatic, psychological, and social changes.

Seventy-year-olds have different feelings about their age. "I'm glad I'm old as I am," says one old woman. Says another, "I don't feel old. I don't want to feel like it because I'm active and I feel like I'm still sixteen." Says a third woman, "I think this period right now is probably as hard as any because I don't have the interest or energy to involve myself in things. And I avoid people so much." A man in his seventies says, "I have no real desire to continue to live and I'm certainly not going to be one of those old people in hospitals where somebody's taking care of me—period." And another man says of himself and his wife, "We're very fortunate people. We have health, friends, a wonderful family, and adequate funds, and what more could anybody want."[1]

Old age is a social category, encompassing people of broad biological, psychological, social and economic differences. Because people travel through life on such different biological timetables, maturing and aging at widely disparate rates and ages, age-linked imperatives, such as mandatory retirement at age sixty-five, are inevitably inappropriate and unfair for large segments of any age category.

Moreover, there is a historical lag in our assumptions and stereotypes about old people. "Despite the rapid expansion of, and marked changes in, the older population, our notions of old age as a phase of life have undergone little revision. We go on marveling at the number of active, alert 'youthful' people in their seventies without recognizing that the same chronological age span now represents a different state than it did in the past (or may in the future)"[2] —with life expectancies different from today's.

Considering "old age" a social category may seem to deny its biological bases and the eventual death of all living organisms. Life does depend on the self-repair and replicative capacities of cells, but as these as well as functional abilities are lost over time, organisms do have life span limits. Leonard Hayflick adds that fibroblasts (connective tissue cells) look different when removed from young and old organisms. But if senescence is a normal process of cell life, can organisms be kept alive interminably by organ replacement? Leonard Hayflick's answer makes one wonder.

> Spare-part surgery for human beings is limited to a few organs, and the spare parts are themselves imperfect. Even if brain transplants were possible, the outcome would be futile. Immortality, after all, presupposes the continuity of self-identify, which someone else's brain would not provide.[3]

Said one old woman, previously quoted, "Life and death go together—that's the natural way."

The social category of old age in North America today tends to be painted gray. For example, in a frontpage headline, "Graying of America," the *Sunday Sun-Times* in Chicago begins an eight-part series with a first installment entitled, "Growing Old: the Worst is Yet to Be." The article touches on old people's loss of control over their lives, loss of family supports, victimization in cities, poverty, difficulties in health care, burdensome increase in numbers, and other problems.[4] Any social category of people who are in a numerical minority in a society and are seen totally or primarily in terms of their problems and the problems they create for other people are likely to become the targets of damaging discrimination as scapegoats for the society's ills. Like racism and sexism, "age-ism" takes many forms and causes much suffering. Human variability and individual uniquenesses, strengths, and potentials are obscured when categorical approaches to people predominate. People are treated as members of a class rather than as persons with differing characteristics. Policy and programs are established as though there need be no options for all old people.

A developmental approach to old people orients us to their lifelong processes, their varied present lives seen as emerging in part from their diverse past lives and leading to their roughly predictable futures. A developmental approach may attend to their continuing and changing patterns of attachment, curiosity and competence, and self-images. A developmental approach conceives of old age and death in later life as normal. Developmentalists increasingly recognize the adaptive resilience of healthy human beings and their proactive (and not merely reactive) capacities at all ages in the life span. Generally, research on aging gives no support to a pathology, all downhill orientation to old age; rather, there is continuing development as well as developmental losses in old age.

With an interactionist approach, developmentalists appreciate the interplay of many forces and thus the need for using research in many disciplines for a useful understanding of old people. Development continues through interaction of bodily and psychological changes with changes in social and physical environments. An interactionist approach to aging suggests the idea of increased boundary shifts in old age. Boundary shifts occur between the old person's inner and outer milieus, as environments must be modified to accommodate what bodies could formerly cope with when somatic deficits increase. Environmental boundaries shift as they offer prostheses compensating for body losses. For example, when one becomes more forgetful, one may have to depend on a notebook in which one lists things one needs to remember to do today or this week. Another kind of boundary shift occurs between past and present, as old people reconstruct their past lives to make sense of it in view of present perspectives and as part of what Robert N. Butler calls a "life review" in which old people, when reminiscing, engage.[5] This and other boundary shifts are illustrated in this chapter.

Finally, a contextual view, as part of the developmental–interactional approach, reminds us of the importance of the flexibility or adjustability and variety of old people's environments, starting with their living place. Living place becomes all the more important for the very old in their later seventies or eighties and beyond as mobility may begin to shrink. The healthy elderly in their sixties and early seventies, and also many others who are older still retain much of the competence they enjoyed in their middle age. Moreover, daily performance may continue at a level which has become habitual, despite bodily losses.

Still, for changes in competence, sometimes sudden, the environments of old people, such as their living places, should be as flexibly responsive as possible. They should also provide sufficient variety in options to accommodate much of the great diversity among old people. This is one of the human service principles guiding the discussion of continuities and changes which follows.

DEVELOPMENTAL
AND CONTEXTUAL CONTINUITIES,
CHANGES, AND LOSSES

In Chapter One, there is a chart of lifelong developmental processes and the contexts that are conducive to their optimal expression. Highlighted at certain periods of life and interrelated—not essentially but normally—in certain sequences, these processes and contexts are as relevant to an understanding of old age as to any other phase of life. By way of introduction to a more detailed consideration of some of these processes and contexts, I shall start with an overview of their meanings for old people.

The macrosociety and living place into which a newborn arrives influence, and are to some extent influenced by, the earliest interaction between a neonate and her or his milieu. In old age, a society's policies and provisions influence the economic security, health care, physical safety, housing and community life, and many other elements of old people's daily lives. Consequently, old people and their advocates help to shape policies and programs relevant to how they live. As previously suggested, with the shrinkage in geographic mobility which many old people experience, their living place—both neighborhood and dwelling space—may make a marked difference in their continuing satisfactions and health. I shall shortly elaborate on living places in old age, drawing on relevant research, as it may relate to developmental changes at this time of life.

Within living places, long-term or new social networks may provide old people with significant attachments, not only to attenuate the feelings of loneliness from which some of the elderly suffer, but also to give support and service, perhaps less of a reciprocal kind of interaction than earlier in life. Ideally many old people have built up a "cash reserve" of indebtedness due them from others whom earlier in life they had helped. Whether interest has accrued is not always a certainty. For the well and the competent, networks of kin and friends are especially important sources of continuing and expanded pleasure when normal adult work years are over and there is ample leisure to enjoy sociability without conflicting obligations. Housing arrangements and options may support or reduce continuing network attachments or the development of new relationships. The latter may be especially important because old age is a time when some of the most intimate and longest of attachments are lost, as, for example, when spouses die and widowhood must be adapted to without the emotional involvements and daily regularities a long-term marital partnership is likely to have sustained.

The loss of attachments or separations in old age may initiate social withdrawal and a diminution of investment in life and its exploration, much as the inadequately attached toddler hesitates to venture out into the new and the strange alone. The explorable arenas that foster curiosity in the crawling infant or the toddler are no less relevant to the daily life of old people—perhaps they are even more so. The old remain open to and curious about new experience when they have kept mentally alert throughout their adult years. Stimulating milieus will be sought out by the elderly able and the still engaged. Problems of boredom afflict those whom earlier life experiences have routinized or mechanized; deprived of their daily jobs or suffering serious somatic limitations of an ambulatory, auditory, or visual nature, some old people are not able to involve themselves in formerly familiar realms. Unimaginative human service workers are unlikely to reawaken a sense of quest in these people. For some old people, however, their needs for adaptation to the changing and novel circumstances of the later years and the closer imminence of death may themselves become a challenge. Modes of adaptation vary widely, of course, and one may pursue one's life interests in a more or less intimate or distanced manner. Note, for example, the position of one of the old men in the Berkeley study who says, "I feel very much the way you might feel at a theatre. You're seeing a very good show and you know the thing is gonna come to an end pretty soon." Another old man remarks in a not dissimilar vein, of distanced engagement, "Well, I'm much more relaxed now than I ever was. I do not feel pressures."[6]

Most of how life is lived in old age hangs, of course, on the competence and other resources one continues to have available from one's earlier life. In addition, the changing feelings one has about self orient much of what one does or fails to do. In view of the salience of boundary shifts in old age between self and surroundings, as suggested earlier, the surroundings become increasingly a determinant of one's aging life's potentials.

Given the framework of this book and current understandings of the later years, my considerations of research on aging continuities and changes begin with studies of living places, an appropriate starting point for policy, planning, and direct practice in the human services.

Living Places in Old Age

The older people become, the more important are their living places to them. Retirement cuts them off from daily social interaction on the job away from home. Economic resources and physical and mental health may decline as people get older. With such decline, people's spatial mobility decreases. They thus become more dependent on the here and now of neighborhood life, its social interaction with neighbors, its physical amenities, its formal services, and other supports.

Questions about living places in old age are complex and fascinating because they require thought about matching or the fit between changing personal needs and widely variable sheltering environments. Much research has gone into these questions, and many of the issues are far clearer than they were some years ago, but practical guidance cannot yet go far beyond the concluding recommendations of a nationwide Canadian housing study:

The overriding objective of policies affecting the housing of senior citizens in Canada should be to provide as wide a variety and range of choice as possible. This means that the government should provide: the necessary income and community services to enable those who prefer to remain in their own homes or to continue living with their children to do so, purpose designated accommodation of the type we have studied, as well as special care homes for those who have suffered a serious decline in health . . . What is important is that sufficient alternatives exist in every community so that old people can choose the accommodation that suits them best.[7]

Note that such recommendations and most of the research on housing for old people spring from an urban and Western industrialized base. Rural settings—unless there are medical problems requiring the attention of big city specialists—seem more easily to accommodate the elderly since rural life is lived much closer to the natural processes of birth, aging, and death. The following discussion assumes also a post-industrial society, where age grading and related categories oversimplify the complexities of large aggregations of people and their diverse needs. In developing African nations, for example, the "towns" (as African urban centers have been called) attract and retain primarily youth and young adults; older people either never migrate from their villages or return "home" when they age. Population distributions by age and migratory patterns in both West and East African urban centers make this fact clear.[8] What follows about living places in old age derives largely from observations in the United States, Canada, and Western Europe, and may have little relevance elsewhere. This cautionary note implies that aging is in part a culturally defined process with quite different meanings in different cultural contexts. For example, in rural Ireland, aged fathers who hold onto their farmlands and farm houses until they die generate housing problems for their forty-year-old and still unmarried sons or "boys" but not for themselves as old people.[9]

Early in this book (Chapter Two), I discussed three dimensions of living places in relation to people's development. First, living places are shelters and other spatial arrangements that foster or limit residents' social and physical activities. For example, living places may or may not accommodate needs for both privacy and sociability, in different degrees by different people and among the same people in differing states of health. Second, living places may provide a more or less desirable base for residents' sense of belonging, identification, and self-esteem. In this regard, not only a neighborhood's location and physical conditions but also its population's composition, transiency or stability, and neighborliness are relevant. The question of population composition in old people's living places immediately raises further questions about homogeneity or heterogeneity along the dimensions of age and health, both physical and mental. Should planned living places for old people be segregated by age—that is, allowing for only old residents—or integrated, with young families and their children sharing a planned housing development? And if only for old people, should it be only for the healthy, physically independent, and fully competent? One's identification with or belonging to a living place depends initially on whether one's self-image can be reconciled with one's neighbors' public identities. For example, it is difficult to feel one belongs in a home for the infirm aged if one sees one's self as neither old nor disabled, despite the objective realities of one's condition or what one's family members think. Finally, the third dimension of living place in relation to residents' development is participation, especially in regard to neighborhood self-government. Living places, and particularly those for old people, may be organized and regulated in ways which allow for very little or no control by residents of the decision making about their living place. Personal feelings of competence are at issue, but I shall discuss this later. Out of the sizable literature on housing for old people, I shall sample some of the ideas bearing on the three dimensions of living place: spatial arrangements, identification and belonging, and social participation, especially in self-government.

Housing for old people ranges from Sun Belt retirement communities for the affluent to public housing for the poor and nursing homes offering different levels of care. No matter what kind of residence, "the design and construction of housing for the elderly must extend beyond the installation of walls, ceilings, floors, and even specialized household fixtures and appliances" to have "the capacity to counter the very real threats of physical and social isolation . . . The design can be a positive factor in stimulating effective employment of leisure time, the development of new roles, and a sense of purpose for those of advancing years."[10] This is not to diminish the importance of physical location, population density, air and noise pollution, traffic volume and other environmental hazards, and the accessibility of stores, health facilities, and recreation.

In fact, such physical rather than psychosocial items were most strongly associated with living place satisfactions in a largescale survey of old people. Drawing upon almost 900 respondents in twenty-eight matched communities stretching across the continental United States—half of them planned and half unplanned living places—a research team found most highly associated with residents' satisfaction the following four "predictors": perception of their community as a safe one, satisfaction with their individual dwelling unit, satisfaction with community recreational facilities, and satisfaction with health facilities, in that order. Note, however, that because the study was part of an evaluation of newly planned community developments, respondents were "a relatively affluent subset of all older persons in the United States" and "Perhaps somewhat different predictors of community satisfaction would have been found for older persons from a middle- or lower-income sample."[11] I cite this study because it describes the perspectives on living place of affluent old people, giving priority to physical features over such social issues as neighborliness.

Two of the now classic, earlier and intensive studies of old people's living places involved poorer people; they were done in San Antonio, Texas, by Frances M. Carp.[12] and in Cleveland, Ohio, by Irving Rosow,[13] and they both stress demographic and psychosocial network components, as against the primarily physical environments of living places. Working-class people more than middle-class people center their social lives in their living place, and the Cleveland study found this true for old people too. Rosow argues, however, that old people living in neighborhoods with a high density of their agemates are better off because "friendships are formed between persons of similar status, notably of age," and "the number of old people's local friends varies directly with the proportion of age peers." Still, he found that "in the middle class there was no relationship between density and local social contacts of men regardless of their employment status." High density of old people did increase the local social contacts more extensively for residents as they aged (became seventy-five and older) and when they were women, not married, and working class (all of whom were retired). Retirement was also found to help integrate "previously self-supporting middle class women into local social life."[14] Generated by the Cleveland Welfare Federation and the Cleveland Metropolitan Housing Authority, Rosow's study focuses on those demographic and related social conditions that seem necessary antecedents to the interaction and morale of old people in their living places. The working-class residents in Cleveland were more likely to identify themselves as old and to profit socially from a more highly age-segregated or more homogeneous-by-age living place.

In Philadelphia, the Community Housing for the Elderly research reports its "conservative conclusion . . . that neighborhood and dwelling-unit factors were *both* related to favorable change and that perceived similarity of near neighbors was perhaps less related to well-being than were the more physical aspects of the environment. It is of interest to note that the effect of dwelling unit size was always such that *smaller* size was associated with improved well-being. It is probably that the most favorable moves were those from large units in unfavorable settings to smaller ones in improved settings."[15] Reduced dwelling unit size presumably increases old people's feelings of competence. Thus report M. Powell Lawton, a long-time researcher on the ecology of old age and especially on housing environments for old people, and his social gerontologist and human services director colleague at the Philadelphia Geriatric Center, Elaine M. Brody, who was principal investigator of the Community Housing research. The reported improved well-being over six months of old Philadelphia residents who had moved into the new housing must be considered against what they had left behind when they moved. More than half of experimental and control subjects gave as their reasons for wanting to move "fear and crime," "poor condition of current dwelling," and "loneliness and isolation"—indicative of the fact that physical factors were not the only impetus for the desire to change residence. By contrast with the Cleveland study, however, the Philadelphia physical and spatial research data "confirm the idea that favorable neighborhood and residential factors are associated with positive effects on the well-being of the elderly." The findings are not meant to downplay the importance of "human factors, such as the natural support systems of family and friends and the institutional supports of services, in evaluating the well-being of older people."[16] It does reaffirm, however, the significance of the physical environment.

In effect, of course, architectural and other planning of old people's living places as physical spaces must be coordinated with social planning. The whole enterprise should be based in explicit biopsychosocial assumptions which draw on relevant gerontological knowledge. For example, a team of British social psychologists and architects have designed and presented detailed floor plans and bed–sitting room arrangements for old people's homes based on their assumptions about the desirability of integrating well and less well residents, thus encouraging assistance by peers. Their "intention is to capitalize on the reciprocity involved in exchanges of goods, services, and sentiments that anthropologists and sociologists claim lies at the core of social relations."[18] This goal might lead to a more remote physical placement of the offices for staff and administration and a juxtaposition of the rooms for residents of different levels of competence. Thus, residents' spatial segregation is not fostered and maintained for the convenience of staff's ubiquitous services and for the prevention or discouragement of "inter-resident exchanges of services or sentiments . . ."[19]

The social interaction of residents with one another and their independence from the staff are encouraged when the administration of homes for old people engages them as much as possible in their own housing management and program planning. Arrangements in a high-rise can begin with the greeting and introductions of new tenants by residents best suited to that responsibility and the election by tenants on each floor of their "floor captain." In Northwood Towers in Halifax, the captains sat on the tenants' association council "which made decisions on social programs and outings." Floor captains also acted as "den mother" and a source of help and referral with health, shopping, or personal matters. "More than half the tenants interviewed said that in an emergency they would contact the floor captain."[20]

With increasing age, most old people's social participation becomes limited to their residence and its immediate environs, but options should be available and accessible in the larger community. The walls of old people's residences tend to thicken against their neighborhoods, like the walls of any institution housing categories of people judged less competent than other people living in the community. In the nationwide Canadian survey of residents of subsidized housing, "a surprisingly low proportion of the residents—only 46 percent—went out for more than an hour each day," a third did not go out at all on a daily basis, and those who did go out were involved primarily in "shopping, informal visiting, going for drives, or simply walking . . . Participation in community activities appears to have declined considerably with entry to the development; indeed, the proportion of residents who never participated in community activities was 50 percent before entry and 65 percent at the time residents were interviewed."[21]

It is difficult to disentangle what lies behind such facts, but more than 60 percent of the studied residents were aged seventy-five and over, almost two thirds of them had blue collar occupational backgrounds, and all of them had experienced the discontinuity of a change from their familiar living places into some type of new age-segregated development. Their two major reasons for moving were given as limited income and inability to maintain their former homes which had often become too large. Moreover, these old people belong to a turn-of-the-century birth cohort whose lifelong community social participation patterns are probably less extensive than those of subsequent generations. The implications for human service planning are clear in the study's conclusions about the residents of subsidized housing for old people, "For most residents of senior citizens housing, the development and its environs represent their world. Except for occasional forays into the community and periodic contacts with relatives anf friends, residents look to their residential environment to provide them with most of the social, physical, mental, emotional, and to some extent spiritual, stimulation that life has to offer."[22] Programming for the development of residents' new social relationships and special interests are an in-house imperative, ideally promoted with maximum resident participation.

I conclude this section on old people and their living places with a reference to one community agency's noteworthy effort to bring selected patients in nursing homes into contact with their agemates who still live in the community. The program was planned so that patients might "spend at least 4 to 5 hours weekly in a setting which focuses on their abilities, as opposed to their disabilities" and so to enjoy a "day out." Arranging for nursing home management and staff cooperation, for wheelchaired patients' transportation, and for integrating the selected patients into the center's programs, in this Baltimore demonstration project, required extensive planning, but "The overall results of this project encourage its continuation as an integral part of the Senior Center program, for it allows existing recreational services to become accessible to a population of citizens who are in great need of social intercourse with the outside community." The continuity of social participation patterns from earlier life into old age is suggested by this project's finding that "Patients previously involved in social groups outside the family or work setting, including church groups and recreational activities, seem more likely to consider Center involvement as meaningful activity."[23]

The major discontinuity is the fact that all these old people—and most of those discussed in this section—have moved, in their old age, into homes and neighborhoods unfamiliar to them. For people who no longer have the energy to be curious about the novel and different, the strain of such change may be considerable. At least those who remain in their accustomed living places, whatever their deficiencies, do not have to make the often painful adaptations which an enforced move and then new daily surroundings demand. Human services should help prepare old people for necessary moves and informatively and empathically support them through reorientations to a new and unfamiliar living place. The sense of loss in leaving a longterm home, lifelong possessions, and a neighborhood social network, may be experienced as a prelude to death.

Attachments, Networks, and Widowhood

With available leisure time, early old age becomes "a stage of reinvestment in friendship," concludes B. Bradford Brown in his review of research on friendship over the life span.[24] In a study of old people's confidant relationships, the general findings are:

Our examination of the composition of the confidant network of the elderly respondents of this study reaffirms what others have found: the old are generally not an isolated population. Importantly, the quality of their relationships which was investigated here, reveals that only six percent of the total sample were without very close emotional support, known as a confidant relation. Further, for most elderly, dependence for this confidant relationship was not restricted to one individual, or one type of individual. Nearly half of the sample had confidants drawn from among friends, neighbors, and relatives.[25]

These findings appear in a study of over 900 old men and women in ten communities, selected for a range of population sizes, across the state of Missouri. Nicholas Babchuk reports similar findings on the lack of social isolation among old people,[26] and Marjorie Fiske Lowenthal and her colleagues give old age retirees second place (after newlyweds who are the highest) in the numbers of friends they have, with an average of six friends for all the old people, and somewhat more for the middle-class women as against the old men.[27] Thus, there is considerable research evidence to counter the popular belief that old age is generally a time marked by widespread social isolation.

Still, loneliness and a need for companionship ranked first as "the one important problem that senior citizens face in life" in a well-sampled study of 552 men and women aged sixty-five and over in Toronto. One in three old people gave this response (as did an even more substantial 45 percent of the women respondents) and another 5 percent felt either unwanted or patronized by other people.[28] Note that this Canadian study is of old people living in a metropolitan area, where social isolation is more possible in the anonymity of urban apartment blocks, but even in the previously quoted Missouri research, which included residents of rural areas, 6 percent of the sample had no close emotional relationship of any kind. In the stable, village-like, working-class neighborhoods of East London, Peter Townsend documents the diminishing contacts that old people have, as they age, with former friends, neighbors, and acquaintances. Generally, instead, family relationships became more and more important. The result is that old people without kin may be quite isolated socially. Of course, some such old people may have made long-term adaptations to being loners, and, in the London study, they are better off than others who had suffered the loss by death of close kin and were "desolates" (rather than "isolates").[29] Distinctions between being alone and feeling lonely are crucial. In old age, the need for help, for example, because of physical disabilities, calls upon different kinds of communication and relationships than does a need for companionship and sociability. The latter, moreover, is not a universal need among old people any more than it is among younger adults. One may be socially isolated and not lonely, or not isolated but still lonely.

Where then does the research on attachments and social networks in old age leave us? Obviously, we are left with a very mixed picture, and not inappropriately so, in view of the very mixed backgrounds and diverse ways of life of old people. In Rosow's Cleveland study, he was able to differentiate among five types of interpersonal orientation among old people: those in the middle class who found ample relationships outside their home neighborhoods, those who had little contact with neighborhood networks or other people and wanted no friends, those who had little neighborhood network contact but did want a social life and so felt dissatisfied, those who had high contact with neighbors and did not want more friends, and finally those whom Rosow called "insatiables" because they had a highly active social life and wanted still more.[30] This is but one set of evidence on the diversity of networks and feelings about them in old age.

Another set derives from the longitudinal study of aging parents in Berkeley, California. Here both interpersonal patterns at about age seventy and their ante-cedents for the same people in their young adulthood, about forty years earlier, are available. While there are four different life style patterns for the 47 men and six for the 95 women, I shall present here the findings on only four of the total of ten life styles. I want to illustrate the proposition that old people's approaches to intimate relationships and larger social networks have their understandable, if not predictable, origins in earlier life. More specifically, the fathers we called "Unwell-Disengaged" were socially withdrawn (disengaged) old men and with markedly poor health (unwell). This same social withdrawal, as well as poor health, had been ap-parent in their young adulthood. By contrast, the "Remotely Sociable" fathers were "hail fellows, well met." They had a large network of superficial acquaintance-ships but a lack of intimate relationships, a pattern present also in their early adult-hood and possibly reinforced by their successful managerial careers, as amplified below. A third group of old men were called "Family-centered" fathers because their wives, children, and grandchildren were so central to their lives, although not to the exclusion of their attending organized groups, sometimes in a leadership role, and their also valuing other friendships. Finally, following these three profiles indicating continuities in interpersonal orientations from early adulthood to old age—from a lifetime of social withdrawal, through extensive and superficial relation-ships, to a lifelong high valuation of intimacy—I present the interesting transfor-mation or radically changed career of a group of aging women called the "Employed (Work-centered) Mothers," who turned from being shy, withdrawn, and dissatisfied as younger women to being very involved socially and high in life satisfactions in old age. The major contextual changes these women experienced, between young adulthood and old age, as described in the passages quoted, perhaps explain the transformation in their life styles.

FOUR LIFE STYLES OF OLD PEOPLE AND THEIR EARLY ADULT ANTECEDENTS (RECORD NO. 24)

Unwell-Disengaged Fathers

Continuity between early adulthood and old age also characterizes the unwell-disengaged fathers. Here the continuities are especially striking, since the central features of their aging life style—their ill health and social withdrawal—were both evident in their earlier lives and thus were not developments initiated in their later years.

In their early-adult years they had the poorest present health (.10) and a cumulative or combined cluster score indicating lowest stamina (.05). Their high involvement in the sick role in old age is paralleled in their early-adult years by their manifesting the most overconcerned or preoccupied attitude toward health of all our fathers. In old age the unwell-disengaged rank themselves as poor in health and have the significantly poorest present health, as they did earlier in life. In old age they have the lowest energy level; in early adulthood they had the poorest stamina. Their health problems—which seem, circularly, to influence their disengaging life style or withdrawal in old age—were manifest all through their adult lives. Thus, as the evidence from our antecedent measures on these fathers suggests, illness linked with withdrawal may provide the roots for a style that spans a total adult life—not merely the later years.

Among the antecedent marital measures of their early adulthood, the unwell-disengaged manifested most conflict with wife over religion (.05) and also most friction over expenditures (.05). In addition, they were rated as showing tension in their adjustment to size and management of income—although socioeconomic-status measures indicate that their families were among the best-off families in early adulthood. Other marital antecedent measures in which they rank lowest are conflict regarding relatives, conflict regarding standards of neatness, and marital adjustment. On only one marriage antecedent measure is there a "positive" note: they share with wife the highest similarity of interests. And yet these couples are unique in the discrepancies between them in age and level of formal education: the husbands are significantly older by more than five years (.10), and husbands average less education (.10) by almost one year, the only marriages in which the husband does not have a higher level of education than the wife. Recall that in old age these fathers are not satisfied with how decisions are made in their marriage, that one partner or the other makes almost all the important decisions, and that neither can count on the other for help. Continuity of marital conflict is apparent among the unwell-disengaged.

In the parenting arena in old age, they are not satisfied with their children's visiting arrangements or with the way that their grandchildren are being reared. On early-adult measures these fathers, compared with all other fathers, had the least close bond with child-S (.05), the greatest discomfort in providing sex instruction for child-S (.05), and a cumulative cluster score indicative of poorest relationship with child-S (.05). The unwell-disengaged ranked highest on hostile relationship with child-S in their early adulthood. Their disapproval of their children's visiting and child-rearing practices in later years thus has early-life origins.

This consistency over their adult years and into old age should not be overgeneralized into support for the conservative shibboleth that "people don't change." Rather, some people change less than others, and our data indicate the personal characteristics of some persons who are less changing. Specifically, as young adults the unwell-disengaged were the most explosive (.05), the most worrisome or tense (.05), and the most nervously unstable (.05) of our fathers. Mental health theory and research support the idea of lesser ability for personal growth and development and change among persons who are "tense" and "unstable." They may be so pre-occupied with defending themselves against anticipated attack that they seem less able to be openly responsive to both outer and inner self-expanding experiences. Continuity of "negative" aspects of life syle among the unwell-disengaged may be interpreted, in part, in such terms. To their unfortunate physical deficits may be added psychic disabilities apparent in early-adult years. If we had more data on these fathers' childhoods, about which we know only that they were more likely than other fathers to be only children, we might find evidence of still earlier origins of their psychic limitations.

An interesting footnote, relevant to their disengagement, is the finding that they made more residential moves in early adulthood than other fathers. While the family-centered fathers made 2.6 moves and fathers in the other clusters made 2.8 moves, the unwell-disengaged made 3.8 moves, suggestive of less meaningful inte-gration in a neighborhood network—or associated, perhaps, with their greater occupational instability. This finding is paralleled by their counterparts among the mothers: the disengaging were similarly the most residentially mobile of the mothers in their early-adult years, with 4.2 moves, as against 2.2 to 2.9 moves for all the other mothers except for the economically worst-off work-centered mothers, who averaged 3.4 moves. Upward social mobility of the disengaging, previously sug-gested, may be associated with their geographic mobility, which in turn may reflect and further their withdrawal from some personal relationships.

Remotely Sociable Fathers

The remotely sociable fathers are the third of the fathers' clusters for whom antecedent measures are highly relevant. Five of the ten significant early-adult measures indicate their satisfaction with their early social status, their finances, and their occupation. Within their early-adult contexts of upper-status occupations and economic comfort, these fathers may well have been prepared for their aging life style of remote sociability—a life style manifested by a large social network but no intimate relationships, low involvement as marital partner, dissatisfaction with mar-riage, lack of close bond or openness in communication with wife, and a low level of interdependence (doing things together) with wife.

Their relatively high occupational status (as owners of small businesses and executives of large organizations) toward the end of their work careers coincides with their early-adult high income (.01) and lack of strain in the family in regard to finances (.05). In early adulthood they were thus very good economic providers with high job satisfaction (.01)—a cluster score combining wife's attitude toward husband's work with husband's own attitude toward his work. Their amount of leisure time was rated "adequate" (.10)—although these couples also had most conflict over recreation. They did, however, agree on expenditures (.10) and had no conflict over money (.01).

These fathers' early-adult high satisfaction with home (.10), a composite score, may reflect social-status satisfactions. But at that stage of life they also evidenced a good relationship with child-S (.05), a composite score on an aspect of family life which by old age has been reversed; that is, in old age these fathers are marked by little expression of affection or instrumentality and not a close relationship with child-S. They are, moreover, aware that their relationship with child-S has, with increasing age, become more remote. This is a change in a facet of life style, an unusual occurrence among our fathers.

The remaining antecedent measures differentiating these fathers in early adulthood characterize them then as both relaxed and controlled and also interpersonally cool and removed. Specifically, they were not worrisome or tense (.10), and they withdrew in the face of conflict (.05). But they were also generally low on expression of affection and were the most private (not sharing) with others about their experiences. We are reminded that in old age they do not communicate openly with the "person most important" to them. In such characteristics, they manifest a continuity from early adulthood. Their old age is marked by their noninvolvement with others in a life style in which many people are "important to me," including many "friends," but no one is very close. This superficial gregariousness is foreshadowed by their early-adult extreme cluster score on withdrawal, indicating that they were the least withdrawing of the fathers as young men.

In summary, these fathers demonstrate a mixture of continuity and change, the latter in the parenting arena. Our data do not tell us why their early good parental relationship with child-S was dissipated. We can only speculate that the high financial rewards of ownership and executive positions in business reinforced an interpersonal style of calm but coolness and friendly noninvolvement with other persons which was functional for economic success but not for the satisfying development of family relationships. Moreover, when their occupational contexts called for social activities outside the family orbit, these fathers may well have found such activities ego-syntonic. With retirement or the diminution of their paraoccupational demands for sociability, they may find themselves, as earlier in life, in some conflict with spouse over "recreation." The vignette in the diary, quoted in Chapter Two, comes to mind: "Harold Clark called us to convince us that we should attend the Serra Club Christmas Party at Spenger's on next Monday. I have tried to convince Marty that we should go but, so far, the answer is no."

Family-Centered Fathers

The family-centered is the only fathers' group for whom antecedent measures are of low relevance to their aging life style. Only two antecedent measures significantly differentiate them in early adulthood from other fathers—and on fewer than half as many measures as any other fathers' cluster are they at either the highest or lowest end of mean ratings. The two significant antecedent measures indicate their early-adult openness to and nonavoidance of the expression of feelings. They were, in the face of conflict, not likely to withdraw or refuse to discuss issues (.10) but more likely to engage in open and flexible discussion or even excessive talk. And they were more likely to be irritable (.10) when provoked. In addition, they were the most expressive of affection, showing an "easy demonstrativeness with family, relatives, friends." They were also rated highest on close bond with wife and on the marital-compatibility cluster, which combines in a single score six measures: adjustment to each other, closeness of bond of both husband to wife and wife to husband, mutual friendliness ratings of spouses, and sexual adjustment. Although these couples did not fully share the management of money, each was responsible for certain items. In the parenting arena, as young adults the family-centered fathers were the best fathers in sex instruction for the children, freely answering questions and volunteering information. Finally, as young adults they were more likely to share most experiences, with only some reticence, while other fathers tended to keep most things to themselves.

Despite the low relevance (few items) of significant antecedent measures, the continuity of the family-centered fathers' style from early adulthood into old age is suggested. For our fathers, generally, old age brings no radical change in ways of living. Early adulthood seems to provide a base for a rather smooth trajectory into almost predictable life styles in old age.

Work-Centered Mothers

A radical change in life style from their earlier ways of living occurs for the work-centered mothers (the E mothers). Aging seems to bring the Es a happy relief from earlier engagement in an unsatisfying marriage and its economic problems. With the loss of their spouses in their middle-adult years (their fifties, on the average), these women ventured into a totally new and apparently highly gratifying style of life, centered in their employment, independence from marital ties, adequate economic rewards, and a new circle of friends—while maintaining a close relationship with child-S.

The differentiating antecedent measures of their early adulthood are set forth in Table 9-1, together with the contrasting life style and context components of the Es' old age. The early-adult Es were lowest in energy level when rated in the 1930s, yet are marked by high energy, accompanied by comparatively good health, in their aging years. The transformation of the Es on the energy dimension is remarkable. Their early-adult profile suggests the kind of retardation that may accompany depression. Their aging life style indicates a complete reversal of any such slowed-down or withdrawn behavior.

More specifically, coupled with dissatisfaction with their home, the Es' in early-adult years were economically strained, if not economically depressed. They had the poorest income of our mothers. On a composite of antecedent measures of their marriage, the Es were significantly the worst off. The Es' early-adult depressive behavior ("mothers' characteristics" in Table 9-1) may well have been a situational response to overwhelming and entrapping poor marital and economic circumstances.

While still in middle age and comparatively young, the Es lost their primary family responsibilities, through the death or divorce of their husbands and the growing up of their children and seem to have experienced a release. In part through meaningful and very satisfying employment, out of their home, they became, as we found them in their later sixties, highly involved as guest or visitor and as worker.

TABLE 9-1   Es' Early and Later Life: Radical Change for Better

ARENAS	EARLY ADULTHOOD	OLD AGE
Age and health	Younger (.10) Lower energy level	More satisfied with health More energy output (.01) Less disabled (.01) Better present health (.01)
Home	More dissatisfied with home (.05) More dissatisfied with home (cluster score) (.01)	More in urban neighborhoods (.05)
Work and leisure	Lower socioeconomic status (.05) More economic strain (.05) More dissatisfied with husband's occupation (.10) Less income Less adequate leisure time (.05)	More working part- or full-time (.01) Higher involvement as worker (.01) More satisfied with present work (.01) Higher past work involvement (.01) More years working (.05) More recreational interests (.05)
Marriage	Lower marital cluster (.10) Poorer sex adjustment Better educated than husband (.10)	More not married now (.01) More widowed, divorced (.01) Generally, marriage is changing for worse these days (.10) Both spouses younger at marriage (.05/.01) Wives younger at termination of marriage (.01)

They are now visiting more than in their forties, have made new friends since age sixty, and have at least one close friend living nearby. They include more nonfamily than family members among those who are close—that is, very meaningful—to them, although child-S is also close to them. In addition, while their leisure time in early adulthood was rated "inadequate," they now have many recreational interests. (Had they had such interests in early adulthood, their familial and economic pressures would probably have prevented their pursuing them.) Thus, when retirement occurs for the Es, their social lives and leisure activities should well sustain them.

The Es were the least "satisfied with their lot" in early adulthood. In old age they are a close second to the Gs, who are highest in Life Satisfaction Rating. With old age, the Es have made a radical change for the better.[31]

Note that the radical transformation in the social relationships and other aspects of life style of the women called the E's seemed to result from or at least followed the death of or divorce from their spouse. Normally, what is called the "role loss" of wife evokes the kinds of suffering which the sizable literature on

TABLE 9-1 (cont.)

ARENAS	EARLY ADULTHOOD	OLD AGE
Parenting	Less adequate sex instruction (.05)	Closer relationship with child-S (.10) More satisfied with children's visiting (.01)
Informal relationships and formal organizations	More withdrawn (cluster) (.05) Shyer social adjustment (.05) Less sharing, more private (.10)	More visiting than in forties (.01) Higher involvement as guest (.05) More weekly visits to others (.10) Rarely or never attends group meetings (.10) More nonfamily close (.01) More friends made since age 60 (.05) Closest friend lives nearby (.10) Less political volunteer work ever (.10)
"Mothers' characteristics"	Lower intelligence (estimated) (.05) Less sense of personal adequacy (.05) Halting use of language (.10) Less poised (.10) Less critical (.10) Less cheerful, more melancholic (.10) Less general satisfaction	

widowhood and marital separation amply describes and documents. I shall make a few observations on what some of these studies of widowhood have revealed and then return to the cluster of mothers for whom loss of husband proved, in the long run, a release from an unsatisfying family life.

It is important to consider widowhood because most wives can expect to spend many of their aging years as widows. Following the initial shock of a husband's death and the period of mourning, widows try to come to terms with their loss and establish a new life for themselves. This is often a slow and difficult process, although the long-term effects, as in the situation of the E's, may be salutary. In most cases, a spouse's death brings about a total life reorienting situation. For widows, it typically requires changes in everyday living routines and sometimes in living place, adjustments to economic threats and losses, modifications in a social life formerly embedded in a married couples' network which may no longer easily accommodate a woman without her partner, adaptations to the sexual deprivations of a lover's loss, and altered ties with children or siblings who feel a new set of obligations to protect an unattached older mother or sister.

Research has documented the poverty of widows[32] and the possibility of their being socially isolated and lonely.[33] Regarding health problems in widowhood, "Serious physical illnesses are more frequent among the bereaved; general malaise, including dizziness and fainting, is even more common. Mortality rates are higher among the recently widowed,"[34] and widows may struggle with feelings of guilt, dependence, lowered self-esteem, and depression.[35]

Analyses of differences in morale and other conditions between widowed and married women, in a study of over 1,200 Los Angeles respondents, ends with the following cautionary note:

> . . . the findings suggest that at least part of the differences we find in morale when comparing married and widowed women result from differences in related factors. The fact that controlling for some of them as covariates removed the differences in morale scores would suggest that lower morale among widows, while indeed a reality, results in part from lower income, lower work involvement, less family interaction, or other factors co-occurring with widowed status rather than widowhood itself. The treatment of role losses such as widowhood as unitary phenomena with similar outcomes for individuals in widely divergent situations needs to be called seriously into question.[36]

One should differentiate not only among the correlative situations of widows but also between the phases of adaptation to their situations, especially in regard to their social network supports and the kinds of support needed, provided, or not provided. Research by Elizabeth Bankoff begins to do just that. Drawing upon a national study of urban self-help systems, she compared about one hundred Crisis Phase "early widows" (in their first eighteen months and still intensely grieving) with about 150 Transition Phase later widows (after more than eighteen months and less intensely grieving). Widows still in the crisis/loss phase find their long-term married friends a source of intimate support in talking over their personal feelings; old friends can help with the grieving process in ways that mourning children may not. Widows in the later transition phase, when they are trying to establish a new way of life, find guidance and approval by other widows most helpful, along with the ongoing availability of neighbors for emergency needs. In this latter phase, in addition to other widows, single women and the widows' daughters can relate helpfully on a woman-to-woman basis. Bankoff's study nicely distinguishes not only among different sources of support but also different kinds—attention, intimacy, companionship for social interaction activities, reassurance of worth and approval of a new life style, emotional support, guidance, and assurance of emergency assistance.[37] At different phases of their long (and perhaps never ending) adaptation to a husband's death, widows have differing social network needs. Still, older women, who are more likely to be living amidst other old women who are also spouseless, often develop very satisfying new attachments.

I can return now to the E's, the no longer married old women in the Berkeley longitudinal study who were happily employed and highly satisfied with their social lives at about age seventy. For them, the role losses of wife and mother in their fifties inaugurated radical and welcome transformations in their friendship and sociability patterns and a whole new style of life which they found a happy second chance. Thus, in addition to the variable conditions associated with widowhood, and the different phases of adaptation to the loss of spouse, human service workers and others trying to understand older women without a marriage partner need to take a life span or developmental perspective and consider what indeed the women had lost in their former total living situation when they lost their spouse.

There is a need too to question the fading stereotype of women's primary roles as wife and mother. It is conceivable that adaptations to the ultimate aloneness of old age are best anticipated by women who have had long experience without a marital partner. At least in the Bonn Longitudinal Study of Aging, in The Federal Republic of (West) Germany, psychologist Insa Fooken compares favorably a group of never married women (mean age 79.7 years) with two groups of widows and a subsample of married women, all in their later seventies. Followed over a twelve-year period, starting shortly after they had retired, the never married women exhibit "growing stability and congruence" and "the most social activity of all subsamples" coupled with an "obvious independence from other people" and "little concern about possible physical impairment." By contrast, the married couples are socially constrained by one another's physical disabilities, and the women are "preoccupied with health and physical impairment" and manifest "depressive reactions, less marital and familial satisfaction, feelings of being unnecessary and dependent" and other "unfavorable experiences."[38]

Clearly, no single set of transformations in attachment occurs in old age. No one pattern can describe how old people develop or otherwise modify their relationships to peers and other persons. Depending on their health, economic circumstances, and living place, they relate to the members of their social networks in various ways and may extend or reduce their social interaction. Much seems to depend also on their ways of relating to people developed in their earlier years. They may continue to relate with emotional warmth as did Berkeley's family-centered fathers, or with superficial pleasantness to many people but little capacity for intimacy as did the remotely sociable fathers. They may be characterized by social withdrawal and avoidance as were the unwell-disengaged in old age—and essentially all through their adult years, manifesting a lifelong series of health problems and preoccupations with them. In contrast to such continuities from early adulthood into old age, they may display a radical transformation in social interaction as did the work-centered mothers, beginning when their familial context changed in middle age and their nests emptied completely with the loss of their spouse. Their unhappy years of family life ended while they could still enjoy a second chance.

Curiosity, Competence, and Retirement

Perhaps the major fear of people approaching old age—at least in Western societies—is that they will lose their abilities, physical and mental, to care for themselves. Loss of competence is also loss of former identity or one's lifelong conception of self as able and autonomous. This is all relative to one's prior life. At age eighty-five, the great Russian-born but California-based composer, Igor Stravinsky, felt humiliated, he said, because "I cannot work long at sustained high pressure and with no leaks in concentration," and, referring to his "hide-and-seek memory," he added, "I have orchestrated the same page twice, greeted perfect strangers in Russian, and performed a variety of other equally scatterbrained acts."[39] He failed to see such new deficits as compensated for by the fact that he was still traveling the world as musician and composer in his eighty-sixth year.

Equally troublesome, although not so much in the public's awareness, is some old people's loss of interest in the new, which a still well-energized curiosity might keep alive. The threat of waning capacities can diminish a sense of adventure and keep one tied to the familiar and routine, whatever one knows one can cope with. Boredom can result, a sense of sameness which fails to make one day different from the next. The dulling of curiosity may be related to the loss of one's emotional attachments and intimate relationships—for example, the death of a partner with whom one had shared former explorations with security. As attachment in infancy seems a necessary base for adventures into the unknown (Chapter Three), so in old age the maintenance of such attachments may be a precondition for continued inquiries of at least a physically active kind. Some curiosity about "what" and "how" and "why" seems a good indicator of involvement in living, even though one is confined to a wheelchair. Had the work-centered old mothers—the E's who were described and discussed in the previous section—succumbed passively to their loss of spouse and not been curious enough to enter a radically new style of life, they might well have passively become the "rocking chair" old people of an early California study of aging.[40]

The issue of competence in old age leads to questions of employment and retirement. As in conceptions of widowhood, retirement has unfortunately been linked with the idea of role loss, and at least some years ago, was tied to the mini-theory of disengagement in old age. In the context of the long history of the American work ethos, loss of job, even in old age, was seen as inevitably a self-damaging or morale-lowering experience. The data on aging people in Kansas City were initially interpreted as pervasive role loss and withdrawal or disengagement of the elderly from many arenas, just as society reciprocally withdrew its options from the aged, reassigning to younger people what it withdrew from the old. Moreover, this mutual "disengagement" was seen as a normal set of processes.[41] In fact, however, a sizable body of more recent research has connected continuing activity, well after job retirement, with high morale or satisfaction, at least in North America. Some of the variables in this formula must be amplified. The across-the-board assumption of retirement from work as a demoralizer seems now grossly inaccurate, especially as younger cohorts of twentieth-century-born middle-aged and younger old people have entered the retirement lists.

As I tried to make clear in the discussion of widowhood in the previous section, "role loss" is an oversimplified conceptualization of an event which occurs in a context including income and other economic losses, sometimes health problems (which may necessitate an early and involuntary retirement), and sizable changes in former social network interaction (at work) and related recreational activities. In short, the transition of retirement involves much more than merely leaving a job. Like widowhood, it has the potential to affect every facet of daily life. It may also free one for a radically new life style, more egosyntonic than one's previous way of life. Every exit in life is simultaneously an entrance.

The relevant research on retirement—much of it useful to human service workers who prepare employees for retirement in preretirement programs—addresses old people's leisure activities after they leave their job, and the correlates of life satisfaction and morale among retirees, including, of course, their economic and health conditions. It should be noted, however, that much, if not most, of the retirement research is limited to males. The in-and-out-of-the-labor-market work histories of many employed but also child-bearing women make a study of their retirement, following such early job experiences that are difficult to pattern, too untidy for orderly and categorizing investigations. Moreover, in addition to the sex variable, different cohorts of workers who matured in different periods and began work with different beliefs, values, and commitments limit the generalizability of retirement study findings. Workers born in the 1880s, at the turn of the century, or during World War I had work experiences with different personal meanings and self-referents. The old man who had been totally invested in his job for fifty years and whose primary family role was as wage earner is in a different place at enforced retirement from his junior by forty years who grew up in a time and society which valued fun and made leisure time equipment and activities widely accessible. For the latter, playing and retirement induce no feelings of unworthiness or guilt. Current generalizations about retirement must be cautiously considered in terms of the sex and generation of the people studied. Moreover, early education is an important antecedent variable—although adult education programs for seniors make this a partially retrievable matter—as are a lifetime's development of avocational interests. What happens in retirement has many early adult life contingencies, some fortuitous, but some that the prematurely wise or wary can, in their foresighted youth, plan for. Competence, I have argued in this book, is contextual in part, and some of the contexts for the exercise of competence in old age are built by the elderly themselves in their earlier years.

In fact, leisure activities carried on through one's middle age, while one is still at work, serve retirees well. For example, a study of postretirement activities of over 200 Midwestern men reveals that their leisure in their late sixties does not differ substantively—only quantitatively—from the activities they engaged in earlier; they were "also popular prior to retirement." Moreover, despite the wide range of activities, "from gambling to reading, horse breeding to birdwatching, golf to team sports," this inquiry found that "activities which are primarily social and/or physical in nature have the most positive effect on life satisfaction"—that is, by contrast with "isolate" or "sedentary" activities, and provided that the retirees were engaged in "doing what you most enjoy," which meant that they were unconstrained by limitations of health, income, or living place.[42]

Living place can, of course, affect the experience of retirement in unanticipated ways. In a cross-cultural investigation of retired teachers and steelworkers in Vienna, Bonn, Nijmegen (Holland), Milan, Warsaw, and Chicago, Vern Begston discovered that, by contrast with all the others being studied, the Chicago school teachers, all males in their seventies, still were "working in one capacity or another—substitute teaching, selling insurance, giving lessons, etc." This was not true of the Chicago steelworkers or of any of the other groups. He wrote:

> Comparing these findings with the rest of the data, it is clear that neither national *nor* occupational factors alone completely explain the situation. Put differently, there appears to be something about living in the Chicago social context *and* having been a teacher that gives a high probability of continuing to work . . . From analysis of the content of the interviews, however, it seems very clear that the social setting in the United States exerts a special push toward, and the career of teacher offers the preparation for, maintenance of activity in the worker role after retirement. This push can be seen as a property of the social structure and as an attitudinal state within the individual—in terms of values, behavioral settings, and life style. At any rate the importance of that constellation of variables which we have been calling the socio-cultural context is clear. A similar push does not seem to exist for the Viennese teacher, nor for the Chicago steelworker, in terms of maintaining activity in the worker role. The high engagement in work activity, therefore, emerges as an interaction of national setting and occupation.[43]

In addition to such milieu determinants of what old people do when they retire, their feelings about retirement—and old age—show a consistent and positive relationship to their economic resources. Social Security benefits and private pensions as well as savings make all the difference. Rising housing and food costs quickly devour a small monthly income. The ability to pursue a hobby, take a trip to visit grandchildren, or simply go to the movies or a sporting event depends on one's available cash. Especially in old age, feelings of adequacy and competence are related to one's economic status. No matter where in the Western world the research was done, the findings on economic resources are similar—in Denmark, England, and the United States as in the studies by Ethel Shanas and her European gerontology colleagues,[44] in North Carolina, or in Columbus, Ohio. The last study of 2,500 retired Ohioans concludes, "Income and economic security may play a more important part in successful aging than previous research has indicated,"[45] and the North Carolina (Duke University) longitudinal assessment of "adaptation to loss of the work role" finds "various indicators of socioeconomic status" to be "important predictors of subjective adaptation in retirement."[46] The research repeatedly indicates also that good health is crucial and that old people's family embeddedness adds to their feelings of satisfaction and competence. But there is evidence too that sometimes low-income retirees may be happy simply to have escaped from unrewarding work, and the unhappiness of retirees with health problems may relate also to their having had to retire early. Voluntary retirements—or retirement plans which allow workers options—result in greater satisfaction when retirement does occur.[47]

The human services in a humane society should give as much attention to helping people leave the labor market as they do to helping them enter. Retirees' ignorance of the entitlements for old people can lead to losses they need not suffer. Ideally, planning for retirement begins early enough in the adult years for some of its long-term effects to be considered. One can approach retirement with a full awareness and use of existing resources, or one can just passively let it happen. The issue of competence or power and its uses is a pervasive one throughout life, and the human services, in regard to work termination, should foster people's meaningful involvement and informed choices.

Having noted at the outset of this section that most of the retirement research focuses on men, I conclude with some observations on women's working and retirement. The rise in the divorce rate and the earlier termination of child bearing have brought more women into the labor market for longer periods of their adult lives. Many women have made considerable psychological investments in their work careers, and while the many implications for their retirement years have still to be studied fully, it is clear that fewer women in the future will suffer the depths of poverty which afflicted old women living alone in the past. There is already a small body of findings that contrasts the retirement experiences of men and women and the morale in old age of women who had worked and those who had not.

A comparison of over 3,500 retired Midwestern men and women, some who had been school teachers and others telephone company workers, reveals no sex difference in the importance their work had had for them. In regard to retirement, while by far most (over 80 percent) were happy about it, "men were significantly more apt to like retirement than women were. Older men in general are more likely than older women to become accustomed to retirement," at least in a shorter time of three months or less.[48] Analysis of a national probability sample of over 2,000 women aged sixty-five and over indicates that those who had worked, whether still in the work force or retired, had higher morale than old women who had never worked.[49] A different adaptation in old age was found to characterize the early sixties of women who had spent most of their adult lives at work contrasted to those who had been primarily housewives. Reports Judith Huff Fox of her white, middle-class women, average age sixty-one, in a sample from the Duke Longitudinal Study of Aging:

> ... women who have worked much of their lives have no fewer social resources and, in fact, appear to be more socially involved than lifelong housewives. Compared to women still in the labor force, retirees have a lower perceived level of social contact, but are more involved in informal interaction with friends and neighbors (and) ... social contact is much more highly related to psychological well-being for retirees than for the others.[50]

Thus new patterns of aging emerge for women—and consequently for men—further diversifying styles of life among old people. A final variant of the stereotyped traditional old couple sitting together in their rocking chairs appears in the National Institutes of Health workshop report on *The Older Woman:*

> There are increasing numbers of couples in which the husbands are retired while the wives are still in the work force. The proportion is likely to increase given the growing numbers of second marriages in which there is a greater differential between the age of the spouses. This is likely to have a variety of consequences for marital [sic] interaction which have not been studied.[51]

Such observations merely touch on changes in relationships between men and women and the effects these may have on feelings of competence and adequacy in old age in the years ahead. Perhaps merely the expected increases in proportions of the population of people aged sixty-five and over will affect old people's sense of power and consequent abilities and activities. Such changing contextual aspects of competence will need to be studied.

Aging Selves

Clinicians and other direct practitioners in the human services who work extensively with old people are especially sensitive to the stigma they bear and their declining capacities. This is because selected segments of the aging population become clients or patients and have critical needs for prostheses and supports of other kinds.[52] Daily work with such old people fosters overgeneralizations about the steady downhill slope the aged are thought to travel. People assume that self-esteem and feelings of adequacy and autonomy inevitably sink. Yet the findings of gerontological research give a very mixed picture of old people's attitudes toward themselves—further testimony to the diversities of the aged. The issue of self-image in old age warrants at least brief attention in this chapter, if only because of popular misconceptions about the self's generally negative descent as people grow older.

The combination of somatic, psychological, and social status changes in old age is likely to induce self-reappraisals. One should redefine one's age identity as an older person; other reappraisals may be retrospective, in the course of reviewing one's life and trying to give integrated meaning to it. Questions about one's self-worth may be prompted initially by one's body monitoring, as one notices facial wrinkles and the beginning flabbiness of muscles which alter one's appearance. Such physical changes, if not accepted, may be damaging to the self. Hearing losses and changes in one's voice sometimes restrict one's accustomed social activities and thus reduce feelings of belonging and the self-affirmations that social interaction gives. Lapses in recall—Stravinsky's previously cited "hide-and-seek memory"—and what psychologist James Birren calls "the slowing with age of information processing"[53] are self-observed as well as noted by others. Moreover, publicly recognized social status changes like retirement and widowhood remove some people's bases for security and adequacy in daily experience and thus may modify their views of self. All such formulations, suggesting a decline in self-evaluations with age, are speculative. At least, they are not consistently supported by studies of self-images in old age.

Regarding "self-image and attitudes toward the self," one critical review of research remarks, "The findings seem divided as to whether self-image is found to be negative or positive in the aged."[54] In a more recent review of relevant studies, psychologist Lillian Troll documents how current understandings have become "much more complex than the original picture of a linear downward path of self-esteem with age."[55] Since there are both definitional and measurement problems that still plague the sparse body of research on old people's self-images, I shall not report details of the mixed and conflicting views that different studies offer. If little else, they do suggest further variety in ways of aging. Rather, I want to underscore the importance of attitudes toward the self for human service work with old people by citing two markedly different efforts to use self-image in practical components of the aging field.

The first has to do with institutionalization and geriatric care. When old people must move into a home for the aged, their perceptions of themselves may be expected to undergo changes. One way of evaluating their adjustment to their new residence after a sometimes traumatic separation from a former living place is to see how their self-image has changed. This is what psychologists Sheldon Tobin and Morton Lieberman did, in a large-scale Chicago study, assessing five dimensions of self perception through such measures as a forty-eight item self-sort: "I am a self-respecting person," "I am a trusting person," "I am rather timid and shy," etc. Assessed while on the waiting list and compared with a sample of old people in the community who were not scheduled to move into a home for the aged, the waiting list people showed lower self-esteem. Reassessed on the same measures after initial entrance to the home and again a year later, the residents saw themselves on both occasions as significantly less affiliative, that is, there was an increase in "self-image as a hostile interpersonal actor," but there was no significant lowering of self-esteem or self-adequacy after these old people had been placed on the waiting list. On the strength of such findings, the provision of supportive services for old people on the waiting list, while they are still living in the community, is strongly proposed.[56]

At the other end of the competence spectrum from nursing home residents are old people who are social activists on behalf of their age peers, although both populations are within the orbit of the human services. To inform community workers about the social and psychological characteristics of aging activists, social worker David Beatty contrasted them with nonactivists, including their "aging group consciousness" as part of their personal identity. He found the social activists significantly more likely *not* to view themselves as younger than they actually were. They were also more likely to view the aged as a minority group, to belong to age-related groups themselves, and to be accepting of death. In short, they seemed generally to have a more accepting attitude toward themselves as old people, and they effectively engaged in organizations on behalf of the aged, such as the San Francisco Senior Citizens Council or Self Help for the Aging.[57] There is no evidence that their self-images led to their participation as activists; the relationship is probably two-way, their self-image being supported by their group memberships and social cause involvements. Nevertheless, it seems unlikely that nonactivists, unaccepting of their own old age, would join agemates in projects to better the lives of old people. How one defines one's self seems to be an important determinant of what one does. Changes in self-image in old age in some way must take into account not only self-esteem and competence but also one's new age identity.

LEGACIES BEFORE
AND AFTER DEATH

With a lifetime's experience and the alleged wisdom of the old, some people do become more "philosophical" and accepting or tolerant of what earlier in their lives they would have avoided or opposed. This seems to be true about facing up to one's own death as one gets older. At the same time, with the increasing interiority, or "turning inward," of old people, thoughts about "how I will be remembered" may lie close to the borders of fleeting wishes for personal continuity or immortality. In practice, the preparation of a will simultaneously acknowledges one's own approaching death and specifies who is to have what meaningful mementos of one's life after one is dead. The most important legacies, however, may be intangible and unplanned for.

One such intangible legacy is movingly described by Robert N. Butler, formerly Director, National Institute on Aging, in his "Personal Note" which opens his Pulitzer Prize winning book, *Why Survive? Being Old in America.* The field of gerontology includes an impressive array of specialists from every professional and academic discipline which through service or research aims to improve the lives of old people. Few if any gerontologists have, like psychiatrist Butler, worked in so many different ways for the betterment of the health and welfare of the aged. He has, among other things, engaged in direct practice with geriatric patients, made theoretical and research contributions to the field, consulted widely with lay and professional organizations, written extensively in both scholarly and popular publications, and been a leader in federal and other governmental policy and program planning. All of these achievements are indirectly the legacy of one old couple, as the following "Personal Note" suggests. It needs no further commentary.

"A PERSONAL NOTE"
(RECORD NO. 25)

What leads a physician to gerontology? A psychiatrist? A young practitioner did not find in his medical or clinical training in the 1950s—any more than today—much knowledge, sympathy or understanding of the mental and physical needs of the elderly; but my childhood compelled this interest.

My grandparents reared me from infancy. My parents separated shortly after my birth, and when I was eleven months old, my mother brought me to live with her parents in Vineland, New Jersey, where my grandfather, then in his seventies, was a gentleman chicken farmer. I remember his blue overalls, his lined face and abundant white hair. He was my close friend and my teacher. Together we rose at 4 A.M. each day to feed chickens, candle eggs, grow oats and tend to the sick chickens in the "hospital" at one end of the chicken house. He would tell me of his younger days in Oklahoma and I would listen eagerly.

He disappeared suddenly when I was seven. I came back from a visit to a neighbor and he was gone. It made no sense. My grandmother said he went to visit relatives in Oklahoma—but he had not told me anything about the trip. With time, I realized I was never going to see him again. Dismay turned to fright and then to grief. I knew before they told me that he was dead.

Why? Why had he died? Why did people die? There was no talk, no funeral, only a "protective" silence that was more confusing than shared sorrow. I felt my silent way through a child's questions and a child's answers. Mostly, of course, I wanted to bring him back. Surely someone could arrange it. Everyone ought to live forever. No, that clearly would make for too many problems: old people would accumulate in hordes and the world would be packed so tight there would be no room for babies.

Well, what about a commission to decide who should live and who should die? My grandfather would undoubtedly qualify for resurrection and continued life—but could I be certain the commission would recognize his special worth? Would there be cheating? Would there be mistakes? This did not appear to be a satisfactory answer either.

It was Dr. Rose, our elderly white-haired family physician, who led me to a solution; I had cherished him for his reassuring presence and care through my serious bout with scarlet fever. If Dr. Rose had been there with the right medicine, I would certainly have had my grandfather with me longer. To be a doctor was clearly the answer. For the first time my anxiety eased.

If love of my grandfather and old Dr. Rose brought me to medicine, it was my grandmother in the years that followed who showed me the strength and endurance of the elderly. This was during the Depression. We lost the farm. She and I were soon on relief, eating government-surplus foods out of cans with stigmatizing white labels. Grandmother found work in a sewing room run by the WPA, and I sold newspapers and fixed bicycles for ten cents an hour. We moved into a hotel. When I was eleven, it burned to the ground with all our possessions. We started again. And what I remember even more than the hardships of those years was my grandmother's triumphant spirit and determination. Experiencing at first hand an older person's struggle to survive, I was myself helped to survive as well.

If this book informs, illuminates, angers and guides it readers, I shall have repaid some of the debt I owe.[58]

NOTES

[1]Henry S. Maas and Joseph A. Kuypers, *From Thirty to Seventy: A Forty-year Longitudinal Study of Adult Life Styles and Personality* (San Francisco: Jossey–Bass, 1974), pp. 137, 139, 144–45.

[2] Herant A. Katchadourian, "Medical Perspectives on Adulthood," in "Adulthood," *Daedalus,* 105 (Spring 1976), p. 53.

[3] Leonard Hayflick, "The Cell Biology of Human Aging," *Scientific American,* 242 (1980), p. 64.

[4] William Hines, "The Graying of America, Part 1, Growing Old: The Worst is Yet to Be," *Sunday Sun-Times,* Chicago, May 2, 1982.

[5] Robert N. Butler, "The Life Review: An Interpretation of Reminiscence in the Aged," *Psychiatry,* 26 (1963) 721-28.

[6] Maas and Kuypers, *From Thirty to Seventy,* p. 143-44.

[7] Michael J. Audain and Elizabeth Huttman, *Beyond Shelter: a Study of NHA (National Housing Act) Financed Housing for the Elderly* (Ottawa: Canadian Council on Social Development, 1973), p. 407.

[8] John C. Caldwell, *African Rural-Urban Migration: the Movement to Ghana's Towns* (New York: Columbia University Press, 1969), pp. 42-43, Table 2:2; A. W. Southall and P. C. W. Gutkind, *Townsmen in the Making: Kampala and its Suburbs* (Kampala, Uganda: East African Institute of Social Research, 1956), pp. 247-50.

[9] Gordon F. Streib, "Old Age in Ireland: Demographic and Sociological Aspects," *Gerontologist,* 8 (1968), 227-35.

[10] *Housing the Elderly/Logements pour personnes agées* (Ottawa, Central Mortgage and Housing Corporation, 1972, 2nd ed.), p. 6.

[11] Ron Toseland and John Rasch, "Factors Contributing to Older Persons' Satisfaction with Their Communities," *Gerontologist,* 18 (1978), pp. 397 and 401.

[12] Frances M. Carp, *A Future for the Aged: Victoria Plaza and its Residents* (Austin: University of Texas Press, 1966); "Housing and Minority-Group Elderly," *Gerontologist* 9 (1969), 20-24.

[13] Irving Rosow, *Social Integration of the Aged* (New York: Free Press, 1967).

[14] Ibid., pp. 294-95 and 297-98.

[15] M. Powell Lawton, Elaine M. Brody, and Patricia Turner-Massey, "The Relationships of Environmental Factors to Changes in Well-Being," *Gerontologist,* 18 (1978), p. 137.

[16] Elaine M. Brody, "Community Housing for the Elderly: The Program, the People, the Decision-making Process, and the Research," *Gerontologist,* 18 (1978), p. 124, Table 2.

[17] Lawton, "Environmental Factors", p. 137; see also "The Impact of the Environment on Aging and Behavior," in J. E. Birren and K. W. Schaie, eds., *Handbook of the Psychology of Aging* (New York: Van Nostrand Reinhold, 1977).

[18] Alan Lipman and Robert Slater, "Homes for Old People: Toward a Positive Environment," *Gerontologist,* 17 (1977), pp. 150-51.

[19] Ibid.

[20] Audain and Huttman, *Beyond Shelter,* p. 193.

[21] Ibid., pp. 331-33.

[22] Ibid., p. 403.

[23] Carol Schreter Hirsch, "Integrating the Nursing Home Resident into a Senior Citizens Center," *Gerontologist,* 17 (1977), p. 233.

[24] B. Bradford Brown, "A Life-Span Approach to Friendship: Age-Related Dimensions of an Ageless Relationship," in H. Lopata and D. Maines, eds., *Research on the Interweave of Social Roles, Vol. 2: Friendship* (Greenwich, Connecticut: J.A.I. Press, 1981).

[25] Leann M. Tigges, Donald O. Cowgill, and Robert W. Habenstein, "Confidant Relations of the Aged." Paper presented at the 33rd Annual Scientific Meeting of the Gerontological Society of America, San Diego, California, November, 1980.

[26] Nicholas Babchuk, "Aging and Primary Relations," *International Journal of Aging and Human Development,* 9 (1978), 137-51.

[27] Marjorie Fiske Lowenthal, M. Thurnher, and David Chiraboga, *Four Stages of Life* (San Francisco: Jossey-Bass, 1975).

[28] *Reaching the Retired/Pour le troisième age* (Ottawa: Information Canada, 1974), p. 108, Table 53.

[29] Peter Townsend, *The Family Life of Old People: an Inquiry in East London* (Baltimore, Maryland: Penguin Books, 1963), pp. 139-53, and 186-205.

[30] Rosow, *Social Integration*, pp. 109-18.

[31] Maas and Kuypers, *From Thirty to Seventy*, pp. 113-20. Quoted with permission.

[32] Peter Marris, *Widows and their Families* (London: Routledge and Kegan Paul, 1958); Helena Z. Lopata, *Widowhood in an American City* (Cambridge, Massachusetts: Schenkman, 1973).

[33] Ethel Shanas, Peter Townsend, and others, *Old People in Three Industrial Societies* (New York: Atherton, 1968); C. T. Pihlblad and D. Adams, "Widowhood, Social Participation, and Life Satisfaction," *Aging and Human Development* 3 (1972), 323-30; G. Arling, "The Elderly Widow and Her Family, Neighbors, and Friends," *Journal of Marriage and the Family*, 38 (1976), 757-68.

[34] *The Older Woman: Continuities and Discontinuities*. Report of the National Institute on Aging and the National Institute of Mental Health Workshop, September 14-16, 1978. U.S. Department of Health, Education, and Welfare, Public Health Service, National Institutes of Health. NIH Publication No. 79-1897, October 1979, p. 38.

[35] I. O. Glick, R. S. Weiss, and C. M. Parkes, *The First Year of Bereavement* (New York: Wiley, 1974); D. Maddison and B. Raphael, "Conjugal Bereavement and the Social Network," in Bernard Schoenberg and others, eds., *Bereavement: Its Psychosocial Aspects* (New York: Columbia University Press, 1975).

[36] Leslie A. Morgan, "A Re-examination of Widowhood and Morale," *Journal of Gerontology*, 31 (1976), p. 694.

[37] Elizabeth A. Bankoff, "Effects of Friendship Support on the Psychological Well-being of Widows," in H. Lopata and D. Maines, eds., *Research on the Interweave of Social Roles, Vol. 2: Friendship* (Greenwich, Connecticut: J.A.I. Press, 1981); Elizabeth A. Bankoff, "Support from Family and Friends: What Helps the Widow?" Paper presented at the 33rd Annual Scientific Meeting of the Gerontological Society of America, San Diego, California, November 1980.

[38] Insa Fooken, "Old and Female: Psycho-social Concomitants of the Aging Process in a Group of Older Women Differing by Marital Status." Paper presented at the Workshop on Life Span and Change in Gerontological Perspective, Nijmegen, The Netherlands, July 8-11, 1981.

[39] "Stravinsky at Eighty-five: An Interview," *The New York Review of Books*, Vol. 8, no. 10, June 1, 1967, p. 16.

[40] Suzanne Reichard, Florine Livson, and Paul G. Petersen, *Aging and Personality* (New York: Wiley, 1962).

[41] Elaine Cumming and William E. Henry, *Growing Old: the Process of Disengagement* (New York: Basic Books, 1961).

[42] Larry G. Peppers, "Patterns of Leisure and Adjustment to Retirement," *Gerontologist*, 16 (1976), p. 445.

[43] Vern L. Bengston, "Differences between Subsamples in Level of Present Role Activity," in Robert J. Havighurst and others, eds., *Adjustment to Retirement: a Cross-National Study* (Assen, The Netherlands: Van Gorcum, 1970, 2nd ed.), p. 48.

[44] Shanas, and others, *Old People in Three Industrial Societies*.

[45] Walter F. Chatfield, "Economic and Sociological Factors Influencing Life Satisfaction of the Aged," *Journal of Gerontology*, 32 (1977), p. 598.

[46] Linda K. George and George L. Maddox, "Subjective Adaptation to Loss of the Work Role: a Longitudinal Study," *Journal of Gerontology*, 32 (1977), p. 461.

[47] Richard E. Barfield and James N. Morgan, "Trends in Satisfaction with Retirement," *Gerontologist*, 18 (1978), 19-23; Douglas C. Kimmel, Karl F. Price, and James W. Walker, "Retirement Choice and Retirement Satisfaction," *Journal of Gerontology*, 33 (1978), 575-85.

[48] Robert C. Atchley, "Selected Social and Psychological Differences between Men and Women in Later Life," *Journal of Gerontology*, 31 (1976), p. 208; "Orientation toward the Job

and Retirement Adjustment among Women," in Jaber Gubrium, ed., *Time, Roles, and Self in Old Age* (New York: Human Science Press, 1976).

[49]Philip Jaslow, "Employment, Retirement, and Morale among Older Women," *Journal of Gerontology*, 31 (1976), 212–18.

[50]Judith Huff Fox, "Effects of Retirement and Former Work Life on Women's Adaptation in Old Age," *Journal of Gerontology*, 32 (1977), p. 202.

[51]*The Older Woman*, p. 49.

[52]Abraham Monk, "Social Work with the Aged: Principles of Practice," *Social Work*, 26 (1981), 61–68.

[53]James E. Birren and V. Jayne Renner, "Research on the Psychology of Aging," in James E. Birren and K. Warner Schaie, eds., *Handbook of the Psychology of Aging* (New York: Van Nostrand Reinhold, 1977).

[54]Ruth Bennett and Judith Eckman, "Attitudes toward Aging: A Critical Examination of Recent Literature and Implications for Future Research," in Carl Eisdorfer and M. Powell Lawton, eds., *The Psychology of Adult Development and Aging* (Washington, D.C.: American Psychological Association, 1973), p. 585.

[55]Lillian Troll, *Continuations: Adult Development and Aging* (Monterey, California: Brooks/Cole, 1982), p. 253.

[56]Sheldon S. Tobin and Morton A. Lieberman, *Last Home for the Aged* (San Francisco: Jossey-Bass, 1976), pp. 270, 56, 129–130, and 196, and Chapter 5, "Implications for Practice."

[57]David J. Beatty, "Social and Psychological Correlates of Social Action in Old Age," doctoral dissertation, University of California, Berkeley, 1971.

[58]"A Personal Note" (pp. ix–x) from *Why Survive? Being Old in America* by Robert N. Butler, M.D. Copyright © 1975 by Robert N. Butler, M.D. Reprinted by permission of Harper & Row, Publishers, Inc. As a contrast to Butler's personal view of old age and for a broad perspective on how social definitions of periods and transitions in the adult life course vary with the perceivers' gender, culture, birth cohort, and historical times, see Gunhild O. Hagestad and Bernice L. Neugarten, "Age and the Life Course," in E. Shanas and R. Binstock, eds., *Handbook of Aging and the Social Sciences*, 2nd ed. (in press).

INDEXES

281

AUTHORS